S0-AYP-941

MILESTONES
IN
MISSION

MILESTONES
IN
MISSION

William Rule III

EDITED BY
BARBARA RULE SUGUE

PROVIDENCE HOUSE PUBLISHERS
Franklin, Tennessee

TENNESSEE HERITAGE LIBRARY
Bicentennial Collection

Copyright 1998 by William Rule III

All rights reserved. Written permission must be secured from the publisher to use or reproduce any part of this book, except for brief quotations in critical reviews or articles.

Printed in the United States of America

02   01   00   99   98   1   2   3   4   5

Library of Congress Catalog Card Number: 98-65598

ISBN: 1-57736-092-3

Cover design by Gary Bozeman

Unless otherwise noted, Scripture quotations are from the King James Version.

PROVIDENCE HOUSE PUBLISHERS
238 Seaboard Lane • Franklin, Tennessee 37067
800-321-5692

I am constrained to add this note of dedication to give credit where credit is deservedly due.

> To my children—Bill, Charlotte, Libby, Paul, Barbara, and John—whose coaxing, I might say commandeering, prompted my attempt to set these matters down in writing for them and their families.

> To my beloved wife—Effie—without whose gentle affirmation and encouragement it would have died aborning.

> To my sister—Barbara—whose multiple skills served me patiently and well as proofreader, stenographer, and editorial assistant.

Thus, it was a family effort, dedicated to that missionary from heaven to earth, the chief cornerstone, who came to redeem us all.

CONTENTS

FOREWORD

Once I picked up *MILESTONES IN MISSION* by William Rule, M.D., it was hard to put it down. This is a wonderful and exciting story of the missionary career of Bill and Effie Rule and the work of the Holy Spirit through these two remarkable human beings. I know that you will find this to be an exciting and inspiring book, just as I did.

Bill Rule makes it clear that the motive for mission is the call of God. In this book he weaves an interesting, exciting, and at times, humorous account of how the call of God began in his childhood and extended through almost forty years of medical mission service in the nation now known as the Democratic Republic of the Congo.

The book closes in 1980 with the return of Bill and Effie Rule to the United States. My encounter with the Rules and with the places and people so well described in the book began the following year. It was in 1981 that I was elected as director of the Division of International Mission of the Presbyterian Church U.S. In that capacity it was a great privilege to come to know the Rules as friends and as supporters of world mission and to come to know first hand the ministry of Christ in the Congo (then Zaire). Reading *MILESTONES IN MISSION* has given me a fresh perspective on this marvelous ministry.

I first went to Zaire in 1981. I was overwhelmed with the suffering of the people but also with the work of the Holy Spirit, both in the church and in the medical mission effort. As I visited in places like Bulape and Tshikaji, I sensed the impact that Bill and Effie Rule had made on so many people's lives. I met both Zairians and missionaries whose lives were changed by this remarkable couple and saw first hand the institutions which their labors had built that had become channels of healing in body, mind, and spirit. This book fills in the details behind the wonderful legacy of Bill and Effie Rule in Zaire.

MILESTONES IN MISSION explains eight stages in a personal missionary journey. It gives new insight into the many transitions that have taken place in the African continent over the last half century. It brings fresh perspectives to the practice of tropical medicine and to the healing work of Christian missionaries.

It is a fascinating first person account of how in response to the call of God a Tennessee native would literally go to the other side of the world to share the love of Christ in love and deed. Through this story we have an account not only of an impressive Christian ministry but also of an impressive family who grew together in love and common commitment to Jesus Christ. Most of all, this is a story that illustrates the wonderful biblical truth that when we lose our life in the cause of Christ we truly find it. The story of Bill and Effie Rule is indeed the story of abundant life in Jesus Christ.

As both a friend and colleague of the Rules, and as Stated Clerk of the General Assembly, I want to pay tribute to Bill and Effie Rule as two of the great gifts of the Presbyterian Church (U.S.A.) to the wider world. My life has been enriched by their witness, and I am confident that you will find inspiration and enrichment in the pages of *MILESTONES IN MISSION*. I hope it will also serve as a clarion call to you to find God's richest blessing through a life based on faithfulness to God's call.

Dr. Clifton Kirkpatrick
Stated Clerk of the General Assembly
Presbyterian Church, U.S.A.
November 1997

PREFACE

One Saturday afternoon in early 1980 I sat in the pharmacy at Bulape Hospital with my friend, Shamba Bidiaka, taking the weekly inventory of drugs and medicines in stock. Shamba was an *Infirmier* or male nurse with twenty-two years of continuous service who by virtue of several years of apprenticeship had gradually been inducted into the job of hospital pharmacist. He was also a responsible and respected deacon in the local church. Drugs were hard to come by and easily lost, often finding their way onto the "black market" in the village market-place. The weekly inventory had been instituted to discourage this drain on limited supplies as well as to protect Shamba's integrity and his good name in the community.

Forty years earlier I had arrived in what was then the Belgian Congo and had begun my medical missionary service. I had met and married my beloved wife, Effie, and we had been blessed with a fine family of children of whom we are justly proud. Now we were packing to leave Africa for the last time, and within a matter of days would be gone with life in the Congo and in Zaire all behind us.

As Shamba and I worked together, estimating the quantities of tablets and capsules, he looked up from his counting, cleared his throat, and hesitantly posed the question: "Doctor, may I ask you something?"

"Sure, Shamba. What is it?"

"When you leave here and conclude your missionary service in Zaire, will there be another doctor from your country who will come out here to take your place and put in a lifetime of work in our land as you have done?"

xiii

Shamba was somewhat embarrassed about how his question might be taken and he hurried on to offer an explanation. "I don't mean that we don't appreciate the help we have received from numbers of people who have come out on short assignment. They have been true friends and a great help. But I am thinking of doctors like you and Mark Poole and John Miller and others who have spent your lives in the Lord's work. Are there going to be others like that who will replace you?"

I didn't answer immediately but searched for a true response to a good and serious query. Lord, I breathed, what is the answer to this brother's earnest question? And the answer came as I replied.

"My friend, this is not my work or your work, but the Lord's work. He loves it and he provides for it. I didn't really come out here years ago because I loved you or your people. I didn't know you. I only learned to love you later when I met you and after we were neighbors. But I came out here as a young man because I loved the Lord Jesus. My love for him told me that he was laying his hand upon me and telling me, 'I want you to go out to Africa and help some people I love out there just as much as I love you.' That's the reason I have spent my life out here. Because Jesus sent me. There are young physicians today who love the Lord Jesus as much as we do, and they are loyal to him. You can rest assured that inasmuch as he needs them in his work in this land he will lay his hand upon them and they will come."

The greatest joy which could come to me from recounting my own experiences would be the possibility of some young doctor or nurse or technician or worker with different skills to be moved by perusal of these pages to give his or her life to carry the gospel of Jesus Christ out across cultural and linguistic barriers to other people who have never heard. There are still many out there. God willing, that young person just might be one of my own children or grandchildren whom I might only contact in this earthly life through these written pages.

Editor's Notes

Barbara Rule Sugue

MILESTONES IN MISSION is condensed from a 1991 manuscript by William Rule III, with the same title. The joyful task of editing my father's manuscript was made easy because he did all the work! I have endeavored to retain the heart and soul of his calling, his education, and God's preparation for his Africa missionary experience.

I would like to express my gratitude and thankfulness for my family—for their encouragement and help. Mom and Dad were always ready to praise and to support my work. My sister, Elizabeth Rule Woodruff, spent hours drawing the illustrations and was a special source of encouragement. I would also like to recognize the help of my Aunt Barbara Rule Moorman in proofreading the manuscript. She lovingly read through it again, and I took all her suggestions and made all the changes she recommended.

God bless my own husband, Noel, for his love in allowing me the freedom to do the things I love to do. And my dear David and Katie, also.

Special thanks to Dr. Clifton Kirkpatrick for writing the foreword.

Providence House Publishers has been extremely helpful. Thank you Debbie Sims and Mary Bray Wheeler, and to Sophie Crane for "hooking" us up!

Finally—and foremost—thank you to my Heavenly Father for His goodness and mercy.

God bless you as you read this book. Our prayer is that you may be inspired and uplifted in your life's journey as you seek to do the will of God, through His Son and our Savior, the Lord Jesus Christ.

MILESTONES IN MISSION

PROLOGUE

The first two intrepid Presbyterian pioneers in central Africa were Samuel Lapsley and William H. Sheppard. Sam Lapsley was an honor student from a patrician Anniston, Alabama, family. William Sheppard came from Waynesboro, Virginia, from a poor but godly family. The two men were appointed missionaries to the Congo Free State by the Presbyterian Church, U.S., in 1889, and they sailed from New York on February 26, 1890. Following several weeks of preparatory business in London, and a visit to meet government authorities in Brussels, they sailed from Rotterdam to arrive at Banana in the mouth of the Congo River on May 10 of the same year.

Almost a whole year followed as they sought to orient themselves in the lower Congo, a land filled with curious cultural observances and fraught with harsh health hazards. They consulted with other missionaries already working in these more accessible regions. They made forays into the interior in various directions, seeking those areas where the gospel had never been proclaimed. Finally they decided to travel up the Kasai River, the largest tributary of the Congo River, and then into the Lulua River to its headwaters of navigation. For more than a month they journeyed upriver on a tiny steamer before they drew up on the banks of the river on April 18, 1891, where they established the mission station of Luebo.

Several months later it became necessary for Lapsley to return to the capitol in lower Congo to negotiate land rights. While at Matadi he was stricken with blackwater fever and died on March 26, 1892, less than a year following arrival in the territory of his chosen missionary endeavor. Sheppard was left to carry on amidst appalling difficulties. Three couples were quickly sent to the field to sustain and strengthen him in the work. Two of the ladies died within four years of their arrival. The struggle for survival was frighteningly grim.

MILESTONE ONE
ANSWERING THE CALL

"Also I heard the voice of the Lord, saying, Whom shall I send, and who will go for us? Then said I, Here am I; send me" (Isaiah 6:8).

1 THE CALLING

Then said Jesus to them again, peace be unto you: as my Father hath sent me, even so send I you (John 20:21).

As one looks back across a vista of seventy years there is naturally some blurring and confusion of images. The longer the shot, the less frequently the target is hit, yet always there are highlights and check-points that stand out. In recalling some of these milestones, the distinct pleasure is to signal out and recapture the especially delicious and delightful pieces, much as one would select from a box of chocolates. But as I contemplate this diversion, my thoughts turn to individuals rather than to events.

In his latter years old Ulysses opined, "I am a part of all that I have met." I would revise the adage from my own experience to read, "I am a part of all WHOM I have met." The power of personality should not be minimized. People are more important than programs.

The obvious place to start is with my family of origin. I shall ever be grateful to God for my beloved father and mother. I remember them as good and godly people. I was continually bathed in an abiding love which they shed upon me and my two siblings. I knew that no matter what happened, they were with me. From early childhood my parents were my rock and my fortress and offered to my life confidence and peace of mind.

I was the firstborn son of William Rule Jr., and Charlotte Gunby Rule. I was born in my family's home on April 30, 1912, in Knoxville, Tennessee.

My formal schooling began in 1918 when Mrs. John Thackston, wife of the dean of the School of Education at the University of Tennessee, offered to school me along with her own son, John Arla. Thus Thackston School was born. Mrs. Thackston was a proponent of some of the new teaching methods of her day. She did not follow a strictly regimented course, but tended to allow the pupil to proceed at his or

*William Rule Sr., William Rule Jr.,
and William Rule III.*

her own pace. Her desire was to make education an exciting and a spontaneous process and to whet the child's desire for knowledge and understanding. I can still remember the day my reading capacity graduated from the one-word-at-a-time category and I began to see whole sentences. The wonder and the joy are still a vivid picture in my mind.

After six years of private school I went to Boyd Junior High School which occupied the old Deaf and Dumb School of Knoxville, later to become the City Hall. I attended Knoxville High School in the fall of 1925. All the boys in high school participated in the ROTC Program.

My parents thought this was a good time for me to learn to play some musical instruments. I took a few piano lessons without much success. Then they approached Mr. Will Crouch, director of the high school band. He gave me a few lessons on a mellophone, and I was a member of the Knoxville High School marching band.

It was in January of 1926 that numerous outstanding citizens of East Tennessee began to get excited over the possibility of having the Smoky Mountain region, along the Tennessee–North Carolina state line, declared a national park. Mr. Dave Chapman, president of a wholesale drug company in Knoxville, was one of the most enthusiastic and energetic along these lines. He and other Knoxville business men conceived the idea of organizing a booster trip across the state of Florida to proclaim the beauty and grandeur of the Smokies and to promote interest and support of the park idea. Florida had experienced a tremendous real estate boom and many wealthy people from all across the United States were flocking to its sunny clime. It seemed to be a logical choice for the location of a booster campaign.

Many prominent Knoxvillians volunteered to join the booster caravan. Judge J. B. Lindsay was tapped to go along as the featured speaker, and he declaimed so many times at the Chambers of Commerce and service club luncheons and dinners that I almost had his speech memorized by the end of the trip. He always concluded by describing the beauty of water in the mountain glades; how it formed rainbows of color in the waterfalls of mountain streams and glistened like jewels on the blossoms of rhododendron. We always waited with bated breath for his punch line when he boomed, "But water as a beverage isn't worth a damn!"

The question may arise, "How did you get included in that trip?"

Well, they wanted some noise and excitement built into the celebration. Something that would arrest people's attention and tune them into what was going on. The decision was made to take along the one hundred piece Knoxville High School band, which would march through the downtown streets of the cities and declare in sonorous tones that the Smoky Mountain National Park had come to town! Mr. Crouch, our director, had pieced together a rather imposing troop and Hugh Smith, our captain and drum major, strutted at the head of the parade twirling his baton high in the air. This was my first year of senior high school. I was not yet fourteen years old and was just about the smallest boy in the band. Mother and Dad had procured a mellophone for me, and Mr. Crouch put me out on the left end of the second line where everybody could see that little boy with the big horn and how red his cheeks got and how his eyes stood out when he puffed and marched!

A special train of Pullman cars carried the whole crowd. Band players slept two in a berth and Richard Williams and I shared an upper. One day, after we had marched around town, we were dismissed to wander on our own before meeting back at the railroad station. Dick and I, still in uniform and with our instruments under our arms, stopped on a street corner and engaged in conversation with a distinguished-looking gentleman and his wife. They wanted to know all about our booster trip, what it was for, and something about Knoxville. We waxed quite voluble in answering questions and contrived descriptions of our beloved homeland. A week or so after returning home I received a small package from New York. It contained a baseball with Babe Ruth's autograph on it! There was also a note enclosed from our Florida acquaintance, one Mr. Frank

M. Stevens, written on his business letterhead which proved that he was an officer of Harry M. Stevens, Publisher-Caterer, the company controlling concessions for Madison Square Garden, the Polo Grounds, Yankee Stadium, Fenway Park, Saratoga Racetrack, and dozens of other famous sports and exhibition centers.

This trip was one of the outstanding experiences of my childhood, one that still conjures up vivid mental pictures that I shall never forget. But not everything was good and beautiful. I witnessed my first fatal accident as we were traveling by bus from one engagement to another. The gentleman who had arranged our schedule was a former Knoxvillian, and he jumped onto the right running board of our bus to direct the driver. We crossed a narrow covered bridge over a river and were forced to pull far to the right because of oncoming traffic. Our hanger-on was pinioned between the side of the bus and the bridge and rolled like a cigarette between two palms. Window glass broke and when there was an open point in the bridge he pitched off and fell twenty feet into the river. He struggled in the

Bill Rule III, R.O.T.C. cadet.

water and there was a cloud of bloody stain all about him. My childish mind seized on the presumption that he had been attacked by an alligator! I can remember Hugh Smith peeling off his puttees and having to be restrained from going in after him. A rowboat quickly put out from shore and he was rushed to the hospital, but we heard later that he had died.

EARLY INFLUENCES

It is remarkable to realize how the church and the Christian community have molded my personality and character. There stands the church, as far back as I can remember. It was a vital part of the lives of my parents and so it was a vital part of mine. Throughout my life I have been able to hark back to truths etched upon my memory in early days, and to apply those truths in difficult and trying situations.

Scouting and the Boy Scout movement also played a large part in molding my activities and attitudes as a young boy. I was a member of Knoxville Council's Troop Six that claimed the honor of having one of the highest percentages of Eagle Scouts among all the troops in the United States, and I was one that attained that rank. For several summers I attended Mr. John Gore's private Boy Scout camp at Wonderland Park, called Camp LeConte. We enjoyed swimming and other summer sports, and we hiked up Mount LeConte, Siler's Bald, the Chimneys, Blanket Mountain, and other highland peaks now part of the Great Smoky Mountains National Park.

Mr. Gore was a fine Christian gentleman and he instilled his Christian principles and faith into his camp life. We had rousing "sings" of gospel songs on Sunday nights, and quite often Mr. Gore himself would close the worship by singing one of his songs of invitation.

Besides my own family and Mr. Gore, Katherine Park also touched my life in a definitive manner. Katherine was a lovely young woman who had attended the Assembly's Training School in Richmond, Virginia, and had returned to our church as "Young People's Worker." I can remember how she encouraged and inspired us with her enthusiasm and excitement about the Christian life and the vocation of serving God. She emphasized to us over and over again the principle that we are born into this world to serve; that we are here not to get, but to give. Jesus gave his life for us and the proper thing is for us to give our lives back to him. I believed that she was speaking directly to me.

William Sheppard

It was only a step from there to choose the avenue of commitment. For a young boy the most exciting, the most adventurous, the most challenging was foreign missionary service! And so the visit of William Sheppard to our church was a momentous milestone in my life.

Sheppard was a black man, born near Waynesboro, Virginia, in the concluding year of the Civil War. He attended the Presbyterian Theological Institute at Tuscaloosa, Alabama, and was sent by the Presbyterian Church, along with Samuel N. Lapsley, to the Belgian Congo. They were the two first missionaries to go into that area. Just one year after their arrival, Lapsley died of malarial fever and Sheppard was the total Presbyterian missionary force in Congo. That was in 1892.

Just what year he was in Knoxville, I cannot remember. It was a long time ago, and I was a small boy. As a backdrop for his missionary message he decorated the pulpit and the wall behind it with an extravaganza of African artifacts, curios, and impedimenta. There were warriors' knives and spears and leopard skins and python hides. An elephant tusk was on prominent display. There were ceremonial dance drums, cowry shell headdresses, and carved figures in wood and ivory. My little boy eyes were wide open and standing out on stems! I was very impressed.

After the message I went forward and spoke to Sheppard. I cannot recall what we said, but what I do know is that he gave me a hippopotamus tooth! It had a hole bored in it through which a string or a ribbon might be run to wear around one's neck. I prized that hippo tooth and some twenty years later took it back to Africa with me. By that time Sheppard was long gone, but his memory was a hallowed legend.

Eugene Kellersberger

I was twelve years old when I met Dr. Eugene Kellersberger. He was one of the church's pioneer missionary physicians to the Belgian Congo. He and his wife established a home for themselves and their two young daughters in the Kasai Province, and it was here that he employed his medical skills in healing the diseases of hundreds of thousands of people who would never have received bonafide medical care had it not been for his ministry of mercy.

One of the killer diseases that flourished in central Africa in those days was *trypanosomiasis*, or African sleeping sickness, carried by the bite of the tsetse fly. It was effectively wiping out whole villages and even whole tribes of people. Dr. Kellersberger found himself locked in a struggle with this major threat. He eventually published a report of nine thousand cases he had treated in his mission clinic, and he was an important link in the effort that finally eradicated this disease as an endemic menace in tropical Africa. But success was not achieved without cost. The malady struck his beloved wife. They were extremely isolated in the back country, and he was inundated with the myriad calls of helpless Africans, so he sent his wife and two little girls to Liverpool where the School of Tropical Medicine was doing the most advanced work on sleeping sickness.

Dr. Kellersberger remained faithfully at his post while his wife received a course of treatment in Liverpool after which she and the children proceeded home to Texas for a period of rest and recuperation. While there a deranged relative shot and killed her in a violent fit of passion. In a state of shock, Dr. Kellersberger closed down his medical practice, packed his bags, and began the weary journey home. As his ship crossed the ocean he walked its decks and

Dr. Eugene Kellersberger.

prayed that God would give him the grace to accept this fate without bitterness. He prayed for the perpetrator of the crime, and when he reached the States he took no part in a prosecuting process. He arranged for the care of his children and then returned to Africa, alone.

While the doctor was in the States, his travels brought him through Knoxville. He was invited to our home for a meal and as we sat around the table, he told his story. I was present and I listened intently with my twelve-year-old ears. My heart went out to this man who was willing to sacrifice so much on the altar of his devotion to his Lord, and I wanted to be just like him. I already felt that God was calling me to the mission field, and now I was convinced that he wanted me to go as a Christian physician.

Through the next sixteen years of preparation, by the grace of God, my determination never wavered. Dr. Kellersberger became my friend—a sort of spiritual father. He wrote me letters from Africa and sent me pictures of gigantic tumors he removed surgically, and also of bright-faced Christians who had come under the redeeming power of the gospel message.

DAVIDSON COLLEGE

As I approached high school graduation, Mother and Dad began to talk to me about the possibility of attending Davidson College in North Carolina. This was a new idea. I had always figured to attend the University of Tennessee—my "stomping grounds." Still, the thought of trying my wings in a new location, of meeting new people and seeing new sights was not distasteful. I was sort of neutral on the matter and conveyed a willingness to do whatever my parents thought would be wise. I am sure they were interested in Davidson because Dr. Tolly Thompson, the revered pastor of our church some ten years earlier, was a Davidson graduate. A significant proportion of the ministers and leaders of the church came from the halls of Davidson. Since my adult life might well be wrapped up in activities and associations of the Presbyterian Church, Davidson would be a desirable place for me to make friends with common interests. These observations were wise, and proved to be correct.

I have many wonderful and meaningful memories of Davidson, among them the impressive leadership of Andrew Bird—president of our chapter of Phi Gamma Delta fraternity. He repeatedly called upon us as a group of young men to make a positive contribution to the life of the community. We thought up projects that would be helpful and we carried them out. Andy, from his podium in chapter meeting, was not hesitant to lecture us like a Dutch uncle, and the fellows took it in good spirit and responded to his admonitions. We were serious about good scholarship, and the stronger students helped the weaker ones. Alcoholic beverages were taboo, this still being within the Prohibition era, and I cannot recall ever having seen liquor in our chapter house. In recognition of that year of activity, our Davidson chapter was awarded the Newton D. Baker Cup by the national fraternity. This cup is awarded annually to the chapter with the best social service program.

On June 2, 1932, I graduated from Davidson College. I was selected to give the valedictory declamation, but let me hasten to add that this was not because my grades were particularly high. It was just a part of our class day exercises. A greater honor which came as a complete surprise was being named by the faculty to receive the Algernon Sidney Sullivan Award, given to the senior "best exemplifying the spirit of Davidson."

MILESTONE TWO
GETTING READY

"Study to show thyself approved unto God, a workman
that needeth not to be ashamed, rightly dividing
the word of truth" (2 Timothy 2:15).

2 MEDICAL SCHOOL

The Lord is my shepherd; I shall not want (Psalms 23:1).

I returned to Knoxville from Davidson expecting to find work for the summer. Business and economic conditions continued to deteriorate through July and August, and Dad could not liquidate the loans at his bank rapidly enough to keep up with the mounting withdrawal of funds. I am sure that one of the saddest days of his life was the day he came home from the bank and informed me that he had written a letter to the University of Pennsylvania to tell them I would not be coming to medical school after all. "I just don't have the money to send you, Bill," he groaned. "I'd give anything in the world to keep this from being so."

My father was not an ambitious, grasping person. He was mild of manner and content with modest means. He dearly loved his family and perhaps his greatest aspiration and pride would have been to put me through medical school. Being denied this pleasure was a cruel blow.

Of course, I was devastated by the news. Wasn't this the direction that the Lord had been leading me for a number of years? Hadn't I turned my life over to Him and hadn't He given me numerous assurances along this line? What should I do now? These questions brought me to my knees and once again I laid everything out before the Lord. Peace came into my heart as I was reassured once again that "all things work together for good." I had turned my affairs over to Him and He would be faithful to see me through.

I began a campaign of visiting affluent friends to ask for a loan to help me start my studies. Within forty-eight hours I had enough to finance my first semester! I sent a telegram to Philadelphia telling them to disregard Dad's letter because I'd be coming!

G. CAMPBELL MORGAN

One of the wonderful things that happened to me that first semester of medical school in Philadelphia was finding Tabernacle Presbyterian Church, just a short walk from where we were living. Dr. G. Campbell Morgan was concluding a pastorate prior to his return to Great Britain. He was an elderly gentleman who had experienced a remarkable career of ministry and Bible exposition recognized by Christendom around the world. It was a tremendous blessing to sit under his teaching and influence.

One of the most dramatic moments I can ever remember took place during one of his Monday evening sessions which he offered once a month. At these sessions he often repeated famous sermons or Bible studies he had given in the past that his many followers wanted to hear over again. People came from all over the city, and it was always a packed house. On this particular evening he was entertaining a question and answer session. The reader will remember that this was 1932. The stage was set for World War II. Hitler's star in Germany was rapidly on the rise, as was Mussolini's in Italy, and military leadership in Japan had become dominant. Against this background someone from the back seats in the gallery called down a question, "What do you think would be the best possible form of government in this world?"

Dr. Morgan strode in his flowing clerical robes to the center of the church platform, and standing erect with a hand on each hip he declared in a strong voice, "a dictatorship!" There was an electric moment of surprised silence before he added, "with the Lord Jesus Christ as dictator!"

Early 1933 had its light and its dark sides. One of the dark ones was that my Dad's bank did not survive the Depression. In January they closed their doors in failure, and Dad was financially wiped out. Then the day arrived for me to pay the second installment of tuition. On that very day I received a letter from Mrs. Powell Smith, a prominent member of our church in Knoxville, in which she said she had felt an inner compulsion to send me some money to help with my schooling. She had gone to the bank and withdrawn the funds, and the next day the bank had failed. She still felt, however, that the money was meant for me, so she sent it. It was a check for $250, which was the exact amount I needed for tuition! Within a few days I received a letter from another lady in our church. Miss Katherine Carson wrote to say that her late father, a University of Tennessee professor, had preserved a fund out of which he helped deserving but needy students, and she was sending me some money from it. At the same time she assured me there would be more from time to time since she knew I must be having a struggle to stay in school. Thus I had enough to see me through that first year. I had not spoken to either one of these ladies, and there was no way they could have known just what my needs were except Almighty God had spoken to them. This is a beautiful example of the way our Heavenly Father cares for those who put their lives and their trust into His hands.

DONALD GRAY BARNHOUSE

Another life that touched mine in a very special way that first year in Philadelphia was Dr. Donald Gray Barnhouse, pastor of the Tenth Avenue Presbyterian Church. I was meeting every week for a time of prayer with a friend of mine from Davidson, Alfred Jackson, who was now studying law at Penn. I learned from Al that Dr. Barnhouse was teaching the book of Revelation, and I decided to attend. Four years later when I was in my internship nearby, he was still teaching the book of Revelation on Sunday nights!

As time went by I found myself in a large cosmopolitan university subjected to criticism and even derision by some of my friends and associates because of my Christian stand and witness. This was distressing to me because these men were not college sophomores trying their new wings of independence; they were mature graduate students with their own convictions—and able to defend them. I didn't always come out on the best end of an argument. At Davidson I had gained honors and position in the student body because of my Christian stand. I had never experienced the truth that Jesus Christ expressed when he said, "If they have persecuted me they will also persecute you" (John 15:20).

I began to recognize that the ineffectiveness I sometimes experienced in discussions was basically because I did not have a ready command of the scriptures. Oh yes, I had studied the Bible; I knew the continuity of the biblical story. But I needed to know the deeper spiritual truths that convey the wisdom and understanding of God. I thought of Dr. Barnhouse and of his remarkable command of the scriptures. I remembered the conviction and assurance I had felt as he broke the bread of life. I decided to pay him a visit with my problem. He invited me to meet with him that evening after the prayer meeting. When we sat down, he took charge of the conversation.

"I think we can move along faster if you let me ask some questions first. What's your name?"

"Bill Rule."

"Bill Rule, Bill Rule, Bill Rule," he repeated, as if to fix it in his mind. "Where is your home?"

"Knoxville, Tennessee."

"Knoxville, Tennessee, Knoxville, Tennessee, Knoxville, Tennessee. Are you saved?"

"Yes sir, I am," I said with conviction.

"Good! You're saved." He paused. "How do you know you're saved?"

This question puzzled me. Nobody had ever asked me how I knew I was saved. How *did* I know it? "Ah . . . " I struggled, "I *do* know I'm saved. I guess I know it the same way you know it. The Spirit within me tells me I'm saved."

Dr. Barnhouse responded, "Yes, that's right, and by the word of God. God has told you what you must do to be saved. You have done it. So because you know that God is true and cannot lie you know you are saved. Now, why was it you came to see me—because of some sin in your life?"

I acknowledged my imperfections but went on to tell him the particular reason I had come to him was to talk about my need for Bible study.

"The first principle of Bible study which you need to recognize is to set aside a time for it every day."

"Well," I said, "I don't want to do just a superficial job. Not just Bible reading. I want to go into it in some depth but I don't know whether I'll have the time to spend every day. How about two or three times a week?"

"No," he replied emphatically, "that won't do. You need to give some of every day. How about an hour a day?"

I was amazed at his suggestion. "Didn't I tell you I'm in medical school? I spend all of every evening on the books. Your advice is just impossible."

He challenged me. "How many hours do you study in the evening?"

"I start right after supper, about seven, and study till midnight."

"That's five hours a night," he said. "I'll give you Saturday night for recreation and Sunday night for worship. That leaves five nights. Five times five is twenty-five. Do you study twenty-five hours a week?"

"Yes, I . . . " I stalled. "Well, maybe not every week."

"Do you study twenty hours a week?"

"Sure, I . . . well, occasionally . . . "

"So you study fifteen hours a week?"

"I get your point," I acknowledged. "I'm just not as efficient or self-disciplined as I ought to be. But it's just that way. That's the way I am."

Dr. Barnhouse looked me straight in the eye and said in measured tones, "I'm going to tell you what I tell my people about tithing. I tell them that if they'll give ten cents out of the dollar to the Lord, He'll make the ninety cents that's left go further than they could have made the whole dollar go. I say to you, if you'll give one hour a night to the Lord, He'll make the other four hours go further than you could have made all five hours go."

I considered the challenge for a moment, and then replied, "When you put it that way there is only one logical answer I can give. I'll do it."

From that day on I studied my Bible daily through all the years of medical school, and finished all my studies creditably.

One Sunday evening in the fall of my senior year I attended the worship service at Tenth Avenue Presbyterian Church. At its conclusion, Dr. Barnhouse asked me to meet with him. After the sanctuary had cleared, he came and sat down beside me. "What are you doing now about regular Bible study?"

"Why, I am studying regularly every night just like you and I set it up with the Lord a couple of years ago. I'm not getting any supervised instruction. It's just what I am doing on my own," I told him.

He looked at me for a moment. "If I had a pain in my right abdomen I might come to you and say, 'Bill, I believe I have appendicitis and I want you to operate on me.' And if you replied, 'Okay, Doctor. I've been studying the book of Romans lately and I believe I can do a first-rate appendectomy,' I would commend you for studying Romans and look for another surgeon! Now, my question is, are you doing it this way, only backwards? Are you so busy studying medicine that you forget that your primary job on the mission field will be to proclaim the Word and to win souls to Christ?"

He paused a moment to let that thought sink in, and then he made his proposal: "If you and the other medical students out at Penn who are planning toward missions are interested, and if we can find a time that is mutually acceptable, I'll give you one hour a week of Bible study."

We met with him to discuss the matter further and we found that the only time we could work it would be from 7:30 to 8:30 A.M. on Thursdays. So for the rest of the year we were up before daybreak, riding the streetcar during the cold winter months and into the spring, down to Spruce and Tenth Streets to meet with Dr. Barnhouse for Bible study; then back to west Philadelphia by 9 A.M. for classes. Three years later when I went back in a residency at the University of Pennsylvania Hospital, these Bible studies were continuing and also included groups of participants from Temple and Jefferson medical schools. Members from these groups made up some of the early chapters of the Christian Medical Society which continues to provide a deep spiritual blessing among Christian physicians and medical students today.

Dr. Barnhouse's contribution to building the Christian life and witness of young medical students was truly remarkable in light of the extremely busy schedule he followed. He preached four or five times on Sundays, once in French. Tuesday night he was in New York City, and Wednesday night in Montclair, New Jersey. Prayer meeting at his own church in Philadelphia was moved to Thursday evening, and then he had a couple of days to get ready and start all over again. At the same time he edited a monthly magazine, *Revelation.* How he found time for a few medical students was nothing short of another miracle of the Holy Spirit.

GOD CONTINUES TO PROVIDE

By the end of that first year in medical school, Duncan Calder and I were low on cash and we had to "bum" our way home for the holidays. Duncan had been a classmate of mine at Davidson, and we roomed together two years at Penn. We spent the first night sleeping in an empty truck parked on a road in New Jersey, and the second night tied together on top of a load of glass jars to keep from rolling off in our sleep. We hooked another ride on a truckload of fresh fish and made it to Charlotte, North Carolina. We were disheveled, dirty, and smelled to high heaven of fish!

During the summer I had a job posting books for a Knoxville bank, and was able to put some money away for another year of school. The second year included courses in pathology, bacteriology, and pharmacology. I found these studies to be challenging and stimulating, and I applied myself to them with a will.

An important advantage that came to me at this time was the job I obtained at the Christian Association of the university. It was a position I retained the last three years of medical school, and it entailed operating the telephone switchboard, acting as reception clerk when the daytime staff departed in late afternoon, and locking the building up at closing time. There were two of us and we alternated evenings of work. In return we had an upstairs room for living quarters and were given a small monthly stipend of $12.50.

Time came for the second semester to start and I was in a financial crisis once again. I had the $250 for my tuition, but if I paid it I would be left with only $50 in pocket. For the next four months I was to receive another $50 from the Christian Association, so that meant only $100 for four months, and I didn't see how I could make it.

I went to the vice president of the university who was in charge of scholarships. I told him my situation and asked for some extra time to pay all of my tuition. Dr. McClelland patiently heard me out, considered the matter for a minute, and then told me to pay the whole tuition and see how far I could go on what I had. His last word was, "If you can't make it, come back and see me."

I never did go back.

I lived for four months on $100. It was tight. My essential costs were three: meals, laundry, and an occasional haircut. I washed most of my clothes but had to send out shirts with an old German grandfather who came and picked them up. There was no such thing as drip-dry in those days. I lived on 65¢ a day. Breakfast dropped out of my schedule. A sandwich and glass of milk became my fare with sometimes an apple thrown in for good measure. I'll never forget those Philadelphia cream cheese sandwiches. And those liverwurst sandwiches—so thick and luscious! Occasionally I got a job waiting tables at Christian Association meetings which earned me a free meal. However, during those lean four months I lost about thirty pounds.

Having completed two years of medical school in good shape, Dr. McClelland's office awarded me a loan scholarship for my last two years. This was loaned me without interest, and I began to pay it back monthly as soon as I graduated. I was allowed to set my own premiums, and four years later I still owed a sizable portion of the loan when I was ready to depart for Africa on my first term of missionary service. Mrs. Poindexter's Bible Class in the First Presbyterian Church of Chattanooga, Tennessee, heard about my debt and they paid if off at the time of my departure.

My last two years of medical school became more exciting because they moved me more closely into the realm of clinical medicine. We were in hospitals and dispensaries observing and participating in the care and treatment of patients. The climax of this clinical work came, for me, when we spent a week at a maternity clinic in south Philadelphia. We held prenatal consultations and, when the calls came in, we went out into the district to deliver babies at home. How important I felt as I sallied forth with my black medical bag containing all the accouterments necessary for a home delivery! This kind of maternity assistance has long since been discontinued but, for us, it was a high watermark experience.

As the years of medical training passed I came in contact with a number of students interested in or planning toward medical missionary service. Several were the children of missionary parents whom we called "mish kids." Years later there were those amongst us who served in Central America and Kenya. One practiced in a predominantly black community in Mississippi. Two sought to meet the medical needs of the American Indian. While we were preparing, we banded together for lunch and a time of prayer once a week.

ALLAN FLEECE

I had spent my second summer at Camp Sequoyah, a boys' private camp north of Asheville. When camp closed I decided to visit the Ben Lippin conference grounds just on the other side of the city. I had attended conferences at Ben Lippin and they had always been a blessing to me. Besides, on this occasion I felt a real spiritual need for renewal. I had lived for three years in intimate contact with non-Christian elements. Things that had once appeared black now had more of a gray appearance.

While I was at Ben Lippin I sought an opportunity to sit down with Dr. Allan Fleece, the conference director, and get some of his advice and guidance. I explained to him this wasn't a question about my beliefs. They were all just the same. It was a problem about my walk. I was some times wandering off the path, and I was in real need of help.

He heard me out and then asked, "Do you know the first verse of the twenty-third Psalm?"

"Sure," I replied.

"Repeat it," he said.

"The Lord is my shepherd. I shall not want."

"All right. Are you in any real need then?" he asked.

"Yes, I am," I replied. "I've already told you."

"Then repeat the first verse of the twenty-third Psalm," he said.

"The Lord is my shepherd. I shall not want," I said.

"Now. Do you have any real need?"

"Well . . . yes . . . I do," I insisted.

"Then repeat that verse again," he said.

"THE LORD IS MY SHEPHERD. I SHALL NOT WANT!" I said with emphasis.

"You see," he explained, "you accept it because it's in the Bible. You give lip service to it, but you don't really believe it, because if you did you would know that since God is your shepherd you don't have any real needs or wants."

With that introduction he began to explain to me that our Christian walk from day to day is just exactly like the faith we had when we first believed, took Christ as our Saviour, and were born again. We were saved by faith. We walk by faith. It's not a matter of our dedication, our desire, our effort. It's a matter of God's all-powerful giving of His Spirit. We let go and let God. Then He works miracles in our lives.

I began to see this truth and I was amazed. I had always thought I had to strive to be righteous, holy, and good. Now I was being told that all my efforts would inevitably end in failure. It is God who is all powerful. It is God who is faithful. He performs for us. I had been a Christian for twenty years and this was the first time I had ever heard this doctrine. I had not received this instruction in my home or in my church. I wondered why it had been left out, but I embraced it as God's truth. It has been a sheet-anchor of my Christian voyage.

3 INTERNSHIP AND RESIDENCIES

And we know that all things work together for good to them that love God, to them who are the called according to his purpose (Romans 8:28).

The senior year in medical school often dilutes itself into primarily a preoccupation and effort toward obtaining an intercept or residency. Fourth-year students begin to cull the publications for information about various positions in various places, even as the school year begins. There is no let up to this search until spring when hospitals begin to announce their selections. Before that time it is the primary thought in mind and the chief subject of conversation.

As I listened and participated in constant intern discussion, the idea kept occurring to me that I should apply for the best, which would be an internship at Pennsylvania Hospital, a downtown institution of great reputation and rich historical tradition. It is the oldest hospital in the United States and was served by Dr. Benjamin Rush, a physician who signed the Declaration of Independence. Rumor had it that only those with high and mighty connections would be accepted. I sent in my application. Now it was almost embarrassing to join the others to talk about internships.

I had an acquaintance with the chief of urology at the hospital since his wife and my mother had attended Agnes Scott College together. I had visited in their home, and I hoped he might put in a good word for me. One day he and his associate invited me to lunch to talk about the matter of my application. They were very gracious and we had a lovely meal together. Afterwards we discussed my plans for the future. I explained to them that I was committed to a medical missionary career in the Belgian Congo. Their eyebrows went up.

"Why in the world would you want to do a thing like that?" they asked.

I explained to them that I felt it was God's will for my life.

They persisted. "You are making application for one of the finest positions for training in the world! Why would you want to throw it away?"

I defended my position by saying that I didn't think it would be a waste, and that there were acute medical needs in the developing parts of the world where Pennsylvania Hospital ought to be proud to be represented.

"You say this is God's will for your life," they countered. "How do you know God's will?"

"Well," I said, "I try to yield myself to God, willing to obey Him in the matters which He shows me. I pray about it and I have convictions in my mind and in my heart that certain things are God's leading in my life. Thus, God speaks to me."

The younger man resounded. "God doesn't speak to me. Why does He speak to you and not to me? Why does he show such favoritism? If that's the kind of God he is, to hell with him!"

I was so shaken by his blasphemy that I couldn't answer him coherently. I mumbled a word of thanks for my luncheon and we parted. I never heard from them further on the matter, and all I could do was take it to my Lord in prayer and leave it there.

In the spring word came that I had not been accepted at Pennsylvania Hospital. The shock left me numb and staggered. I went to my room, got down on my knees beside my bed, and wept from the bottom of my heart. Why God? Why? Why? I thought it was so right. I had counted on it so strongly. Now everything is washed away. I don't even have anything to fall back on. Why?

Gradually my composure returned and God seemed to be saying to me, "Hold onto your faith. Don't let it fail. I still have plans for you. You are still in my hand. Some times it is important for me to teach my children the lessons of faith, through the face of defeat. Remember, I love you."

The next day was Sunday and Duncan Calder and I were having our midday meal together. Duncan had just accepted an internship at Philadelphia General Hospital. He knew something of the shock of disappointment I had experienced the day before, and he was trying to cheer me up.

"Bill," he said, "my second choice was Bryn Mawr Hospital, out on the Main Line of Philadelphia. It's a good hospital, well staffed, and with good learning facilities. I looked into it thoroughly. I happen to know that they will be making their final decisions on interns tomorrow. Dr. Richards is the chairman of their committee. I have his phone number. Why don't you call him and ask if they will consider you?"

This seemed to be a door opening before me, and the only one in sight. I didn't even wait to finish my lunch, I went to the phone and called. Dr. Richards himself answered and when I explained why I was calling, he said, "My! You are quite fortunate. I was on my way out of the house and came back to take this call. I wouldn't have been available for the rest of the day, and our committee is meeting tomorrow morning. Bring your letters of recommendation and come out and meet with the committee at the hospital."

On Monday morning, I made the fifteen-mile trip to Bryn Mawr as fast as I could go and was ushered in to meet the committee. They asked me some questions, and then as I left the room Dr. Richards went out with me to say they would be making their final decisions within the next few minutes if I wished to wait. Half an hour later he shook my hand and told me I had been selected for an internship at Bryn Mawr.

God really had matters all planned out for me from the beginning because in less than forty-eight hours after receiving Saturday's devastating news, I had my internship! I still feel that I was acting within God's will when I applied to the first hospital, but He had a very important lesson to teach me that has blessed me all of my life.

On June 10, 1936, I graduated from the University of Pennsylvania with a doctorate in medicine, but I was not there to receive it. My examinations had been completed a week or ten days earlier, so I lit out for Knoxville in order to have a few days with my family before starting my internship at Bryn Mawr.

BRYN MAWR

Not many days later I was arrayed all in whites and had taken up my duties as a fledgling physician. Bryn Mawr Hospital was a privately endowed and administered institution located in the township of the same name on Philadelphia's Main Line. It was of medium size and catered to an affluent community. The hospital was well staffed and well equipped. It afforded excellent instruction and opportunities for a tenderfoot doctor.

The internship offered a general hospital experience and was called a rotating internship of a year's duration which comprised six services of two months each. I had the fortunate assignment of starting out with some of the less exacting responsibilities such as clinical laboratory work, outpatient department, and manning the ambulance on emergency calls. I finished the year with the more strenuous duties of obstetrics, surgery, and internal medicine.

Much of the conduct of medical practice in those days was predicated on the paucity of specific medications, compared to the extensive armamentarium which we enjoy today. During my four years of medical school the use of antibiotics or even of sulfa drugs was never once mentioned. They had not yet arrived on the scene. Furthermore there were no antihistamines nor contraceptives nor steroids nor tranquilizers. The only diuretics were mercurial. There was no specific treatment for tuberculosis. In fact, the only specific curatives I can recall were quinine for malaria and neosalversan for syphilis. Insulin for the control of diabetes was the one great medicinal breakthrough of that vintage which was acclaimed by one and all as a miraculous victory. If the doctors of that day had been polled to determine the one drug they would have chosen if only one were available, the winner probably would have been morphine!

During my internship, the first sulfa product became available for clinical use. It was called prontosil and was administered intravenously. We tended to retain it the winter of 1936–1937 for children with pneumonia, which was the number one killer in those days, running about a 20 percent mortality. It was called "Captain of the Men of Death." Prontosil saved a lot of those babies and small children.

The other signal advance which profoundly affected the practice of surgery as we knew it then, permitting the many rare procedures that are merely routine today, was the introduction of the science of anesthesiology. We had no closed system anesthesia, much less mechanically controlled respiration and circulation. Many of the frequently employed emergency operations of that day (such as appendectomies, mastoidectomies, tonsillectomies) are seldom seen today. This is, of course, because of the effective intervention of antibiotics to control various kinds of infection.

There were other events and activities which occupied that first year of medical practice. Some of the nursing staff of the hospital asked me to teach a Bible class once a week, which I did for several months. Political events transpired at that time that will never be forgotten. It was in 1936 that Edward VIII, serving as king of the British Empire, surrendered his throne to marry the American woman he loved. It was also the year of an American presidential election. I shall remember it always because it was the first one in which I cast a vote. The age of maturity and political responsibility in those days was twenty-one, but I had to wait until I was twenty-four to exercise my political prerogative.

Franklin D. Roosevelt was elected president in 1932 during the Great Depression, but four years later he was still supporting strong government controls that I understood were meant to be temporary . . . so I voted for Alfred Landon from Kansas. Roosevelt won a second term with a devastating landslide over brother Landon.

OBSTETRICAL RESIDENCY

Late in my intern year I addressed myself to what I should do next. I was convinced that I needed some more training before embarking for missionary work in Africa. But what kind of training should it be? I had enjoyed my obstetrical service most of all, and I felt I had done well at it. Certainly obstetrics was a branch of medicine that could be well put to use in any part of the world and in any sort of culture. Thus, I placed my application for a residency in obstetrics with the University of Pennsylvania hospital, the teaching hospital where I had studied as a student. I really had little expectation of obtaining the appointment, so it was with surprise and gratification that I received notice of my acceptance.

The Hospital of the University of Pennsylvania, conveniently referred to as HUP, is located on Spruce Street, just over the Schuylkill River in West Philadelphia. It stands as a beacon and an integral part of the oldest medical school in the United States. It was here I had performed my first physical examinations on real live patients, had trailed along on ward rounds with my eminent professors, had teetered on the edge of an amphitheater bench drinking in all the marvels of modern surgery. It was in this institution that I had heard Dr. Stokes declaim on the vigorous resistance of the *Treponema pallidum*; I listened to Dr. Schumann expound on the history of the obstetrical forceps; I enjoyed Dr. Perry Pepper reading from the twelfth chapter of Ecclesiastes. Now I was returning to HUP as the Resident in Obstetrics!

My job description in the department was to take an active leadership in the prenatal clinic, to oversee the activities of the interns who rotated regularly through this phase of hospital service, to make postpartum rounds, see that records of the patients were accurately maintained, and to write up birth certificates on all the newborns before sending them to the bureau of vital statistics. Normal deliveries were considered to be the prerogative of the interns, and they assisted most of these patients. Whenever there was a reason to anticipate an obstetrical abnormality or the possibility of a difficult or dystocic delivery, I was always the house officer in charge, keeping in constant touch with the staff member on call. I roomed and took my meals in the hospital.

The clinical chief of our obstetrical service was Dr. Carl Bachman. He was a relatively young professor and had the unusual experience of being invited to Bangkok to organize and set up an inclusive maternity service for the government of Siam. He had been quite successful in this venture and was called from there to a teaching position in Canada. He had come to Philadelphia as an associate professor of obstetrics only a year prior to my arrival.

There were, of course, many valuable lessons learned from Dr. Bachman and his associates. I learned to do low cesarean sections by mobilizing the bladder and making my extraction of the baby through the lower uterine segment. This became particularly valuable in Africa where it was so often necessary to section a thirteen or fourteen-year-old nullipara, not yet physically mature enough to spontaneously deliver a term baby. Still, this girl could go back to her village with the full intention of bringing another offspring into the world every year or two for as long as her childbearing facilities would last. Invading only the lower uterine segment helped to protect this oft-used organ.

Analgesia and anesthesia were still in their rudimentary phases when I was at HUP. Barbiturates were about the only oral medications that we had for labor distress. Nembutal rendered patients wild and woolly. So for this reason we relied more often on the use of opiates.

Closed system anesthesia was yet to come into its own. Open drop ether or venethine were often used, but we also did a lot of cesareans under local anesthesia. This experience was singularly helpful to me in Africa where I was often working without the help of an experienced anesthetist. I much preferred xylocaine infiltration of the skin and peritoneum, which was entirely adequate in my African patients.

But perhaps the most valuable lesson I learned from Dr. Bachman was not directly connected with performing professional techniques. I called him one day to report on a patient in difficult circumstances. We were giving her a "trial of labor" and she wasn't responding very successfully. I told Dr. Bachman I thought we were going to have to section her.

"Why do you think so?" he asked.

"Well . . . she's been in labor for quite a while and she's not making any progress."

I was surprised by his next question. "What are the reasons against sectioning her?"

"Against? Why, there aren't any. I just told you, I think she needs to be sectioned."

"I'll come and see her," he replied. He did, and we eventually performed the necessary surgical intervention.

The following morning he called me into his office. We sat down together and he produced a large tablet. With a heavy crayon he made a line down the middle of the page. At the top, on one side, he printed the words "Reasons For," and on the other side he wrote "Reasons Against."

"Now," he said, "let's put down the reasons for performing that cesarean yesterday. What are they?"

I thought of several and was surprised that he could add a few more.

The he said, "What about the reasons against surgery?"

"There weren't any," I said. "That's why we did it."

"No," he answered. "There are always pros and cons, and we need to face them. We need to put them down because if we aren't willing to look at both sides of the question we never have any real expectation of coming up with a valid answer. So, here they are. Let's write them down."

Again I was surprised to see him list a number of disadvantages that yesterday's surgery might have entailed. He showed me how he weighed one set against the other to help determine the right procedure. He never had to do that again. On numerous occasions through the years I have sat down with my paper marked by a black line down the middle, and while my decisions have not been of the earth-shattering variety, they have been decisions I could comfortably live with because of this approach.

As the period of my residency in a large, well-staffed teaching institution drew to a close, it behooved me once again to evaluate my professional training in the light of ultimate services I expected to render on the mission field. HUP presented a great opportunity for learning, but with so many chiefs and subchiefs ahead of me, there were fewer opportunities for performance. My mind projected to a coming day when I would be thrust precipitously into what promised to be a solo practice in which I would be called upon to take care of everything that might come down the road. I was itching to get my hands more effectively into the center of the action.

One option was to continue with more study in the field of gynecology. But specialties were not sought after in the 1930s as they are today. This was prior to the great explosion in medical knowledge which has demanded limitation and concentration in particular fields. Here again, as I looked forward toward service in Africa, or possibly some other mission field, I realized that should I arrive on the field a qualified specialist; there was little expectation that I would actually pursue my specialty. There would likely be too many other medical demands. So it was that I began to look about for an appointment which would broaden my capacities and experience, particularly in surgical skills.

Ashland State Hospital was advertising its needs for a surgical resident. It was a small institution located in eastern Pennsylvania and it promised considerable surgical opportunities. I made application and was accepted.

SURGICAL RESIDENCY

This portion of the state is known as the hard coal region. One hundred years ago there was a booming industry as anthracite coal was extracted from the deep mines and transported to the Pittsburgh steel mills, as well as to other industries and millions of household hearths and furnaces. Then the bituminous coal of Kentucky and Tennessee came on the scene. The process of open-face mining was much cheaper than sinking deep shafts and shoring up long tunnels with heavy timbers. Hard coal bowed to the inevitable, and one by one the companies closed down their activities.

The miners in that area, however, knew only one occupation—mining. So when the legitimate mining companies closed down, individuals resorted to "wildcat" mining. They continued to exploit existing facilities and even sank their own shafts. They would lower themselves on cables wound round the axle of an old automobile chassis. State safety inspectors had to close their eyes to these activities not to incite armed rebellion among the beleaguered miners. Obviously there were more accidents and casualties resulting from wildcat mining. In order to help protect the people, the state government established several government-supported hospitals throughout the area. Ashland State Hospital was one of these government hospitals.

On the day of my arrival I found two practicing surgeons in the hospital. One was the chief of staff. I was one of three residents, and there was a full-time radiologist and pathologist.

I was immediately assigned to the receiving ward and shortly had a call to come see an accident case with a hurt leg. The young fellow was lying on the examining table under a white sheet surrounded by four or five of his mining buddies. Their faces were completely black, covered with coal dust, which gave me the impression that they were wearing masks. They were laughing and joking together, and the injured one was smoking a cigarette.

I walked in airily and casually greeted them as I threw back the sheet. My breath caught. There was no leg! He had caught it in a swinging boom and there was a clean amputation at midthigh. Retraction of blood vessels had controlled hemorrhage and a quick check of his vital signs showed he was in good general condition. I rushed to the phone to call the chief and tell him we had an emergency case for the operating room.

"Okay," he replied. "Take him on to OR, clean him up, and get started. I'll be with you in a few minutes."

I followed instructions, anesthetized and prepped him, and I began probing gingerly. Large arteries had to be ligated and the sciatic nerve had to be stripped and cut back. I surveyed the protruding femur; it had to be shortened in order to afford muscle and skin coverage of the stump.

The chief came hustling in, cast several appraising glances over my shoulder, and pronounced, "You're doing okay. Carry on." Then he departed from the room! I was left alone with my first surgical procedure at Ashland State.

This was my first experience (and hopefully my last) of state-controlled medicine. Everybody was on salary, including all the doctors. There were no true work incentives, no penalties for indifference or laziness. Worse than that, the whole organization was set up on a political basis. President Roosevelt had just swept Democratic government in a long-standing Republican bastion, and all across the state of Pennsylvania the Democrats were "reaping the spoils." Our hospital administrator was an untrained local ward heeler. Some of our doctors, those who had voted Republican all their lives, were now paying dues to the Democratic party in order to keep their jobs.

It was amusing but also pathetic to watch our wards fill up at Thanksgiving and Christmastime. The politicians would round up the lonely and vagrant across the county and send them to the hospitals for free holiday meals, and the next day they would all be discharged.

I knew I was needed at the hospital and that my job didn't depend on political favors. One ward politician came to me at the beginning of the summer months and seriously proposed that he had eighty-five children who needed to have their tonsils removed. He wondered how we could set up a schedule for me to take care of all of them during school vacation. No physician had examined them or judged that they needed tonsillectomies. Needless to say, I flatly turned down the honor!

One interesting experience I had at Ashland was to encounter, diagnose, and treat my first case of leprosy. In the years to come I would be involved with leprosy victims by the thousands, but it was here in Pennsylvania that I saw my first case.

Ashland State Hospital furthered my education in another area. Our radiologist at Ashland was quite a Civil War buff, and it was soon obvious that I was the first resident from below the Mason-Dixon line ever to be seen in those parts. He immediately began bombarding me with Civil War trivia, and when he recognized my woeful ignorance on the whole subject he was aghast. He supplied me with a copy of Fletcher Pratt's *Ordeal By Fire*, which I perused during the evening hours. Soon I found myself thoroughly engrossed in the extended panoply of those stirring events. I studied my lessons well, and he was no longer able to completely befuddle me with logistic problems and questions. In fact, I developed the capacity to lance a few barbs in his direction.

But the situation continued to afford me one uncomfortable aspect. I was being lauded by my colleagues as a dyed-in-the-wool Southerner. What they didn't know was that East Tennessee had been predominantly Union in its sympathies. My grandfather had been an officer in the Union Army of East Tennessee! I must admit I put off breaking the news and having my exalted image besmirched, but finally the time came and I resumed my ordinary place among mortal men.

As the year wore on, my days of residency training were rapidly coming to a close. It was time to begin preparations for going to the mission field. I wrote to our mission board in Nashville, Tennessee, to inform them that I was completing my third year of residency, and that I was formally making application to go to the Belgian Congo in late 1939. They replied that there was no opening in Africa at the time, but there was one in Korea. This was a sobering thought for me. I had dreamed in terms of the Belgian Congo for so many years that it was sort of difficult to get my thinking turned around. I wrote them again to say that certainly if the Lord was leading me to go to Korea, I wanted to move forward in His will. But I still had six months of work at Ashland, and we would hold the matter in abeyance.

Shortly before I left Ashland they wrote me again from the board to say that during the intervening six months the six doctors under appointment in the Congo had been reduced in number by two. One had resigned and another had been forced to return to the United States suffering from African sleeping sickness. This left an opening for me to be appointed as a new medical missionary to the Belgian Congo!

The person who had resigned was my friend, Dr. Eugene Kellersberger. Among the reasons he resigned was to make a place for me. I was always sorry about this, and disappointed that I missed getting to serve with him on the mission field.

On August 31, 1939, I concluded my work at Ashland. All evening I spent packing my belongings preparatory for departure the next day. While I packed, news reports on the radio began to interrupt regular scheduled programs with increasing frequency, telling of the invasion of German troops into Poland. After I finally went to bed, a fellow resident wakened me to listen to Adolph Hitler regale the Reichstag with his rabble-rousing bombast which was translated for us as he spoke. By morning both England and France had declared war on Germany. World War II had begun.

As the war mushroomed, expectations of getting to Africa began to fade. A requirement of the Belgian government was that I take a course in tropical medicine before practicing in the Congo. But where could such studies be followed? Our other missionary doctors had studied tropical medicine in London and Liverpool, England, and at Brussels, Belgium. But these countries were now experiencing the aggressive might of the German war machine and it was impossible to go there. I languished at home and sought out temporary opportunities to practice medicine while waiting to go. I filled in as a house officer at Knoxville's Presbyterian Hospital, tending to IV infusions, doing physical examinations, and teaching various Bible studies.

MILESTONE THREE
STARTING OUT

"And I am sure that when I come unto you, I shall come in the Fullness of the blessing of the gospel of Christ" (Romans 15:29).

4 DEPARTURE FOR AFRICA

And he said unto me, My grace is sufficient for thee: for my strength is made perfect in weakness. Most gladly therefore will I rather glory in my infirmities, that the power of Christ may rest upon me (2 Corinthians 12:9).

As the year 1940 counted off its weeks and months, the German military might extended its domination over most of Europe. First, Norway and Denmark, then Belgium, the Netherlands, and France fell to the swiftly invading Panzer Units. British troops eked out a hairbreadth withdrawal at Dunkirk, and the Battle of Britain was on. The Belgians set up a government-in-exile in England and assumed control of their colony in Africa. The rich mineral deposits in the Congo would be of strategic importance in the war effort.

In June the governor general of the Congo saw fit to waive the requirement for new incoming doctors to complete the tropical medicine course for the obvious reason that there were no schools of tropical medicine! It was not until September that this news arrived in the United States—an indication of the disruption of communications caused by the devastating effects of a global war.

This news meant that I could now proceed to the Congo! The next hurdle would be to obtain a means of passage. Much shipping was now diverted to the war effort, and German submarines and raiders on the high seas rendered travel quite hazardous. Besides that, there was one more fly in the ointment. Congress enacted legislation in September calling for a peacetime draft. American youth began signing up in October, and then the huge administrative effort took place to appoint draft boards and to instruct members of these boards as to their duties and prerogatives. These members were ordinary citizens, none of whom had ever served on a draft board before, and since this was a brand new experience, everyone was thoroughly confused.

Africa.

In the meantime I was informed that reservations had been made for me on a ship sailing from New York to Cape Town the first of November. I also learned I had to get permission from my draft board before I could leave the country. I applied for this permission, and informed them that I needed a prompt release as my sailing date was only ten days hence. The board replied that they could give me no such permission until they knew my draft number, and there were tens of thousands of draft cards which had been collected in a helter-skelter manner. They lay in great masses in large bins in draft offices. Whole pages of the newspapers were daily devoted to printing names and numbers; not alphabetically, merely listed information, one card after the other. I scanned the papers carefully from day to day, but my name and number did not appear.

The departure date drew nearer and nearer. I took this matter earnestly to the Lord in prayer, and said, "Father, I know You don't have to look at those cards. You know my draft number, and You knew it before it was ever given to me. I am sure that if You want me to go to Africa and if this is necessary to my going, You can certainly supply it. So I just leave it in Your hands, and I thank You for taking care of all of the matters which need to be handled."

A day or two before my planned departure from Knoxville, I had a call from the lady who was the new secretary for the draft boards, and she said: "Dr. Rule, a strange thing happened here today. I had a whole mess of cards on the table to gather information from them, and I was just idly turning them over and happened to turn up one with your name on it. I immediately recognized that this was one from which we wanted to get the number, so this is to inform you that we now have your number. The board is meeting today and the matter of your overseas departure will be before them." Later that day I was told to come by the office and pick up my permit to leave the country!

Thus the Lord intervenes in the lives of those who will turn to Him and put their trust and confidence in Him. It has happened to me so many, many times, and is one of the warm and comforting spots of my existence. I know that my Heavenly Father acts daily on my behalf, in matters which are sometimes of major importance and also often in quite incidental and commonplace affairs.

THE VOYAGE

At this juncture I shall go back to letters and statements written forty-five years ago to give a more accurate account of my departure from Knoxville, arrival in New York, and voyage aboard the *El Nil* down the eastern seaboard of the United States and South America, and from thence to Cape Town.

November 4 was election day. I had already cast my vote, again for the losing candidate. But more importantly for me, this was the day that we finally cast off and began our journey towards Africa! Thank God that I need have no fear or apprehension at this time, for I knew that "His grace was sufficient for me."

The *El Nil* was an Egyptian ship and the captain was taking various precautions. We observed blackout on the open sea. There were about a hundred passengers aboard and forty-eight were missionaries. We hugged the eastern coast of South America and rounded the bulge of Brazil to put in at Recife where we were allowed to go ashore. Recife, a city of four hundred thousand at that time, is eight degrees below the equator, and it afforded us a real taste of tropical climate and verdure, with stately palm trees exhibiting flowing tresses in the breeze. The city's architecture flashed pleasant multicolored designs before our eyes.

As we set forth more deeply into the South Atlantic, I was confronted with my first medical problem as a missionary doctor. Two-year-old John McMurray, son of fellow missionaries, came down with a fever. It climbed steadily to 105 degrees, keeping us busy applying sponge baths and administering antipyretics in an effort to reduce the fever from such a danger zone. He refused to eat or drink and the problem arose of maintaining an adequate fluid intake. I culled my newly acquired textbook of tropical medicine. The fever subsided within a few days and I realized I had observed my first case of dengue fever. This is a viral disease, carried by the bite of a mosquito and characterized by fever, headache, general body pains, and a rash. Apparently John had gotten his mosquito bite as we lay at anchor in Trinidad harbor.

This experience points up the ultimate challenge of commitment of overseas missionaries living under the physical disadvantages often encountered in developing countries—the protection and safety of their children. I was finding a deeper appreciation of this dimension of missionary life as I heard Jean McMurray, little John's mother, recount in the course of daily conversation the serious illnesses which her two older children had experienced in Congo. The oldest child, Harlan, had been suddenly seized with terian malaria and within six hours was in a coma. He was so critically ill that the doctor

Sailing to Africa on the El Nil, *1940.*

deemed it wise to give him three intravenous injections of quinine within a twenty-four hour period. Their little girl, Nancy, suffered repeated convulsions with her malaria. Both children developed African sleeping sickness and were treated over weeks and months with injections of tryparsamide. Yet here was the McMurray family, delighted to be on their way back to the Congo after an agonizing two-year delay in the States. Why this inscrutable response? Because of their firm conviction that God had laid His hand upon them and called them to their work and if God so called, He could protect and keep the children in His own mighty and loving way.

All the young missionary men aboard, like myself, had narrow experiences getting by their newly-formed draft boards and leaving the United States. Their difficulties had been fantastic. Howard and Marjorie Horner were new recruits for service with the Disciples of Christ mission. Both were doctors. Howard had applied to his draft board to leave the country. The matter was studied and he was turned down. "If we're going to go into this war you are one of the fellows we'll need," they said. "You have skills which will be needed in a war effort, and we would call you up." It looked like the way was barred for him until the director of his board called to ask him if he was an ordained minister, as this would exempt him from being drafted. It seems the Disciples ordain all of their missionaries, in whatever profession. When he went back with this added information there was a raising of eyebrows, and it wasn't until his director made a personal trip and appeared before the draft board to explain that Howard's ordination was for real and that he could marry people and bury people like any other minister, that they finally reluctantly let him go.

Maurice Brantley, a Floridian on his way to the Baptist mission in Nigeria, was unable to get permission to leave the country right up until he was on his way to New York to catch the boat. Howard McCamey, a dentist from Dallas, Texas, had to engage legal aid to effect his departure.

But the most fantastic tale was told by Elwood Bartlett. On registration day for the draft, Elwood was trying to find passage to Africa from California. He was unable to find a ship going his way and the Methodist mission board ordered him to New York to sail on *El Nil.*

He drove his car across the United States, consigned it for shipment to Africa, and presented himself on the day of embarkment, ready to begin his journey.

"Where is your draft board's permit for you to leave the country?" The ship's purser asked.

"What do you mean 'permit'?" He replied in amazement. "I didn't know I needed any permit."

"Of course you do. You won't be able to go on this ship."

"But I have to," Elwood explained. "My car is in your hold!"

"Then you'll have to contact your draft board if you are to come on board. Where did you sign up for the draft?"

"In California!" Elwood exclaimed. But he had done no more than register on the day of universal conscription, and immediately head east. He didn't know where his board was located or how to get in touch with them. He rushed to a phone and contacted local New York draft boards which, of course, could give him no help. Then he called the State Department in Washington. Time was drawing nearer for embarkation. He must have done a good job of presenting his cause and he was able to put the purser on the line who, in turn, was satisfied enough with the permission to forgo regulations and allow Elwood to board.

As we put out into the New York harbor, Elwood stood at the rail and heaved a sigh of relief, but the snafu really had not been untangled. He still had his woes ahead of him. Months later, as he served his church at Elizabethville in the Belgian Congo, he received a communication in an important-looking envelope with block letters emblazoned upon it: WANTED FOR DELINQUENCY BY THE UNITED STATES ARMY!

Our ship plowed deeper and deeper into the South Atlantic where porpoise and flying fish provided interesting interludes. Even whales were occasionally sighted. The heavenly bodies gradually changed positional relationships to the ones I had become accustomed to for my lifetime. Polaris, the north star, slipped early on, below the horizon and was lost to view for the next four years. Orion now swung in the northern skies and by arising before dawn I was introduced to the glories of the southern cross. In daytime, too, the sun had shifted northward, and for the first time in my life my shadow was cast to the south.

Thirty-two days out of New York we approached the southern tip of Africa and sighted Cape Town harbor. God in His providence had shielded us from German raiders and submarines. We had encountered no suspicious signs, yet a sister ship that followed us a few months later on this same course was intercepted and sunk. How inviting the sight of terra firma appeared, beckoning to us to come ashore! The dramatic appearance of Table Mountain with its flat expanse rising above the city at its feet was breathtaking, and when a white cloud rolled over its precipice and slowly tumbled down the facial cliffs, it gave the impression of a giant cloth brushed from the table, falling in slow motion.

What an exciting moment! Africa, here we come! Twenty years of anticipation, and now my feet were going to touch that dreamed-of soil. Closer and closer I was coming to the land of my foresworn dedication, and to the task I was convinced God had called me to perform.

CAPE TOWN AND VICTORIA FALLS

Cape Town is a beautiful city and we enjoyed the lush foliage of its December summertime. We had six interesting days in which to discard our sea legs and get our land legs under us once again. Then on December 12, we boarded a train for the interior—a mode of living which would be ours for most of the next ten days and for nearly three thousand miles! The trains were all wood burners and they lit up the skies at night with billows of racing sparks. This augmented everything to be grimy and precluded raising windows (not protected by screens) which added to the sultry temperatures.

Our first respite from this continuous travel came at Bulawayo in Southern Rhodesia. Here we were given time to go to a hotel for a much-needed bath, and even to take a dip in the hotel swimming pool. We also indulged in a fine multicourse meal and, best of all, we had ice water! As I asked for my second and third glass I noticed my waiter eyeing me with disapproval and finally his concern for my well-being overcame his embarrassment. He sidled over to advise me in a *sotto voce* that drinking so much cold water in the tropics was dangerous. I nodded and refrained from requesting a fourth glass.

It is at Bulawayo that Cecil Rhodes is buried, and we visited his grave. It is carved out of solid rock on a wild desolate mountaintop which speaks of enormous strength and granite willpower. The place memorializes a man who, without all the advantages of foresight, played a major role in shaping a continent—sometimes for good and sometimes in ways that have not been so good.

We crossed the Zambezi River, from Southern over into Northern Rhodesia where we stopped at Livingston. After checking into an elegant hotel with the McMurrays, I took the fifteen minute walk over to the brink of Victoria Falls. What a breathtaking encounter that turned out to be as I watched the waters plunge twice the distance that Niagara Falls descends.

Some thirty-one of *El Nil*'s passengers were on this train trip into the interior, and most of them were at Victoria Falls. We took a sight-seeing trip up the Zambezi where I had my first glimpse of hippos and crocodiles in the river and monkeys in the trees. Yes, this was truly Africa. I was becoming convinced.

THE BELGIAN CONGO

We left and traveled into the Belgian Congo. It was late at night in a tiny border post called Sakania that we were held up for hours as custom officials went through the baggage of those of us who would be residing in Congo, and finally issued permits of residence to us. We continued on to Elizabethville, capital of the southern province of Katanga and the second largest city in Congo. We were here for a couple of days and enjoyed meeting and visiting with our Methodist missionary brethren working in this area. It was here that Elwood Bartlett left us to take up his proper missionary responsibilities.

From Elizabethville we boarded the train for the last lap of our two-month-long journey. Now we were in homeland country where the McMurrays could lean out the windows to greet crowds of Africans in their Tshiluba tongue.

On the morning of December 22 we arrived in Luluabourg and left the train with no backward glance of regret. We were now in the center of our mission area. Bill Worth and Day Carper were present to receive us. They packed us into two A-model Fords and escorted us over rough and rutted roads the thirty-five miles to Mutoto. This was home for the McMurrays.

Christmas was upon us and I spent my first tropical Yuletide at Mutoto with palm fronds instead of evergreens. I was reminded that Christian worship during this season is more in recognition of the advent of our Lord than a commercial bonanza where everybody antici-pates tissue-wrapped presents and turkey dinner.

Orders from the colonial government had reached me requiring that I present myself in Leopoldville, the capital, for a month of medical orientation and observation before striking out on my own. So a week after arrival at Mutoto, I made my way back again to Luluabourg and boarded a plane for the trip to Leopoldville.

The airplane afforded a birds-eye view of the topographical features of the Congo. I had always imagined that the land consisted largely of widespread forests and dense jungles, but what I saw below me was open, rolling country which the French call *savane*. It was liberally traversed by large rivers, mostly flowing northward. The rivers and numerous smaller streams were bordered by ribbons of forest which gave way within a hundred yards or so to open country again.

The land area of this Congo basin drainage is approximately 1.5 million square miles. The system of navigable waterways reaches out into the inte-rior over a distance of nearly eight thousand miles. Near Leopoldville the Congo River backs itself up for some thirty miles in the Stanley Pool from which it breaks through the encircling Crystal Mountains and tumbles tempestuously through two hundred miles of cataracts to the sea. All imports arriving in Congo by ship must be off-loaded at the port of Matadi and taken around these cataracts by rail to Leopoldville where they are loaded again on riverboats to travel into the interior.

Leopoldville of 1941 was little more than a village of less than fifty thousand (of whom three thousand were Europeans). The main street was under construction. It began at the railroad station and stretched westward in the form of a simple dirt path. The city, known today as Kinshasa, has grown into a metropolis of over two million people!

I presented myself to the *Medecin-en-Chef* and was introduced to other functionaries of the Colonial Medical Service. I was assigned to observation in the clinical laboratory and to visitation in the government hospitals. I also made visits to a nearby leprosy colony. Because verbal communication was difficult and I only spoke a smattering of French, the authorities deemed it wise to send me for a week of work at the nearby American Baptist station of Sona Bata with two veteran missionary doctors, Dr. Glenn Tuttle and Dr. A. Osterholm.

After two months in Leopoldville, I flew to Luebo. The business office of the APCM (American Presbyterian Congo Mission) was located here. Mr. Allen Craig was the secretary/treasurer of the mission, and Mr. John Morrison was the "Legal Representative"—a position required by Belgian law. But the most indispensable job at Luebo was running the mission press. The Reverend Mr. Hershey Longenecker turned out hundreds of thousands of pages of school books, song books, Sunday School lessons, Bible commentaries, hospital forms and records, and monthly periodicals for those who could read—all in the Tshiluba language.

The dean of the missionary corps was the Reverend Dr. Mott Martin, a true pioneer who arrived in Africa in 1903 and survived the sinking of his riverboat as he journeyed up the Congo River to Luebo. He spent much of his time sitting in consultation with his African friends to judge, with them, in arguments and charges and countercharges. Dr. Martin considered these occasions to be unique opportunities to instruct the people in Christian ethics and morality.

The physician at Luebo was Dr. Tom Stixrud. He was self-confident, vigorous, dynamic, and strong. He had a captivating personality and had built an impressive medical work at Luebo. He was also quite popular among the Belgian colonists and officials.

I worked with Dr. Stixrud for two weeks, and while a boarding guest in missionary homes I was entertained by many tales and anecdotes of missionary life. Mr. Vass once ordered from England a "box of crackers" and received birthday favors which exploded when pulled apart. Mr. Morrison's food order to England included a request for four quarts of mixed jams. The order arrived minus that item with the explanation that the strange request was being filled and would be shipped as soon as the jams were thoroughly mixed.

There were five hospitals on the mission field and the only other doctor besides Dr. Stixrud and myself was Mark Poole at Bibanga station. Mark, my contemporary, had studied at Johns Hopkins while I was at Pennsylvania. In 1936 I went to New York to see Mark set sail for his first term of service. At that time he was single, but he married Sara while studying tropical medicine in London.

I enjoyed working with Mark for nearly three weeks at Bibanga. I began to get my hands into the intricacies of vesico-vaginal fistulas, sliding hernias, scrotal elephantiasis, and other conditions I had seldom or never observed. It was also meaningful for me to finally see and work in Dr. Kellersberger's hospital. It was to this hospital that I had addressed my letters of correspondence to the doctor for nearly twenty years.

The last day of March I assisted Dr. Stixrud with a cesarean section. Two days later I was taken to Lubondai station where I would direct the medical work. Now I considered myself AT HOME at last. It had been a long journey. All told, over 13,700 miles.

5 SETTLING DOWN AT LUBONDAI

Nay, in all these things we are more than conquerors through him that loved us (Romans 8:37).

Lubondai station was founded in 1925 as a fifth post of the Presbyterian mission. It had been laid out in an orderly fashion. Pathways edged with flowering shrubs cut across a grassy campus. An imposing red brick church and primary school for African children faced one side of the open area, and a row of attractive houses for missionaries were on the opposite side. At the western extremity of the station was a complex of buildings housing Central School, a boarding facility for missionary's children. Curriculum was for fourth grade through high school. A quarter of a mile away at the other end of the station was the hospital complex (two buildings and a scattering of huts for overnight guests). This was to be my bailiwick for some fifteen years of my life in Congo.

There were two large wards in the forty-bed hospital—one for women and one for men. There was a small room used for isolation, and an adequate operating room with an adjoining scrub/work room. Sterilization was provided by a steam boiler fired with logs cut from the forest. The boiler also propelled a steam generator which charged a bank of wet-cell batteries for thirty-two-volt electric lights until 10 P.M. Thereafter kerosene lanterns were used. Water was collected from rain runoff in a large cistern, then pumped by hand to an elevated reservoir so that running water passed by gravity to the work rooms of the hospital. A record room, pharmacy, and clinical laboratory were all housed in the dispensary building which adjoined the hospital proper.

My first official responsibility was to study the Tshiluba language. I was given a textbook of Tshiluba grammar which helped me appreciate the logic of the construction and order of words. However, there were acute medical needs at the hospital so I spent many hours there from the start.

Adapting to African medical service required considerable flexibility, ingenuity, and compromise. I was immediately confronted with the fact that the hospital was much more than a mere institution for housing the sick. It was also a hotel! Patients came from long distances with limited means of transportation, often on foot, so families came with their children and brought goats and chickens for food. Outbuildings had been constructed nearby to take care of this overflow population, but at night many of their relatives crowded into the hospital to keep their family member company and to enjoy the warmth of a log fire in the fireplace. When I determined that this could not continue, I bricked up the fireplace, and I made a new regulation that only one family member could stay with a patient at night. Making rules is one thing. Enforcing them is another. Occasionally I found it necessary to get up in the middle of the night, go to the hospital, and physically remove violators before they eventually got the message.

A second amazing observation was that there were no sheets on the beds. Sheets were a useful practice to help maintain postoperative cleanliness and provide some propriety! I had already learned it was advisable to securely seal-incised wounds with adhesive plaster to keep probing fingers from exploring the curious results of surgery. Well-laundered and regularly changed sheets would help. We had sheets in stock, so why not use them? The missionary nurse, Margaret Liston, told me it was impossible to keep sheets on beds. Patients wrapped them around as skirts and wore them all over the compound.

Now one of my characteristics is persistence (sometimes referred to as stubbornness). I determined to lick the problem. All beds were made each morning with sheets and a lightweight blanket. My colleagues pursed lips and shook heads, but I battled it out with friend and foe and once again, they eventually got the message.

The third regulation brought to my attention involved the hospital attendant who was "on call" during the night. He may have thought he was on call but it would have been a loud call to arouse him. He was not monitoring the medical situation nor the patients' conditions. He simply slept through the night like everyone else. It was a real blockbuster when I told him to stay awake all night and be responsible for the patients. I set an urn of strong coffee on the night desk and gave him specific responsibilities to accomplish during the night.

How quickly it became apparent that the basic thrust must be educational in an evolving society. Whether medical, theological, or pedagogical, there are lessons to be taught, information to disseminate, and explanations to be made. A case in point: open windows in the operating room, not even screened, where crowds gathered to watch as delicate operations were performed. This had to change.

CHIEF NTOLO

Just outside the gates of Lubondai station stood a large African community, Ntolo's village. Chief Ntolo was the paramount chief of some eight or ten villages that stretched for about five miles. All these villagers were interrelated and this larger tribal group was called the Bakwa Tshipanga (the people of Tshipanga).

Chief Ntolo was a regular attendant at public worship, and he certainly knew the gospel message, but he had never made a public profession of faith nor been taken into the membership of the church. This is a particularly difficult step for African chieftains for two reasons. First, because so much of the animistic beliefs and customs are built around the local village hierarchy, which means the chief stands at the center of spirit and ancestor worship and perpetuates all taboos, fetishes, and amulets against evil so intimately interwoven into the culture. Second, in a polygamous culture, status and standing are often determined by the number of wives a bigwig possesses. A paramount chief must have a harem, otherwise he is not worth his salt in the eyes of the people. However, the church frowned on this practice and forbade membership to male practitioners, though more lenient with women in plural marriages who exhibited true faith and cleavage to Christian principles. Women were considered to be in situations over which they had no control. Families, not individuals, determined nuptial alliances and the woman involved would be the last person consulted, if at all.

CONGO COURTSHIP

When I arrived at Lubondai I met a lovely young lady who had a warm friendly smile, and gorgeous black wavy hair. Her name was Effie Crane, and she had come to Congo a year before to teach the mission-aries' children at Central School. Our friendship ripened into affection and then into genuine love before too many months had passed.

I proposed to her on Halloween night, and there was much whooping and hollering when we announced our engagement to the student body. We soon found out, however, that "tying the knot" was not going to be easy!

Belgian law was guided by the customs and requirements of the Roman Catholic Church. There must be two distinct ceremonies, civil and religious.

Furthermore, our birth certificates were required, and we did not have them. The territorial administrator floored me when he told me that before we could be married we would have to get permission from our parents! I tried to explain to him that I didn't need my parents' permission, that I was twenty-nine years old and could make the decision for myself. But he smiled benignly and shook his head. "No," he said. "You'll have to have your parents' permission."

Our missionary friends with years of experience in the Congo shook their heads and tried to let us down easily. "This takes a lot of doing and a long time," they said. "It will certainly be a year or more before you can be married." But I rebelled at the idea. We wanted to be married as soon as possible. Besides, Effie's school vacation was coming up in late December and early January, and if we didn't get married then we'd have to wait until the end of the school year in May or June.

Mrs. Carroll Stegall, the petite, vivacious wife of the good Reverend at Lubondai, agreed to go with us into Northern Rhodesia as our chaperone and bride's attendant. I wrote my friend, Elwood Bartlett in Elizabethville, and he offered to get us over the border at Ndola. December 31 was our target date, and we set out from Lubondai on December 27, 1941.

It was a grimy, two-day train ride to Elizabethville. We bought Effie's engagement and wedding rings there, and the following day we drove 150 miles to Ndola. The city hall authority informed us that for a certain number of shillings I could get a license which would become valid in two weeks, and for a pound I could purchase one which would allow us to be married immediately. With deep gravity I said that I would like to purchase one one-pound license.

Of course we wanted a religious ceremony, and we were directed to one Mr. Smith, pastor of the Free Church. He was a young man, large, and of fair and friendly appearance. He agreed to marry us and said he would arrange for some music for the occasion. The ladies went off to do some shopping and that left me free, with Elwood's help, to solve the last two problems on my list. They were: 1) flowers, and 2) arrangements for a marriage feast.

Flowers presented no difficulty. There were several flower shops around town, and we ordered a bouquet, a corsage, and boutonnieres. Appropriate facilities for a combination wedding feast/New Year's Eve celebration were harder to find. Our hotel, the Rutland, was booked. We looked around and finally came upon a rundown passenger hotel near the railroad station. It didn't look like much, but

I was desperate. The proprietor was enthusiastic about entertaining a wedding party, and he assured us that he could provide what we needed—even a wedding cake.

Wednesday, December 31, dawned bright and fair, and it was with minimal patience that we awaited the five o'clock hour to conduct ourselves to the Free Church for the grand event. The thought suddenly occurred to me that our respective families had no idea we were outside the Belgian Congo, much less that we were in the actual motions of getting married. Five o'clock was probably too late to send a cablegram, so we looked up the telegraph office, a little prematurely, to send the message to Effie's parents. We told the clerk we wanted to send a message to Charleston, West Virginia, and he produced a tremendous volume which must have contained all the telegraph offices in the world. He searched and searched but couldn't seem to come up with the desired location. Finally he asked, "Here is Charleston, South Carolina. Won't that do?"

"No," I replied, "Charleston is the capitol of West Virginia. Surely it is in your book."

He looked some more. "How about Charleston, Ohio?"

"No, that won't do either," I told him.

"Well, here is Charleston, Tennessee. I hope that will be okay."

When I told him it wasn't okay he rather testily asked, "Why not?!"

I patiently explained. "It's like if you had an Ndola, Southern Rhodesia and an Ndola, Northern Rhodesia, and if you wanted a message to go to one place but sent it to the other, it would never get there."

Obviously, Charleston, West Virginia, had mistakenly been omitted from the directory, and we were at an impasse as to how to get a message to the Cranes. Then we recalled that over in the West Virginia panhandle there is a Charles Town, so perhaps we might send it there and they might recognize the street address and forward it to Charleston. This we did and found out later there was no delay whatever in receiving the message. Apparently, they had frequent mix-ups between the two cities which are quickly straightened out.

Now came the wording of the message for which I was going to have to pay several dollars per word. I wondered whether the location of our wedding would appear on the telegram or whether I should include the words in my message. "Will the location, Ndola, Northern Rhodesia, appear on the telegram?" I asked.

"Yes, it will say 'Ndola,'" he said.

This left me unanswered and undecided. I knew our families wouldn't have the slightest idea where Ndola was, so I checked again. "Will it say Ndola, Northern Rhodesia?"

"Oh, everybody knows where Ndola is," was his airy reply.

I walked out of the office contemplating the conversation just completed in the light of current events. A terrible world war was in progress in which people of many different languages and cultures were finding it difficult, even impossible, to understand one another. Here was a fellow who spoke the same language I did, yet I thought he was crazy because he didn't know the difference between Charleston, South Carolina, and Charleston, West Virginia; and he thought I was crazy because I didn't know that everybody knows where Ndola is located.

Promptly at five o'clock we stood in front of the tiny Free Church where Mr. Smith came out to greet us. We found that we had six local friends to attend our marriage. Mr. Smith and his wife and their small daughter were present, a kind lady who played the foot-pedal organ, and an elderly retired missionary couple who came along to lend moral support.

The sanctuary was small, perhaps thirty feet in depth, and the organist managed to get through only a few bars of the wedding march before Effie, on the arm of Mrs. Stegall, traversed the full length of the center aisle. Elwood and I were waiting for them up front, and when they reached us we four turned and faced the minister. In a ceremonious manner he handed us each one a hymn book already opened to the proper page, and we joined in to sing "Love Divine, All Loves Excelling." Effie and I are the only couple I know who participated in singing in a quartet at their own wedding!

Mr. Smith then proceeded to preach two sermonettes, one from the Old Testament and one from the New. They were brief, well chosen, and effectively presented. The ceremony proceeded smoothly, and Effie and I were pronounced man and wife before man and God.

Evening arrived and we made our way to the railroad hotel to discover what unknown delicacies had been provided for our nuptial banquet. Our jolly host had extended himself beyond perfunctory preparations. He had decorated the room, set a lovely table, and put the little pot in the big one. Dishes were brought in and carried out, and course followed course in typical Continental fashion. The food was delicious and the conversation gay, and we had a wonderful time! He even provided a beautifully decorated wedding cake with white icing and a miniature bride and groom mounted on top. When we cut into it we found that it was a fruit cake, the customary wedding cake employed by these people! So we delighted ourselves by following the suggestion, "when in Rome, do as the Romans do." At the end of this perfect day we enjoyed listening to the firecrackers, explosions, bells, and whistles as the old year was ushered out and the new 1942 was conducted in.

*Bill and Effie Crane Rule, married
December 31, 1941.*

ON THE ROAD AGAIN

At Lubondai station, our medical forces were depleted, and we had little expectation of reinforcements from the homeland because of the ravages of World War II and the disruption of normal travel. The next three years devolved into a series of frequent journeys from one mission station to another. Needless to say, it was rough on us newly-weds! Effie carried on her teaching duties at Central School, and I answered medical calls from all over the mission area. During the year 1942, I was at Lubondai a total of 173 days and "on the road" for 192 days! In 1943 the situation improved; I was away from home only 119 days.

Another reason for this continued displacement was the increased incidence of illness among the missionaries and their families. Furloughs were long overdue because there just wasn't any assured or safe passage to America. Everybody was suffering from overwork and fatigue. Another even more alarming factor was a marked increase in the incidence of African sleeping sickness. This tropical disease is caused by the invasion of a flagellate or trypanosome into the blood stream, lymphatic, and central nervous system of the human body. It is introduced through the bite of an infected tsetse fly. The Belgian government had been conducting a valiant battle against sleeping sickness, but the disruptions of World War II resulted in the loss of skilled public health personnel and permitted a resurgence of the disease.

In a two-year period, there were twenty-four cases of sleeping sickness under treatment among our Presbyterian missionaries and their families. This constituted about 25 percent of our personnel. I was often routed out of bed in the wee hours of the night on emergency calls. Traveling dirt roads in vintage cars was an additional challenge. During rainy season the roadways were washed-out ruts and gullies. During dry season, the roadways became almost impassable because of deep, engulfing sand. There were no garages, no filling stations. We carried gas cans and learned to be auto mechanics!

Tire trouble was a common experience on the road. Once I took a group of the Central School Boy Scouts on the ninety-mile trip to Lake Munkamba for an outing. Thirty miles from Lubondai, we suffered a puncture. At noon, both rear tires went out simultaneously! We waited five hours while two of the boys hiked to an African village and brought back the necessary items for repair. We patched the tires, but a mile down the road one of them gave out for good. We recovered an intact inner tube, inserted it into the defective casing and limped into our campsite about 7 P.M. I still had to go on to Mutoto to give some injections, so I left immediately on the additional thirty-five-mile trip. Halfway there I had my fifth flat. I finished the trip on two leaking tires, stopping every two or three miles to pump them up.

The following account in my diary was entered on December 14, 1941:

> Two weeks ago I had quite an experience. It was necessary for me to travel the 180 miles to Luebo to see one of our missionaries who was sick. Just before reaching Luebo the hydraulic brake system on the car went bad and I had to limp in very carefully and uncertainly. The purpose of my visit completed, we started in bright and early Monday morning to repair the automobile. It was a longer job than anticipated and when we finally finished it was already 4:30 in the afternoon. However, I had a lot of work waiting for me at Lubondai and decided to start back. Night fell as I reached the seventy-five-mile mark and when it was good and dark, the brakes went out again. I spent about an hour by flashlight before getting them in shape to go on. Then, not knowing the road and it being very dark, I missed my turns a couple of times and had to retrace my steps. This took me about thirty miles out of my way. Shortly before midnight I came to the Lulua River to find that I had missed my crossing and was at the next ferry downstream. The ferry was on the other side and although I finally roused the men I could not persuade them to come across for me. I can't say that I really blamed them. I could hear hippos in the river, snorting through

the darkness and I figured that they were afraid to venture forth. I decided to turn around and go to the upper crossing, but in backing, my hind wheels went over a four-foot embankment and when I got out to view the situation, I found the automobile at a precarious angle with the wheels spinning in thin air over the water! The car was resting squarely on its chassis. I had a fellow with me and sent him back up the road for help. Men came and we built a fire to see by. We tugged and pushed and used poles under the car for leverage, but it was five hours before we got reinforcements and finally lifted the car into the road.

I went on up to the other crossing, arriving just before dawn. The hippos were there too and I could see their heads bobbing up and down in the water as I waited for the ferry. I was put across in broad daylight and had no further harrowing events except for running out of gas a couple of times. Fortunately, I had bought a fifty gallon drum at Luebo but had no equipment for pouring from that heavy container into my gas tank. I finally rigged the rubber tubing of my stethoscope as a siphon and drew enough to get me home!

IN THE OPERATING ROOM

I was not only on my own on the road, but also in the operating room. I was the total medical community, the entire Academy of Medicine. I was confronted with conditions I had never seen, and called on for skills I had yet to develop. Time and again I went back to my medical books for help.

In most cases we saw the same things in Africa that we see in the United States, the only difference being that because of ignorance and neglect, or perhaps there was just no medical help available, the conditions were complicated or greatly exaggerated. I saw many large colloid goiters, but I remember one woman who had such a large goiter that her head was forced upward in extension, and it was difficult for her to see where she was going. After surgery, the smaller lobe weighed one pound, and the other one pound nine ounces!

One of my first four surgical cases was a leprosy patient who had been hobbling on a stick for more than ten years. He had a knee fixed at right angles. Examination showed he had suffered a dislocation with a posterior displacement of the patella and fixation between the femur and the tibia. Surgery was a relatively simple matter, but it was necessary to release and lengthen tendons and use skin grafts. Then he had to learn how to walk again. It was a long process, but we were successful.

During my earliest days in Africa I introduced the phenomena of blood transfusion. There were no donors. No blood banks. Africans were more than a little suspicious and afraid. But an opportunity arrived when a little old woman came in who was eaten alive with hookworm. What she needed more than anything was blood. I explained to her husband that if he would give some of his blood we might help her, but if not she would surely die. Wonder of wonders, he agreed! His blood was compatible and in no time we administered the first blood transfusion ever given in the entire Kasai region of the Congo. We rid her of her hookworm infestation and sent her home healed and contented. What an opportunity this afforded to point out to our medical staff the spiritual analogy that Jesus Christ gave his blood for us that we might live.

Teenage Mpampa was the son of Mundemba, the paramount chief of the Bakete tribe south of us. Mpampa was a victim of polio which is common in the Congo. Both his lower legs had suffered attack, and he had marked atrophy of the calves and hyperextension of both feet. He had to walk on his tiptoes, and in this manner he came to us—more than a hundred miles—to seek help.

I was dismayed. I was no orthopedist. Yet here sat the boy before me because there was nowhere else to go. I took a deep breath and tried to explain that I could not cure him. I could not help his legs, but perhaps his feet could be straightened so he could walk flat-footed.

"I never have done an operation like this," I told him. "And I don't know whether I can do it well. Your feet and legs will be in plaster casts for weeks. You will be in pain. I can't even promise your feet will be any better than they are now."

I stopped to wait for his answer and I'll never forget his response. "Doctor, operate. If God wants me to walk again, I'll walk."

Mpampa did walk again, much better than before, and the Lord blessed both of us in a very special way.

My medical services always caused tension with the local witch doctor. Africans went to him for treatment of diabetes, epilepsy, and often tuberculosis among many other complaints, but there were two areas in which he could not compete with me—surgery and obstetrics. My skills could offer a satisfactory resolution. The witch doctor could not.

Obstetrics was my great love and the chosen specialty for which I had been best trained. Bearing children is an integral function in all communal societies, especially in central Africa. Pregnancy and the delivery of a new member into the family are accepted as routine situations that demand little prior consideration, and so have minimal influence on the flow of ordinary events. It was not uncommon for a woman to walk a mile or so to the field to work, go into labor and deliver her baby (sometimes assisted by other women in the field), wrap it away in a safe, shady spot while she completed her work, then walk home to prepare the evening meal. But no village is without its toll

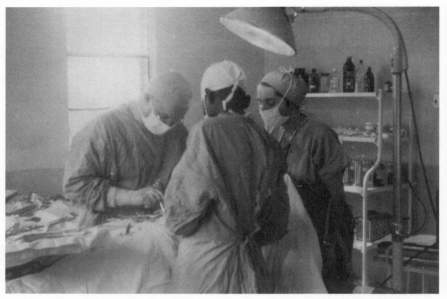

Dr. Rule and assistants in Lubondai operating room.

of both fetal and maternal mortalities. The three conditions which most often caused difficult and operative deliveries were: 1) pelvic disproportion; 2) abnormal presentation of the fetus; and 3) hemorrhage. Pelvic disproportion was often encountered in girls of fifteen years or younger, put into a marriage before reaching physical maturity. Hemorrhages were unexpected and terrifying, taking their toll of maternal life. How we needed a blood bank!

I remember a woman who came to us in labor at Lubondai with her progress handicapped by a difficult occiput posterior position of the fetus and a rather small pelvis. She was making very little progress, and I decided a cesarean section would be the safest mode of procedure. But night was coming on and we had no electricity in the hospital, so in spite of our hurried preparations for surgery, the operation had to be completed in darkness. Our anesthesia was open drop ether, so it was quite impossible to use a lantern, and we had to call for flashlights to complete the procedure. Several people stood around the periphery and shone lights onto the operative field! This was only my second cesarean at Lubondai, and I left the hospital in such a frame of mind as to hope this might be the last!

There are such things as tropical diseases, meaning that they are encountered almost exclusively in countries with tropical climate. Often this is true because the carriers or vectors of the disease are mosquitoes, gnats, ticks, snails, or flies found only in the tropics. A distressing condition which was frequently encountered a generation ago is tropical ulcer or phagedenic ulcer. These are gangrenous, rapidly extending, and sloughing ulcers characteristically seen on the lower extremities or involving the muscles of the buttocks. Numerous spirochetes and fusiform bacilli are found in the lesions. An even more repugnant form attacks the muscles and tissues of the face. It is called noma or *cancrum oris*.

I write repeatedly of huge tumors, overwhelming infections, and of grossly neglected pathology. African maladies are not uniquely different but simply neglected out of both ignorance and hope. Medical care was so rarely available that their mind-set was not to seek help. Of course we encountered tropical diseases not found in temperate regions, and our number one killer was malignant tercian malarial fever. Malnutrition was a common problem in infants and children, and could be combated best by educating the people.

The following entry in my diary was made on December 21, 1942:

> Up at 6 A.M. and to the hospital for prayers with the staff. Dispensing of drugs, bandages, soap, etc. Home for breakfast with Effie. Conversation with Mrs. Stegall concerning plans for the new nursery. Then worship and prayers with Effie and the boys in our household. Paid the school teacher from the leprosy camp. Laid out a walk in the backyard and paid ten men for planting grass there. To the hospital for ward rounds. Examination of patients in the dispensary. Home for lunch at 1 P.M. Examined several specimens and tests in the laboratory. Sold some cloth to several villagers. Filled my kerosene lamps. Trimmed a bush in the backyard. Supper. Corrected student nurses' exam papers. Visited in another missionary home. Took my bath. Family prayers. Worked on layout of new hospital charts. To bed at 11:30 P.M.

BUILDING ADDITIONS

The director of a Belgian firm for gathering, ginning, packing, and shipping cotton, La Compagnie Congolaise (CCC), came to pay us a visit. He was impressed with our medical work and said his company would like to help us in some way. We told him of our great need for an obstetrical addition where we could conduct our deliveries and house the postpartum patients for a few days. Plans were drawn up and the CCC agreed to foot the bill. Mr. Stegall went to work. He had to burn the brick and cut the lumber. It was he who ordered the nails and other hardware, as well as the metal roofing to cover the structure. Then he laid the stone foundation and poured the cement for a floor to guard against the ever-invasive termites.

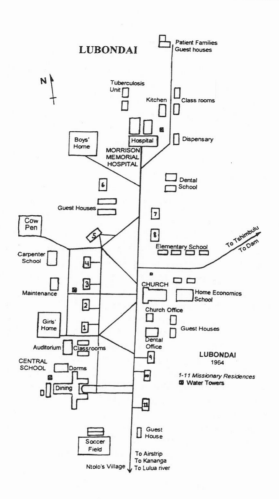

Lubondai map.

He ran up the walls, put in the doors and windows, and thus built us a maternity ward with delivery room and a dozen obstetrical beds.

At another time he dammed up one of the local streams to create a lovely lake which afforded a picnic and swimming area for many years. He installed a hydroelectric plant to deliver round-the-clock electricity to Lubondai. No more surgery by the help of flashlights! We had real surgical lamps in the operating room.

Our medical work could also thank Mr. Stegall for the renovation of facilities for taking care of orphan babies. Orphans, in central Africa, become immediately and invariably the problem and the responsibility of the missionaries. If the mother dies in childbirth and the baby survives, there is absolutely no hope for that child to receive sustenance unless a missionary takes it, provides care and cleanliness, and purchases, prepares, and administers the milk.

MASHONDO PIERRE

Mashondo Pierre was my chief African helper at Lubondai. He was a member of the royal family in Ntolo's village, and he was only a young boy when he began volunteer work with Dr. Cousar at the hospital. When I arrived some sixteen years later, he was the most dependable and experienced member of the staff. I relied heavily upon Mashondo.

But he was not well. He was lean and drawn in appearance and soon ran out of endurance and energy. I examined him carefully from time to time, with a growing conviction that he had a solid mass or tumor in his chest. I had no X-ray equipment then, but the most likely assumption was that he had a malignancy. As he became weaker we proposed to relieve him of some of his work, but he would hear nothing of it. He was determined to keep on going.

He lived in the village, about half a mile from the hospital, and the day came when he could no longer pedal his bicycle to work so he employed young village boys to push him to work. Eventually the pulmonary lesion broke through, and he had a draining fistula in his chest, but he still would not give up. Finally we built him a mud and stick hut beside the hospital so that he could continue his faithful appearance at work. But time was running out for him, and the day came when he returned to the village to stay. A week or so later, word came to us that he had died.

I went to the village in the afternoon to attend the funeral. He was a man of dignity among his people, and a great crowd came to mourn his passing. The people of the Bena Lulua tribe bury their dead just under the eaves of their own house, in the midst of the village. The rest of the family moves out, a white flag is placed on top of the hut to show that it is now a grave site, and the place is abandoned and allowed to eventually tumble down and be washed away by the winds and rains.

When I arrived, the grave was freshly dug with the body of Mashondo lying beside it. There were no boards to make a coffin, and custom was to wrap the body in woven mats for interment. There was great wailing going on, and people had painted their bodies with white chalk and were dancing around to much beating of drums. All of this was to appease the spirits, and to show respect for the ancestors whom they worshipped. I was distressed and heartsick as I sat there looking upon the scene. I kept

thinking, this is not what Mashondo would have wanted. I entertained the
idea of interrupting the proceedings to give him a Christian witness, but
they were lowering the body already into the grave. Hands smoothed and
corrected the cloth for the final disposition, and suddenly there was a
great shout. A group of Christian leaders to one side had escaped my
notice, and now they burst forth in glorious song:

UP FROM THE GRAVE HE AROSE!
WITH A MIGHTY TRIUMPH O'ER HIS FOES.
HE AROSE A VICTOR FROM THE DARK DOMAIN,
AND HE LIVES FOREVER WITH HIS SAINTS TO REIGN.
HE AROSE! HE AROSE! HALLELUJAH! CHRIST AROSE!

There was no more moaning or drum beating. An awed silence
rested on the crowd, and the pastor went on to conduct a service of
prayer and worship appropriate for the home-going of one of the
saints.

Thus it went, some of the travels, the trials, and the triumphs that
I encountered during those initial years on the mission field. Through
it all, Effie and I looked to God for His guidance, for we were there to
serve Him. And He in turn blessed us in many ways. One of those blessings was the birth of our firstborn, William Rule IV, on February 1,
1943.

6 TRAVELING HOME AND A NEW ASSIGNMENT

*Have not I commanded thee? Be strong and of a good courage; be
not afraid, neither be thou dismayed: for the Lord thy God is with
thee whithersoever thou goest (Joshua 1:9).*

By late 1944 World War II was winding down. The Germans were being
pushed back into their own little corner, and were no longer as aggressive on the high seas. Effie and I began to think seriously about getting
home on furlough. Nearly five years had elapsed since she left home
and during that time she had acquired a husband, a son, and she was
pregnant with our second child.

Dr. Mark Poole was forced to return to the United States because of
sleeping sickness, and for some months I had been the only physician
for the entire mission. Now Dr. Robert King had arrived, and news
came that Dr. Tinsley Smith was on his way. This took some of the

responsibility off me, and we began to make preparations to leave.

Packing up our household meant storing all our belongings in the attic, selling food supplies to neighbors, and boarding with them while we waited to be booked for passage. On September 12 we learned that a ship was sailing from Cape Town within a month. In a flurry of activity we made preparations, but three days before our departure to South Africa, we received word that the ship had cancelled. What a blow!

We spent a month at Luebo waiting for travel arrangements to be made. Finally we moved to Leopoldville because we had heard that Pan Am was flying in every two weeks. They were flying the famous old China Clipper ships from Africa to the United States and back. At Leopoldville, an amphibian plane was landing on the extended waters of the Congo River at Stanley Pool. To date they carried only freight, but word was that passenger service was about to start. Travelers clamored for reservations, and we secured places on the third flight (whenever that might be). We found out that there were some two hundred missionaries in Leopoldville hailing from all over central Africa, and all seeking passage to the States. Ships sailing in that direction from Matadi were few, and time schedules were not publicly released because of war security. In mid-November Pan Am officials announced there would be no passenger travel, and our discouragement hit bottom. I made reservations for a local flight back to Luluabourg.

But God's ways are always wise and all-seeing. While waiting for our flight, I heard that a small plane was flying up the west African coast from the French Congo every two weeks. Without delay I crossed the river to Brazzaville, capitol of French Congo, to make inquiry. Yes, it was a small eight-passenger plane, and civilians were often bumped by military priorities. But it was worth taking a chance, and I signed up. There was no room on the plane leaving immediately, but they put us on the list to go in two weeks. Now all we had to do was make contact with Pan Am further up the coast. Both French and American planes stopped at Dakar, but we heard there was plague in Dakar. Our option was Monrovia, Liberia, where Pan Am hopped off to cross the south Atlantic.

Back on the Belgian Congo side of the river there was much to be done. Francs must be changed from Belgian to French denominations, all luggage repacked, diapers washed and dried, letters written, and reservations to the mission cancelled.

The day before our departure to Brazzaville, we were informed that we had been preempted by military personnel. What to do? The only really valid thing anyone can do. Go back to the Lord and submit it all into His loving concern and care. We waited another two weeks for the next flight. It was now mid-December.

On December 12 another call from Brazzaville came through saying that we'd made the flight. We boarded a train to Pointe Noire, then on December 17 the small amphibian plane took off for Liberia, and we were aboard! Effie and I breathed a prayer of thanks to God Almighty.

We made overnight stops in Duala, Cameroun, and in Abidjan, Ivory Coast. The third morning we flew into Monrovia where we deplaned on a nearly deserted dirt airstrip. Within fifteen minutes of our arrival, we learned that the shuttle plane which would convey us to Fisherman's Lake (where Pan Am flew out) had suffered an accident and was no longer functional. In addition, the American military had reportedly cracked down on civilian air travel from Robert's Field to Fisherman's Lake. There was no other way to get to Fisherman's Lake, some fifty miles up the coast. Once more our hopes were dashed.

There was a Lutheran mission in Monrovia, so we packed our baggage in a taxi and went to ask for refuge. At the mission head-quarters I knocked at the front door. A gentleman opened it, and his eyes went wide with surprise as he exclaimed, "Bill Rule!" I stared. It was Lee Bowers. We had known one another during our student days in Philadelphia. He welcomed us and introduced us to Miss Otto who mothered us in a beautiful way. The love of Christ exuded from her every word and action. In heaven Miss Otto will be one of the first saints I want to greet.

In town I went immediately to change my francs to American dollars. This in itself did something for my morale. Real American dollars in my pocket for the first time in four years! I must be close to home.

Next I visited the Pan American representative in Monrovia. She operated out of her own home. She made radio contact with Fisherman's Lake and brought me the following message: "Come immediately to Fisherman's Lake. The American military won't transport you, but the British will. Try them." The lady explained that "come immediately" meant there would be a plane departing very soon. Because of security measures, definite times of departure were never divulged. She also said that because we were American citizens we needed to get permission from the U.S. military before the British would ferry us to Fisherman's Lake.

"You have one piece of luck." She said. "The American commanding officer is having lunch right now with the American ambassador at the embassy. If you hurry you can talk to him there and avoid a trip to Robert's Field." I went immediately to the embassy.

The commanding officer was one Colonel Currie. I met with him and the Ambassador and explained our situation. Then I asked for permission to be ferried there by the British aviation people. The Colonel proceeded to read the title clear for missionaries in general, and me in particular. He said he was tired of missionaries scuttling around the countryside and expecting to bum their way with the army anywhere they wanted to go. He said he wasn't out there to transport missionaries, he was there to win the war, and if I could show him my passage was essential to the war effort, he would let me go.

I was surprised at this outburst, but I tried to explain that we had been en route for nearly three months, that my wife was in her last month of pregnancy, and that we had assurance of passage to America if we could get to Fisherman's Lake. Besides, I was not asking for American transportation, only for his permission to travel with the British.

The Colonel was adamant. "There is a war on," he kept saying. "Show me you are indispensable to the war effort and you can go. If not, then you can't." He kept using that phrase "indispensable to the war effort" until I finally bristled. "Colonel Currie, who is indispensable to the war effort? Are you? Is President Roosevelt or Mr. Churchill? I am an able-bodied American citizen, and a physician. I am enrolled in the draft. When I reach home my draft board can call me up to active service if it so chooses. What more contribution can one make?" But my words cut no ice.

I concluded, "Well, Colonel, I want you to know it has been just as unpleasant for me to ask this favor as it has been for you to listen to me."

Next I went to the United States Navy. Obviously if there was no air passage, the only alternative was to travel up the coast by water. They gave me a pleasant and friendly negative.

FISHERMAN'S LAKE

For two days I spent my time frequenting the waterfront. Many small craft were tied up along the quay with quite a bustle of loading and unloading. They were manned almost exclusively by Africans who spoke a pidgin English which was very difficult to understand at times. I kept asking about boats going north to Fisherman's Lake, but most were going south. Eventually I began to look for an idle craft as it occurred to me that we might privately engage one of the boats to make the trip.

About noon on the second day a man pointed out beyond the retaining wall of the bay to a boat coming in and informed me it was coming from Fisherman's Lake. And, more importantly, he said it would be returning to Fisherman's Lake. Needless to say I was waiting to meet it as soon as it touched the pier. It was nothing more than an oversized rowboat, some twenty-four feet long. Each side cradled four or five oars. I addressed myself to the helmsman.

"Have you just come from Fisherman's Lake?"

"Yeah."

"Are you going to return?"

"Yeah."

"When?"

"This afternoon."

"What time?"

"About four o'clock."

"Do you take passengers?"

"Yeah."

"How much does it cost?"

"Two dollars a head."

"Would you have room for me and my wife and little boy?"

"Yeah."

"Good! We'll be here. Hold places for us."

"Yeah."

"By the way, could you rig a tarpaulin for my wife to protect her from the sun and rain?"

"Yeah."

"Okay. We'll be here. Don't go off without us!"

There was little time to reflect upon what I was doing. We were about to make a fifty-mile boat trip in the open ocean! We committed ourselves into the hands of our God and prepared for the trip. I bought a heavy ticking mat to stuff with straw for a bed. I bought a flashlight, sunglasses, a straw hat, and some food. At four o'clock we were at the water front.

Effie and Billy squeezed under a stretched tarpaulin alongside an elderly gentleman whose legs were paralyzed. Though he was in obvious pain, he was the soul of courtesy and never uttered a complaint throughout the trip. I sat on the gunnel beside the helmsman throughout the voyage. The oarsmen were inspired occasionally to row furiously. They needed the encouragement of rhythm, so one would beat energetically with a couple of sticks on the side of the boat and the rowers would sing and cry out as they pulled with all their strength. Of course this lasted only ten minutes or so, and then they rested for an hour before reenacting the performance. Thus we began to row out into the Atlantic Ocean!

As night approached we moved along off the shore but near enough to keep the dark outline of land in sight. A beautiful evening gave us a calm sea and a nearly full moon.

At dawn I realized we were changing direction. Gradually the coastline closed in on both sides and I knew we were entering the river leading to Fisherman's Lake. How long would it take us? The answer rested on the willing muscles of the oarsmen, and I fought against anxiety as I urged the helmsman with, "I'll pay double if your men will get us to the lake within two hours."

Finally the water widened into the beautiful lake. To our right I saw a small town on the southern tip. "What's that?" I asked the helmsman.

"Robertsport," he said.

I felt apprehensive. "Where are we going?"

"Robertsport," he said.

"Where is the Pan American base?" I was almost afraid to ask. He made no reply, but swept his hand generally in an easterly direction.

"Will you take us over there?" I asked with a slight note of desperation.

"Have to go to Robertsport first and unload," he said.

Just then there was considerable activity visible at Robertsport. A power launch was taking off, and it came across the lake rapidly, in front of us. It was shiny white and printed on the side I read PAN AMERICAN! With my heart in my throat I jumped up to wave my jacket and yell. They neither saw nor heard, and sped on out of sight. I believe for me this was the low point of the entire odyssey.

At Robertsport the draft of our boat was too deep to get us up to the shore. An oarsman carried me piggyback to shore and returned to help others. While I waited for Effie and Billy, I noticed an olive drab, military launch. The motor was running and uniformed men were making ready to depart. I ran to ask them how I might get to the Pan Am air base and they obligingly replied, "Hop aboard. We'll take you."

I was frantic. "Wait, wait," I cried. "My wife and baby!"

I ran back to the row boat and shouted to Effie still aboard, "Have them bring all our luggage too! Right away! I have a ride to Pan Am!"

I was ecstatic and began transferring our bags. In the middle of it all I realized my wife was in tears. She got my attention and in a plaintive voice said, "I'm not going till I change this dress. Look, it's dirty and split down the back!"

I gasped. "You want to risk missing that plane?" I yelled and motioned, "Get on that boat!" Weeping, she did as she was told. Once aboard the launch, I put my arms around her. The faith and courage she had exercised in all these recent weeks would remain always in my memory.

Fifteen minutes later we were at the Pan American base. Our hosts were most gracious and polite. They put us up in the infirmary where we had a welcome rest after our twenty-hour trip in the row boat. We were advised that the China Clipper would depart the following afternoon. So, on December 23 we boarded the Clipper ship to complete the last segment of our long journey.

For sheer luxury in the air there has never been anything like the Clipper. It had upper and lower lounging decks, berths for sleeping accommodations, and large walk-in bathrooms. We had four male flight attendants. Billy had the run of the ship, and he enjoyed himself immensely.

We celebrated Christmas in Port of Spain, Trinidad. It wasn't so special in the manner that Christmas usually is, but there has been no

Christmas that we have been more conscious of the glory of the Lord or more grateful for His advent. Once more aloft we were served a complete Christmas dinner. We landed in San Juan, Puerto Rico, in time for high tea, then went on to Bermuda.

On the morning of December 26 we flew into New York, right into a howling storm. Our plane was buffeted considerably and most passengers were miserable. But not Billy and me. I moved him from window to window to point out the Statue of Liberty, Brooklyn Bridge, Statten Island. He was most interested in the snow on the ground. "Look, Daddy, look! Milk!"

Once in our hotel room in New York, I called home. My mother, father, and aunt had no idea where we were. Aunt Polly answered.

"Hello, Auntie! This is Bill."

A moment's hesitation. "Where in the world are you?"

"In New York."

Again she hesitated, then whispered in a voice I could barely hear, "Thank the Lord!"

I couldn't agree more.

HOME ASSIGNMENT

We spent our first furlough (now more commonly known as the home assignment) in Charleston, West Virginia, with Effie's parents. Bill and Katharine Crane were pastoring the Ruffner Memorial Presbyterian Church, only a block away from the magnificent gilt-domed state capitol. Our second child, Charlotte, was born in Charleston on January 25, 1945.

In May, Germany surrendered and the terrible fighting of World War II in Europe came to an end. We were in Montreat, North Carolina, at a world mission conference when we heard that the atomic bomb was dropped on Hiroshima, Japan. I remember that the word came to us on a Sunday morning when Congressman Walter Judd, a former medical missionary to China, was scheduled to speak in church. He had to return to Washington at the last minute, and Dr. Charlie Logan, a venerable retired missionary to Japan, filled in for the senator.

The most demanding aspect of home assignment is carrying the message of missionary endeavor to the people in the pews. Promotional work is absolutely essential to maintain the vision of the world evangelization and to encourage support. During the year of 1945 I spoke in churches and to various organizations 186 times, in ten southern states, to an estimated audience of over twenty thousand.

I heard that Tulane University in New Orleans was conducting a six-month course in tropical medicine. I enrolled and began my studies in early 1946. The knowledge I gained was interesting and helpful. I reviewed all the latest investigation on the diagnosis and treatment of diseases I had encountered in Africa. I also had the fascinating experience of traveling to Carville where I observed the management of leprosy under optimal conditions.

As our home assignment came to a close in the summer of 1946, we made preparations to return to the Belgian Congo. We spent several weeks in New York trying to gain passage to Africa and finally, on August 20, we were able to fly only as far as London on BOAC (British Overseas Airways). I spent the better part of a day visiting offices of various airlines in London but with little success. Then BOAC informed us that a small plane was leaving the following day for Lagos, Nigeria, and there was room on it for us. Investigation revealed that Sabena, the Belgian airline company, had service from Lagos to Leopoldville three times a week. So we made reservations and put all into the hands of our God.

The effects of World War II in London could not be avoided. Rationing was still a way of life, and bombing had reduced whole areas of the city into piles of rubble. In Bordeaux, France, the airstrip was pockmarked with bomb craters and on all sides there were burned-out wrecks of German *stukas* and fighter planes, simply bulldozed out of the way and abandoned.

We were the only passengers on the Sabena flight from Lagos to Leopoldville. We spent several days in the capitol city getting all our papers in order, then on September 6 we flew to Luluabourg, arriving almost two months after setting out from home.

BIBANGA

We received a new assignment and proceeded to settle at Bibanga, located in the eastern Kasai province. It is situated on a hilltop just forty miles from Bakwanga, the diamond mine capitol. But Bibanga is separated from most of the rest of the our mission territory by two large rivers, the Lubilanji and the Mbujimayi. During the rainy season these rivers often overflow their banks and isolate Bibanga.

The station is located in the heart of Baluba country, a people long receptive to the Christian gospel. They established a strong church and were eager to accept advanced education offered by government and church.

The medical work at Bibanga was initiated some thirty years earlier by Dr. Eugene Kellersberger, and the Edna Kellersberger Memorial Hospital stood as a tribute to his deceased first wife. For me it was a deeply meaningful moment to stand in Dr. Kelly's hospital and in his place at Bibanga because his dedication had been my guiding star for many years, and now I was to carry on in his bailiwick.

There had been no doctor in residence for several years and the work had declined. The modest complex was composed of six brick buildings with fifty beds. At the Bibanga leprosy camp, five miles away, five hundred victims of the disease were under treatment.

The routine activities of my daily life kept me well occupied. Each day began with the hospital staff at worship, a report from the night attendant, staff meeting, and ward rounds. The remainder of the morning included surgery and outpatient clinic needs. There were afternoon prenatal clinics, visits to the leprosy colony, instruction of student nurses, setting laboratory procedures and reading the results, and filling pharmacy prescriptions.

One of the first and most far-reaching medical problems I ran into at Bibanga was the intestinal and hepatic infestation of *schistosomiasis*, also known as *bilharziosis*. I had not seen it much at Lubondai because the schistasome has a secondary life cycle in the bodies of certain water snails which do not exist in the Lubondai area. The water is too acid to support them. But Bibanga is in limestone country where they flourish.

The young larvae penetrate snails and undergo certain changes before leaving their host to enter through the skin of people wading or bathing in the water. Eventually they lodge in the small blood vessels of the intestine and liver where they cause degenerative changes which can be fatal.

In the 1940s our drug of choice for treatment was tartar emetic which had to be administered intravenously. Eighteen injections were given on alternate days after which the patient was examined at intervals to make sure the infestation had been eliminated. If not, a second course of treatment was given. Obviously those under treatment were compelled to stay in the hospital, sometimes over a period of months. We waged a continual battle in the effort to reduce the incidence of this disease.

Aside from my medical work, I had the welcome responsibility of superintending the adult Sunday School, teaching the teachers the weekly lesson. Effie and I enjoyed working with the choir. A less enjoyable responsibility given to me was overseeing the station's herd of cows!

It was absurd to expect a city boy to handle farm animals. To me, milking a cow simply meant backing one into the garage and draining the crankcase. Yet, since there was no one else to do it, this job fell on me. We did not keep the hundred head of cattle penned in, except at night. During the day, herdsmen led them across the hillsides to find their fodder and water. Many species of ticks abounded in the high tropical grass, and the cattle needed to be dipped regularly. It was always a battle to herd them into the sluice and get them thoroughly submerged in the medicated water.

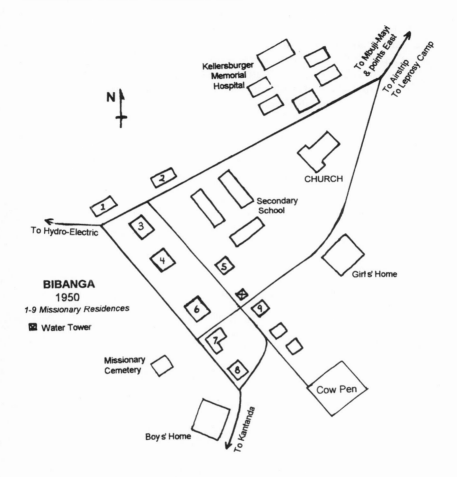

Map of Bibanga.

Finally there was the surgical vendetta of castrating the young bulls. Here I became quite the cowboy as well as wielder of the scalpel. I could wrestle one to the ground with the best and, sitting astride the fallen foe, resort to my surgical arts. Needless to say, not all that labor was for nothing. We enjoyed some nice beef cuts from time to time, and our African friends benefited by increasing their meager protein intake.

March brought Effie to the end of her third pregnancy, and Mark Poole, who had delivered Billy at Lubondai, came again to superintend the ceremonies. A bedroom at our house had been cleared to serve as the delivery room.

On March 21, 1947, Effie proceeded to give birth to our third child. In the dark I tried to start the generator for some light while Mark Poole assisted Effie, but I inadvertently flooded the carburetor. So while Mark groped in the dark, baby Elizabeth Hampton obliged and deposited herself into his searching hands. Such is obstetrical practice and such is birth in the interior of Africa.

MILESTONE FOUR
EXTENDING THE EFFORT

"Enlarge the place of thy tent, and let them stretch forth the
curtains of thine habitations: spare not, lengthen thy cords,
and strengthen thy stakes" (Isaiah 54:2).

7 EXPANDING THE WORK

Delight thyself also in the Lord; and he shall give thee the desires of thine heart. Commit thy way unto the Lord; trust also in him; and he shall bring it to pass (Psalms 37:4–5).

From the beginning of my medical work in Africa I recognized the need for a program of instruction for our Congolese male nurses. Girls were not yet pushed academically, but remained at home and in the fields with other women.

Some of our medical workers had become quite proficient by reason of familiarity and repetition of tasks. But rationale was often missing. Our nurses needed to be better educated.

The colonial government recognized medical helpers in three categories. The fellows with the least training were called *aides infirmiers*, or as we would say, nurse's aides. Next, a three-year course plus a two-year *stage* (period of practical application), awarded a diploma of *infirmier diplome*. The third category (now discontinued) was called a medical assistant. Only one school offered this training and it was located in the capital city. When independence came to Congo in 1960, the medical assistants were sent to schools in Europe, given a limited medical course, and returned to be recognized as physicians.

At Mission Meeting we began to think about training medical personnel at the *infirmier diplome* level, and a decision was made to "Ask Dr. Rule to experiment with a class," i.e., keep records on cost, equipment, textbooks, and report at the 1947 meeting. As soon as a sixth doctor was available, the Mission would endeavor to establish the school on a permanent basis.

Preparations began. Entrance exams were sent to all mission stations. We assembled a teaching staff and classes began after school commencement in August 1947, so when Mission Meeting rolled around again in November, we were well on our way. Anticipation of a second year, however, required more help. There was none. It was not

73

until six years later that sentiments changed to the point of making higher medical education a priority.

Medical equipment is always relatively expensive and hard to come by on modest mission budgets. But in the 1950s we received some heartwarming assistance from home base through a churchwide program to provide significant funds for missions. With these added dollars we availed ourselves of an electric suction apparatus and a high frequency cautery for the operating room, a new microscope for the laboratory, and, best of all, the first X-ray machine ever at Bibanga. A group of doctors in Dallas, Texas, gave me an honest-to-goodness operating table—one with a hydraulic lift for regulating the height of the operative field. Another group of men in Huntington, West Virginia, supplied me with some urgently needed surgical instruments.

In 1958 the old Knoxville General Hospital was dismantled. It had been a hospital facility in Knoxville for fifty years. My grandfather was on the original Board of Trustees. However, more modern facilities had replaced its usefulness and most of the old equipment was scrapped.

Mrs. Elizabeth Price McClure, a childhood friend, spearheaded a herculean effort to pack up and ship many of these items halfway around the world to our mission. In September of 1959, four mission doctors gathered at the railway siding at Luluabourg where the cargo had arrived at last. We tore open the huge wooden cases and brought forth the prized goodies to be divided between six mission hospitals.

Unpacking the cartons of hospital equipment sent from Knoxville General Hospital, 1958.

There were beds, an operating table, surgical spot lights, bed pans, surgical instruments, metal tables, and a host of other things.

As for me, I received beautiful new hemostats with ratchets that I could depend on to hold when clamped upon a bleeding artery. Operating room lights replaced ordinary overhead bulbs. A new surgical scrub basin replaced scrubbing under an ordinary faucet. A badly needed fracture bed provided traction for broken bones. Now cement walkways were laid from wards to surgical areas for a four-wheel cart instead of four nurses grasping a bed at its four legs and awkwardly carrying the patient across uneven ground. Finally, I had a portable laboratory incubator, perfected by the military for field service during World War II. This gave us our first facilities for bacteriological culture and diagnosis and provided a rational approach to the many diarrheal diseases and dysenteries encountered by the African population. How proud and delighted we all were!

At Bibanga, the battle continued against tropical malaria, sleeping sickness, hookworm and roundworms, filariasis, schisotosomiasis, tuberculosis, and leprosy. Women in dystosic labor were brought in every day or so, and it was necessary to nurse them through the crises or perform surgical deliveries. We encountered many pathetic circumstances.

One time, a whole series of victims came to us from a nearby village suffering from abdominal pain, nausea, and vomiting. But they also had neurological symptoms, suggesting poisoning or botulism. Most of them died. On another occasion, a husband and wife came to us with a full-blown case of rabies. They died within an hour or so of each other. Their small child had died two weeks earlier with rabies and had infected the parents.

Surgical experiences provided their share of pathos also. Tropical ulcers are often extremely difficult to control. They became the site of multiple bacterial and spirochetic contamination, and necrosis extended rapidly through the adjacent tissues. Under such circumstances they were designated as phagedenic ulcers. I recall a patient who was brought to the hospital with his entire lower leg involved in a huge ulceration which had undergone sloughing, and much of the tibia was denuded and completely exposed. Circulation had been destroyed and the only option was amputation. The poor fellow was suffering marked agony but when confronted with the possible loss of his leg, he resisted. I waited, expecting that the pain would force him to agree, but he kept holding out. Then a remarkable thing happened. A second patient arrived with an almost identical situation. And there they were, side by side, both in acute pain. But the second patient was not as stoical as the first, and he quickly opted for amputation. The following day we visited him for postoperative exam and dressings, and he was a relieved and smiling patient. Patient number one observed him for a few hours and then decided that he, too, would undergo the amputation.

Another victim arrived with a huge fibroma about the size of a large grapefruit, growing within the maxillary sinus. The whole side of his face was grotesquely deformed with his left eye pushed up and out of line with the right. I took one look, threw up my hands, and exclaimed there was nothing I could do for him and he would have to go somewhere else. But a familiar scenario unfolded. He didn't go somewhere else, and the next day he was back again, and the next, and the next. Of course I knew why. He didn't go somewhere else because there was nowhere else to go. Either I was going to try to help him or he wouldn't get any help.

I managed to put my patient to sleep and complete the surgery. I must admit he was no candidate for a beauty contest, but we had removed the tumor and got his left eye back down in balance with his right one and, for me and him as well, this was success. A week or so later I had to go to Luluabourg, about 150 miles away. I knew he had come from Luluabourg, so I asked him if he would like a ride. As we reached the city close to nightfall, my passenger spoke. "There's going to be great joy down there in that city tonight," he said. "When I walk in the door it will be the first news my family has had of me since I left many weeks ago. I guess they have figured I was already dead. And when I take my wife and my children in my arms there will be great joy. Thank you!"

Tuberculosis was one of the major health problems in central Africa. Not only did we see many cases of pulmonary tuberculosis, but there were always cases of Pott's disease under treatment. Pott's disease is tuberculosis located in one or more of the vertebrae. The disease destroys the structure of the bones which collapse under the weight of the body and often impinge on nerve roots which causes extreme pain.

One of the local men came to us with only mild lumbar deformity, but he had terrific pain down his legs and muscle spasms. We put him to bed in hyperextension and with traction. After several weeks the pain and spasm not only disappeared but there was considerable correction of the deformity. Then the question was where do we go from here? Obviously, he couldn't be left in bed for the rest of his life! Our only choice seemed to be an effort at the spinal fusion, but I had never done one.

It was quite an operation to behold! We didn't have the proper instruments, and I had to take the graft from the tibia with a small hand saw and a bone chisel! When we were ready, we turned him over and fastened the graft into place between the split anterior spines. There wasn't enough plaster to put him in a body cast, so we hyperextended him and molded a plaster brace to his back, then strapped it to him with bands of adhesive across his chest and abdomen. In spite of us and by the grace of God, he really got a fine result. Our success with him brought equal results for several others. Later we were able to immobilize Pott's disease patients and treat them medically, and to a large extent natural healing processes eliminated the need for surgical correction.

At the close of World War II, the Belgian government began to extricate itself from the chaos caused by German occupation. The exiled government relocated again in Brussels, and reconstruction began to take place. Colonial mineral riches had made a significant contribution to the war effort, and now millions of assets were being returned to the Belgian Congo. A rather commendable stipulation was to use such assets primarily to enhance the well-being of the Congolese people. An administrative body was formed and titled Fonds du Bien-Etre Indigene or Native Welfare Funds. I was invited to serve on a regional consultative commission (1948) to provide information and make suggestions for use of the funds. Health, education, and civic improvements were made in the Kasai because of these funds.

On April 5, 1949, Dr. Cousar came over from Lubondai to officiate and celebrate with us on the arrival of Paul Crane Rule. He was a fine bouncing, nine-pound, five and one-half ounce baby, and he brought great joy to his parents and his ecstatic brother and sisters. Paul's arrival in this world was almost coincident with my dear Aunt Polly's departure. News of the baby's arrival was sent home by amateur radio. At the time Auntie was bed-ridden with her terminal illness and, barely conscious, she was told of the arrival. We understand that when she heard the news she smiled and nodded her head, and a few days later went home to be with her Lord whom she had loved and served across the years.

SPEAKING GOD'S WORD

On a mission station the opportunity to reach out to people with the good news of salvation in Jesus Christ presents itself in numerous and variable ways. For expatriate missionaries the job begins right at home among the bevy of local retainers seeking profitable employment. The cook, the houseboy, the washjack, the night sentry, the children's nurse—all are candidates for the presentation of the gospel and for nurturing in the faith. The doctor addresses himself to his medical assistants, and to the many patients who come from far and near for physical healing. The school teacher has crowded classrooms full of listening ears and open minds, and there is no ban on religion being taught in the schools. Maintenance engineers avail themselves of

The church at Bibanga where Dr. Rule often preached and taught Sunday school.

workmen to talk with while burning brick or dressing lumber, and the
mission pilot engages his helper in serious conversation over the
handle of a long wrench and other tools as they work together.
Evangelistic missionaries make a capital effort to get out into the
outlying villages to establish preaching points, to install resident evangelists, and to baptize Christians and help organize a self-sustaining
church.

My medical work did not afford me the opportunities to get out into
the villages for evangelistic meetings as often as I would have liked, but
sometimes this was possible and Sunday afternoons were an ideal time
to drive out and visit some of the nearby communities.

I remember preaching one Sunday in a village I had never before
visited. There was no evangelist and no church shed. I called the people
together out under the trees, and when I tried to lead them in some of
the more familiar Christian songs I noticed that numbers of them knew
the words and sang right lustily, especially the children. After the
service I asked how long it had been since a missionary had visited the
village, and the residents opined it must have been five or six years.
Then I asked if any native evangelist had visited them and they replied
in the negative. Finally I asked how all the little children knew the
hymns so well, and they pointed out a young boy about twelve years old
and told me he had gone to school at Bibanga through third grade. He
dropped out, but when he returned to his village he began to share
some of the things he had learned. This boy had taught them the songs

and led them in worship exercises. Multiply that story by the thousands of third grade graduates in Zaire and estimate the potential results!

THE STORY OF KABUYA

Sometimes an extraordinary example of God's saving grace is discovered on one's very door step. Such was the case of Kabuya, our night sentry. A night sentry came to work late in the afternoon with a huge log of wood on his shoulder to cut up for kindling for the kitchen stove. This was for heating bath water and also for his own fire which he kept going through the night. He was also our watchman to see that all was quiet in the "fence," and if we needed to send a message to the hospital or to one of our neighbors, he was our telephone. I sat with him one evening, close to his small fire, and he recounted for me his spiritual pilgrimage. Because it gives glory to our Heavenly Father, I share it now with you.

"My mouth was continually full of dirty talk and lies," Kabuya began. He spoke of his younger days in years gone by, describing a life of sin and degradation. He was a habitual drunkard and lived in gross immorality. Eventually he married a woman who bore him a child, but when the child died in infancy he accused her of "eating its life" and sent her home to her family.

He married a second wife, and she too had a child that died only a short while after birth. Kabuya began collecting charms and fetishes to protect him from further misfortune. He went to the medicine men and surrounded himself and his wife with their witchcraft. Another baby was born and once again it soon died. The bereaved parents redoubled their efforts to find an antidote. They spent all their money buying fetishes, idols—any charms the heathen mind could concoct. In fact they became so knowledgeable of the varied remedies that Kabuya began making medicine of his own, and gained quite a reputation as a sorcerer.

About this time he got a job in the diamond mines where a large population of workers, drawn from all quarters of the country, promised a lucrative field for the plying of his nefarious trade, even as he drew a daily wage. He made medicine for many people selling goat horns stuffed with special charms, or crudely fashioned metal bracelets, and other objects. These fetishes were used to get them out of trouble, protect their health and strength, or to throw a curse upon someone. But these were not his only sources of revenue. He became an expert gambler, and he competed in an ancestral version of our American crap game with loaded dice, and many innocent victims were fleeced.

One day his wife became seriously ill. She was taken to the company hospital where she hovered at death's door, and another baby was lost.

This time at the fourth month of conception. Her eventual recovery brought no change of heart, and the pathway of idols and heathen rituals was again followed in the blind search of the human heart to cast out darkness and despair, which only the "peace that passeth understanding" can dispel.

Time went by and Ntumba, Kabuya's wife, again bore a baby boy. The parents watched over the wee life with anxious eyes and hearts and, sure enough, when the baby was a month old he became ill. In the spirit of futility and fear Kabuya visited the most notorious witch doctor he knew and asked for help.

"Remove all your old medicines and charms," he was told, "and go to the women of the next village who make medicine. Ask them to enter the ritual of smearing their bodies with white clay to make medicine for you. This is the only thing which will save the child's life."

Kabuya did as he was told. He paid the women two hundred francs and two chickens, and they smeared themselves and the baby with white clay. They put a fetish around his neck and gave the father four idols and the horn of an antelope. This was very strong medicine. Then Kabuya and Ntumba returned home with high hopes. But the baby only grew worse, and he went back to the women with four more chickens, fifty more francs, and a pair of spectacles.

"My child is worse," he said. "I want to leave both the child and his mother in your hands. Do anything you wish to stop the child's sickness."

Then he left them with the women and went back to his work at the mines. Five days later he decided to go see how his baby was getting along, but when he returned home from his work he found his wife and child already there. The baby was much worse, and the mother, fearing he would die away from home, had brought the child home. The father and mother gave up all hope.

During the early afternoon of the following day, which was Sunday, Kabuya was at home and was actually putting his clothes in a box to hide by burying it in the ground. He knew that when the child died and the many relatives and friends would come to wail with them, some of them would steal the clothes. As he packed the box he heard an automobile horn in the village street, which was not unusual since cars passed by daily. But this time something impelled him to stop and listen, and he felt a strong urge to follow the horn and see who it was. He found the parked car where a missionary was just beginning to preach to a small group. There was a stir as he approached, and the whispered question, "What is the medicine man doing here?"

Kabuya sat quietly on the edge of the group, waiting for the missionary to finish, and then he went up to him and said, "Today I want you to write down my name because I want to know your God."

He was impressed by the force which had impelled him to follow the horn, and knowing all his old remedies had failed, his misery had directed him to look for something new. He took the missionary to his house and a large crowd followed, curious to see what business the witch doctor had with the man of God. Kabuya collected all his idols and fetishes and spread them on the table.

"These have been my gods," he said. "But I am putting them away. I want you to pray for me to your God. Everything else I put my hope in has failed."

"Do you want me to pray for the life of your child?" the missionary asked.

"No, I am not asking for the life of the child. But I am very, very miserable. Pray that God will do with us as he sees fit. We throw ourselves upon His mercy."

The missionary prayed, and then he spent some time explaining to Kabuya his God's way of salvation through Jesus Christ, and he urged the African to give his heart to Jesus and be cleansed from his sins. In parting he promised, "If you will persevere in this step you have taken and not turn back again to old and evil ways, God will bless you."

That night the mother cried for the fetishes Kabuya had given the missionary to take away. "Why did you give them to him?" she chided. "Now you know for sure the baby will die."

"No," Kabuya explained. "I gave them up in order to accept the Lord Jesus. I am putting all my hope in Him."

During the night hours the child took milk and cried for the first time in nearly a week. Eagerly the loving parents watched over him, and when morning came, although the baby was still drawn and feeble, the illness had diminished. He went on to a complete recovery!

Kabuya went to the local Congolese evangelist with a song in his heart and a light in his eye.

"I am a Christian now," he announced. "What shall I do?"

The evangelist suggested that he regularly attend the worship services, which he began to do. He also entered the catechism class and began to learn more of his newfound faith. The people of the village were amazed that this leader of heathen practices should make such an about-face, but his break with the past was complete. He even changed his name saying the old man was dead and that he was a new man in Christ. He had been Kabuya Kashingi, and now he was Kabuya Paul.

The next time the missionary came to the mines Kabuya told him, "I want to go with you to the Mission. This place is the site of all my former sins. Temptations are on every side and I want to get completely away from them. I want to go to the Mission and learn more about Jesus."

"You must go to school first," the missionary said, "and learn how to read so you can read a Bible."

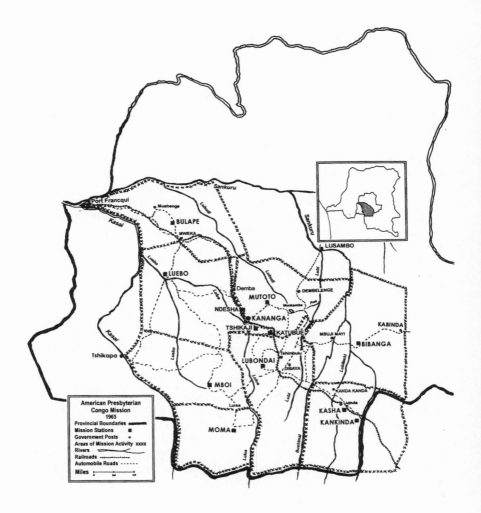

Map of Kasai.

So Kabuya worked on the afternoon shift and went to school in the morning, taught by the evangelist, until he had completed the first two grades. Still he wanted to leave the mines and go to the Mission. He decided to go to the office and ask for a six-month vacation with the hope that at the end of that time they would not hold him. His friends scoffed at his temerity in making such a request.

"Anyone who gets a vacation for one month is lucky," they said. "Nobody could get six months!"

But to the wonder of all Kabuya asked for and got a six-month vacation. The first thing he did was help the evangelist construct a mud and stick shelter for worship. Soon another missionary passed by, and again Kabuya asked to go to the Mission. He was willing to do any kind of work if it might mean a chance for further schooling and more knowledge of God and His word.

"Have you received your dismissal from the mines?" asked the missionary.

"No, but I have a six-month vacation," Kabuya said.

"But I cannot take you to the Mission unless you have your permanent dismissal."

Kabuya thought this over. Obviously the only way he could go was to get his dismissal, and the only way he could get it was to ask for it. This time the people did more than laugh. They expressed their concern.

"You have just been fortunate enough to get a six-month vacation, and now before it has expired you propose to ask for your dismissal. You will be thrown in jail!"

"So, all they can do is throw me in jail," was Kabuya's laconic reply, and he went to the office to make his request.

Here Kabuya's faith in his newfound God failed him to some extent, and he fell back into his old way. He confronted the overseer and said, "My father has died and left ten wives and nine children, and I must settle his estate. You don't want me to bring them all here, do you? So give me my dismissal and let me go to my own village to take care of them."

True, Kabuya's father had been a local chieftain and had ten wives and nine children, but Kabuya was misrepresenting the facts because affairs had already been taken care of. The overseer agreed, but said he would have to take the request to the director of the mine for final approval.

Now even the native pastor and evangelist were apprehensive about the outcome. But Kabuya insisted, and stubbornly went to the director, and again the door was opened before him and consent was given.

So Kabuya and Ntumba and their baby boy, Mulumba, came to Bibanga, and Kabuya began going to school. But it was in the effort to leave his mornings free and still afford him some means of livelihood that he was given the night sentry job. Ntumba also attended the catechism class, and in due time both Kabuya and Ntumba were baptized. Kabuya became an evangelist, and for many years he has proclaimed the saving message of the Lord Jesus Christ across the length and breadth of Baluba land.

He and I sat together that evening as I listened to his story. He cocked his eye toward the thatch ceiling of his native hut, stirred the coals of his dying fire, and with a pensive look, he thought of the events of those momentous months. Again he heard the horn and felt the compelling force which had drawn him to the gospel of Jesus Christ. Again he stood before his employer to receive the amazing vacation, and the even more amazing dismissal. He shook his head. "You know," he said softly, "they even gave me my blanket and raincoat which they always take from dismissed workmen, and a whole extra month's wages on top of that!" Reverently he continued. "God has surely led me step by step, away from my old life of sin to the Good News of Jesus Christ!"

8 MOVING BACK TO LUBONDAI

I will sing unto the Lord, because he hath dealt bountifully with me (Psalms 13:6).

After sojourning for seven years at Bibanga and increasing its number by two, the Rule family had to pick up and move back to Lubondai. During the move mother and children traveled to Lake Munkamba for a few days of overdue vacation, which also gave their daddy (especially irascible under such circumstances) a chance to maneuver without any kids underfoot.

Lake Munkamba is a lovely sky-blue lake, about three miles long and a mile wide, lying approximately in the center of our mission area. It is fed by underground springs and is far from any rivers or streams and so, having no inlets or outlets, it is free of crocodiles and hippopotami. It affords fine swimming and skiing and other recreational facilities. For many years the Africans were afraid of spirits which they believed inhabited the lake. Mr. Hoyt Miller, John Knox Miller's father, was the first person to take a native canoe out on the lake, and when no disaster followed, he talked the local chieftain into going out with him. Thus ended the taboo. This afforded the mission

A retreat at Lake Munkamba.

first chance at obtaining a large concession from the government, making it a choice location to develop a retreat/recreation area and campsite for missionaries. The lake has afforded blessed rest and pleasure through the years.

Eventually merchants, government officials, and other Europeans recognized Munkamba's charm, and cottages and homes began to appear all around its banks. It became the favorite vacation spot in that part of the country.

So while my family vacationed, I packed and drove three truck loads of belongings which included furniture, refrigerator, sewing machine, bicycles, and Effie's big upright piano. The trip was 150 miles one way. This meant a total of 300 miles round-trip each time, including crossing large rivers by ferry boat four times for each load. My lack of training in the art of moving furniture exhibited itself when I lost three mattresses off one load and proceeded for 50 miles before I knew it! I retraced my steps, stopping at each and every village to inquire about my lost property. I finally found them, safe and sound and undamaged. By now there must have been thousands of Congolese across the countryside who knew that *Ngangabuka Kabamba* (my Tshiluba name) was moving from Bibanga back to Lubondai, and he had lost three mattresses!

A DREAM COME TRUE

After seven years at Bibanga station, we were going back to Lubondai because the mission had endorsed a school for *Infirmiers* (School of Nursing), and I was to be the director! It was a dream come true!

This new venture was possible now because of the arrival of four young doctors from 1950–1952. Dr. John Miller and Miss Margaret Liston and myself were to serve as faculty for the school. A six-member board of trustees was appointed and instructed to draw up a constitution and bylaws. Classroom instruction was to begin in January 1954 with an initial class of fifteen male students.

In spite of all our enthusiasm for realizing the dream, it was not an easy task. All the instruction had to be in French and we needed books. The students were not only studying in a foreign language but were acquiring a foreign medical vocabulary. Dr. Miller gave his first lecture on entomology with care and precision, patiently laying the groundwork concerning the insect kingdom. At the end of the lecture there was a question: "What kind of a disease is entomology?"

It isn't easy for the young African student to listen and to use deductive reason. He has been taught from infancy to learn his lessons by rote, to memorize the answer. If a question required a specific response, he was completely floored. When we told them we would lecture and they were to take notes on what they heard, they were dumbfounded. They had no idea what we were talking about. Once when giving an examination, I told my class if they answered with the exact words of the printed text I would give them a passing grade. But if they replied in their own words, I would give them a higher grade. One fellow objected: "How can I give a better answer than the one in the book?" It was exciting to watch them struggle and then to see their intellectual capacities expand as they experienced the process of higher levels of learning.

Basic courses included anatomy and physiology, use of a microscope, and nursing care techniques. In later years our subjects expanded to include general pathology, bacteriology, and pharmacology. Eventually we included foundational concepts of internal medicine, surgery, obstetrics, and other clinical practices. Students also had classes in Bible and witnessing during each of their study years.

Besides curriculum and classroom demands there was the dilemma of creating a physical plant. As soon as the rains stopped in May, we assembled a crew of workmen to build a four-room dormitory for sixteen students. We added a second unit and later a third building with two classrooms and an office. A chapel in the center of this complex was converted into a dining hall. We christened the teaching center the *Institut Medical Chretien du Kasai*, popularly called the "IMCK."

The Belgian government recognized our schools and sent a government physician each year to assist with "jury exams," and to grant government certificates to *Infirmiers* after a two-year practicum in a government hospital. Our graduates performed well and we were proud of them. The IMCK's reputation was established.

*A nursing school student
conducts an experiment.*

GOD'S GRACE ABOUNDS

During all the hustle and bustle of the move and opening the school, Effie gave birth on August 5, 1954, to our fifth child, Barbara. Barbara's growth and development were normal and healthy during the first four months. Then she began to run some of the dreaded fevers of malaria. On Thanksgiving Day she was better, and we had a lovely family meal together. But the following day her fever went back up, and she became listless and toxic in appearance. By midafternoon we gave her an intermuscular injection of atebrine, after which I proceeded to the hospital to conduct my regular prenatal clinic.

A short time later our African helper, Ngandu, came running to the hospital for me. *"Muana kena bimpe to!"* He gasped. Translated verbatim, he said, "The child isn't doing well." But this understatement is the accustomed manner used by the Congolese to announce impending disaster. I needed no further explanation and raced the two hundred yards to our home. The baby was convulsing in Effie's arms. The little girl was comatose. Her breathing came in short, ineffective, stridorous gasps. I quickly administered a respiratory stimulant, but her breathing failed completely. I began to give her artificial respiration, the way we do it with little fellows, folding her in the middle and then hyperextending her. Although she would grunt as I pushed air from her lungs, there was no inspiratory effort and the blood drained from her face. Her little limbs, which had been rigid in convulsions, began to relax in the flaccid aspect of death.

I thought she was gone. I lay the small body on the couch and, kneeling beside her, began to give her mouth-to-mouth insufflation. This was also a good position in which to talk to the Lord as I worked. Effie and I were both praying, and a wonderful peace came into our hearts, even during that moment of crisis.

As I breathed air rhythmically into her lungs, the stimulant I had injected began to take effect and she made a few feeble efforts at respiration. I nursed her along for about fifteen or twenty minutes until she was able to go it alone. We sat with her for the next three hours until she regained consciousness, and then we took turns for the rest of the night. Effie was as steady as a brick through it all, and I found myself leaning on her for added strength and courage.

Barbara went on to run ten days of intermittent fever and there were other anxious moments, but she came out of it. How we loved that baby girl and feasted our eyes on her, sort of a backlash reaction to the depths we had gone to in the valley of the shadow, and of having come so close to losing her.

Malaria did not constitute the total gamut of hazards to which our children were exposed. Some of the ills were the ordinary risks we all experience, even in the bosom of our mother country. At ten, Libby broke her arm while hanging by her legs from the limb of a tree. A couple of years later she suffered a more exotic accident. Two baby foxes had been brought to me and I had put them on leashes running on a long horizontal wire behind the house so they could move about and play. Late one evening the children discovered that both foxes had been killed and torn by some predatory animal. While they were surveying the damage, Libby was suddenly attacked from behind by a stray dog which savagely bit and tore her lower leg. I took her to the hospital to repair her wound, but the matter of greater import to all of us was a question of the dog's health. Was it rabid?

In central Africa, rabies is an ever-present danger and concern. We left the dead foxes where they lay and the dog, as I suspected, returned. We cornered it and confined it to a heavy wooden box. It didn't take long to recognize that the dog was rabid. It would go into a furious tantrum when offered water, which is typical of the disease—a fear of water.

Libby had to take the shots to protect her against contracting rabies. I had to take them too because though I had worn heavy gloves while catching the dog, I had been scratched during the struggle. In those days the treatment meant twenty-one injections, one every day, in the abdominal muscles. It wasn't any fun, but we both completed the series unscathed.

MEDICAL WORK AT LUBONDAI

The obstetrical load at Lubondai increased. More women came to our prenatal clinics and there seemed to be a much larger proportion of dystocic labors and deliveries. The Bena Lulua are, on an average, a smaller people than the Baluba tribe, so in the Lubondai area women were smaller and had smaller pelvic measurements. Naturally pelvic disproportion was more often encountered. Another factor might be in the difference of promiscuity in sexual relations. The Baluba are a proud people who guard the virginity of their daughters and at the time of marriage receive a public ceremonial gift substantiating purity. The Bena Lulua are more casual with their morals and young girls are often given in "trial marriage" before the union is formally solemnized by the delivery of a dowry, so immature girls often become pregnant before adequate physical development to allow natural childbirth.

One Sunday evening while we were grouped around the piano singing gospel songs, a man came to the door saying his wife was ten miles down the road in labor with only the baby's arm visible. He and I got in the car and went to get her. Near the place he had left her we met a crowd of the village people bringing the woman in a hammock. We transferred her to the car and were back at the hospital in a few minutes where I gave the anaesthesia and John Miller did a version-extraction. We got a fine baby girl and the mother got along okay, but the point is she had received no prenatal care. She never approached a physician until she was in deep trouble.

A week before, I operated on a woman having her second child. The first was delivered by cesarean section at the diamond mines, and did not live. This second time, instead of seeking medical aid, she went off homeward into the countryside just at term where she went into labor and remained thus for seventy-two hours before she was brought by government ambulance to us. The mother and baby lived, but once again we decried the lack of prenatal care and gross neglect.

Dystocia can be a devastating tragedy, but the complication we ran into more often and carried a higher mortality rate was placenta previa. I was called to the hospital one afternoon to find a woman suffering a gushing and exsanguinating hemorrhage. Not a moment could be lost if we were to save her life, and I did something I'd never done before. I performed an unsterile vaginal examination. There was a mass of placental tissue in the cervix which was only five centimeters dilated. What to do? There was certainly no time to sterilize instruments for a cesarean section, so with my patient under anaesthesia I did the second thing I had never done before and incised the cervix enough to get at the fetus, did a version and extracted placenta and baby, then packed the uterus and sutured the cervix. All of this within fifteen or twenty minutes of my first exam. The patient got along fine, but she would have surely died in another few minutes.

At Hemptinne Mission, some thirty miles away, the Catholic sisters provided a large obstetrical service. They were tireless and devoted workers, but sometimes they ran into complications they couldn't handle, and then they brought them to us at Lubondai. One Sunday morning just at the conclusion of our worship service the sisters arrived in a truck bringing a patient who had been in labor with her first baby for a couple of days. The head of the dead child was crowning, and I did a wide episiotomy and was able to extract the infant with forceps. It was macerated with a terrible odor and there was much necrosis of the vaginal mucosa. Exploration of the uterus revealed a Bandl's ring but no rupture. I repaired the episiotomy, but three weeks later we were dealing with both vesico-vaginal and recto-vaginal fistulas which necessitated repeated surgery.

The sisters were back again in a month with another primigravida (first pregnancy) who had been in labor for twenty-four hours with the head unengaged, pulse of 160 and fever. We sectioned her and again the baby was dead. Antibiotics saved the mother.

It is easy to understand that with so much neglected dystocia repeatedly presenting itself we had more than our share of vesico-vaginal fistulas. I can remember that one day John Miller and I transplanted the ureters of two patients into the rectum. John did the first one on a woman who came in with practically the whole bladder sloughed out after childbirth. I did the second on a poor patient for whom we had unsuccessfully attempted to close her fistula on four occasions. I am sure the above recitations give an intimation of the obstetrical emergencies we often encountered in Africa which in the United States and other highly developed countries are seldom if ever seen.

Many of these exaggerated situations were pathetic and elicited much sympathy and compassion, but there were also humorous occasions adding their share of amusement. I conducted a family planning clinic at Lubondai, but my clinic was weighted much more to the side of correcting sterility than to the matter of birth control because in Zaire the accent is on having lots of babies. An elderly chieftain came complaining of sterility. He was the most unique example I ever encountered with this disability since he had twenty adult children. Seven younger ones were still at home, but currently there were no babies or toddlers. At that point in time he had nine wives, and he brought the three Protestant ones with him for examination!

Another consideration to deal with was the African lack of insight concerning lapse of time. The question, "How old are you?" invariably brought forth a puzzled frown and a vague reply which implied that the person not only did not know but had never really seriously considered the question. An even greater puzzler was when we sought to get the history of the illness and asked, "How long have you had this pain (or symptom)?" Eventually the reluctant answer was, "I don't know." An instance pointing up a total disregard of time was when a Congolese man accosted me in the path one day, pulled a worn and yellow slip of paper from his pocket, and handed it to me. "See, I have returned," he said proudly, "like you told me to." I read the slip. It was a discharge note from the hospital on which I had added that the patient should return in a few weeks for follow-up. He was responding after a fourteen-year lapse!

I have already commented on the exaggerated and excessive findings we so often encountered in the African pathological conditions, and have explained that these were usually due to ignorance of the disease process plus a stoic disregard and negligence of evolving results. One day I drained a plural effusion and removed 2,300 cc of fluid from a man's chest. That was nearly two and one-half quarts, and constituted something of a record for me. A week later I relieved him of another 2,250 cc!

Appendicitis was rare in the Congo but occasionally we ran into grossly undiagnosed and unappreciated cases. I examined a woman in the clinic and found all the pelvic structures indurated and matted together. My first impression was that it was a far advanced malignancy, probably inoperable. But we scheduled her for surgery where I found an abscess posterior to the uterus involving a tube and ovary and loops of bowel, and in the center of the mass was the remains of the appendix! This was one of those rare cases of African appendicitis that had ruptured and walled itself off. God's provision of our natural bodily defenses is marvelous to behold!

In February and March of 1956 we had an experience which very few American doctors have ever had and probably never will. We worked with an epidemic of smallpox. At the hospital at Dibaya, thirty miles away, I saw fifty cases, and among those poor people there was a fifty percent mortality. During three weeks at Lubondai we vaccinated some fifteen thousand people, and that was some job! It meant about a thousand a day.

CLIMATE AND COMMUNICATIONS

Few subjects are so regularly abused as that of weather. Both African and missionary are greatly influenced by the weather. It controls travel, building, planting, reaping, and more. At the height of the rainy season there is a hard rain almost every day. Great thunderheads build up in the heat of the morning sun to discharge their contents along with a formidable display of thunder and lightening. A rainstorm doesn't last long, sometimes no more than ten minutes, but while it comes down it does so in deluges. In Africa, we ask the same question all people ask when they glance at gathering clouds. "Is it going to rain?" And I have always been amused at the African's stock reply as he cogitates and says, "It's up there," and nodding they add, "but only God knows whether it's coming down."

Dry season is more uncomfortable than rainy season. From mid-May until well into August, there is no rain. The arid climate dries out the skin, and sandy particles get into eyes and between teeth. The roads dry out and, contrary to expectation, this is the season when vehicles bog down the most in deep shifting sands.

Communications have also been a battle in the heart of Africa. The hammock, supported on swaying African shoulder, afoot, was replaced with the motorcycle, then by stock cars, and more recently by four-wheel-drive vehicles evolving from the war. Weeks and months of transoceanic transport gave way to flying the same distance in mere hours. Written communications, originally sent from station to station by runners, later acquired the dignity of government postal service, and finally the marvel of radio appeared on the scene.

A specified section of radio frequency in the forty meter band was set aside by the authorities for official business communications across the length and breadth of the colony, and equipment was quickly installed on our several mission stations to send and receive radio messages. Finally there was a general mission "network" for each station to pass along questions and information. If any two points had a particularly important matter to transact, they could set up a *sked* (schedule) and meet on the air by appointment. Thus medical information and advice could be transmitted over the radio, often reducing the need for cross-country emergency visits.

Such use of the airwaves quickly suggested the possibility of making contact to the home country. Mr. Carroll Stegall was the first member of our missionary force to obtain a license from the colonial government to operate an amateur radio station. He had the distinction of being the first such ham radio operator in the entire Belgian Congo.

I studied my books and in 1948 I applied for my license and obtained the components necessary to operate on the ten meter band.

Effie and Bill Rule with Effie's parents, Bill and Katharine Crane and family, in Athens, Georgia, during furlough, 1956.

Late in the year I began to make some DX contacts—which is ham radio lingo for overseas conversations. It was an entertaining evening pastime which took some of the strain and stress off the day's work. Of course I was interested in making contacts close to home, but that was not easy. Whether the mountains created a barrier or the radio wave bounce wasn't right, I don't know. But I couldn't raise Knoxville. I contacted Nashville to the west and Kingsport to the east, but not Knoxville.

Then one evening (December 10, 1949), while I worked the band, I heard a rather faint signal, "CQ, CQ, CQ." I was just about ready to close down and go to bed, but "CQ" means "I am calling anybody who wants to come in." And then I heard, weakly, "This is W4AZD calling CQ from Oak Ridge, Tennessee . . . " My ears pricked up. Oak Ridge is only eighteen miles from Knoxville!

Conditions were poor, and I realized there wasn't much chance of getting through, but I sure was going to give it a try. "W4AZD, W4AZD, W4AZD. This is 9Q5DQ calling and returning. Do you hear me?" Imagine my joy when he came back. His name was Porter. I told him I was from Knoxville and asked him to contact my family.

Porter Orr and his family and my family became close friends. Later, he moved to Knoxville where we were members of the same church. While I was in Africa, we had hundreds of radio contacts and conversations across the span of twenty years. He has been a dear friend.

A GRIMY BOAT AND A WEARY DRIVE

The trip back to Africa after furlough in 1957 was quite an adventure and must be told. Before we left Knoxville, we received a wonderful gift. Mr. Brantley Burns, a dedicated elder of our church and a beloved friend, presented us with a gorgeous blue and white Chevy station wagon. We equipped it with balloon tires and extra-strong springs to lift it off the gutted African roads, and we were most grateful for the roominess to accommodate our still-growing family. Our baby John was born during this furlough, bringing the family count to eight, which meant more baggage on top of baggage.

In Knoxville, preparing to return, I drove one day down a side street and an object caught my eye. It was a fire-engine red, two-wheel trailer parked on the side of the road with a "For Sale" sign on it. On an impulse I stopped, looked it over, and bought the thing. So when we broke camp in Knoxville and headed for New York, we not only had a Chevy to carry cargo but also a trailer. Both were packed to the brim.

It was after dark when we approached the Big Apple, and I struggled to negotiate all the heavy metropolitan traffic and watch for the sign to the Holland Tunnel to channel us from Jersey to Manhattan. We saw the sign and entered and someone noted that we were going under the Hudson River. Three-year-old Barbara was standing behind me at my shoulder as I turned the car into the narrow tunnel, but she had not been briefed on what it meant to "go under the river." Still she was up to the occasion. If all her family was going, it must be all right, and as we moved along I heard a soft little voice behind me say, "Everybody hold your nose!"

We sailed on the S.S. *Burkel*, an old U.S. World War II victory ship which had been sold or given to Belgium, and we sailed under the Belgian flag. It was primarily a cargo ship and only boasted six or eight state rooms. It burned crude oil and it was greasy and grimy and dirty, and we just kept washing ourselves and the children, morning, noon, and night. We put our toddler Johnnie in a playpen and the captain condescended to string up chicken wire around all the outside railings to keep our passel of kids out of the drink. We had a really pleasant trip as we sailed across the narrow part of the Atlantic and hugged the west African coast, calling at a number of the national African ports where we observed the natives and bought fresh fruits and trinkets. At the end of thirteen days the blue ocean turned a muddy brown and we knew we were nearing the mouth of the mighty Congo which flings its red silt sometimes two hundred miles into the Atlantic Ocean. The Congo also pours two million cubic feet of water every second into the sea, and up it we chugged to the principal port of Matadi.

As we had previously done, Effie took the younger children by train to Leopoldville and from there by plane to Luluabourg while Billy and

Charlotte and I followed with the heavily loaded vehicles. Our 250-mile trip from Matadi to Leo took us some twelve hours. From Leo we followed a new highway inland and for the first 35 miles it was smooth sailing. Eventually, we were trapped in sand three times and worked an aggregate of six hours trying to get out. We were near a village the first time and some Africans came out to help, but we ended up having to unhook the trailer and push them one at a time, car and trailer, through the clinging sand.

We had to cross a river by a small rickety ferry, and it was too short for both car and trailer. Again we had to unhitch the trailer and muscle it up by hand after we had put the Chevy across. Hitched up once more we waved good-bye to the ferrymen, drove fifty feet, and were trapped in another hopeless sand pit! Again there followed unhitching and pushing, inch by inch, until we got the two sections through. A worse experience took place in the middle of nowhere and during the maximum heat of the day. We worked for two hours shoveling quantities of sand to effect an American four-lane interstate and we just breezed along. Then came the rude awakening as we ran off the asphalt into deep, dry sand where the construction stopped! There are two ways you can get stuck on African roads. One is in mud and the other is sand. They are equally horrendous. It was dry season and so we were dealing with sand.

The first day we traveled for fourteen hours and covered 150 miles, a little better than ten miles an hour! Just as night was coming on we hit a stretch of bad sand about 10 miles long. It seemed to never end. We coaxed our motor along and were fortunate enough to get through some threatening brush fires, uncomfortably close on both sides of the road. About 8 P.M. we could go no further. We were so completely exhausted that we gave up and slept in the car.

We were a sight to behold. Charlotte moaned over her filthiness, but Bill and I finally persuaded her to enjoy the dirt since there was nothing she could do about it. We had eaten almost nothing all day, fearing it would make us more thirsty. We had a quart of drinking water and a dozen cokes and they were about gone. The kids were good sports, though, and did little complaining. Bill's innate deliberateness, Charlotte's fastidiousness, and my short temper exhibited themselves now and then, but were usually put down by the other two who were absorbing the gaff.

About five o'clock in the morning while it was still dark, I saw the lights of several autos coming toward us, which proved to be three or four trucks of Belgian workers and a whole bevy of African help. They stopped to survey our predicament and I heard the Congolese speak Tshiluba which amazed me since we were a long way from the Tshiluba-speaking part of the country. But when I spoke to them in their

mother tongue, they were even more amazed. We had an animated
conversation. I identified myself as Ngangabuka Kabamba from
Lubondai, and a couple of the fellows said, "Oh, I know you!"

We learned that this was a survey team, charting maps of the Congo.
They had begun their work in the Kasai region and therefore had gathered their working team from that area. Now, here they were in the
Lower Congo with the Tshiluba-speaking help still with them. They
went to work and there were so many of them they completely lifted our
car out of the sand, and then the trailer, all in a jiffy and we were ready
to travel once more. The Belgian engineers told us their base camp was
only ten miles up the road and that when we came to it we could get
cleaned up and their cook would fix us something to eat. Hot water for
bathing, a change of clothes, and good food on the table completed a
richly, refreshing experience, and after the accommodation we
proceeded on in much better spirits.

The next day was our longest. We traveled from five in the morning
to midnight, and managed to cover 280 miles. We crossed six ferries
and finally reached Kikwit where we were bedded down by our Baptist
friends. At one point that afternoon, when we were hot and tired and
completely out of any drinks, we came to a small store on a lonely road,
manned by a Belgian. We entered his place and the first thing we saw
was a large refrigerator. Our faces lit up.

"Do you have anything cold to drink?" I asked eagerly.

He opened the door and we saw a quart bottle of carbonated water.
All the rest was beer. I considered the situation and then turned to the

One of the many ferries on the African waterways.

kids. I handed them the fizz water and told them to go to the other end of the room with their backs to me, then I bought myself a cold bottle of beer. Let me herewith attest to the fact that it was perhaps the most refreshing drink I ever drank!

After Kikwit we were making good time on a rather bumpy road when lightening struck again. Suddenly the angle iron braces from the body of the trailer to the hitch attached to the car buckled and cracked, dragging on the ground. Apparently we had too much weight forward and were moving too fast for the resistance of those braces. By good chance we discovered a Catholic mission just over the hill where the Congolese priest agreed for us to leave the trailer load temporarily with him. This way we could pull the empty cart along even though the connecting braces were dragging the ground.

We reached another Baptist mission station which took us in for the night, and they told us about a Portuguese farmer/trader who operated a welding rig. The following morning I went to him with my dilemma. He straightened the braces and reinforced them with more angle iron, doing a neat job. I was much impressed with his layout where he had luxuriant gardens in the valley all watered by bamboo pipes and runways from a water source higher up on the hill. The system worked simply by gravity when he turned them on or off. He also harvested palm nuts and had a press to make the palm oil which he sold to soap manufacturers. He even had runs made of chicken wire where he raised wild francolins, an African genus of quail or partridge, quite a table delicacy. I let him know I was impressed with his place, and his response was, "That's the difference between me and you missionaries. I build in the valley to get close to water. You build on the hilltop to get close to God."

That afternoon we traveled 92 miles to Mukedi, a Mennonite station. And incidentally this was the only day we had no adverse experiences. The following day was Sunday and we worshipped with the Mennonites before we hit the road again. We covered 117 miles and spent the night at Tshikapa with Congo Inland Mission friends. We had to cross one large river, the Luange, where it became necessary to transfer from one ferry to another in midstream. We were slowed when we developed a dry socket in one of the trailer wheels. We had no axle grease with us, so we removed both wheels and redistributed the grease. From Tshikapa we had a 216-mile lap to Lubondai, and great was the rejoicing to finally be home again and have that hard grind behind us!

I think of one more amusing incident. Several weeks after reaching Lubondai, I happened to reach under the driver's seat of the Chevy and brought forth a fifth of very fine imported whisky! Where in the world did it come from? I searched my brain, trying to recall, and then it came back to me. One of my Presbyterian brothers came by to bid us farewell in Knoxville. He had offered me a fifth and I had thanked him but turned it down. He must have slipped it under the seat anyhow. I smiled as I considered how many people might have discovered that bottle and confiscated it along the way. But all of them had overlooked it, and now it fell into the hands of the missionary ladies at Lubondai to use in our Christmas fruit cakes!

9 BANTU THOUGHTS AND BELIEFS

As in water face answereth to face, so the heart of man to man (Proverbs 27:19).

Like any other nation, developing nations are made up of people. When one crosses cultural lines to proclaim the gospel or teach the ABCs or provide medical care, it is of the utmost importance to get to know the people. What do they think? How do they feel about your being there? What makes them tick?

Before we set out to teach Africans our system of philosophical thought and cultural action, it behooves us to make an effort to understand theirs. If we can do this we may avoid some of the errors made by our white predecessors who were convinced that the civilized western Christian concept was unassailable, and they demeaned the pagan without giving him his rightful hearing. Out of this proud postulate came the theory of colonization.

Christian scholars have applied themselves to the study and understanding of Bantu philosophy, endeavoring to seek out the fundamental thought processes which underlie the Bantu concept of life or being. This is where we deal with the spirituality of the people, and where the Christian missionary is most particularly interested in making a valid contact. He or she uses, with great success, principles of life learned from the Bantu way of thinking, thus teaching Christian concepts and relating them to images in their own culture. When we fail to explore the mind of the Bantu, we deprive ourselves of the privilege of offering them a spiritual body of teaching they are surely capable of understanding.

Bantu concepts and behavior are always centered in a single value which we shall call *vital force* or *life force*. Our two words "life" and "force," it would seem, are relatively synonymous in the African mind. *Muoyo* in the Tshiluba language is the word for life, and it is the common greeting.

Muoyo instead of "Hello." The idea behind this seems to be that the most precious gift a person can possess is life, or force, so we greet each other and wish each other this great gift. Sometimes the greeting is even more explicit.

Ndi nkuela muoyo or "I throw you life."

Another important word is *bukole* or "power" or "force." When two friends meet, one might say *"Udi ne bukolo, anyi?"* Or, "Are you strong?" "Do you have force?" Thus, "force" is interchangeable with "being," and that's just exactly what life is, i.e. *force* or *being.*

A third important word is *muntu*, usually translated "person." This can be used for anyone but it is always the name given to the original man, so it would be their "Adam." When it designates the original or first person it also includes a fantastic amount of "life" or "force" which he had and which he passed down to all his millions of descendants. So, the *muntu* within you, or the *buntu* as they express it, is your "force" or your "being" or your "life." Take your pick.

This *life force* can be cultivated and increased or it can be neglected and can wither. They even think of it in the anthropological sense of being tall or short, fat or slim. This may be a reason why it is so painfully difficult to depose elected officials in a democratic process, despite the fact that the candidate has been elected for a limited period of time. Come the end of that period, he invariably expects to linger in office and those who cast the vote are loathe to unseat him. It has to do with decreasing or offending his *vital force*, which is a bad thing to do.

Our good friend, the Catholic Archbishop Bakole of Kananga, has written about the *life force* from the Christian point of view in his book *Chemins De Liberation* (Paths of Liberation). Here follows his introductory paragraph I have tried to translate from the French, because I feel it carries much insight and balance as an African merges his *life force* and the gospel message:

> To live, to live abundantly, to augment and reinforce the inner life, this is our deepest desire. Because life is the most beautiful gift that we have received from our parents and through them from God, the source of all life. Thus the first responsibility imposed upon us is that this life should be developed, strengthened, and made as attractive and happy as possible. This we also should transmit to children, to members of the family, to friends and to all people with whom we together form the great Zairian family. Since life is a great gift, but also a difficult task, we are responsible to one another in it.

Variations and extensions of this idea of *vital force* have shaped and colored Bantu concepts for generations. Objects in the world and in the universe also possess force. All living beings, including all animals and insects, qualify. Even flowers, ferns, and fruits, but particularly trees are venerated. Moreover, inanimate entities are the obvious harbingers of force and are to be respected. This list will include streams, rivers, wind, thunder, and lightning, even rocks and boulders.

So *force* is a prize of great value for which people strive with all their being. It is the object of prayer and invocation to the gods, to the spirit world, and to dead ancestors. Bantu religious expression resolves into two main streams: animism and ancestor worship. The animism of the *vital force* being in inanimate objects and natural phenomena. Ancestor worship is perhaps a phase of animism. The more recent departed ancestors are closest at hand and therefore yield more influence or force, and are the ones most frequently invoked. The ancients have declined in *vital force* and are not in ready contact and are of less importance and deserve less attention.

In the Western mind, *vital force* is a rather static phenomenon, but the African might be affected quite dynamically by a number of factors. The African tends to externalize the happenings of the day, separating them from the dynamics of his own being, whereas we internalize them. For example, if I had an accident on a bike, I would say, "I fell off the bicycle." The African would never say it like that. He would say, "The bike threw me." He never puts the action on himself, but on the object.

In the mind of the Bantu, the dead also live but they have a diminished life with reduced vital energy. The spirit continues to live in the dead cadaver, but it can escape and wander about. He believes the soul not only leaves the body at death but at other times as well. This explains a dream. The body lies inert on the bed, but the soul escapes and has all sorts of adventures, some of them delightful and others quite terrifying.

Because their *vital force* is dynamic rather than static, there can be encounters, even conflicts, between operative spirits. A person living or dead can directly or indirectly reinforce or diminish the power or being of another person. If one force is greater than another it can paralyze it, or diminish or even destroy it. With spiritual conflict ever-present, the African lives in a state of unease or even frank fear of the unknown. When will lightning strike? Or a tree fall across my humble dwelling?

In order to combat the fears, a large portion of the population resort to *Buanga*, which is medicine or magic medicine. It is usually bought from the medicine man to protect against the suspicious medicines of others.

Technical skills impress the African. The white man seems to have mastered a great many of the natural forces, which indicates to the black man that there is a very potent reservoir of *vital force*. He also concludes that this is the reason the white person is unimpressed with their conflicts of their *vital force* and never seems concerned about making medicine to protect himself. Apparently he has a strong enough force to withstand anything which might be hurled at him from the African arsenal of magic.

The Bantu believe in a Supreme Being who is the Creator. He is *Nvidi Mukulu*, the all-powerful One, and his existence lies at the root of all religious conceptions, even though it degenerates into animism, fetishism, ancestor worship, and magic. There are ten to twelve thousand folk religions throughout the world today, and some eight thousand of them have been studied in depth. Findings indicate that fully 95 percent of the religions acknowledge that there is one Great Spirit or Creator. Most of them explain that there is a great distance between God and mankind which is difficult to bridge, and so they do obeisance to the nearer spirits with whom there is communication. Worship is more out of fear than reverence. This Creator has force and power within himself, and he gives existence and life, allocating the power of survival.

Mankind or *Muntu* is the dominant force among all the created and visible forces. His fullness of being consists to a greater or lesser extent in his participation in the force of God. Here is the place for Christian theology. Jesus has talked about this life-giving force. John 10:18 says, "No man taketh it [my life] from me, but I lay it down of myself. I have power to lay it down, and I have power to take it again. This commandment have I received of my Father."

In this way he speaks of his own *life force*, and he also speaks of his force in the lives of others upon his death. Now this is something the African can understand and believe. The sacrament of Holy Communion is also very meaningful to the African. He finds no problem when Jesus said, "Except you eat the flesh of the Son of man, and drink his blood, you have no life in you" (John 6:53). This speaks to him about a concept he has known from childhood—the *life force*!

The weakest link in the Bantu's concept of spirituality has to do with a low moral ethic plus neglect in holding the line in matters of good and evil. When a theft is committed, the great shame is not the misdemeanor but the embarrassment of being caught. Lies and deceit are judged more on the exigencies of the moment and what is necessary to escape trouble, than on the pragmatic commandment, "Thou shalt not bear false witness." To protect dignity and one's *life force* the use of falsehood might be considered subtle and clever. Adultery is not so much an infraction of morals as the abuse of another man's dignity and personal force. Everything may be corrected by paying a fine. Such low moral standards are born out of the primitive consideration of persons. It is a law of *vital force*, and not of property and its use or misuse. The worst evil in the Bantu's mind is harm done to the *vital force*.

It is into these situations and attitudes that the light of the gospel of Jesus Christ shines. Certainly the other person is extremely important, and we should love our neighbor as ourself, but this can only be realized with validity after we have first addressed ourselves to the cardinal principle of loving God with all our heart and soul and strength and mind. So what have I gleaned in my forty years of observing the Bantu personality? What characteristics have I recognized and learned to deal with in my daily interaction with my African brothers and sisters? Let me list them:

1. *Resilience.* Perhaps the most predominant nature of the African personality is that of buoyancy. The ability to quickly regain poise in the face of adversity. I have admired their remarkable resilience. Often enough they fail to realize their hopes and aspirations, but they don't miss a step. They keep plugging away. Political defeat is endured with stoic acceptance, but you can depend on it: they'll be back again at the next election. In America we have an axiom, "If at first you don't succeed, try, try again." The Bantu have developed this attitude to a science.

2. *Bargaining and Compromise.* The African is contented, comfortable, and at his best in a bargaining situation. You only need visit the village market place to see this quality in action. If there's anything that dismays the customer, it is a firm price on an item. Eliminating the dickering process takes all the pleasure out of the purchase. This attitude carries over into all areas of human relationship, including politics. Since bargaining ends with a compromise, it is imperative to take your first stance way out ahead of the position you expect to eventually agree on. The Africans have an expression, *Kuteta mai,* (that we also use) which means "test the water." One can always keep in mind that the African's first word is never his last, under any and all circumstances. This explains some of the outrageous positions Patrice Lumumba took during the early days of Congo independence. The western nations stood aghast, but what they failed to recognize was that "the first word is never the last."

3. *Insight.* The Bantu are extremely wise in their ability to size up the other party; to recognize what makes him tick and to exploit that observation. I was in the uncomfortable position over and over again of feeling that the Congolese in question knew me better than I knew him. And in their dealings with the missionaries they surely capitalized on this propensity. Time and again they appealed to his or her "higher nature" to gain their ends. "Don't you have any *luse* (love or mercy)?" Or, "Preacher So-and-So has great *luse.* Why aren't you like him?" Nobody likes to have benevolent qualities called into question, especially missionaries!

4. The Extended Family. The extended family relationships are more important and intimate among the Bantu than in the western world. They are very dependent upon one another to help build houses, care for the sick, clear and cultivate fields, obtain the marriage dowry, plus conduct other financial transactions. They truly have no place to turn but to the structured family circle. They look to the established leaders of the *diku* (immediate family) and the *tshiota* (tribe), and these may not necessarily be their direct parents. The leader of a family may be an elder uncle who may have more authority than the true parents.

Most marriages are within the tribe and the people all venerate common ancestors. During the early years of the Republic, tribal loyalties far outweighed national loyalty. But time is changing this to some extent as urbanization is gradually breaking down tribal affinities. In the city your neighbors may come from a dozen different tribes and so your friendships become more cosmopolitan.

5. Situational Ethics. Kierkegaard and Sartre introduced the concept of existentialism in the field of Christian philosophy, but among the Bantu this thought of "honoring existing circumstances" has long been known. Here again the value of the person and his own *vital force* takes precedence over rules and regulations. True morality is based on the needs and even the wishes of the individual. You help the fellow in trouble no matter what he has done, and no matter what you have to do. There is the story of Hercules who refused to help the man free his cart from the mud because the man wouldn't get off and push. The African says Hercules was a "bad person" because he had the strength to deliver the beleaguered man but didn't do it.

An African girl entered our school for nurses but began to have some psychiatric problems. It became evident that she would have to drop out, but we were urged to take her back because it would affirm and support someone in trouble. Then there are those incidents where we were importuned to take someone by car to his destination simply on the basis that he was far from home and night was coming on. It made no difference what agreement you had made, the situation changed the complexion of the matter. On this basis, their contracts are some times dishonored and thrown in the trash. A new situation has made the earlier agreement invalid. This is situational ethics as it works itself out in Africa.

6. Importunity. The Bantu concern for their own personal *life force* automatically puts them into extremes of importunity—the demand for personal consideration over the best corporate interests. One year we gave entrance examinations for a class of nursing aides at Bulape and after the class was chosen a couple of days later two young men arrived to take the exam. They had come a long way, and the trip had been difficult and expensive. They were informed that they were too late; the exam had been given and the class selected. The matter was closed.

"But we didn't know the date of the examination." This was meant as justification and why some special exception should be made for them.

"But we can't reopen the candidacy and give the exam to everybody," I objected.

They were amazed at my reply. "We're not asking you to give it to everybody," they explained. "Just to us!"

When I still refused, they were affronted and angry. I had personally demeaned them. It was impossible for them to see my point of view, and it was impossible for me to see theirs. In their simple society the relationship of one person with another is paramount, and making exceptions is the way of life. When I refused I was saying, in effect, "You are not worth making an exception for." I had offended their self-image.

As I looked into my own heart and tried to be honest, I had to admit that I was really not concerned about whether they got into the school or not. I was concerned about the school and about conducting it fairly. I would have liked having them if they were superior students and I didn't want them if they were inferior. In any case I intended to abide by rules and regulations. I am the product of a more complex urban society where the individual concedes to the group. But as a Christian I am concerned about the person, and I was concerned about those boys. In spite of the antagonistic feelings I had caused, I tried to make spiritual amends, and they were the subject of my prayers.

7. *Improvidence.* The African anticipation of future events and the preparation for them is quite poor. This is probably because of a basic difference between the more affluent and the less affluent. The "well fixed" are content with the present and are looking toward the future. "How will I be doing five years from now? Ten?" But the poor person must give his attention to the present. "What will I have to eat today?" Or, "Where will I sleep tonight?" There are so many questions for the present, there is no time left to think about the future.

This helps explain some of their attitudes toward property. Your cattle and your fields are important because they represent your daily sustenance, but land ownership is hardly significant when in a year or so the entire village will be moving to a new site a kilometer or so down the road. This makes the concept of upkeep or maintenance difficult for the African. Automobiles and trucks are worn out in short order because they are abused and not kept in good functioning condition. Missionary doctors despair over the way hospital records are lost or destroyed since preserving some of them is of historical value. The African sees them as advantages of the moment, i.e. notepaper or toilet paper.

8. Autocracy. Let us keep in mind that the acceptable African form of government, handed down through the years and across generations, is an autocracy. The man in charge is the paramount chieftain who brooks no challenge to his authority, and any who question the status quo are in danger of losing their life. The populace, mentally regimented to this mode of social control, adds their voice of approval. This is the reason there is no such thing as a true democracy in black Africa today, nor any indication there might soon be one. If there is going to be any dissenting opinion it will not be within the body politic. A secession and withdrawal must be instituted wherein the minority voice will become the majority opinion. Autocracy breeds fragmentation because if all sides are to be heard, a split occurs. We are reminded that an effective democracy is a form of government which permits and lends dignity to a minority opinion, which is truly essential for the existence of democracy.

9. The Significance of a Gift. In this characteristic the Westerner and the African are poles apart. In the west we think of a gift as an expression of generosity and affirmation of another person. It might be in recognition of achievement and so constitute a prize of accomplishment. It might be for no reason at all except out of love, admiration, or affection. A gift is not normally in payment of an obligation. It is at the discretion of the giver. Appreciation is a proper attitude of the recipient. It is not the gift which is important, but the thought behind it.

On the other hand, the African senses the interplay of vital forces in such a transaction. The force of the donor is increased in the very act of giving, and that of the recipient may be enhanced if the gift is a handsome one, but may be decreased if the gift is cheap. In any case the recipient has honored and blessed the donor by being fit to receive, so the donor owes a sense of gratitude to the recipient.

The recipient may return the gift if unworthy and suggest that the giver try again and up the ante! "You don't look a gift horse in the mouth," we say. But the African says, "Of course you do!" And he returns it if it doesn't measure up.

"God so loved the world that he gave . . . " (John 3:16) must be carefully presented. There is nothing we can do in receiving His gifts that will enhance His goodness. We simply accept on the basis of our own great need and His free gift.

TRIBAL CUSTOMS

There are a number of taboos which govern community behavior in African society. In many instances they have little or no relationship to health status, but they are all around and you never know when one might complicate the treatment of illness or the protection of public health. One commonly found taboo is the disapproval of in-laws looking at one another. A young man never looks directly at his mother-in-law. If he wants to talk with her he sends word that he is coming, and he stands outside and talks over the fence or through the bamboo wall of the house. Now this can be a problem if the son-in-law is a medical auxiliary and his mother-in-law is a patient seeking assistance.

There are certain foods which may or may not be eaten. Ordinarily, the Africans among whom we lived would not eat crocodile meat. I can't say that I blame them. The crocodile is a scandalous scavenger, and the only meat I have ever timidly sampled from its muscular tail I found to be greasy and flat, the taste almost revolting. But among Africans there are two exceptions to this taboo. If one's name is *Ngandu* (crocodile) then he is permitted to eat *ngandu*. And if a family member has been taken by a crocodile (not uncommon), then not only are they freed of the restriction, but they are charged to eat crocodile meat at every opportunity. "It ate us. We eat it." However, I can think of no examples where this has played a part in medical treatment.

Sexual practices might have a real bearing on the incidence of venereal disease and procedures for its control. The Bena Lulua are rather lax along this line, setting up "trial marriages" which can easily be broken and another "tried." So there are health factors to consider, as well as moral factors.

Another concept of the Bantu people that must always be kept in mind is their understanding of the *life force* and their solemn concern for it. Concern for a dying patient is more for the person's spirit and what its activities will be after death. Time and time again families have carried moribund patients away from the hospital to take them home, fearing that death will come in a strange locality and the released spirit will wander and be upset. It was naturally disconcerting to me when they made off with a patient they thought was dying, but whom I thought had a good chance of recovery!

They have a method to entrap the spirit and keep it in the expiring body until they reach home. They plug up the mouth and nostrils which are the obvious passageways, and this is of no great moment for the dead person but quite tragic and conclusive in a living one. We had to watch carefully to keep this from happening, and I am sure there were times when we failed.

Finally, there are the African herbs and medicines. I seldom found any practitioners among the Bantu who would freely confide in me, in spite of the fact that I was also a "witch doctor." They called me *Ngangabuka* and they called their medicine man *Ngangabuka*. But when it came to explaining native medicines, they backed off, even though I was friendly and non-judgmental with them. I recognize that there are herbal potions which are effective in the treatment of disease. Some are applied internally and some externally, with a somatic effect. But some may be quite dangerous, and probably the most ominous threat is that dosage is seldom considered or measured. Any herb which might have true curative qualities can turn into a killer if the wrong amount is taken. This is often seen in small children who are given the same dosage as their parents. Because of this I was never able to sincerely advise my African friends to visit the medicine man.

THE SPIRIT WORLD

One cannot practice medicine in central Africa without feeling the proximity of the spirit world. Indeed one must deal with the practical aspects of such a world since it exists in the minds of the African people. They generally accept the existence of a Creator, who is one person with dominion over everything. But he is distant and relatively inaccessible. The spirit world which is intimately about them is more meaningful and of practical import in their daily lives. The spirits are of the departed dead (called *bakishi* or in the singular, *mukishi*) and they may be friendly and benevolent (in whose good graces one strives to remain), or capricious (amusing themselves in their manipulation of humans), or often downright hostile and diabolical in their treatment.

In our American culture we have become extremely materialistic, and the world of the spirit seldom enters into our thinking. Not so with the black African. The spirit world is in every rock and tree, in every event from harvesting manioc to a clap of thunder. The physician deals with this kind of atmosphere almost daily, in the minds and lives of the people he encounters.

I have referred to the fact that several times I performed reconstructive surgery on epileptic patients who while in an unconscious epiliptic seizure were "treated" with burning behind their knees. This was apparently the accepted manner of "making it too hot" and uncomfortable for the *mukishi* causing the convulsion. If burned, the *mukishi* might leave the victim and go elsewhere.

I shall never forget a patient who died of massive bilateral lobar pneumonia. I was called to see him just as he was about to die. I examined

108

him. His pulse was failing and his feeble respiration faltered, then ceased. Some friend or relative was standing at the foot of the bed, and I told him, "He is gone."

The relative became suddenly alert. "Is he truly dead?" He wanted confirmation.

When I nodded my head he turned in agitation toward the deceased body and omitted a wild diatribe of invectives. He stretched out his arm, pointed his finger and shouted at the top of his voice. He stopped suddenly, turned on his heel and stalked out of the hospital. Here was a man with a highly emotional conflict inside him. While the dying man was unconscious there was no use to speak to him. No one knew where the *mukishi* was. But as the patient died, the relative didn't want the *mukishi* to leave the body and get away before hearing him out.

On another occasion an old chieftain came to us with abdominal pain and vomiting. Surgery revealed a widespread carcinoma of the stomach. We did a gastroenterostomy to relieve the obstruction and to allow him easier eating, but we were unable to do anything about the life-threatening tumor. He was released, but three months later he returned with another intestinal obstruction which we released. However, he was already in the final stages of his cancer and in a few days he passed away. Before he died, his retinue of followers began dressing him in preparation for carrying him home. They didn't want the release of the *mukishi* at Lubondai where it might wander around, get lost, and never get home. It was wiser to carry the dying man to his village which would please the *mukishi* and establish good relations between it and the people. They came to me to ask permission for the patient to leave the hospital. I was torn by this request between my sympathies for friends and loved ones and my concern for the comfort and dignity of the dying patient. I was forced to say no.

"I cannot agree to your dressing this dying person and then bumping him along in a hammock to take him home. If you do it you will do it without my advice or permission."

"But you don't understand," they said. "He is the big chief, and if he dies here and his *mukishi* escapes here at the hospital instead of back home, we will all be punished!"

Once again I took the opportunity to remind them that God is not a being, faraway and unconcerned with our problems and troubles. He is our Heavenly Father who knows us and loves us. He takes us home to himself when we die. The important thing isn't where a man dies but that he puts himself into the hands of God by means of belief in Jesus Christ.

"Look at me," I said. "Here I am a stranger in your country. My family and my clan are in the foreign land. But if God wants to call me home to Him today, I'm ready to go. And you needn't be afraid of my *mukishi* hanging around here to bother you because God will take it."

Unfortunately, as I mentioned, families didn't always know when death was approaching and all too often a patient was carried away in the night by family when we could have saved the life. More than once I warned, "If you take your loved one, he/she will die, but if you stay your loved one will live."

Inevitably there were those who died in the hospital. The pattern for conveying the corpse homeward was almost always the same. One group was nonvocal, and they were occupied with carrying the body wrapped in fiber mats. The women went before them, painted with white clay, the sign of mourning, and dancing and wailing at the top of their voices. A larger group was out in front of everybody else, on all sides, and bringing up the rear, and they were sweeping the ground with palm fronds as the cortege moved along. This encompassing group was directing the liberated and errant *mukishi* along the way to prevent it from getting misplaced or lost.

Mukelenge Kaseya was the chieftain of a village near Lubondai. Mujinga, his wife, was a *Muena Lubika*, which means she was a diviner who talked with the spirits. People came to her for advice and for healing, and her ministrations were always benevolent. She was similar to a psychic or fortune teller.

One day I happened to be in the village while she was plying her trade and I stood by to watch. Her face and arms were marked with *luhemba*, the white clay used in various African ceremonies, and she was going through a series of incantations which the person seeking her assistance was to repeat after her. While she spoke, her eyes were at times glazed and fixed, as though in a trance. She held a large gourd half filled with *luhemba*, and on its surface lay several small articles including a small coin, a match, a scrap of cloth, and kernels of corn. Mumbling in her singsong cadence, she would shake and tilt the gourd from side to side, and when she stopped it was the order found of the various objects which she "read" to give advice to her client.

The man before her complained of rheumatic pains and her advice was for him to avoid the public market place for three weeks. If he did not go near it, the aches and pains would ease and stop. There was a fee, of course, for her services.

A month later, Mujinga presented herself to me at the hospital. She had a badly infected eye with swelling and pustular discharge. She was in considerable pain and distress.

"Why did you come to me?" I asked her. "You are a healer. Haven't you made medicine for yourself?"

Her abject humility was disarming, "You know and I know that you have the wisdom and the medicine to heal my eye. That is the reason I have come."

There was no time to lose in order to save the vision in her eye, so we put her in the hospital for strong doses of internal and external antibiotics. When she recovered, she was duly impressed. So much so that she gave up her divination and made a public profession of faith. Then she came back to the hospital to ask me for a job because, she said, she wanted to work for the healing of her people the proper and Christian way. We put her to work caring for our female patients where she served faithfully for many years.

10 THAT ANCIENT SCOURGE—LEPROSY

And the King shall answer and say unto them, Verily I say unto you, Inasmuch as ye have done it unto one of the least of these my brethren, ye have done it unto me (Matthew 25:40).

I have chosen to deal with my experiences in the field of leprosy in a special chapter because the treatment of this disease has been such a unique service in missionary medicine. Also, the reaction of leprosy patients to the Christian Gospel has been singularly heartwarming.

From biblical times, leprosy has carried a stigma in the minds of many people. The word "leper" has had such a demeaning ring that it is no longer used. We speak of a person with leprosy as a "leprosy patient." There are those who also seek to eliminate the word "leprosy" from current usage, instead using the words "Hansen's disease." G. H. Hansen (1841–1912) was the Norwegian physician who discovered the leprosy bacillus more than 140 years ago. It was one of the first pathological bacilli ever recognized, and it was Hansen's work that led Robert Koch to discover the tuberculosis bacillus.

When I arrived at Lubondai in 1941, I found that a leprosy colony of some three hundred patients was an important part of my new medical responsibility. Located about five miles from our mission compound, the village was composed of row after row of mud huts with thatch roofs where the leprous patients lived with their families. I was surprised to find that there was little or no effort at isolation within the family. Healthy spouses lived year after year along side their leprous mates, and the most alarming factor was that children ran around everywhere. In the center of the community there were two buildings of stone foundation, brick walls, and metal roofs. One was the medical dispensary with facilities for giving treatments, bandaging sores, storing supplies, and doing the basic laboratory work including urinalysis and the preparation of slides for tissue examination. The other was a neat and attractive chapel where worship was regularly conducted.

During this era the employment of chaulmoogra oil was the basic treatment for leprosy. It is true that oil from this East Indian tree does have some ameliorative effect on the progress of the disease, but such large intramuscular injections are required and are so painful that there has always been the search for a better remedy. About the time I arrived someone had suggested that the injection of diphtheria toxoid would stimulate resistance to leprosy. American Leprosy Missions (formally called the American Mission to Lepers) sent me generous quantities of this preparation and I began an investigation among our patients at Lubondai which included taking pictures of the lesions of each recipient and regular examination of all results. We never found evidence of any real therapeutic value, so the experiment was finally discontinued which saved me considerable time and effort.

American Leprosy Missions was always extremely helpful in the management of this disease. Funds were allocated annually which helped immensely in the treatment of the disease. I especially appreciated these favors because they came from the hand of my idol and mentor, Dr. Eugene Kellersberger. The same man who had largely inspired the care of leprosy patients in this Kasai region, who had personally managed this leprosy colony at Lubondai, and who was now the executive officer of American Leprosy Missions.

These years gave me a new experience and a new insight into the manifestations of this ancient malady. I learned in a practical way what I had been taught in medical school, namely that leprosy is basically an invasion of the nervous system by the leprosy bacillus. It eventually destroys nerve cells and interrupts motor and sensory pathways. This provokes the anaesthesia and the deformities of face and figure which are so characteristic of leprosy's outworking. But I learned something new: that before the nerves die they hurt. Leprosy doesn't always take away all feeling, but some times it aggravates feeling to an unbearable point. I was called upon again and again to provide relief for pain which was excessive over prolonged periods of time. I used up all my armamentarium of analgesics and pain killers and still the victims groaned.

One treatment discovered and used with seemingly the most effective results was daily but alternate intravenous injections of thiamine chloride (vitamin B1) and calcium gluconate. Patients kept returning and asking for more of these injections which I interpreted as rendering some effective relief.

Anaesthesia is, of course, the eventual and the most dramatic effect of the infection. Many of the deformities, particularly those of the extremities, are not due to the direct invasion of the bacillus into those tissues, but are due to trauma to the fingers and toes. The patient may wear a pair of ill-fitting shoes that pinch and rub and cause blisters, but the wearer has no knowledge of the problem because he has no feeling.

Evenings tend to turn cool and Africans have little if any covering, so they habitually maintain a small fire or hot coals in the middle of the hut, huddling around it to keep warm through the night. One day when I arrived at the leprosy camp I was horrified to find a woman with deep and destructive third degree burns on both her feet. She had slept too close to the fire, inadvertently sticking her feet into the red hot coals. Anyone else would have immediately jerked them out, but she had slept peacefully through it all. The surgical restoration was a sad occasion as it was necessary for me to remove significant parts from her feet, all because she had no pain perception.

Another problem encountered at the leprosy camp were chronic ulcerations in the feet. The tissues are not healthy and active and they heal very slowly. Many patients must contend with long-standing ulcerations which suppurate and emit foul odors in spite of everything. Here again I harked back to an old remedy I had learned in Philadelphia called the Unna Boot. It is concocted of gelatin, zinc oxide powder, and glycerin which is applied to the offending part with a paint brush and then sheathed with a gauze bandage also impregnated with the Unna paste. This can be left without replacement for a week or two which not only saves bandages and labor but has a truly healing effect on the ulcer.

But perhaps the most rewarding aspect of the care of leprosy patients, at least for the Christian worker, was the profound appreciation those people expressed, and their enthusiastic response to spiritual dimensions of physical healing. The percentage of patients making commitments of faith was always greater than that of the conventional populace, and their giving, though small considering their economic status, was always with joy and true celebration. I recall one Sunday morning when Lumbala Nicholas was preaching about repenting of our sins and reminded his hearers that we should correct the wrongs we have done to others if we expect God to forgive us. He quoted Jesus' statement, "If you bring your gift to the altar and there remember that your brother has something against you, leave your gift there before the altar, and go your way. First be reconciled to your brother, and then come and offer your gift." After the service one of the patients came to me and asked for a permit to travel and permission to leave the camp for a few days. I asked him why he wanted to go and he recounted an event which had taken place a couple of years earlier. He had been walking along the highway on an approved trip to his home village when he encountered a group of strangers. They jumped on him, beat him up, and took his money. As he proceeded he met the government official in the next village and told him what had happened. Policemen went back with him, found the offenders, and brought them back for trial.

"The only trouble is," the patient told me, "I only had fifteen francs in my pocket, but I saw a great opportunity to get more from my adversaries. So I reported that they had taken three hundred francs. The officer accepted my story and made them pay up." Now the penitent man wanted to amend the wrong he had done and pay back the men. I gave him a note allowing him to go and look for the strangers.

LEPROSY AT BIBANGA

In 1946 when I was located at Bibanga, I found that I had inherited an even larger and better equipped leprosy colony with about five hundred patients. Again this was the imaginative handiwork of Dr. Kellersberger, and it was largely his dedication and success in developing this work that had led him to the directorship of American Leprosy Missions. When Dr. Kelly found it difficult and time-consuming to obtain chaulmoogra oil for his patients, he solved the problem in a very logical manner. He planted an orchard of chaulmoogra trees and produced his own oil. A large cast-iron press stood before the dispensary door, anchored in cement and with long rotating bars for manually compressing nuts off the trees that grew luxuriously in a fertile valley bathed by the waters of a meandering stream below the camp. The able members of the camp climbed the steep hill regularly, each with a basket of nuts on his head, then trudged round and round the press, pushing those long handles and watching the precious oil trickle into a waiting container.

But by the time I arrived at Bibanga the new sulfone treatments for leprosy were being introduced, replacing the chaulmoogra oil as well as the faithful assembly line. The parent sulfone first recognized as effective in the treatment of the disease was diamino-diphenylsulfone, commonly referred to as DDS. But it was too toxic and was discarded for some of its allied salts. The three we used were Promin and Diasone (by mouth) and Sulfetrone (intramuscularly). These medications were administered twice a week, starting with small doses and gradually increasing them as the patient adapted to them. After a while we noted that the DDS dosages could be considerably reduced and still give a good therapeutic result. Toxicity was reduced and DDS by mouth became the accepted medication of choice. Now we had a formidable tool for combating leprosy.

In 1951 American Leprosy Missions sent a representative, Mrs. Mamie Gene Cole Husk, to the Congo to get an on-the-spot view of the leprosy work to be used for promotional and fund raising purposes back in the States. Mamie Gene was an old friend and it was a great pleasure to have her in our home while we escorted her around the Kasai

Province to see the leprosy work on several mission stations. I took her first to Mutoto, then eastward to Lusambo, and from there to the Methodist station of Minga where Dr. and Mrs. Bill Hughlett were our hosts. From Minga we journeyed to Tunda where Dr. W. B. Lewis had an active leprosy service.

On our way back to Lusambo and westward, returning to our Presbyterian mission area, we were caught in one of the most torrential rains I ever saw in Africa. The roadways were all flooded and became muddy mires. Driving was painfully slow and a number of times I had to dig us out of mud up to our wheel hubs. There was a stream we had to cross to reach Lusambo and it was a torrent. Water had risen well above the overpass which was no longer visible. I got out, took off my shoes and socks, and rolled up my pants to make a creeping examination of the road. Finding it still intact, I made the bold but foolish decision to cross. I drove out to the center of the bridge. The motor coughed and died, and water began to well up over the floorboards. Somehow we would have to be either pulled or pushed out of there and we were all alone with no help in sight.

At this juncture it was a good thing I was then a strong and athletic young man, so I put the car in neutral and with Mamie Gene steering, I bent my back to it. Nothing moved. I cut down a tree and trimmed the branches to make a pole. (We didn't travel in Congo without an axe and a shovel.) I put it under the rear axle pried the car forward, inch by inch, stopping often to rest from the violent exertion. We finally reached the other side an hour or so later, and then it was necessary to dry off spark plugs and wiring and blow out the exhaust pipe so the engine would start. We did make it home!

Dr. John Miller took Mamie Gene to visit the leprosy colonies at Luebo and Lubondai after which she returned to Bibanga to have Christmas with us. I believe she enjoyed her African tour in spite of flood and flounderings, and I am sure it was useful for taking the story of leprosy to the church people back home.

MADRID LEPROSY CONGRESS

The American Leprosy Missions very magnanimously sent me, along with several other missionary doctors, to attend the Sixth International Congress on Leprosy, held in Madrid, Spain, October 3–10, 1953. There was much excitement in the Rule household as preparations for my journey were made. Effie would keep the home fires burning and ride herd on the four children. With my bags packed I drove over to the state post at Tshilenge to get my permit to return to the colony. The young administrator reviewed the matter and finding that I would be gone only a week or ten days he opined that I didn't need a permit. So off I flew to Leopoldville where I caught the Sabena plane for Lisbon, and from there took another plane to Madrid.

This was my first visit to Spain. I was intrigued by the late start of the city's business day. At ten o'clock in the morning the streets were still empty. People were just getting up and eating breakfast. Evening activities hardly started before midnight. Movie houses opened around 10 or 11 P.M. It was most remarkable! Another surprise was the cheap accommodations. I stayed in the Hilton Hotel for only $1.50 per day! Taxi service anywhere in the city was usually no more than twenty-five cents. A phone call or a subway ride was a matter of pennies.

The meetings of the congress were like attending the United Nations. Since there were delegates from all over the world, papers were read in many languages with headphones for interpreters. All aspects of the disease were covered: bacteriology, immunology, treatment, public health control, etc. The big question which fired off the most sparks was the matter of clinical classification of the disease.

I was particularly delighted to find one of my Davidson College classmates in Madrid. Roger Enloe was president of the YMCA our senior year and we were close friends. He was in Madrid as a fraternal advisor or as a listening post for the mainline churches to learn what was going on religiously in Spain. Remember that this was the era of Francisco Franco, the Fascist head of state. Roger was not a missionary. He would not have been admitted under such designation. His job was to encourage and advise the Spanish church without position or authority in it. The church was truly persecuted. The constitution of the country gave the right for people to worship as they pleased privately but not publicly. Any "propaganda" for religion was forbidden except that of the state (Roman Catholic) church. Protestants could meet together, but the building in which they met could not look like a church. There could be no signs or advertising of meetings, and no religious literature could be printed or imported, including Bibles. Neither could the church engage in public social services such as help for the poor, orphanages, and the like. That also was "propaganda." In other words, a Spaniard was, to all intents and purposes, a Catholic, and he must be able to walk down the street, engage in his business, live in his home, and never have it brought to his attention that there was any other confession but the Catholic one.

On Sunday some of us wanted to find a service where we could worship with our Spanish brethren, so we went to the hotel clerk and asked if he could tell us where a Protestant church was. Obviously embarrassed, he hemmed and hawed and finally said we could go to the British embassy and worship with the Church of England people.

We told him we would much prefer attending a service with Spanish believers, so he finally directed us to a building which looked like an office building. We had followed his instructions, but we were not sure if we were in the right place until we saw a number of people going in a gate. We followed them and as we poked our heads in the door and found the seated congregation, I will never forget the looks of alarm and fear. When we took our seats and bowed in prayer, we felt the tension relax. After the service they greeted us with happy smiles and warm handshakes and were delighted that we had come. They admitted they were always on the alert. Only the week before, vandals had broken in and destroyed Bibles and hymnbooks. They had no recourse with the authorities.

A special treat was introduced to me by Roger when we went to dinner one evening. Never before and never since have I partaken of a dish of suckling pig! And here they came, pig on platter, intact from snout to tail. I was to eat the whole thing, skin and all. Baked to a delicious crispness, it proved to be one of the most enjoyable and extraordinary meals I ever had.

The congress concluded and I returned to Lisbon to catch my plane back to Congo. I had the genuine pleasure of fellowshipping with the Presbyterian missionaries on assignment in that city. I also observed the fine job they were doing among the Protestant Christians in Portugal. Mike Testa was their able leader under appointment by the Northern Presbyterian Church in the USA, and the Herbert Mezas had only recently arrived from our Southern Presbyterian Church. These men bundled me in a car and we lit out for northern Portugal where they were to participate in a Portuguese pastor's ordination. We spent the night in a very plush hotel which was almost empty as the tourist season was over. I continued to be amazed at the low rates in these countries.

The following day we visited the famous Catholic shrine at Fatima, managing to do so on a very special day. It was October 13, anniversary of the day the Virgin Mary appeared before the three small children on that spot in 1917 when she instructed them to tell the church to pray for the conversion of Russia, for the unity of the church, and for world peace. Two of the children died but the third was, at that time, a revered nun. Fatima had been declared by the Catholic Church to be a true miracle, and with much pomp and show, an imposing basilica was built including a hospital and a seminary. It became the biggest tourist attraction in Portugal, even rivaling Lourdes in France.

It was drizzling rain the day of our visit, but we joined some ten thousand people who stood bareheaded at the outdoor mass. Many had made pilgrimages barefooted, coming from long distances, even crawling in

Bill Rule, third from right, and Dr. Kellersberger, far right, attending the Leprosy Congress in Madrid, Spain, 1953.

the dirt and slush on their hands and knees as a sign of humility and contrition. For a few cents people could have various objects consecrated by placing them on the exact spot where the Virgin had stood. They brought prayer books, crucifixes, rosaries, and all kinds of personal objects, hoping a little virtue might ooze into them. The most distressing sight of the whole performance was the large crowd of sick and afflicted waiting inside the cathedral, hoping to be cured by a miracle. Many were disabled children. Some seemed expectant, some were crying, some down-hearted and discouraged, some unmoved by it all. I was gratified that such large numbers were looking to God for help, but the carnival atmosphere with the obvious hope of making extra money was distressing to me. Saint Paul's words to the Roman church came to mind, "And they, being ignorant of God's righteousness, and going about to establish their own righteousness, have not submitted themselves to the righteousness of God" (Romans 10:3).

We also visited Leiria where the most beautiful cathedral in the country has been dedicated as a national shrine. It is there that Portugal's unknown soldier is buried. The next day back in Lisbon I visited the Sabena office to verify my reservation for the following day. They asked to see my passport and, finding no visa for reentry into

Congo, they said I would have to get one before they could clear me for travel. I explained that before leaving I had made a special trip to get the permit and had been told it wasn't necessary. The Sabena official was polite but told me this did not permit them to ignore regulations and I would have to take the matter to the Belgian legation. This I did, emphasizing that I had been attending an international congress on leprosy, and that my wife and four children were in Congo. The officer heard my story and I think he believed me, but he said only the minister could give me permission!

I hastened to the American Consulate where I found a vice-consul who had lived in Maryville, Tennessee, and knew my family! He called the Belgian office to intercede for me and gave me a nice letter of identification. But after I waited an hour or so, the minister turned me down. My only recourse now was to send a cablegram to the colonial government in Leopoldville asking them to send permission for my return. I also sent another message to Mr. Ohrneman, secretary of the Congo Protestant Council, so he could go to bat for me. In the mean time, all I could do was wait.

It was another twenty-four hours before my permission came through from Leopoldville, but Sabena could not give me another reservation for three weeks! At least they were good enough to mark it so I could travel either Sabena or Pan American. The Pan Am people couldn't do much better. I couldn't get a seat with them for ten days. However, hope springs eternal in the human breast, and I was determined to meet every plane headed for the Congo. After all, I was only one person with one hand bag. The next plane was four days later and I was johnnie-on-the-spot, ready to go. The agent looked at my corrected ticket and nodded for me to have a seat. Boarding time arrived and the passengers trooped by. Finally the last ones passed through the gates.

I was full of disappointment and started to leave, when the agent gave me a sharp whistle and exclaimed, "Quick! Get out there! There's a place for you!"

LIFE AT THE CAMP

One of the "fun times" at Bibanga was when we took a particular movie to the leprosy camp one evening. Several years earlier a professional photographer had come to make movies of mission activities. He made a two-reel film of work at the Bibanga leprosy colony and called it "Song After Sorrow." Since it was made at Bibanga, the American Leprosy Missions graciously presented us with a copy.

At its African premier, we loaded the projector and started up a motor generator for electricity. We also took a loudspeaker and microphone to give explanations of pictures. We might as well have left the public address system at home because from the moment that first familiar scene flashed on the screen before that select audience there arose a shout and hubbub which did not abate until the last picture faded away. The Saturday morning Wild West shows I so faithfully attended as a boy couldn't hold a candle to this for excitement. Intermittently close-ups were shown of some individual still in the camp. He might be weaving a mat or thatching a roof or receiving his regular injection or simply smiling into the camera. At these moments the excitement was deafening! Dr. and Mrs. Kellersberger also appeared on the screen and when they saw the founders of their leprosy colony, away from the work nearly ten years, their cry of greeting "Muoyo!" filled the air as though the Kellersbergers had suddenly appeared in person.

As with the Africans, so it is with us. Occurrences in our own lives are the really important events. These are the things which are important to God as well. We might consider that His camera is constantly trained on us, faithfully recording each moment. Thinking of this we will be more faithful in living each day so that when the picture is finally released it will be a praiseworthy recording.

For me, the most humbling experience was passing the elements in celebrating holy communion. Serving as an elder in the church I have participated in this worship service many times, but never has it been as moving as when I served the elements in the leprosy camp church. I have always been forcibly struck by the difficulty these deformed and twisted people have in partaking, and as I have moved among the waiting worshippers it has occurred to me that the physical difficulty they experience in accepting and partaking of the elements are a symbol of the spiritual hindrances which must be overcome to effectively "come to the Lord's table." Time and time again it has been necessary for me to take a morsel of bread off the plate and place it in a palm with no fingers. Or to place the cup between two stumps of fists to be raised shaking and spilling to lips that named the name of Him whose blood was shed. We do not often think of difficulties out of which we attend the Lord's table. Our temptation is to accept it all too matter-of-factly. But here was a picture of physical handicap symbolizing spiritual disease. If mutilated hands make partaking of the Lord's body and blood difficult, how much more do the mutilated lives of men and women separate them from Him? It is only through His grace that we are enabled to come near enough to experience the reality of the sacrament. Mutilated lives keep us all from fellowship with the Lord, but even as He spoke a word to cure the leprosy victims of old, so He speaks to us today to make us whole and clean in His precious blood.

TENDON TRANSPLANTS

I was impressed in reading about the reconstruction being done on the leprous hand. The pioneer in this field was Dr. Paul Brand, a British missionary who had done his original work in India. He was the first to transplant tendons in the twisted and disabled hand. Among the leprosy patients at Lubondai there were numerous crippled hands, so during my next furlough I went to Tulane and took a postgraduate seminar on the transposition of tendons and the effective suturing of them to restore movement and function to paralyzed fingers. I even accompanied our teacher to the leprosy colony at Carville, Louisiana, and assisted him with surgical restoration of a number of cases.

Back at Lubondai we carefully picked several patients we felt we might effectively help with this kind of intervention. After surgery, there were certain finger exercises we encouraged them to practice many times a day. The basic one was to bring the tip of each finger into apposition with the thumb. Some times this was difficult, some times painful, occasionally impossible, but we encouraged them to keep at it every day. It got to the place that when patients saw me coming, even those who had no hand problems, would raise their hands and begin doing the exercise!

The providential spin-off of this specialized treatment came a couple of years later when one of our missionary colleagues suffered a so-called accident for which we had to do extensive tendon repair. Kemp Hobson was viciously attacked by three villagers who had knives and spears. He was seriously wounded and had lost considerable blood by the time they got him to us at Lubondai some six hours after the attack. But let me go back to the beginning.

Out in a village one of our African evangelists had been accosted by a follower of the pseudo-religious movement called *Bampostolo* (The Apostles) which was a heathen mixture of animism and tribal lore wearing some of the trappings of Christianity. The movement had come up from the southern Congo and probably originally from the Rhodesias. The *mupostolo* was jealous because more villagers worshipped with the evangelist than with him, and he threatened to burn down the evangelist's house and the little chapel. The evangelist called Mr. Hobson who went to the village to try to reason with the interloper but sensing hostility, he left and reported him to the state official who returned with him along with two unarmed policemen. The *mupostolo* saw them coming and with another man and a woman went into a hut to get a spear, knives, a bow and arrow, and even some hammers. As they approached the *mupostolo*, without warning he launched the spear at Mr. Hobson.

Just then a white worker for the cotton company and his wife drove up which was a miraculous intervention because if they had not come it is possible that both of the other white men could have been killed. The state official had a pistol but could not get it into action as the attack continued on Hobson. The two policemen and all the villagers ran for the high grass. The cotton company employee took out his .22 rifle and passed it to the state official who fired, killing one of the assailants, but while he was shooting, the *mupostolo* slashed him and he dropped the gun. The official ran to his car but could not get it to start. Meanwhile the *mupostolo* picked up the gun and fired at him, then ran to attack him with a knife. The official escaped and ran for the cotton company car into which Mr. Hobson had already been helped. He managed to get in and they drove away. The *mupostolo* burned down the house and chapel as he had threatened.

When Hobson reached John Miller and myself he was in mild shock with the loss of blood, so we first transfused him. His left hand was more than half severed at the wrist, and his right elbow was laid wide open. We worked for three hours repairing the damage. Eleven tendons in his wrist had been cut and had to be sutured during the repair, and here my training in the approximation of tendon sections became especially valuable. More serious than the tendons was the separation of the ulnar nerve. There were four bones fractured at the wound sites. Both arms were in plaster casts for a month, but he gradually regained good use of both members and we were all grateful to God for what we considered an exceptionally good result.

MOVING THE LEPROSY CAMP

An important leprosy conference was held at Lubondai in late August 1954. It was conducted by Dr. Robert Cocheran, world renowned British leprologist who was technical medical advisor for American Leprosy Missions. Dr. Cocheran's credentials were impressive. He was advisor in leprosy to the Ministry of Health of the United Kingdom, and was associate editor of the *International Journal of Leprosy*. He had taken a leading part in the Leprosy Congress at Madrid the year before. But beyond his professional skills he was a great Christian.

His one big peeve was that both government and missions were institutionalizing far too many leprosy patients. Many of the tuberculoid cases he declared to be closed cases. They were showing little or no change from year to year. Bacilli could not be demonstrated. They were not infectious. They should be discharged and sent back to their villages, with possibly some continuation of treatment. This would not be detrimental to public health and would be without danger of spreading infection. On the other hand he would detain the lepromatous cases, which were a small minority. He felt that the disease in this area was of low endemicity and did not appear to be a public health problem. Institutionalization was costing both the government and the missions too much in loss of time and money.

In the light of Dr. Cocheran's stand, we decided to take a hard look at our leprosy situation. We had a camp of several hundred patients who seemed to be functioning smoothly and efficiently. True, a number of our patients could be discharged. But the government camp at Tshimuanza was only twenty miles away. The government had invested large sums of money to make it a real showcase. A handsome and completely equipped hospital had been constructed, solely for the treatment of leprosy. A resident leprologist was there to take care of needs. Was it practical, wise, or reasonable to continue to compete with them, twenty miles up the road?

The next logical step was to send our patients to the government camp. The drawback was that the Tshimuanza complex was tied to the Catholic mission of nearby Hemptinne. All administrative work and much of the nursing was in the hands of Catholic nuns. We were willing to send our patients to Tshimuanza but how would they be received? Many of them were baptized protestants. Would they be permitted their own worship? Would we be allowed to establish a church there? Could we have a resident evangelist?

We put these questions to the doctor and received most open and cordial response. He reminded us that religious freedom was the law of the land and that this hospital was a government institution and not a church camp. So we told him that if we were allowed to build a church and a home for a resident evangelist within the compound in the non-infective area, at our own expense, we would move our patients to Tshimuanza. The doctor went to the proper authorities and contacted us to say that all was in order.

We constructed an attractive chapel and built a house for our evangelist. Then I began to make a careful physical examination of each of the patients and compile a complete history. Some were not so happy about moving to a new location after calling Lubondai home for many years. But we gently encouraged them and over a period of weeks we sent them, truckload by truckload, to Tshimuanza. I made three copies of the records: one for the Tshimuanza authorities, one for the evangelist, and one for myself. Finally the transfer was complete. Our old camp was empty and deserted.

Things went very smoothly at first. Our African pastor was well received and our chapel filled with an enthusiastic group of worshippers each Sunday. Some of us from Lubondai went out each week to visit with our friends. Then the whole ball of wax began to come apart.

First, the government moved the doctor-leprologist to another location, leaving the spanking new hospital without adequate management. All administrative and policy decisions were left in the hands of two senior sisters with some very strong concepts of Catholic autocracy. Protestant patients began to be discriminated against with the implication that it would take a Catholic confession to solve the problem. Distribution of blankets, food, clothing, and other perks were given to Catholics only. Some weakened and embraced the Catholic faith.

Next, special pressure was put on the invalid patients. Water for their daily needs was hauled up from the valley. Able folk performed the work with burdens on back or head, but the sisters considerately sent paid workers to carry water for invalids. However, the Protestants incapacitated were informed they would receive no water unless they revised their confession. They apologized to me for what they were forced to do and told me they simply had no other choice. We went to the sisters with our charges of gross discrimination and failure to stand by promises made. They were evasive and denied the charges. However on successive Sundays they stood in the roadway, ordering patients to alter their steps from the protestant chapel to the Catholic Church. When I was advised of this I went to Tshimuanza over and over on Sundays and stood in the pathway before the ladies to countermand their instruction. Our confrontation became increasingly sharp as time went on.

Finally three scenarios took place which profoundly altered and rectified the situation. One was the arrival of Congo's independence. Under the constitution established by the Africans complete liberty of religion was observed. The Catholic Church was no longer the "church of the state" as it had been under the Belgians. There was no more built-in position of priority and superiority. In fact there was a growing feeling of comfort to stand shoulder to shoulder with the Protestant Church to face the unknown future under a new government. Secondly, John XXIII became the pope of Rome in 1962 calling a Vatican Council to examine many issues including the whole question of ecumenism. In the Catholic Church a new breeze was blowing. Closed doors were opening and intolerant mindsets were softening. But the nuns at Tshimuanza finally overstepped once too often.

One of our strong Protestant believers, in declining health and also badly crippled was badgered unmercifully to make a Catholic profession. He was forced to concede because he was totally dependent on them, but he sent his small offering for our collection plate each Sunday with words of assurance that while his lips had changed their profession his heart had not. His wife, free of leprosy, was a faithful member of our church, and the Sisters saw an opportunity to get at her through her ill husband. They told her if she didn't become a Catholic they would discharge her and her husband from the camp. She refused, and one day a cart drew up before their hut on which all their belongings were piled plus the patient, and they were wheeled away to the first large village they came to. The cart was returned to the leprosy camp. With no way to continue their homeward journey and no means of sustaining themselves, the neglected patient died.

A cry rose from all directions. The Protestant community and all the patients at Tshimuanza denounced the series of events and the Catholic sisters. Word spread through surrounding villages where chieftains and other dignitaries joined in, and the affair finally reached the African government. There was a reprimand of the Catholic Church with the conclusion that a mother superior visited Tshikaji to review the whole matter. She had brought the two sisters before the assembled Tshimuanza populace, declaring that they acted in a non-Christian manner and against the best interest of the church. The sisters were removed and new personnel was brought in to continue ministry to leprosy victims.

These are a few pictures of the evolving management of leprosy in Central Africa. Today we believe that leprosy is a dying scourge, not just in Africa but all over the world. It will probably be gone long before its first cousin, tuberculosis.

Treating leprosy patients has been a rewarding experience. Leprous patients continue to respond to the sulfones, and they continue to respond to the gospel of the Lord Jesus Christ.

MILESTONE FIVE
MARSHALLING THE
RESOURCES

"Casting down imaginations, and every high thing that exalteth itself against the knowledge of God, and bringing into captivity every thought to the obedience of Christ" (2 Corinthians 10:5).

11 RUMBLINGS OF INDEPENDENCE

Stand fast therefore in the liberty wherewith Christ hath made us free, and be not entangled again with the yoke of bondage (Galations 5:1).

The Belgian government's practice of paternalism toward the people of the Congo is well documented. Based on their estimation that the Congolese were naive, essentially passive, unmotivated, and without political ambition, the Belgians completely overlooked a people's innate hope for civil self-determination. Inevitably there would come a day when the Congolese people would want to assume control of their own country.

Maintenance of this paternalism had not been easy. It required cooperative efforts of government, state church, and big business. Brussels appointed a resident governor general. The Roman Catholic Church was awarded large land holdings and for a period of time had a monopoly on government subsidies for education. The business community had a tremendous concentration of economic power. It was estimated in 1952 that five holding companies controlled about 70 percent of all Congo business, and the state held strong interest in all five. Through these three agents the Congolese were supplied with food, clothing, housing, education, and medical care. But what the bureaucracy failed to understand was that imposing care is no substitute for nurturing human relations into useful and practical function.

Several events in 1958 were of significant importance. At the International Exposition in Brussels, Congolese manned several of their pavilions. Fellow countrymen from far and wide met one another for the first time and were able to share social and political hopes. The second event was the visit of General Charles de Gaulle to Brazzaville. Brazzaville is the capital of French Equatorial Africa, directly across the Congo River from Leopoldville, the capital of the Belgian Congo. In addressing the Africans, de Gaulle assured them that those who wished

127

for independence could have it as soon as they wanted. This rare offer was noted on both sides of the river. Two days later a motion to the minister of the Belgian Congo was presented by a number of the African leaders who eventually held positions of high responsibility in the liberated government. These men were Patrice Lumumba, Joseph Ileo, and Cyril Adoula. The motion made specific demands for a dated program of "decolonization and total emancipation."

The third event in December of 1958 was a Pan-African Conference that was held in Accra, Ghana. Several Congolese leaders were invited to attend, and the Belgian government concurred. The Congolese were all treated as governmental dignitaries, and Lumumba was elected a member of the permanent organization. He made a short but impassioned speech, displaying his habitual disdain for moderation, and castigated Belgium severely for "injustices and abuses." On his return to Leopoldville, he delivered himself of another fiery public oration which undoubtedly helped set the stage for the riots which occurred on January 4 and 5. The police, and then armed troops, were called out which resulted in some fifty deaths and nearly four hundred other casualties. The dead have naturally gone down in history as martyrs to the cause of independence, and January 4 has become a Zairian national holiday.

This train of events called forth, on February 13, 1959, a declaration from the Belgian government which, for the first time, spoke of Congolese independence. Belgium introduced this concept by saying, "Belgium intends to organize in the Congo a democracy capable of exercising its prerogatives of sovereignty and of deciding on its independence." The Congolese scrambled to form political parties and power bases which often arose from tribal loyalties. The year 1959 was punctuated with numerous confabs and councils, and by outright tribal warfare throughout its course.

Our Presbyterian mission effort found itself embroiled in the midst of this confusion and tension as the two largest tribes we traditionally worked with, the Baluba and the Bena Lulua, began to go at it with hammer and tongs. As the day of independence drew closer and closer, the anticipations and perplexities of that strange event made the people restless and agitated. This translated into tribal cleavages which were nowhere more pronounced than in our own mission area where the two dominant tribal groups, the Baluba and the Bena Lulua, set themselves against one another in a decisive confrontation.

Historically this was the country of the Bena Lulua. More numerous than the Baluba, they were a physically aggressive, warlike group, but paradoxically they were also languid. The Baluba were more serious of purpose, looking toward the future, wanting to get ahead, taking more interest in education. They were larger and perhaps stronger than the

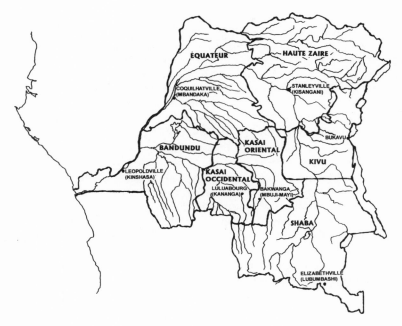

The Congo, 1960.

Bena Lulua, but were more deliberate and contemplative.

The center of Baluba population was to the southeast of the Bena Lulua, east of the Lubi River. Because of their physical and mental capacities and their passive nature, the Baluba had been the prime target for the Arab slave traders during the eighteenth century. Many fled westward to escape and this led them into the heartland of their Bena Lulua neighbors. At that time the Luluas accepted them, even defended them, and gradually Baluba villages began to dot the Lulua region until by my day one could journey down any particular road and encounter alternating tribal villages for mile after mile.

The carefree Luluas who were content to pursue such tribal interests as hunting and fishing and raising crops, suddenly began to wake up to the fact that the new government would belong to the ambitious, better-educated Baluba. During the tense days of 1959, Africans and missionaries coped with change.

"Independence" became the magic word heard on all lips, but no one really understood. One day during a lull of medical chores I asked my head medical helper, Lukusa Andre, what the coming independence meant to him.

He pondered for a while, then groped to explain. "*Ngangabuka* (Doctor), you ask me what independence means to me. Let me answer by saying what I hope and expect it to mean personally. When you go over to the territorial office at Dibaya to transact business with the administrator you walk up the steps to his office door. He sees you coming and he steps out to shake your hand, call you by your name, and invite you inside. He offers you a chair and invites you to sit down and, folding his hands and leaning across his desk, he asks you with a smile what he can do for you. When I go over to Dibaya to see the administrator nobody comes to the door to see me. I sit down on the steps and wait until it is quite convenient to give me an audience. That may be a matter of hours or a matter of days. When I finally go into his office I am not offered a chair. I stand before his desk, hat in hand, and state my case. A note is made. It may be handled today or I may be told to come back tomorrow. What does independence mean to me, *Ngangabuka*? It means that I'll be treated like you are when I go to Dibaya."

The year 1959 was perhaps the most demanding year of my missionary life. Besides my regular medical work in a busy hospital and classes at the nursing school, I had the added responsibility of the medical secretaryship of the Congo Protestant Council, plus the title III surplus powdered milk program (more than eighty tons every three months to distribute to 108 mission stations).

A FAMILY VACATION

The Rule family spent a joyous Christmas at Lubondai but set forth bright and early the next morning for a previously planned vacation visit to Bulape and Luebo. We arrived in Luluabourg just before King Baudouin who, in process of a surprise visit to Congo, was scheduled to lead a grand parade down the main streets. We, of course, interrupted our journey long enough to see the king. We saw him in Brussels in 1951 at the time of his coronation. Now people lined the route he was to take and I observed that they were well spread out along the way. Apparently the authorities did not want a concentration of large crowds at any one point. Soldiers and police cars patrolled and an army helicopter flew just above the treetops surveying the streets. Eventually the king and the governor arrived in an automobile which moved along at a rather rapid pace. There was polite applause, and I heard shouts of "Independence!" as they passed. The atmosphere was good-natured and passive.

We enjoyed our visit at Bulape with missionary friends, but we noted that they were working under some tension. This was because of the revival of the practice of the poison cup among the Bakuba which had been effectively outlawed by the colonial government for a number of years, and now was coming back into practice. The poison cup is administered by a few older men of the tribe, instructed in the art, who know the proportions of the various herbs used. The purpose of the cup is presumed to discover and destroy witches. The old man visits a particular village and singles out several people he claims are witches. The only way they can prove their innocence is to take the poison cup and survive. Only witches will die. Nobody thinks of refusing since that would brand them a witch in the eyes of the whole community, and they would be ostracized and driven away.

Furthermore, the family of each victim singled out must pay a fee for the privilege of their relative's taking the cup to vindicate him or her of the charge. Usually old people, especially widows, are chosen. You might call it a sort of primitive euthanasia program, or population control in reverse. Obviously the dosage of the noxious substances is varied since some survive. This is essential for a continuing practice because if there were a 100 percent mortality the enthusiasm to participate would surely diminish. Another possibility of avoiding death is through nausea and vomiting.

As we arrived at Bulape villagers came to say they were giving the cup in a nearby community, and Dr. Mark Poole left immediately to see if he could stop the activity and help any victims. Bill Mulcay drove the thirty miles to the state post at Mweka to report the incident. Mark arrived to find that they had already given the cup to ten people. Five were dead and a sixth died after his arrival. He brought back one old woman who died the next day. Three managed to survive. The dispenser of the potion was apprehended and naively explained to the state official that it had been a long time since the cup had been given and the old men who knew the art were dying out, so they decided to take some younger men out with them and teach them to administer the cup. The chief dispenser was caught and arrested, hopefully to quell the outbreak, but it was not before several hundred people had died. Here we see the demonstration of the breakdown of foreign control and the reversion to ancient heathen customs and practices.

We returned to Luluabourg, without mishap, on New Year's Day where we stayed with the Vass family at Ndesha Station. I had promised the children we would celebrate the new year by going to a movie, and they were excited. I suppose I should have known better than to take them into town since we had heard that hoodlums were at large and there was trouble in the city. But after supper I started out with our four eldest and Lillibet Vass.

Going into town not a creature was stirring. The curfew in Luluabourg during those days seemed to be enforced. There was quite a crowd at the movie, and all was gala and seemed calm, and afterward we piled into the car and headed for home. The mission station is about five miles from downtown Luluabourg, and on the way we must pass through the native quarter. We descended the long lonely hill just beyond Katoke and climbed the one on the other side and I bore to the right to go to Ndesha when I saw a group of half dozen young boys carrying brickbats. One fellow ran up to the side of the car and peered in. I gave him my sweetest smile and greeting.

"Stop!" he shouted. But I didn't, and for three reasons. First, I was a little uneasy with the children in the car. Second, it was New Year's and I didn't know how many might be drunk and hard to deal with. Third, I presumed this was the only bunch I would pass and I could get on beyond them rather quickly. So I shoved on the gas and as I did so, they let loose with their rocks which thumped against the car but without much damage.

I thought we had gotten off lightly but a hundred yards on down the road I saw a second group, larger than the first. The die was cast, so I made at them as hard as I could to throw them off balance and force them off the road. They threw their rocks, and from there on for over a mile it was run the gauntlet past group after group. The objects they threw kept getting bigger and bigger and some had to heave with both hands. They had large tree trunk mortars and pestles as big as your leg, used for beating their manioc flour. As we rushed on I heard the tinkling of window glass and I shouted to the children behind me to get down on the floor. A couple of barricades had been placed in the road, and as I slowed to get around them I took some of my heaviest blows. The last one came just before I slowed to turn into the road to the mission station when a man stepped forward with one of those wicked sticks they fashion with a hard wooden knot at one end and he crashed it completely through the front windshield. We were traveling so fast that it was wrenched from his hand and lodged in the windshield glass.

When we reached the mission station we toted up the damage. Three windows had been smashed out plus the front windshield, and there were numerous dents and slashes all over the chassis where machetes and rocks and boulders had been heaved. A front door was severely battered and swung with difficulty. But we were all deeply grateful that nobody was hurt. The shatterproof glass had saved the day, otherwise it might have been a different story.

I had been particularly anxious for Paul in the front seat with Libby. He was on the outside, against the door where the worst blows fell. Later, in recounting the adventure, I expressed my anxiety and Paul promptly reassured me: "Oh, Daddy, you needn't have worried about me. My head was down under the dashboard all the way!" Libby was praying aloud and fervently the last half of the gamut, and I'm sure her prayers helped pull us safely through.

I called the police and they came an hour later. Their hands had been full in various quarters. Two Congolese were killed during city rioting and some twenty in the whole area over the weekend. A young lady teacher in the Catholic school traveled the same route we did and received the same treatment. The police looked over the damage and told me to report to headquarters the following day where a written description of our experience was recorded. I was assured that the government would pay all repair costs. The incident was reported on both Leopoldville radio and BBC from London, without mention of names.

In January/February of 1960 a meeting was held in Brussels with both Belgians and Congolese making decisions about details and dates for a political turnover. Fifty-five Belgians and ninety-six Congolese were official delegates, plus eighteen other European advisors. The first Congolese government would be composed of members chosen in provincial elections. There would be two houses: a chamber of deputies and a senate. The new constitution, to be confirmed on June 30, 1960, would include freedom of speech and religion, individual liberty and corporal integrity, right of public meeting, and right to own property. Momentum grew inexorably and swiftly toward the day of independence.

AN EMERGENCY RETURN TO THE U.S.

On March 17, 1960, I had to return to the United States for emergency gall bladder surgery. The older children, Billy, Charlotte, and Libby, then ages seventeen, fifteen, and thirteen respectively, stayed at Central School under the care of Walter Shepard. Upon arrival stateside I proceeded directly to Philadelphia for medical consultation, and Effie accompanied the children to Nitro, West Virginia, where her sister, Kitty Ross, lived. Kitty heroically took in our three, along with her own six, while Effie joined me in Philadelphia!

During my recuperation period, we rented a house in Knoxville where Effie's and my parents lived. Bill Crane had been called to Second Presbyterian Church, Knoxville, to serve as minister of counseling. Walter Shepard was becoming increasingly tense with the responsibility of the Rule children left to his care. As soon as school was out in June he very wisely decided to ship them to their parents. It was good to have all our enlarged family located in the same community and to be together during this time.

Finally Congo independence was just around the corner, slated for the last day of June, and political parties were becoming increasingly rambunctious in search of effective power bases with which to inaugurate the era of emancipation. Prominent among these groups and quick to take extremist positions was the Mouvement National Congolais under the leadership of Patrice Lumumba. A spin-off from his group was one headed by Albert Kalonji, headquartered in Luluabourg and which festered the conflict between title holders of the land, the Lulua tribe, and Kalonji's Johnnie-come-lately Baluba tribesmen. Speculation was rife as to what was really going to happen when the Belgians turned the reins of government over to the Africans.

We anxiously followed the unfolding news of troubled events in Congo through both newspapers and television. Accounts trickling homeward of the evacuation experiences of our fellow missionaries were not encouraging.

INDEPENDENCE

True to the script drawn up by its Belgian overlords, the Congo moved steadily toward independence on June 30. Six weeks earlier, on May 19, the Belgian government had promulgated a *Loi Fondamentale* to serve as a temporary governing instrument until the Congolese should fashion their own constitution. The temporary government was fashioned after that of Belgium, providing for a prime minister and a chief of state and leaving a door open for the Belgian hope that the Congo might accept the Belgian king as its chief of state. Thus, on June 30 King Baudouin and all of his royal retinue arrived in Leopoldville to surrender and transfer the reins of government into the hands of the Congolese. With much pomp and ceremony he made his speech of transfer, and Joseph Kasavubu, preferred by the Congolese as their indigenous chief of state, declared his acceptance with the same pomp and dignity. The only sour note was sounded by the new prime minister, Patrice Lumumba, who, with his gift for radicalism and ribald rhetoric, sneered at the king as he said, "Now you can no longer call us *makaka!*" *Makaka* is a word meaning "monkey," and was often used as an expression of disdain by Belgians speaking to Africans. The Congolese hated the epithet.

The first four days of independence were declared a national holiday. There were minor tribal altercations. The Bayaka and Bangala were skirmishing with the Bakongo in the Lower Congo region, and there was intermittent conflict between the Baluba and the Bena Lulua in the Kasai. Eighty people had been wounded in Leopoldville and a curfew was imposed. Two hundred houses were burned in Luluabourg and again a curfew was established. But by and large, independence was accepted by the masses with equanimity and a wait-and-see attitude.

On July 11, Moise Tshiombe declared the secession of the Katanga from the Republic of Congo. United Nations troops began to arrive four days later to restore order. The impetuous Lumumba government issued an ultimatum to the United Nations directing them to remove all Belgian troops from the Congo within seventy-two hours, and if the deadline was not met the government would call upon "Soviet Russian troops" to deal with the problem. This order was rejected by Ralph Bunche with the statement that the UN was "not in the habit of accepting ultimatums." The first Belgian troops did leave Leopoldville on this day.

In wake of the wholesale evacuation of Europeans there were by late July only four doctors in all of the great capital city of Leopoldville. Three of these were missionaries, and one of them was Dr. Tinsley Smith of the Presbyterian mission, serving in the big general hospital. Tinsley and his wife, Catherine, were on a plane flying from Johannesburg to the U.S. which stopped in Leopoldville. Missionary friends urged Dr. Smith to deplane and stay and help with the desperate medical needs of the great city. After committing the matter to prayer, the Smiths decided to stay. They eventually returned to the Kasai rather than traveling to the U.S.

In early August, the Katanga rejected the entry of United Nation troops into their territory which left the UN in a quandary. They had been charged to stabilize circumstances in *all* of Congo. To stay out amounted to a tacit recognition of Katanga's autonomy, but to go in meant war. On August 20, Ralph Bunche resigned as Dag Hammarskjold's personal (UN) representative in the Congo. He was replaced by Rajeshwar Dayal of India.

Reports began to leak out of the interior about the formation of Albert Kalonji's *Etat Miniere* (Mining State), later to be called the Autonomous State of South Kasai. This cut the established Kasai Province in two, divided the Baluba and the Bena Lulua, and also divided the Presbyterian mission area and the church.

The intellectual leader who organized and formed the South Kasai government was Pascual Ngalula, but the charismatic figure who captured the imagination and the loyalty of the masses was Albert Kalonji. He had been their original political spokesman and was closely aligned with Lumumba. But they fell into disagreement and Kalonji retreated from the national political field to concentrate on the leadership of his own Baluba clan. When the Baluba were forced to strike their tents at multiple points in the Congo and to retreat to the land of their ancestral heritage, a land that many of them had never seen, Kalonji became the Moses leading them through the wilderness to their promised land. Now he assumed the title of *Mulopwe*, which not only named him prince or ruler of the Baluba but also carried overtones of his being the god-man to whom they owed worshipful obedience.

At this time it became known that the Russians were supplying Lumumba with the war materials which had made it possible for him to invade the South Kasai. One hundred Russian trucks and ten Ilyushin-14 planes had been sent to the Congo. Heavy fighting continued in the South Kasai where Congolese forces around Bakwanga were still pinned by the activity of Baluba rebels. The center of the conflict seemed to be near Tshilenge, Luputa, Gandanjika, and Mwena Ditu which were all in government hands.

Australian medical personnel working in the Kasai area had organized a Red Cross field unit and were seeking to render medical aid to the many wounded, plus bury the dead. Our Presbyterian missionary, David McLean, offered them his services as guide and interpreter. At one point they found themselves in a very heavy crossfire and an American correspondent was shot and killed. Dave was the first person to him but was too late to be of service. During the heat of battle the two sides were mixed and confused, and the Red Cross unit lost its identity and its immunity. Dave was captured by a group of soldiers who, without any time-consuming formalities, proceeded to smash and beat him to within an inch of his life. Some nine months later when I was with Dave at Lubondai he was still waiting for further healing of his face and mouth before heading home to his wife and family back in the States. He hoped most of his terrible deformities would heal before they saw him.

On September 5, Chief of State Kasavubu, resorting to Article 22 of the *Loi Fondomentale* which permitted him to dismiss the prime minister and his cabinet, ousted Premier Lumumba and named Joseph Ileo as provisional premier to form a new government. Lumumba, not to be outdone, declared that Kasavubu was no longer chief of state and that he alone was in control of the country.

More Russian planes and trucks began to arrive in Stanleyville from whence the planes ferried Lumumbist troops to bolster the government forces in South Kasai. Judging that Lumumba would now turn more wholeheartedly to his Russian helpers, the UN command closed all of the Congo's airports to outside traffic.

The U.S. Embassy in Leopoldville declared, "The Failure of the UN to dislodge Tshiombe and the Belgians as quickly as Lumumba desired led the Congo Premier to call on the Soviet Bloc for assistance, thus to provide the entering wedge for Soviet penetration."

On September 14, General Mobutu declared a military coup to "neutralize" the impasse between Lumumba and Kasavubu, and to assume authority in a "simple and peaceful revolution." At the same time he ordered the Soviet and Czechoslovak and other communist diplomats and technicians to leave the country within forty-eight hours.

These acts were profoundly significant in projecting the Congolese image to outside governments and pressures, but it was also an important indication as to how the political winds were blowing internally. Mobutu had been only second in command in the army, but he had been able to win wide support among the Military Police and also a newly created commando battalion based at Thysville. He was also well known in the capital city and was Kasavubu's friend. Two days earlier President Kasavubu had demoted General Lundula without reaction, and command had effectively passed to Mobutu.

Lumumba was placed under house arrest and some thirty of his aides were also arrested. Guards were stationed around the parliament building and all deputies and senators were denied access. Thus Mobutu consolidated his gains and denied all recourse to others for transacting government diplomacy.

A RELIEF AGENCY FORMED

The dire need for medical help, which in large measure had departed from the country, was clearly evident. The burden grew upon my heart that I was now available and should be helping in some capacity in that needy land.

Effie and I talked over the matter and earnestly prayed together about it. We were settled in a comfortable home we had leased for a year. The children would soon be in school again. Both Effie and my parents were nearby, and my brother Gunby lived only blocks away.

In late July I wrote to the Board of World Missions to inform them that I was now physically able to return to Congo to help fill the medical need. If the Kasai area and our own hospitals were in questionable safety, I offered to work with Church World Service, the International Missionary Council, the United Nations, or any other appropriate body.

In August word began to come through about a new effort to meet the emergency medical need in Congo. Doctors from the *Institut Medical Evangelique* in the Lower Congo, evacuated and on their way home, began to have second thoughts by the time they reached Accra, the capital of Ghana. They returned to Leopoldville and began to make plans for a Congo Christian medical relief program. A committee of three doctors began to call upon churches and Christian organizations for help. These doctors were David Wilson, Glen Tuttle, and Warren Berggren. They named Robert Bontrager as president and Allan Stuart, treasurer. Reverend Roland Metzger was dispatched stateside to establish a liaison office in New York. Church World Service offered drugs and food, and the Christian Medical Society promised medical supplies. There was already a quantity of rice and powdered milk on hand.

One objective was to contact all missionary doctors in the interior to offer them assistance which was no easy task as lines of communication were badly disrupted. Another objective of the committee was to encourage doctors who had proceeded homeward to return to Congo as quickly as possible. The stark need must be presented in no uncertain terms.

I received a letter from Bob Bontrager in late August in which he outlined the developments which had taken place in their organization in just three weeks. The great medical need had been crystallized into a crying demand for more doctors. Where there had been eight hundred doctors in Congo before independence, there were now some two hundred. About one quarter of these were missionary doctors who also comprised the majority of those in isolated areas. The one major effort of the organization was to appeal to Christian physicians to offer short term medical service. This was called "Operation Doctor."

The other major need was for assistance to refugees, most critical among the Baluba in the South Kasai State. Archie Graber, a Mennonite missionary, was called to go to Bakwanga to help the Baluba with their problems of food and housing. Some 200 to 250 thousand people had been driven back into the historical Baluba country where they were simply squatting on the bare ground. And there were more to come. Those who had fled in terror did so with only what they could carry on their backs or heads. Starvation was rampant as is always the case under such circumstances, and the little children suffered most and were the first to die. This project was called "Operation Refugee."

Bontrager's letter to me explained that a full-time executive officer would be necessary to administer the whole program. The two operations were to be combined under one management and called The Congo Protestant Relief Agency. He was asking me to come and assume the administrative position.

Now this invitation left me on the horns of a dilemma. Would I be returning to work, as in the past, under the direct supervision of the APCM and within the area of our Presbyterian mission, or would I serve as the executive secretary of CPRA in Leopoldville? A whole month went by before that question was answered. On September 13 the Board of World Missions met and ratified my return to Congo, but they reneged on making the decision about where I would go. They stipulated that I could return either to Lubondai or go to Leopoldville, and that the final decision would be made by consultation between me and the mission. At the same time they began to make arrangements for my return trip, instructing me to try to get a visa of entry into the Congo. This would require some doing since the Congo did not yet have a consulate nor an official presence in the United States! So I boarded a Pan Am plane in New York on October 4, headed for the Congo but not entirely sure where I would go once I arrived on African soil! I had no Congo visa and it was only by the hardest that I persuaded Pan Am to take me aboard.

Glen Tuttle, my Baptist colleague who had helped to establish the *Institut Medical Evangelique* (IME) at Kimpese, had been in New York trying to help get CPRA on a firm foundation. We were traveling together. Mrs. Timberlake, wife of the U.S. Ambassador in Leopoldville, was also on the plane, along with her three children. This was a reassuring indication. We arrived at Njili airport in the early morning hours of October 6 where surprisingly I had no trouble with entry into the country. Alec McCutchen was waiting for us and took Glen and myself home to Limite where we tumbled into bed to sleep off the jet lag.

12 Congo Protestant Relief Agency

Therefore, my beloved brethren, be ye steadfast, unmovable, always abounding in the work of the Lord, forasmuch as ye know that your labour is not in vain in the Lord (1 Corinthians 15:58).

Our Presbyterian mission owned two houses in Limite, a neighborhood only four or five miles from downtown Leopoldville. Alec and I would occupy one of the houses and we would protect and utilize the one next door as circumstances dictated. I registered at the busy and booming American Consulate and made contact with the founding fathers of CPRA: Bob Bontrager, Allan Stuart, plus my traveling companion, Glen Tuttle. That evening we went over to the Baptist Missionary Society (British) and had an interesting visit with Bishop Leslie Newbigin who had dropped in at Leopoldville to get a firsthand view of all the things he had been reading about in the newspaper. A number of others were present and we talked together about the church and some of its needs.

In the morning Alec woke me abruptly, calling attention to the fact that we had been robbed during the night! Only two days in Congo and I had already been relieved of several hundred dollars worth of traveler's checks. Let me quickly add that American Express lived up to their advertisements, even in the heart of darkest Africa, and they canceled my checks and handed over the cash without a whimper.

What a day! But it had just begun. I had no valid driver's license. My *Permis de Conduire* for Congo had been left among my other papers at Lubondai and was not available. Alec and I went to a local police station to see if I might obtain a new one. As we approached we found a dozen or so policemen banging on the front door. They were shouting and appeared to be both agitated and frustrated. Alec parked the car and we sat wondering what was going on. Suddenly the door was opened and another policeman, in immaculate uniform and shiny puttees, appeared and shot through the startled group before they knew what had happened. He ran on down the street as fast as he could run. The others hesitated for only a moment, and then they pursued as fast as they could go, waving their sticks at his back and shouting indistinguishable epithets. We watched them disappear, and the door of the empty police station swung idly upon its hinges. We questioned two or three onlookers who told us that the police had not been paid their weekly wages and they were demanding satisfaction from their superior officer!

So it appeared that I would get no license from the police station. But where to turn? I thought then of the possibility of getting an international driver's permit, so Alec and I went to the International Tourist Club where we found one Congolese attendant. I asked him if he could issue the permit I needed, and he assured me he could. He took out a booklet of the printed forms and inscribed my name, age, and other credentials, and finally he demanded, "Let me see your Congolese Permis de Conduire." I explained that it was up in the Kasai Province and I couldn't possibly get my hands on it. "Oh, that's all right," he said. "Just let me see your American driver's license." I explained, with some embarrassment, that I had left it in the United States. This stumped him for the moment, but then he shrugged his shoulders and pulled the form towards him with a final request: "Let me have a picture that I can affix to your permit." With dismay I began to see the possibility of a driver's license slipping away. I had left my small packet of passport photographs at home that morning and had to tell him I had none with me. He sat thinking, and then he slowly pulled open his desk drawer and took out a small picture of some nondescript white male. When I realized he was going to paste it on my driving permit, I interrupted him.

"Don't do that," I said. "I have my own picture at home and I will put it on the permit."

"But I must stamp our seal on the license," he explained, "and part of it must extend over the picture." Then carefully placing a small square of blank paper on the form just where the picture would be affixed, he stamped the seal with only a small fraction of the circular arc marking the paper. He removed the blank square triumphantly and said, "Attach your picture just where I placed this paper. Then you will only need to complete the circular border of the seal onto your picture!" With a jubilant smile he handed me my new driver's permit. Alec and I could only shake our heads with incredulity as we left the office.

MAKING CONTACTS

My first ten days back in the Congo were spent making contacts and visiting responsible people who needed to know what we would be attempting to do as Protestant missions. The first visit was to the Congolese government's Ministry of Health, to meet the student/minister, Mr. Marcel Tshibamba, and his staff. Dr. Bellerive, a Haitian doctor assigned by WHO (World Health Organization), was present for the entire conversation and did most of the talking. As our meeting proceeded I was surprised and somewhat disturbed to sense that the thrust of his questions and remarks was an effort to get at the political significance of our presence. I reminded him that the missionaries had been there long before politics, that we had propounded our ideals and beliefs openly, and that we were happy to serve the people in any way we could be of assistance.

From there I went to talk with Mr. Timberlake, the American ambassador, where I aired my concern about being equated with political finagling. He was sympathetic but pointed out that in the present atmosphere of political intrigue and counter-intrigue, each new idea or project must expect to be examined in the light of political implications. The incongruities of the situations which almost daily presented themselves were often laughable, but also often tragic.

One day I went to the provincial offices to see the minister of health. I walked into the building and went up and down the halls, poking my nose in every office. There was not a soul to be found. Finally someone came through and I asked him if he knew where the minister of health might be found. He told me that he was probably out working in one of the dispensaries! On another occasion a young Belgian teacher, who lived across the street from us, came in one evening and with incredulity announced, "One of the students in my law class is now minister of justice!" Thus in those early days the Congolese were striving to plug the holes in the dike.

Another visit I made was to the Red Cross representatives in Leopoldville. It was confusing to discover that there were two Red Cross organizations sort of competing for preeminence and recognition. *Le Comite International de la Croix Rouge* was directed by a Mr. Borsinger with Mr. Senn, their troubleshooter, traveling the interior, looking for fields to conquer. Just down the street was the *Ligue des Societes de la Croix Rouge* with Miss A. Spahr at its head. Red Cross is very disciplined in its commitments and cautious in its involvements. I dealt with them on a number of occasions in matters about which they were tentatively considering but upon which we were already acting.

During my first days back in Congo I received a letter from the Presbyterian missionaries, now some twenty-two members strong, gathered in the Kasai Province. In a mission meeting from September 27 to October 6 they had agreed to my placement at Leopoldville as director of CPRA until the end of February. At that time, I would be expected to return to the Kasai to conduct refresher courses for our graduating *infirmiers* prior to their final oral exams, required in order to receive the state certificates as *Infirmier Diplome.*

MORE TRAVELS

During the month of October I had occasion to make a week's visit to the Kasai where I enjoyed a reunion with the missionaries and revisited many of the sites of my previous twenty years of missionary service. I was distressed to find the capital of our Kasai Province, once a meticulously cared for lovely city, now the site of decadence and desertion. The modern air terminal was grimy with dirt, and ill-smelling since none of its plumbing was functioning. There were broken down, abandoned, and partially stripped cars on all the streets. Only a few shops and stores remained open. Most of the downtown buildings were intact even though the facades of many were pockmarked from the results of July gunplay. United Nations and Congolese Army soldiers were much in evidence.

Violence was still the order of the day, and the man with the gun called the plays. During those days I was in the Kasai, this situation brought tragedy home to us.

Maboshi was one of the most effective and admired leaders in the church. In the formation of the new independence government of the Kasai Province he was named minister of education. He was neither Baluba nor Lulua, but a member of the Bakuba tribe. He had asked Charlene Halverstadt to take a position in his office as technical advisor. He was walking down the street one evening in Leopoldville on a business trip, when a band of ruffians shot and killed him. How distressed we were to see the new government deprived of real Christian leadership, and how difficult it is to submit to the Lord in matters we cannot understand.

Another tragedy beset Kesu, our mission chauffeur at Moma Station. Everyone was attracted by his sunny disposition and quick willingness to be useful. He was transporting some church people from Moma to Lubondai in the station pickup, and as he was traveling a narrow road where tropical grass towered above the vehicle on both sides of the path, a bicyclist came tearing through the growth and violently slammed into the side of his car. The cyclist was killed and as Kesu stopped his truck, the villagers grabbed and beheaded him in a matter of seconds.

Thus it went. One pebble cast into the pond makes waves all across it. One act of violence bred a dozen. Because of the Kesu incident, it was necessary for the authorities to go to Moma the same night and evacuate all the Bakete, the fellow tribesmen of those who had murdered Kesu. They could have been wiped out by the resident Basala Mpasu. All this meant that the mission school at Moma was without teachers, and so was closed.

Also about this time Hank Crane had a narrow escape. He was traveling in his car toward Bakwanga when a truck load of Baluba soldiers stopped him. They loaded Hank into their vehicle and transported him pell-mell along the extremely bumpy road, with no explanation and a machine gun poking him in the back. They took him forty miles to Bakwanga and finally decided to let him go. By the time he got back to his car, he found that it was gone, obviously commandeered by the Baluba troops. Hank was born and raised in Congo, and he spoke Tshiluba like the Africans. He had always thought he had special rapport with them, but this experience scared him nearly to death. He later said, "Every time I spoke to them or asked a question in Tshiluba, it just made them madder. I finally realized I had to shut up or I might get shot."

My first formal act in Luluabourg was to visit the Provincial Ministry of Health. The minister was out of the city but I had a good visit with Mr. Loma Kjesa, the director of the large public hospital, and also with Dr. Nicholas, another Haitian physician assigned to the Province of Kasai by WHO. He begged for help from our Operation Doctor program, saying the Kasai Province was in greatest need of medical assistance of any of Congo's provinces. There were only three doctors in the entire province employed by the government. One was at Luluabourg, one at Lusambo, and the third divided his time between Mweka and Mushenge. In the city of Luluabourg itself with a population approaching one hundred thousand there were only four doctors and one dentist.

At Lubondai I enjoyed visiting with all my friends, missionary and African. I had the opportunity to go into the attic at our house and pack a barrel of pictures, scrap books, and other prize keepsakes to send to Effie. I also retrieved my stamp collection, particularly the Belgian Congo stamps which I was loathe to lose. While I was up in the attic, I also tried to hide my guns so they would not be discovered and carried off by some interloper.

From Lubondai we flew to Bakwanga where I wanted to see first-hand how Archie Graber was managing with his effort to aid Baluba refugees. I also wanted to make contact with the breakaway government of South Kasai. We found Archie just beginning to get himself situated along with the two young Mennonite fellows who had come to help him. They were conscientious objectors working off their obligations for military duty by helping serve the displaced people of

South Kasai. We received a ready reception from Mr. Kazadi Nicholas, the minister of health, and an audience with Prime Minister Joseph Ngalula. These men were very pleasant and seemed much less formal and pompous than their counterparts in Luluabourg or Leopoldville. They also impressed me as more able executives. Mr. Ngalula, in particular, was an impressive personality. They received the information about CPRA with interest and approval. It was obvious that their people would need a tremendous amount of assistance in the days ahead.

We visited Bibanga and admired the courageous work Hugh Farrior was doing there. He was the solitary missionary on the spot. From there we returned to Lubondai, and John Davis, Bill Washburn, and I flew to Moma where we visited with Earl King Jr., and then continued south to the Methodist mission of Kapanga where we were taken in overnight by Bill Davis and Dr. Duvon Corbitt. We had also visited Tinsley and Kit Smith at Mutoto where he was maintaining the medical work in spite of the fact that he was not very well.

Upon our return to Leopoldville, there was more unrest in the capital city. During the evening of October 21 and on into the following day, occasional bursts of automatic gunfire could be heard from across town. Some of the tribal groups were apparently going at each other. I felt some disgust with the apathy and unwillingness of UN troops to commit themselves to public order and safety. They seemed to simply stand around and watch the goings on, not even intervening when acts of violence occurred right under their noses.

The Ministry of Health finally responded to us about our Operation Doctor program after carrying the matter all the way to government cabinet level. They had considerably modified their demands. They withdrew their requirement that our visiting doctors speak French, and they agreed to our right to place these transient workers. This suited us just fine and we were happy to agree with their provisions. We also had permission to transport medical drugs and supplies inland by UN planes to doctors serving in remote areas which was a welcome breakthrough.

About this time the officers of CPRA had to get their heads together for a trouble session. We were dismayed that we had become such a political football between the ecumenical giants. In the beginning Church World Service had endorsed our Operation Doctor and Operation Refugee programs and had agreed to promote a campaign of $300,000 to pay costs. Next the Committee on Interchurch Aid of WCC announced that they were assuming responsibility for a secondary school program and they naturally expected CWS to help them foot that bill. So CWS (Church World Service) was on the horns of a dilemma, and there was the threat that they might have to back off from our

program. Cables were fired in both directions at a great rate, and finally
CWS stuck with us. But we never came close to the $300,000.

13 REFUGEES AND EMERGENCY FOOD

*But they that wait upon the Lord shall renew their strength; they
shall mount up with wings as eagles; they shall run, and not be
weary; and they shall walk, and not faint (Isaiah 40:31).*

Intertribal conflict continued to distort and destroy normal village life
all over the country, creating homeless populations of fleeing refugees
seeking sanctuary over and over again. This was particularly true in the
region of Kasai. Word came to us from friends in the city of Luebo that
approximately twenty thousand Baluba refugees were jammed into the
urban area of that city to protect themselves from local Lulua reprisals.
This immediately raised the specter of inadequate housing and insuffi-
cient food. The Red Cross was quite reluctant to get involved. How often
we thanked God for the leading which had prompted our mission to
place a global order with Church World Service, back in February, for
food and clothing to meet essential needs of anticipated refugee populations. So what had happened to this food? The story of its
meanderings is worth recounting at this point.

In March, before independence, the APCM had asked Church World
Service to send us 150 tons of beans, 150 tons of rice, 100 bales of mens'
and women's light clothing, and 100 bales of children's light clothing.
These supplies were duly collected, packed, and loaded aboard ship in
New York for the trip to Matadi, Belgian Congo. But by the time it
reached the mouth of the Congo River the country was in turmoil and
Matadi was under control of rebellious troops. So the ship moved on
south and deposited its cargo at Lobito, the port of Angola. There it sat,
in the storehouse, until we began to look for it in October. When we
finally tracked down the shipment, we paid the storage cost to the
Angolans and redirected the supplies by rail into the Congo to be
deposited at Mwena Ditu for the starving and destitute Baluba. But when
the shipment reached Tenke where it should have turned north onto the
main rail line to the Kasai, there was ominous news that Lumumba's
troops were advancing down the railroad into the Katanga. The supplies
were redirected southward where this time they were stored in a ware-
house at Elizabethville. By the time we traced them down and once
more paid storage costs, the central government troops had withdrawn,

so they were shipped northward again, destination Mwena Ditu.

Now other altercations blocked the way. The ambitious and expanding Baluba of the South Kasai were intent on pushing back the smaller tribes of Bakete and Bena Kanyoka in order to control the railroad line running through their parts of the country. In retaliation the Kanyoka had stormed the Catholic mission station at Kalenda, killing the abbé who was a Muluba. The well-equipped hospital suffered extensive destruction, and the few remaining whites had been run off. Now the Baluba were mopping up with the Kanyoka.

Archie Graber, alerted to receive the shipment of foodstuffs and clothing coming up on the train from the south, proceeded to Mwena Ditu where he engaged a storeroom from the oil refinery. The space was substantial and could be locked against thieves. He lined up a team of natives to unload the cars and transfer their contents to the storage space, but fighting between the Baluba and Kanyoka was coming nearer and nearer. When the train finally arrived and the particular cars had been sidetracked, open gunfire was uncomfortably close and stray bullets kept whining through the air. Archie and his men worked feverishly, and as soon as possible he paid them off and locked the storage doors. The Africans hightailed it to a safer place, but the fighting tribes were upon Archie and he found his only refuge underneath the railroad cars where he hugged the ground until the battle passed by.

These supplies were a miraculous godsend to the Baluba people. Archie Graber corralled two Mennonite helpers and a couple of trucks for the job of organizing and distributing. They brought food and clothing from Mwena Ditu and dispensed it on schedule all over the destitute Baluba area. When the UN and the Red Cross came through some time later with greater airborne quantities of supplies, Archie had such a well-organized program in progress, and he was so well-known and respected by the populace, that he was asked to go with the UN trucks as well.

THE POLITICS OF FOOD RELIEF

In comparing Sendwe and Kalonji, both were leaders of marauding and ruthless Baluba gangs, but Kalonji had managed to look more respectable than Sendwe in the international picture because of his break with Lumumba. But in dealing with them man to man, I'd much rather deal with Sendwe than with Kalonji. I perceived Sendwe to be a more open and honest character. Kalonji was a fox.

This distribution of food to the needy and the political implications that such a program might foster, did not fall without recognition upon the sharp imagination of Albert Kalonji. He came to my office to express his friendship and appreciation for all we were doing for the Baluba people through our Operation Refugee, and then he happened to mention that he had a DC-3 plane going to Bakwanga and wondered if we might have some foodstuffs on hand to send to the needy people. I understood, of course, that this was a political ploy that Kalonji would be using to enhance his image in Baluba land. On the other hand, I did have food and there was no question that the Baluba needed it, so why not let Kalonji do our transportation for us? I told him we would have the supplies at the airport the following day. Before he was to depart, Bob Bontrager quickly had a large rubber stamp made. It was over six inches long and it said *MU DINA DIA YESU*. These words were stamped on all sides of the boxes we trucked out to Kalonji's plane, so supplies were delivered to the South Kasai with the message in Tshiluba for all to read: *IN THE NAME OF JESUS!* A couple of months later I had occasion to visit the South Kasai. I found our empty boxes everywhere I went. Some had been torn and discarded. Some were utilized to house odd collections of schoolbooks or papers. All of them still declared *IN THE NAME OF JESUS*. I believe we got our message across.

Months later, Albert Kalonji again came to my office. After an exchange of pleasantries he handed me a bill for one million francs! He informed me that this was the amount we owed him for the transport of food to the South Kasai. I restrained myself from any blatant protest or show of surprise, and just as solemnly told him we would consider it and let him know. The following day I posted a proper letter to him in which I noted that he had charged us one million francs for transport and added that we had turned over the foodstuffs to him to use in his own way among his own people, so we calculated that the value of those supplies was also about one million francs. "Therefore," I concluded, "seeing that the value of your favor to us and the value of our favor to you were approximately the same, we presume that our account with you is a closed matter." I never heard any more from Kalonji.

Our CPRA Committee deemed it advantageous for me to try to visit the various capitals of the provinces in an effort to see how much medical service was being accomplished, especially in areas where the greatest need for assistance existed. In early November I flew first to Coquilhatville (now called Mbandaka), the administrative seat of the Equatorial Province. The Disciples of Christ (Christian Church) had a strong work in this area and I sought them out to help me make my survey. Gary Farmer, their field representative, happened to be at the mission compound. He was a big help, conducting me around and introducing me to all the Congolese officials I wanted to meet. I met Dr. Faniel, the Belgian Provincial doctor, and Dr. Axelson, a Swedish physician heading up the WHO contingent. He had a French doctor and a team of three Canadians working with him, and as far as I could see these were the only doctors in the province other than the missionary, Dr. John Ross, engaged in an active practice at Lutombe.

Another benefit to the situation at Coque which should be mentioned was the presence of United Nation troops from Indonesia. They seemed to be more energetic and friendly than any I had encountered, and they appeared to have established a good rapport with the Congolese. These soldiers were on track early in the morning for calisthenics and vigorous marches. They were assembled regularly, not only for combat practice but also for cleanup and public works programs. The Congolese soldiers were quite impressed with their discipline and energy.

From Coquilhatville I flew to Stanleyville, capital of the Orientale (or Eastern) Province. I was met by Dr. Jim Taylor of the Baptist Missionary Society (British), and he took me to their Yakusu station where their large hospital and a school for *Infirmiers Diplomes* was located. I had the pleasure of seeing four of our Batatele students who had left Lubondai when the tribal conflicts began, coming here to complete their medical training. This part of the country had been a Lumumba stronghold and was instilled with much of his radical political philosophy. Their indoctrination taught them that everything in the country was now theirs since the country itself was theirs. Property was surely theirs since it was composed of the materials of their country and fabricated by the labor of their own hands. Thus the missionaries had been instructed by the government to choose a Congolese and teach him the responsibilities of legal representative of the mission to soon replace the European representative. It was apparent to me that there was much more antiwhite sentiment here than we had experienced in the Kasai.

Back in Stanleyville the following day I met the provincial minister of health. He was Mr. Guestau Etienne, a former student at Yakusu and quite cordial. I also met Dr. Dambreville, the WHO doctor assigned to this province. It was apparent that Orientale Province was better off medically than either Kasai or Equateur. There were eleven doctors in Stanleyville itself, and forty-two in the entire province. The economy, on the other hand, seemed to be almost at a standstill. There was little or nothing in the stores. I shopped around trying to find so simple a thing as a comb for my hair, but was unsuccessful in my search.

My third stop was Bukavu, capital of Kivu Province. This lovely city, on the banks of Lake Kivu, is part of a beautiful terrain of mountains and lakes. There was less deterioration here than in any of the other capitals I had visited. This was probably because of its proximity to the Uganda and Rwanda borders, and European residents felt a greater security than further in the interior. They had elected to remain on the spot and to conduct life as usual, so there was less evidence of radical change.

When I went in search of officials in the Ministry of Health I learned that they were in process of replacing the Belgian Provincial doctor with a Congolese medical assistant. I found no one in the office. I did meet Mr. Norbert Kalumba, director of the hospital, from whom 1 learned that the medical situation in Kivu was better than either that of Kasai or Equateur, more on a par with Orientale. Eleven doctors were right in Bukavu, ten were employed by the government.

COORDINATING RELIEF EFFORTS

A week after my return to Leopoldville our worker on the scene at Bakwanga, Archie Graber, arrived unexpectedly, relating some lurid tales of hunger and starvation among the Baluba. He predicted that the next four months were going to be an extremely critical period during which many would die because the refugees to the South Kasai would not have time to clear fields and plant and harvest crops. Archie was working himself to exhaustion distributing food all the way from Mwena Ditu to Lake Munkamba, and needed still a bigger program to meet all the need. The Ngandanjika area was still too dangerous to enter because of continual vicious tribal fighting.

The Red Cross contribution was being orchestrated by Monsignor Mels and was going almost exclusively to Catholic school children. It was obviously not making a blanket contribution. The African Commissar for Relief was pressuring Archie to take the CPRA sign off his truck, and Archie felt that even his own personal safety was being compromised.

The United Nations food relief coordinator, Mr. Beruti, called a meeting of those participating. Mr. Borsinger, the Red Cross representative who had just come back from Bakwanga, opined that there were between 250,000 and 300,000 refugees in the South Kasai. He classified them in two groups: those experiencing ordinary hunger but in adequate physical condition, and those who were ill from starvation and malnourishment. He estimated that on a basic intake of 1,500 calories per day that forty tons of foodstuffs daily would be required to sustain them! From this estimate he was bidding for ten six-ton trucks to accomplish the distribution!

Then another monkey wrench appeared in the machinery. The Congolese government of the South Kasai began to recognize the relief effort as a significant event of international interest, so they came out with some new guidelines for relief distribution. They would take over the whole program themselves and there would be no more recognition of religious input. Those making donations in cash or in kind might have a seat on an advisory council and the right of observation of activities, but no active part in it. Now wheels began to whir, not only in our minds but also with the Red Cross and United Nations. Everybody had a word to interject, but after reflecting they were not sure just what that word should be. Now the classical manner of handling crises in Congo came into play. Namely, just sit back and allow time to pass. The more it did the less obvious were the issues. Gradually tempers cooled, excitement died, reform became blurred, and situations returned to the normal status quo. Those who had been providing food for the starving Baluba continued with their errands of mercy.

Here it might be well to introduce an important character of our CPRA drama. He was Mr. Ori Miller, a Mennonite millionaire. He spoke with restraint but he thought big. He had made his money manufacturing shoes, exclusively for women and children, so he couldn't be backed into a corner by the government and forced to make footwear for soldiers. He was the moving spirit of the Mennonite Central Committee which has had the vision to create and assist in worthwhile services all over the world. Our CPRA effort was right down his alley and he latched on to it with enthusiasm. One day Ori sat down with Bob Bontrager and myself, and the upshot of our deliberations was a cablegram from the three of us to our CPRA office in New York asking for: 1) Two hundred tons-per-month of foodstuffs for the next six months; 2) Eighty dollars per ton for transport; 3) Ten thousand dollars to be used for obtaining and transporting doctors to Zaire. There were other items and the cablegram was long enough to be persuasive. It cost us forty dollars. This was pure Ori Miller! I got a nibble from a Belgian physician who wanted to come to Congo and work for us under CPRA, and I complained because I had no funds to make it possible to deal seriously with him. With a faint smile Mr. Miller encouraged saying, "Invite him to come. I am sure that if he does, the funds will be forthcoming."

Most of us considered CPRA a temporary, interim project, an effort to assist the protestant missions and the Congolese government during those initial days of independence. After that it would be discontinued. Not so Mr. Ori Miller. He saw it as the type of service which should go on and on through the years. It was a program to build upon, dreaming up new ministries and services to help the Congolese people in the name of the Lord Jesus Christ.

REFUGEES

I made a trip back to the Kasai in mid-December. At Bakwanga I was delighted to run into our own missionaries from Bibanga, Day Carper and Hugh Farrior, as well as a sprinkling of Mennonites which included Mr. Ori Miller. I also met Dr. Frank Lowenstein of the UN, a specialist in nutrition. He was preparing to make a reconnaissance through the South Kasai and invited me to come along.

In the morning, we made the automobile trip to Ngandanjika. We were told that there were sixty thousand people around Ngandanjika, and twenty thousand were refugees. Two representatives of the minister of health traveled with us. We went to the hospital and saw a dozen or so cases of kwashiorkor (severe malnutrition). Most of the other installations we visited were Catholic. Some five thousand children in the Catholic schools were getting Red Cross milk. We had supper at the Catholic mission and spent the night there.

The following day we visited three villages among the Bakwa Kalonji. At Kasansa there was a Catholic dispensary, maternity, and orphanage. Here a thousand students were receiving Red Cross milk. At Tshibata we visited with Mutombo Katshi, the paramount chief of the Bakwa Kalonji. He was the most powerful of the Baluba medal chiefs. At Bakwa Kashila 2,600 school children were receiving milk, all Catholic students. Again it was becoming evident that the Red Cross effort was pretty exclusively Catholic. We visited the hospital at Katanda, just twelve kilometers from Bibanga. Here we found a number of cases of kwashiorkor. The majority of the workers were our own Bibanga medical workers. No milk.

The third day of our journey we crossed the Lubilanji River westward, and visited the dispensary at Nkwadi where 500 people were lined up to receive medicines which were nonexistent. Here there were 3,600 refugees, mild kwashiorkor, no milk. Yet down the road there was a Catholic school where 2,500 school kids were getting milk daily. I was grateful that so many children were receiving nutritional aid, of course, but I was distressed with the inequity of the distribution.

We returned to Bakwanga where the rain was coming down in sheets. I went to see Mr. Charles Muzada who was in charge of the Red Cross work, and I pointed out to him how obvious and deliberate it was that Catholic schools were getting milk and Protestant schools were not. He was embarrassed and promised to correct matters. The following day we camped at the airport, hoping to bum a ride to Leo. Sure enough, a Swiss plane came in with food supplies and they gladly obliged.

AERONAUTICAL ADJUNCTS TO RELIEF WORK

On December 3, I received a call from Mr. Grady Parrott in Brazzaville to tell me he was coming across the river and asking me to meet him and help him around in Leopoldville. Grady was the executive officer of Mission Aviation Fellowship, an organization of Christian pilots who came out of World War II wondering how they might use their recently acquired flying skills for the Lord. Their vision was to set up a flying service for missions and churches in third world countries which would be conducted with high professional quality and the best of safety regulations. They had already expanded to South America, Africa, and islands of the South Pacific, and hearing of emergency needs in the Congo, Grady wanted to come have a close look at the situation. I went down to the beach to meet his ferry as it came across Stanley Pool, and we spent several hours together during which I outlined some of our aspirations for Operation Doctor. We discussed ways and means by which aviation might help.

Later I had a phone call from a Dr. Gorecki, a Polish radiologist practicing medicine privately before independence, and staying on afterward with a strong interest in the political currents fluctuating around the capital. He had quite a flair for sniffing them out when not openly apparent. He asked me to come to his office which I did, and he introduced me to another Pole, Mr. Micuta, the civil affairs officer of UN for the Province of Leopoldville. They were concerned about the Kwango Kwilu District to the east of us where they reported there was only one doctor. I knew this wasn't quite accurate since I could count two missionary doctors I knew in the area, but they were right that it was a sadly medically impoverished region. They raised the question as to the possibilities of sending an aerial team to fly from post to post to administer medical care, and as they spoke my pulse quickened and I began to feel goose pimples. I told them an aviator had just arrived in town a few hours earlier to talk about the same possibility, and they both just threw up their hands and breathed the one word: Providential!

Dr. Gorecki gave me a sheaf of confidential notes he had jotted down concerning the medical situation since independence, and I took them home to read. I gathered that he was a person who wielded considerable influence in an unofficial manner. There were a number of letters from Tshibamba, the minister of health, seeking his advice on various matters. So I took Grady to see Mr. Micuta, and I believe the Polish gentleman sold him his ideas about a flying team of doctors because for the next three days I conducted him from pillar to post. We had to get him a temporary Congo visa, and then we went to WHO headquarters to talk with them about the project. From there we visited the Red Cross offices (both of them). They were primarily interested in the safety of the participants who would be flying out in the hinterland. We went to the *Bureau of Geographique* and bought aeronautical maps which Grady pored over. Finally he was ready to declare that he had a plane in Nairobi and a pilot in Mali and he would commit them both to the job in Congo, ready to initiate the program by the first of January!

We went to the Shell company to talk with them about gasoline supplies, and to the *Bureau of Aeronautics* with questions about a license for the plane, letter markings to be painted on the wings, and radio frequencies. Everything was all set, and Grady was ready to return to the States. Before Grady's arrival I had begun to do a little flying again myself. I had taken my physical exam and was issued a student license. The local Air Club was looking for new members, so the prices were very reasonable and my American dollars were attractive. A little flying in the afternoons was good recreation and relaxation. I was assigned a preceptor and it wasn't long before he gave me permission for cross country flights. In January I decided to visit the hospital at the *Institut Medical Evangelique a Kimpese*, our largest union protestant medical installation, and I prepared to fly down. An airfield at Lukala was only 7 kilometers from Kimpese, and the flight from Leopoldville was only 150 kilometers.

I had no trouble on landing. The guard was pleasant and helpful but the administrator of the territory came racing out in his car to see what was going on. By the time he arrived Glen Tuttle had met me with his car to transport me to Kimpese. We explained my position and why I had come and this satisfied the administrator, but he added apologetically that he would of course have to report my arrival to the authorities at Thysville. I assured him that would be just fine, and Glen and I departed.

We had a nice afternoon visit. We walked over to the hospital where I looked in on some of the installations then proceeded to the guest house to wash up and dress for supper. Out the window I saw an ambulance arriving but gave it only casual attention since I figured that an ambulance arriving at a hospital was a rather normal occurrence. But then I noticed that it was loaded with armed soldiers. I watched them pile out with celerity and come running to throw a cordon around the guest house! An officer knocked and asked for the aviator who had just arrived, so I began trying to identify myself and justify my flight. He seemed rather agitated and wanted to know why I hadn't let them know I was coming. I said I didn't know that it was necessary, that I had filed a flight plan in Leopoldville and figured that the airport commandant would handle notification. He wanted to see my passport and other papers, and then asked for a *laissez-passer* (permission to circulate). I had a pocket full of these since I made a habit of asking for one everywhere I went. Fortunately I had one signed by the *Chef de Surete* which is the equivalent of the chief of the FBI. When the officer saw this he unbent for the first time. His eyes lighted up and he exclaimed, "Ah, that is very valuable!" Now he accepted my presence and the presence of my plane, reminding me to tell the *Chef de Surete* that he was on the job down there. Finally he called his men, got back into the ambulance, and returned to Thysville.

Gradually the import of my situation began to sink in. After all, Lumumba was under detention only sixty kilometers away and everybody connected with that arrest was on pins and needles. The following day the Leopoldville newspaper carried a squib about "an unidentified airplane" being spotted in the vicinity of Thysville, and that the security around Lumumba had been increased. I eventually learned that my landing at Lukala was the very first plane since independence six months earlier! Then the pilot had been the son of ex-Governor General Ryckmans of the Belgian Congo, and he had been arrested and taken to prison in Thysville where he was later murdered. The Good Lord was taking care of me! I returned to Leopoldville the following day with no further mishap.

In the big city I continued to try to set the stage for the flying doctors' program in Kwango Kwilu. I went to the office of the Provincial Minister of Health where I received a cool reception. This was apparently because they would not endorse a program for which they were not running the show. Reaction was much more genuinely receptive at the National Ministry of Health, and after that I approached the tribal point of view. I called on Mr. Cleophas Kamitatu who was at that time the mayor president of Leopoldville Province, but more significantly the leader of the Bambala people in the Kikwit area. He was friendly and receptive to the whole idea of medical help and said he would assure us security among the local people and would be glad to send guards with us to protect both doctors and pilots. Kamitatu was a bright and attractive person. I was more impressed with him than with any of the Congolese leaders I had met, unless it might be Joseph Ngalula of the South Kasai. These two struck me as having the most on the ball.

The following day I went to see Mr. Albert Delvaux who held ministerial rank in Lumumba's government and who was the leader of the Bayaka in the Kwango. These were the two tribes among whom we would be working. Mr. Delvaux was also very much in favor of our projected program and said that he would be glad to help us any way he could. On January 6, I had another call from Brazzaville that John Strash and his family would be crossing the river for him to take up his job of flying for Mission Aviation Fellowship (MAF). Alec and I temporarily housed them in the vacant mission house next door to us. As I had previously done with Grady, I began to chauffeur Strash around town until he was orientated. We went to the embassy to get him signed in and then to the Civil Aeronautics office where he asked for permission to bring his plane into the country. He talked to the U.S. Air Force attaché at the embassy and got some maps and plenty of advice. Of course I took him to meet Dr. Gorecki and then to Miss Spahr of the Red Cross. We visited the Ministry of Health, the UN Air Movement Control, and had an interesting conversation with one of the pilots of the Seven Seas Airline.

Seven Seas was an American charter airline which had been engaged by the UN to fly emergency food supplies into the South

Kasai. Apparently they were cleaning up on the deal. This particular fellow had been at the Goma airport the day before where he had a run-in with the Lumumbist troops. He reported that they had a heavy field piece trained down one end of the runway and a series of machine guns down the side. He felt that they were deliberately trying to provoke him into some condemning statement or rash act to give them reason to shoot him. They accused him of carrying arms for the Belgian paratroopers, so he invited them into his plane to show them that all he had were crates of tomatoes. Then they said that although he had brought in a crew of five he could only take out four. Naturally he wasn't going to fly off and leave one of his men, so he continued to palaver with them. When he inadvertently told them he was going to Usumbura they categorically refused to let him take off. Finally they decided he could go to Leopoldville and to this he readily agreed, although he knew he didn't have enough gas to get there. They told him if he did go to Usumbura and ever came back there, they would shoot him on sight. Obviously he went to Usumbura, but he had no intention of ever returning to Goma!

A week following the Strash arrival, Wes Eisemann and his family arrived in Leopoldville as a second MAF pilot on the scene. John Strash took a commercial flight to Nairobi to pick up his plane and fly it back. Within another week he had returned and great was our rejoicing to have a lovely Cessna 185 for the flying doctor program.

On January 25, John and Wes took off for Kikwit to make the first trial-run of the proposed program in Kwango Kwilu. A little later I followed in a Flying Club Piper Cruiser, landing at Kikwit just as Mr. Kamitatu was reviewing an honor guard which had been drawn up to salute him. He was admonishing them to behave correctly and with calmness, assuring them that the government would protect their interests. This lecture was obviously in light of the violence which had taken place there a month and a half earlier, but I deemed it was also an effort on his part to pave the way for a safe experience in our flying venture. Later he spoke with me and was very friendly, wishing us well.

I found a bed that night at Dr. Ernie Schmidt's house and while relaxing there, the first vice president of Kamitatu's local political party, *Parti Solidaire Africain*, came to see me. He delivered himself of a long political harangue to which I politely listened, and afterward took the opportunity to tell him something about the politics of the church of the Lord Jesus Christ.

In the morning we went to see Mr. Dikatele, the *Commissair* of the district. He was sending messages on ahead to advise officials of the arrival of our plane before John and Ernie and the two Congolese deputies being sent with them took off for Gungu, then Kahemba. At the same time in my plane, Wes and I flew northward to Vanga, an American Baptist Mission station. At that time there was no air strip at Vanga, so we circled the compound to get attention and when all the school children piled out of their classrooms to watch us, we dropped a note to Dr. Frank Anderson to tell him we would be holding a medical meeting that evening in Kikwit and hoped he could come down and meet with us. Vanga is about seventy-five kilometers from Kikwit. The other plane had flown over Mukedi, dropping a note for the Mennonite physician, Merle Schwartz. He came in to join us the next day.

The following day Strash and Anderson and the deputies flew to Masi Manimba, to Kenge, and to Kasonga Lunda. The rest of us went to see Mr. Kibende, the director of the Mission Medicale du Kwango Kwilu. He was one of Merle's old medical boys and was quite pleased with a review of our project. Later in the day I flew back to Leo, content that we had taken the first good step in providing airborne medical care for a needy area. This was indeed true and MAF continued to provide aeronautical aid through the entire period of upheaval, and is working there today.

14 OPERATION DOCTOR AND MORE POLITICS

Wait on the Lord: be of good courage, and he shall strengthen thine heart: wait, I say, on the Lord (Psalms 27:14).

The waning days of November and the early days of December brought some quickened events of import to the capital city. On the evening of November 21, Alec and I heard gunfire from across town and of course wondered what was going on. We knew that for several days the Congolese government had declared the Ghanian ambassador *persona non grata* and were calling on him to leave the country. He had not responded and, as a precautionary measure, the UN had installed a cordon of Tunisian soldiers around the embassy to create a buffer zone. On this particular evening Congolese soldiers went to tell the ambassador his time was up and that they had come to escort him to the airport. As a result the firing broke out. Ghanians, Tunisians, and Congolese each swore that one of the others started it. Gunfire continued intermittently through the night, but it was too far away to keep either Alec or myself from sleeping.

The following morning broke bright and fair, and all seemed normal and calm. Boys and girls could be seen on their usual way to school. In mid-morning we decided to reconnoiter and find out what had happened, so we drove over to the Ghanian Embassy. It was deserted. The soldiers were gone. Foxholes had been dug all around the place and in adjoining residential yards. One side of the embassy house was well pockmarked with fire from small arms. An army truck and a small civilian car had been deserted and left in the street, all shot up. These were our observations but the more serious part of the story was that two Congolese and three Tunisian soldiers were killed. One of the two Congolese was their commanding officer, Lieutenant Colonel Nkokolo. This was personally distressing news as Nkokolo was one of our strong protestant church members in Leopoldville. He had been in our office only the afternoon before, discussing with us the work and potentialities of CPRA. The story we were able to unfold was that Nkokolo walked unarmed to the embassy door and knocked. It was opened, someone fired close range and he fell. It was never determined who did it.

Six days later President Kasavubu triumphantly returned from his visit to New York and the United Nations where he was successful in seating an Ileo Kasavubu delegation instead of a pro-Lumumba group advocated by the more radical third world nations. With pomp and circumstance he paraded through the city for a better part of the day.

Meanwhile, Patrice Lumumba, under a soft house arrest in the city for a couple of months, saw his star gradually declining, but he had other plans on his mind. While the public was welcoming the returning president, the prime minister gathered a group of his followers and, without any fanfare, a convoy of vehicles rolled out of Leopoldville. Their departure was so unobtrusive it was not generally known for several days. It was quickly concluded that they were on their way to Stanleyville to join forces with Antoine Gizenga and his opposition regime. On December 2 Baluba soldiers captured Lumumba at Port Francqui. A few more miles eastward he would have been in sympathetic territory with no obstruction to reaching his goal, and the eventual history of the country might have been considerably altered. Instead, he and his cronies were imprisoned, Lumumba under observation of the military at Thysville.

Three days later vicious fighting broke out at Kikwit between the local people and the occupying soldiers of the national army. Certainly part of the explanation of this disruption could be laid to the recent Lumumbist activities and the unrest, doubts, and questions raised thereby. Details of the trouble gradually filtered into Leopoldville. A group called *Jeunesse* (a youth organization) of the Kwilu district began to signal out members of the BaCongo tribes who lived in and around Kikwit, assaulting them and destroying their property. Soldiers intervened and the young men let one of them have it, hitting him in the head with a hammer. As he fell, his head was further cracked open with a blow from a heavy machete. The soldier was rushed to the hospital but he died the following day. That was signal enough for the army. They went through the village areas of Kikwit shooting and burning, and completely drove out the population. Fortunately the people had anticipated the massacre and had taken to the forest, so there were not the casualties there might have been. The only doctor in the district was our missionary colleague of the American Mennonite Brethren, Ernest Schmidt. He was directing the hospital at Kikwit where he counted fourteen dead and fourteen more seriously wounded.

A final brutal casualty of these perilous days, sad to relate, was the murder of two British missionaries of the Congo Evangelistic Mission in the northern Katanga. All members of the mission had been gathered at Kamina where Mr. Hodgson and Mr. Knauf decided to push northward towards the Kasai border to see how fellow Christians in some of the village churches were faring. Late in the day they stopped at a road-block where, in spite of identification and explanation of their activities, they were placed under arrest and marched toward the village of a tribal chieftain. But before they arrived, the accompanying crowd worked itself into such a frenzy that they set upon the two men and butchered them. The story goes that each one tried to protect and save the other. The older of the two reasoned that his body would provide them strong medicine for conquering their enemies. Mr. Knauf reminded them that his companion was too old and worn out and that they should take him. Mr. Hodgson countered that his young friend was untried, not worth much, so they should take him, the old hunter. The Baluba *Jeunesse* decided to play it safe and kill both of them, taking their hearts and testicles to make their medicine. The men were not tortured and they died praying. Christians who were present asked for their bodies but were driven off. The older missionary had been on the mission field for forty years, and the other for twenty-one.

I attended church the following Sunday with Mr. Sendwe. Those were his Balubakat followers who had perpetrated the crime, and I expressed to him our sadness over the death of our friends. He too declared his disappointment and sadness. I asked if he had known the victims but he did not. Then I asked if he knew Mr. Warmsley, the legal representative of their mission, also a sort of father figure among them. He told me that Warmsley had married him and his wife. We talked about the lack of discipline and control among the young people, and I told him I would be praying for him in the days to come because we need more God-fearing men in positions of leadership in the land. It is also sad to relate that later Mr. Sendwe himself made a trip into Balubakat country to try to counsel and calm the radical elements, and he was also set upon and murdered by his own people.

OPERATION DOCTOR

We had waited for weeks to see some results to our Operation Doctor challenge, but nothing was forthcoming. This was disappointing and our impatience was beginning to show. Mine was heightened by the arrival of a little-old wizened-up Swiss lady who appeared in our midst in Leo. She was deaf as a post and so feeble she looked like she might keel over at any time. Yet here she was, all alone, on her way back in the interior to sell Bibles! She was going into a section which had seen its share of the political unrest and was still strongly pro Lumumbist and anti-white. Yet there she was going and expecting, by the grace of God, to do an effective job. And I'm sure she did. But I looked at her and thought about the difficulty I was having in getting strong, able-bodied men injected into this crying medical need, and my frustration was further fomented.

Finally we had a breakthrough! Our first doctor arrived from the States. Dr. Witt was sent to the Luluabourg area and to possibly go to my old post at Lubondai to fill in for John Miller who had gone on furlough. But here again the arrival of Dr. Witt brought us a sobering reflection. Dr. Witt was a lady physician! Where were the men?

A week later Oliver Hasselblad flew in to help us out for a while. I had just received a plaintive call on short-wave radio from Dr. Bob White on the Methodist Mission at Wembo Nyama. Two of their doctors had gone home, leaving him as perhaps the only doctor between Luluabourg and Stanleyville! He was inundated with work and had to complete piles of administrative papers. His elective (non-emergency) operative schedule was months in arrears, and he was begging for a helper "to come and just operate from morning till night and relieve me of some of this pressure."

This was right down Oliver's alley and he jumped at the opportunity. We sent him to Wembo Nyama and he had a ball! A month or so later when he returned he was most enthusiastic about the impact he had been able to make, and more seriously he felt he had been a true bulwark to Bob, helping to protect his composure and health. Bob had been in danger of buckling. Oliver Hasselblad moved on to the presidency of American Leprosy Missions, based in New York, and exerted a worldwide impact in the control and treatment of that ancient scourge.

Thus the ice was broken and we began to get support from several different directions. First, I received a call from a Swedish colonel of the UN Air Force who said they recognized the important contribution we were making in Congo and wanted me to come over and talk with them about ways they might be able to help us. I went to see him and he told me that the Swedish air teams had appreciated what missionaries had done to help them, and were impressed with the job they were doing among the Congolese people. He offered to carry more medical supplies inland for us, and even to include milk and foodstuffs.

My second call was from a Mr. Osen of ICA (International Cooperation Agency), forerunner of the Agency for International Development or AID. He was to return to the States in a couple of weeks and would be speaking before civic and religious groups and wondered what to tell them about missions. He too had been favorably impressed by the work and he wanted to give us a good boost. You can be sure I filled up his ear!

A third call was from Mr. Ngweti, the *Commissair* of health of the national government. He wanted me to go see the minister of the interior of Leopoldville Province to tell him about our flying program. I called on the minister of the interior and he was most cordial and interested. He assured me he would do everything necessary for the safety of our planes and personnel. Mr. Tshibamba, Ngweti's superior and the minister of health, also called. They had been unable to secure doctors from Belgium to meet their needs and were looking anew to us for help, even specifying, "We need a radiologist and a chest surgeon here in Leopoldville." They were completely in favor of our flying team to the Kwango Kwilu, and wanted to call a news conference and give it radio publicity. But I sort of shied away from this, at least until we had established a going service.

There were invariably a few sour inclusions from time to time. One evening Alec and I were working the ten meter band, enjoying a contact with Porter Orr in Knoxville and through him a visit with Effie and the kids. We were having a great time when there came cries of alarm from the street outside. We rushed to the door to see what had happened and learned that thieves had broken in next door and were in process of trying to cart off our dining room furniture. Neighbors across the street had seen what was going on, and their cries alerted us. We retrieved all the possessions and chased the culprits down the street, but our radio contact was ruined. I spent the rest of the night in the vacant house.

By February of 1961 the push of Gizenga's armed forces was in earnest. A Lumumbist vanguard drifted casually into Luluabourg setting the stage for a takeover. Commercial planes had been fired at and air traffic had been temporarily stopped. I went to town to visit the UN headquarters and was surprised to find some three or four hundred men milling about there in an unorganized manner. As I approached the crowd a Lulua young fellow sidled up to me, called me by name, and began talking in Tshiluba. I asked him the significance of the crowd, and he casually explained, "Oh, we are just some fellows who have come to ask the UN to fly us to Stanleyville so we can join Gizenga's army." He was perfectly serious! He had no concept as to how ludicrous the statement was.

From there I went around to the American Embassy and met with another thunderbolt. Mr. McIlvaine, the U.S. Consul, informed me with a smile that word had come from Luluabourg that all the soldiers there—Mobutu's, the Lumumbists, the *gendarmerie*—all had stacked their arms together under lock and key with the Ghanians saying, "Now we'll go have a beer!"

You never can tell in Congo just how things are going to work out. This is true not only on the streets but also within the confines of one's own home. Alec was our cook. I helped wash the dishes. Alec couldn't cook a lot of things, but one food he did concoct well was gravy. We bought our bread from a local bakery and we often enjoyed Alec's gravy over either bread or toast. However, the bakery wasn't completely reliable, and often we reached home late in the afternoon to find the bakery completely sold out. There was no way of anticipating this and we never knew until one of us presented himself to make a purchase. This sold-out-bread happened to us one afternoon when Alec had a particularly delicious smelling batch of gravy on the stove. Beautiful gravy, no bread. What could we do about it? In effect, we really had no supper at all. Then Alec remembered that his wife, Peggy, had stashed away a carton of popcorn packages before leaving for America. "I wonder how gravy would taste on popcorn," he mused.

"Let's give it a try and see," I suggested. So we did, and we found that gravy on freshly popped warm popcorn is one of the most delectable dishes in this world! We enjoyed it again and again.

CLIMACTIC POLITICAL EVENTS

In late 1960 and early 1961, the Congo was politically splintered into four fragments, each claiming autonomy. The Leopoldville government was increasingly controlled by a Kasavubu/Mobutu alliance while publicly being administered by a cabinet headed by Joseph Ileo. There had been a declining Lumumba influence, throttled by his arrest, first in Leopoldville and then at Thysville. Vice President Antoine Gizenga had moved to Stanleyville and set up a regime which he claimed to be the authentic Lumumbist government, and therefore the rightful government of the nation. Albert Kalonji, *Mulopwe* of the South Kasai, and Moise Tshiombe, president in the Katanga, each claimed that their respective states had seceded from the Congo, formulated their own constitutions, established their own governments, printed their own stamps, etc.

In February of 1961, seven Lumumbist functionaries were tried by the Baluba in a kangaroo court of village chieftains at Bakwanga, and thereupon were executed. In response to this, fifteen political personalities were shot at Stanleyville, including the minister of communications in the Lumumba government, deemed not hardline enough against Lumumba's enemies. On February 15, two white men were shot and killed at Luluabourg, and the following day a Catholic priest was set upon in Leopoldville by two Batatela and two Lulua youths. The first report was that he was dead, but we later heard he was in the hospital.

It was in this cauldron of political unrest and intrigue that word arrived late, having been kept under censure for some three weeks, that Patrice Lumumba was dead. The news came that he had fled, somewhere in the Katanga, and that villagers discovered him and killed him. This report was entirely fishy as everyone knew that the Katanga was the last place Lumumba would have willfully gone. Hadn't Tshiombe sworn to do him in if he could get his hands on him?

Gradually more reliable accounts emerged. The prime minister had been put on a plane the evening of January 17, along with two of his cabinet ministers, and flown to Elizabethville after which they were never seen or heard from again. Who did him in, and under what circumstances has never been divulged. Obviously the prime responsibility fell upon Moise Tshiombe, but he could not have acted alone. Kasavubu and Mobutu had to assume blame at the sending end of the line. But others too were involved and European nations must accept their part in the suspicions. I talked with a friend from the Katanga months later who claimed to have been on hand at the airport when Lumumba arrived. He told me, and I have no certainty that this is true, that Belgian men handled Lumumba when he arrived. He was unceremoniously pitched from the plane to the tarmac below and apparently he was the object of obvious beatings and torture. Was our own American government involved? I hope not, and they have always claimed innocence.

VISITORS FROM AMERICA

A month after the Lumumba fiasco, we at CPRA were visited by some friends from the United States. A threesome from the Christian Medical Society came to look things over, and I served as their Leopoldville host. Their leader was Raymond Knighton, the executive director of the society, and the other two were members of their executive committee: Dr. Gustav Hemwall from Oak Park, Illinois, and C. Everett Koop, who later served as the surgeon general of the United States. I took them around to visit dignitaries in Leopoldville, and then we journeyed to the *Institut Medical Evangelique* at Kimpese where they could see missionary medicine in action. We traveled by car through the country, and I left my visitors in the hands of the Kimpese staff the following day to return alone to Leopoldville. I say "alone," but I had a car full of Congolese I picked up along the roadsides.

Only a week later there was another visit from Governor G. Mennen Williams of the U.S. State Department and his party. They had been sent

Left to right—G. A. Hemwall, C. E. Koop, Ray Knighton, and Bill Rule, February 1961, Leopoldville.

to observe some of the American missionary work in Congo. Although arrangements were made by the embassy staff, I was asked to accompany the party to visit the American Baptist station, Sona Bata, where there were schools and a hospital. "Soapy" Williams (as I called him) was a fraternity brother and I had followed his activities in the Phi Gamma Delta magazine as well as in the public media. He had been a nationally publicized governor of Michigan, and a widely-supported Democratic candidate for the presidency. At that time, he held a high position in the State Department of newly elected President John F. Kennedy, where my old Davidson College schoolmate, Dean Rusk, was head man.

Governor Williams spoke at an American Men's Club luncheon. He was not as eloquent or as entertaining as Senator McGhee of Wyoming was earlier in December, but "Soapy" was the consummate politician. He shook hands in all directions and posed with proper backgrounds for the photographers. The famous Mennen Williams smile was highly conspicuous. The following day we set out for Sona Bata, ten carloads strong! I traveled in a car with a Mr. Sanger from the office in Washington, Steve Stephanitis, agricultural expert of the embassy, and the consul from Angola. They sort of put me on the spot with probing questions about situations and solutions in Congo. I ventured that our political positions in this land should be shared with the African leaders in an effort to gain their acceptance and cooperation. If we failed to take them into our confidence, no matter how good our plan, they wouldn't like it. Secondly, as I saw it, the one vital need in Congo was a functioning judicial system which could mete out at least token justice. There was no haven of protection for anyone. It is important to remember that with the Congolese, their first word is never their last. They are born hagglers. Their most comfortable procedure is to initiate an extreme position from which they can drop back while seeking a compromise.

The seventy kilometer trip brought us to Sona Bata where speeches of welcome were given. School girls came out of class and danced for the governor, the choir sang for him, and the cameras ground away at a great rate. We had a picnic lunch on the grounds after which we visited the hospital.

In January and February, we began to receive some large, expensive, and quite significant shipments of medicines, dressings and bandages, and other hospital linens and supplies. Extra space had to be cleared to house these materials. We had the halls so blocked with boxes and cases it was hard to get through. Finally a reluctant permission came through from the U.S. that American planes would be allowed to move our supplies for us. This was a big help. It meant that UN planes began to transport medical supplies for us to Stanleyville, Luluabourg, Bakwanga, and other points.

In December our food relief program for refugees in the South Kasai was going in high gear. Archie Graber was recognized and respected over the whole territory. When the UN began to transport its food in Ghanian trucks, the people were suspicious, so Archie's trucks led the way to help make them acceptable. But by February several nations had gotten into the act with global amounts of food, and we were pretty well shoved into the background. The United States offered all the cornmeal and powdered milk the Kasai government would accept, and Scandinavian countries provided large quantities of dried fish.

We began to try to fill other needs of the people in the South Kasai. Housing was a problem. Many refugees had no protection against the heavy March and April rainy season which was upon them. We managed to get hold of a large supply of pup tents to ship to Archie Graber at every possibility. The art of woodcarving was encouraged as a means of gainful employment.

In early March the Congo Protestant Council held a garden party at the residence of Mr. R. V. deCarle Thompson, our general secretary. It was an enjoyable affair with delicious refreshments. Mr. Kasavubu put in his appearance and shook everybody's hand, and Mr. Kamitatu sent his vice president. The diplomatic corps was out in full strength, and the Salvation Army band added its decibels to the occasion. But in spite of celebrations, the general situation continued to deteriorate. The president of our air club was out walking his dog one evening and they were both ambushed and killed.

Pastors Isaac Kanyinda and Samuel Bukasa from Bakwanga sat with us one evening and gave graphic accounts of the fighting between the Baluba and Lumumba's troops back in August. They told us the government troops drove into Bakwanga with pictures of Kalonji on their trucks and everybody accepted them. Then they began beating people and knocking them about. On a Sunday morning some of the tribal chiefs, plus a crowd, went to the soldiers to ask why they were behaving as they were. The soldiers opened fire and killed two people. This infuriated the crowd so that they set on the soldiers and killed two of them with their bare hands. From this episode the conflict escalated.

They told of refugees who were slaughtered at the police station; of soldiers who went to the Catholic cathedral and sprayed rooms with automatic gunfire; of a battle across the Mbushimayi River. They felt that the power of the Lumumbist drive was finally broken when thirty-five *Jeunesse* from the Katanga who were well-armed surrounded 150 Lumumbist soldiers in the night. They practically wiped them out. Word at this time from Lubondai told of soldiers coming from Dibaya to commandeer all the station transmitters, which meant that my personal one was included. They had gone up in our attic and smashed some trunks and boxes, so I kissed my .270 rifle good-bye since it was out in plain view.

Later we heard that several of the WHO doctors had been roughed up. The doctor at Luozi was badly beaten, and those at Luisa and Kabinda also had trouble. By that time I had my plane ticket to leave Leo and return to Lubondai and Bibanga for the next three months. I put it all in the hands of Almighty God.

15 BACK TO THE KASAI

And I entreat thee also, true yokefellow, help those women which laboured with me in the gospel, with Clement also, and with other of my fellow-labourers, whose names are in the book of life (Philippians 4:3).

After completing six months with the Congo Protestant Relief Agency in Leopoldville, it was time to return to the Kasai Province. I had specific directions to conduct refresher classes for our graduated *infirmier* students in order to prepare them for the governmental jury exams.

These exams were necessary before they could qualify to receive their official certificates as *Infirmier Diplome*.

I flew to Luluabourg on Easter Sunday morning. Stanleyville soldiers of Antoine Gizenga, some two hundred strong, had rolled quietly into town, obviously following some "understanding" with the commanding officer of the local *gendarmerie*. This prompted the chief of the national army to beat a retreat to Leopoldville. But then elements of the central secondary school (high school) began to agitate against the Stanleyville government, which drew some of the army personnel away from the side of the invaders from the northeast.

Their officers had agreed to lay down their arms but the rank-and-file soldiers refused. The Stanleyville troops saw things weren't going their way, so the third day after their arrival they began to withdraw. The few who did not were arrested. On the following day Kalamba, the Lulua chief, came with twenty thousand of his followers to demand the release of the chief of *gendarmerie*, also arrested. Everyone recognized that the wisdom of valor in this case was to accede to the pressure and allow the incident to pass off as quietly as possible. However, the crowd did get a little unruly and one civilian was killed. Then others "made medicine" to protect themselves from the soldiers' guns and attacked four of the national army men, severely beating them and killing one. Now the soldiers went into higher gear and attacked some of the known Lumumbist sympathizers' homes. There was shouting and firing throughout the night and the following morning thirty or forty were dead including some women and one child. This desultory action bespeaks the African logic of "testing the water." Had the Lumumbist soldiers found themselves genuinely welcomed by the public, an entirely different chapter might have been written in the Zairian history.

The following day I caught an automobile ride with Charlie Ross to Lubondai. It was good to get my hand back into the practice of medicine which was meaningful and good for me. My second night I was called in to the hospital for a difficult delivery in which I did a version and extraction which were successful. The next night I did a midforceps delivery on a primigravida suffering from secondary inertia. It felt like old times.

While at Lubondai, I went up into our attic to see how our belongings had fared during the invasion of the African soldiers. I was amazed to find that apparently nothing had been disturbed. There stood my rifle leaning against the brick chimney in plain view! I cornered Nolie McDonald to tell her of my findings and to again ask if the soldiers really did go into our attic. She told me that they certainly did because they asked her for the keys and she surely wasn't going to withhold them.

"But," she said, "it was in the middle of a very hot and cloudless day. I'm sure the temperature up there must have been 150 degrees." They had stayed for only a minute or so before tumbling down the stairs with their faces streaming with sweat.

The lead soldier had complained, "That doctor has more boxes and trunks than I can count!"

"Well, he has a large family and has been out here for a long time," Nolie soberly replied.

Four days later Wes Eismann passed through Lubondai with an empty MAF plane and I was able to send several trunks and boxes with him to Alec in Leopoldville. Alec managed to get them into the hands of American army aviators who brought them to the States where eventually they were delivered to Effie in Knoxville.

Now it was time to bend our efforts toward review seminars for the *infirmier* students and, if we could round them up, hopefully also for Sandy Marks's dental students. Lucile McElroy was there to help with the recapitulation, particularly from the standpoint of bedside nursing techniques. We had more Baluba graduates than Luluas, and because of tribal strife the ten Balubas were all working at Bibanga hospital. At Lubondai there were only three Luluas with prospects for taking the government exam. We decided to go to Bibanga first.

We ran some risk traveling from Lulua territory to Baluba country. I knew that Archie Graber was planning a trip from Luluabourg to Bakwanga in a UN truck convoy, so I decided to accompany him. We started out twelve trucks strong and arrived with ten of them still intact! I rode with a Pakistani chauffeur and it was worth one's life to be so involved. The dirt roads were neglected and in awful condition, that's true, but even on the straightaway he struggled manfully to keep his car on the road. Occasionally he would ram into the truck in front of him, and each time he changed gears it sounded like he was totally stripping them. Slowly but resolutely we covered the 125 miles between the two provincial capitals.

Halfway along we would come to that welcome spa which missionary families always strained with anticipation to sight. That was Lake Munkamba. Two or three miles before reaching this point a large village, Mpanga, was situated on a prominent elevation at a crossroads. As we reached Mpanga we were amazed and distressed to find every hut in the village burned to the ground. Some of them were still smoking which meant the destruction was as recent as a day or two earlier. There was no sign of life. Obviously the villagers had fled before the assault.

As I studied the havoc around me, however, I noticed a complex of school buildings on the other side of the road intact! The fresh whitewash of their walls shone in the sunshine. I breathed a prayer of thanksgiving. Bill Washburn had scraped together the materials to build this regional school, and he and the local people had sweated

168 MILESTONES IN MISSION

together to construct it. The school served in the education of children
over an extended area, and the marauding antagonists had affirmed the
work being done by leaving the buildings standing.

We stopped at Lake Munkamba to eat our lunch—a bottle of warm
pop and a sort of rolled up pancake with a concoction of beans and
sauce inside, prepared by the Pakistanis. I took advantage of the few
minutes of rest to nose around the mission compound. The dormitory,
Luebo house, the Miller's, and McElroy's, all appeared to have intact
roofs, but this was still early on. As the fleeing Baluba left Lulua
country, hundreds of them settled along the eastern shore of the lake.
They took anything they could find to build shelters and the metal
roofing off of these houses was first to go. Eventually all the houses
were vandalized and all roofs, doors, windows, furniture, and anything
else which might be used by the refugees, was taken. I counted about
twenty-five wrecked and abandoned cars along the route from
Luluabourg to Munkamba. They were without wheels, upholstery, and
often complete motors as desperate people who had lost everything
tried to recover and replace something.

We arrived at Bakwanga after dark. The following day I visited the
Ministry of Health to make arrangements for the provincial government's examination of our students. While in Bakwanga I went to a
makeshift museum to see the cannons which were fashioned and used
by the Baluba in their warfare with Lumumbist troops. There were
dozens of them and they certainly were amazing creations.

From Bakwanga we made the forty-mile trip to Bibanga in a relief
agency truck, crossing the Mbushimayi and Lubilanji Rivers on hand-
and-pole propelled ferries. We had to wait at the Lubilanji for an hour
and a half while the ferry men worked themselves into the frame of
mind to come across and get us.

Bibanga Station was a concentration of bachelors. Cam Wallace
and Charlie McKee lived in one house and Hugh Farrior and I in
another, but we all ate together. I thoroughly enjoyed seeing so many
of my old Congolese friends. Kokesha and his wife, Mbuyi, came to
pay their respects and brought me a huge stalk of bananas. Tshiela
Makasa brought me a chicken and Majiba Andre added another. It
was good to visit with Lukusa Andre who had been with me at
Lubondai for so long, and with Kanda, the head medical boy at Mutoto
in years gone by, as well as with Bibanga stalwarts Kapitaine Stephan
and Lubilanji Samuel. I gave the ancient Tshiela a piece of cloth in
Effie's name and she prayed for our entire family most vehemently.
She told me she didn't get much sleep at night because the angels
were always talking to her. She said they told her what a wonderful
person Albert Kalonji was, and that all the missionaries who had left
for the States must hurry back to the Congo!

During the next ten days, the ten *infirmiers* and I engaged in daily classes to upgrade their knowledge for the examination. This included all the basics: anatomy, physiology, pharmacology, pathology, internal medicine, surgery, gyn-ob, and a number of other branches. Eventually I returned to Lubondai to go through the same process with the three Lulua students. Nine of the ten later passed the jury exams and were awarded their *Infirmier Diplome* certificates.

RECOVERING MY RADIO

At Lubondai I sought to retrieve the short wave radio transmitters confiscated by the territorial officers. One belonged to Lubondai Station and the other two were the private property of Sandy Marks and myself. I made the first forty-mile trip to the territorial offices at Dibaya with two of our Congolese leaders. We had heard that there were Baluba soldiers there, but I figured if the two Africans were not afraid to go, then I ought not to be! We passed a dozen or more barricades, some manned by armed villagers and some by no more than "Boy Scouts" with sticks, but we took it easy and talked our way through. We found Dibaya peaceful with no Baluba present. I saw the fellow who had taken our rigs. He was an old acquaintance, but said that the administrator was not there that day so nothing could be done about it and I would have to come back.

Two weeks later I tried again with Tshisunga Daniel and Ilunga Andre to help support my demand, but again the administrator was away and nothing was accomplished. I waited only two days before I made a third visit to find the administrator present but in conference, so I simply barged in and made my request. He had not even heard of my previous visits and told me nothing could be done about my request at that time. But he did encourage me to believe they were easing restrictions about radio equipment and that we might get them back.

"Come back next Tuesday or Wednesday," he said.

I thus made the fourth journey to Dibaya. He was reluctant to make any concession, but we argued our point and finally he told me I could take one transmitter. I told him that if I could take only one I would choose the mission's rig. This was agreeable so he sent me with Tshinkenke Muana, the fellow who had confiscated the property, to get the transmitter. I found them all safely stashed away and in good condition, and as I disassembled the Lubondai components Tshinkenke began to feel sympathetic and apologetic about my having made all those trips.

"*Ngangabuka*, I'm going to take it upon myself and let you have your rig too," he told me.

I thanked him, and then I asked, "Now what about Sandy's rig?"

He said, "You tell Sandy to come on back out here to Congo and go to work and I'll give it to him."

A CONCERT

Toward the end of this period at Lubondai, Betty Jean Mitchell asked me to transport her and her thirty-five member choir of Congolese boys and girls to Luluabourg where they were to participate in a musical concert for the public. Betty Jean, our one black American missionary, was doing an outstanding job of teaching the young people and maintained a fine rapport between herself and the African people. I was delighted to accommodate her and prepared the mission truck for the trip. We departed at 5:00 A.M. while it was still dark, hoping to make good time across the hundred miles to Luluabourg. We were traveling along beside the railroad tracks as dawn slowly broke with a heavy mist swirling, cutting down on our visibility. Suddenly I came upon a road barricade made of sticks and poles. During this period of intertribal conflict, villagers set up barricades at the drop of a hat, with no prior notice and no explanation for their existence. I busted right into this one which sent particles of the broken barricade flying in all directions.

As I applied the brakes to stop I heard a musket discharged behind us, and my heart was in my throat as I came down out of the cab to check the young people in the back, fearing that some might have been hit. Fortunately they were all unharmed. On the other hand, the guardians of the barricade were furious with me, and I was amused to find two of them squatting in front of the truck, the muzzle of their guns only inches from the two front tires. I heard one say to the other, through clenched teeth, "If he moves this truck an inch, blow the tire off!"

I began to express my distress over destroying their barricade, but I noticed that the more I apologized the madder they grew. It became obvious that silence on my part was the better part of wisdom. I confined my remarks to one statement: "I didn't do it on purpose."

Their first thought was to turn the truck round, traverse the many miles back to Tshimbulu, and put me in jail. I patiently listened to them talk this over and occasionally interjected my reminder, "I didn't do it on purpose." Then they remembered there was a railroad telephone at a nearby railroad station. They could call Tshimbulu to ask the police officer there what to do with me. A half hour went by before the messengers returned saying they were unsuccessful in contacting Tshimbulu. Their third decision was to fine me, but the question was how much? They couldn't agree on a figure, but by this time their anger had abated and finally they signaled for us to get back in the truck and proceed upon our journey. We lost no time in complying with the suggestion.

The following day the concert was held. I attended part of it, but then had to go out and look for diesel fuel to get us back home again. Since it was Sunday no service stations were open. Finally I bummed a bit off a friend and siphoned it directly from his tank to mine. It was 5:15 P.M. when we finally pulled away from the city. Fifteen miles down the road we came to a barricade manned by government soldiers. It was a dull Sunday afternoon and they were looking for some amusement, so they made us all get out of the truck and line up. We were not allowed to speak French or Tshiluba—only Lingala—which none of us knew. They made cute remarks about the girls and said that each one of us must have a permit to circulate in order to leave Luluabourg. I was sure none of the Africans had anything like that. I pointed out that I was the only foreigner in the crowd and that I might need one, but all the others were citizens of the nation. They jumped at this and wanted to know where my permit was, but I was already way ahead of them. I kept my pockets full of permits, so I began to produce them, one by one.

As we sorted this out, an unusual sight came walking up the road. A Congolese had been waylayed and half his scalp was lifted from his head. He was covered with blood from head to foot. The soldiers forgot all about permits and told me I'd have to take him to the hospital. So we piled in the truck and back to town we went where, after depositing the wounded man at the hospital and losing another hour, I realized I had also used enough fuel to preclude our getting to Lubondai!

In spite of all these mishaps we proceeded on through the night, and as we approached the vicinity of yesterday's altercation I reduced my speed to little more than a crawl. I certainly didn't want to run into that local barricade again! Sure enough, they had rebuilt it and posted a lone sentinel. I stopped and he sauntered over to peer in the window of my cab. He plied his questions as to who we were and where we were going. I joked with, "Why you know me, I'm the fellow who gave you all that trouble yesterday morning."

He considered my statement for a moment and then posed the question: "Did you say that you gave us trouble or that we gave you trouble?" (It is confusing in the Tshiluba and can be understood either way).

I laughed and replied, "Let's say that we both gave each other trouble." He chuckled and began to talk. It was apparent that he was lonely and bored and welcomed some companionship and conversation. We visited for a few minutes, then bade him good-bye and continued on our way to Tshimbulu where we again had to extract some diesel fuel from a friend's tank in order to make it on to Lubondai. We reached home about 11:30 P.M.

THE UNITED NATIONS

About this time the United Nations organization began to concentrate their forces. Relationships with the Congolese government were rapidly deteriorating. Troops were pulled out of Lodja, Luputa, Luisa, and Kamponde. This left the Baluba soldiers in the South Kasai free to roam in any direction they chose. It also left Bill Pruitt in a rather lonely position at our Moma mission station. He went to the state post of Luisa where he found an angry and bitter town. They had been sacked by Baluba soldiers who had taken the Red Cross Finnish doctor, stood him against the hospital wall, leveled their rifles at him, and shot over his head. They had stolen everything he possessed except the clothes he was wearing.

Bill himself had a narrow escape. He was walking along a forest pathway when the ground beneath him gave way and he fell some ten or twelve feet into an elephant trap the Africans had dug. Stakes with spear-like points had been driven into the ground across the floor of the pit, and fortunately he was not impaled, but he suffered a severe laceration of his scalp and had to be rescued by African friends who found him.

I must add, however, that the presence of UN troops at Luluabourg did help keep the peace and prevented civil conflict from breaking out. Except for their presence, the local people and the national army would doubtless have been at each other's throats.

GOING HOME

With the conclusion of student examinations my work was done and I was ready to turn my face homeward to be reunited with my beloved family. One last task before I left was to sell my beaten and battered Chevy station wagon. Repair had been a slow process through all these months. I bought glass for the broken windows, a new windshield, and lastly a new battery. I had the engine tuned and then we fired it up and listened to the sweet music of a running motor. The mechanic said the car was worth one hundred thousand francs, but he knew I was leaving the country and wanted to get rid of it, so he only offered me sixty thousand. He told me I owed him thirty thousand for the work he had done. I listened to his recitation with some cynical reserve, but I was in no position to bargain with him. I took his sixty thousand and wished him well with the neat profit he would realize. Then I turned my face westward.

At the airport in Leopoldville, we boarded a Boeing 707, flew all day stopping at Douala and Marseille, and landed in Paris about 10:00 P.M. What an agreeable contrast to go through customs once again where basic politeness prevailed and where there were no soldiers with guns.

Two days in Paris gave me occasion to check off several "musts" which included the Louvre Art Museum, Notre Dame, and the Eiffel Tower. Napoleon's tomb at *Hotel des Invalides* was breathtaking, and of course there was a ride on the metro. Everything in Paris is on a grand scale. The buildings are astonishingly large, and while not as tall as those in New York, they convey a massive impression. The opera is immense and I could easily imagine how the phantom could get lost in it! The Louvre dwarfs even the opera and must be much larger than St. Peter's in Rome and the Brussels Palais de Justice rolled together! Even the pigeons are as large as ducks!

My beloved wife was waiting for me in New York, and my fine and admirable children would be at the end of a much shorter line in Knoxville. I would soon see family and friends and faithful church members who had been supporting all my efforts. God is good. He grants us such rich blessings in serving as his coworkers! Thank you, Lord!

16 UPHEAVAL IN THE EARLY SIXTIES

Hear me, O Lord, hear me, that this people may know that you art the Lord God, and that thou hast turned their heart back again (1 Kings 18:37).

Back in the United States for the summer of 1961 it was time for me to get caught up with my family members who had been living on very short rations during my absence. Effie has often recalled that this was the hardest, most trying year of her life. The children had all made it through another year of school from Johnnie's kindergarten to Bill's high school graduation. Through the generosity of friends both Bill and Charlotte were given a year of study at the prestigious private Webb School in Knoxville. Charlotte was sophomore class president, and Bill graduated Salutatorian and received a promptness award. I was distressed that I arrived too late to attend the ceremonies. Paul had a wonderful summer at Camp Sequoyah in the North Carolina mountains where Bill and I had preceded him as campers. Bill spent his vacation at Montreat, North Carolina, as one of the custodians of the World Mission Building, before he entered Davidson College for his first year.

Fall lengthened into winter and once again we began to feel the tug of getting back to our work in the Congo. A real concern was whether Central School was to reopen and offer continuing education for our children. Word came that the school would be open, but

174

Charlotte's situation gave us reason for reflection. She was in her third year of high school and needed the challenge of scientific subjects such as physics and chemistry. How could we assure her the quality education she deserved? We began to get reports that Rift Valley Academy in Kenya was a fine school with an excellent faculty and run by the Sudan Interior Mission. When we heard from them that they would be willing to take Charlotte in the middle of the school year, we took this as a leading from the Lord and made plans for her to fly from Knoxville to New York to London to Nairobi from where she would be met and driven a short distance to the school. So there she went in January of 1962, a seventeen-year-old high school girl, all alone, traveling halfway around the world to continue her education!

Meanwhile the rest of the family obtained bookings on the Belgian freighter, SS *Burkel*, from New York to Matadi. The *Burkel* was a diesel-guzzling victory ship from World War II days on which we had sailed in 1957, and it was just as greasy as ever. Paul enjoyed the voyage because he was frequently invited to the bridge to pilot the ship. I sometimes wondered whether we would reach Matadi or Singapore!

We were supposed to depart New York on January 23, but we didn't get off until the following day because the stevedores wouldn't work. January 23 was the day John Glenn was scheduled to make the first orbital rocket flight around the earth, and everyone including stevedores were glued to their television sets to watch the proceedings. Glenn was delayed for a month but in the meantime we made our way into the Atlantic and turned up the Chesapeake Bay to put in a call at Baltimore.

We reached Matadi on February 12, and in due time we heard from Charlotte and her safe arrival at Rift Valley Academy. I say safe arrival, but certainly not uneventful. The poor girl got to New York to find that her excess baggage would cost more than all the cash she had with her, so the only thing to do was reduce the cost by sending much of it as unaccompanied baggage, meaning its time of arrival was entirely problematical. She reached school without further incident and a few days later was informed that her other articles had arrived and were in storage at the Nairobi airport. They made an automobile trip to town to pick up her things and after loading the car they parked and locked it and went to a restaurant for lunch. When they returned to the car what was their shocking astonishment but to find that the car had been broken into and all of Charlotte's baggage had been stolen! She was a brave girl and says today this was one of the most valuable lessons she ever learned—that material things are not the basic, most important treasures of our lives.

MISSIONARY WORK RESUMED

Back in harness at Lubondai we were occupied for several weeks trying to get a handle on the situation. What had transpired politically, socially, economically during the seven months since I left Congo, and how did it all affect our missionary approach to the job at hand?

It was decided by a close vote at the April Mission Meeting to open Central School for missionaries' children at Lubondai in August. The project almost died aborning. Several days in advance of the meeting Effie and Nolie McDonald and Eleanor Goodrum went to work to clean up the school and make it ready to house the folks coming to the conclave. They laid out sheets and spreads and towels and all needed equipment for guests. But a day or two before the scheduled meeting someone broke in and stole all linens and other provisions.

At that time, just prior to Mission Meeting, Presbytery was also in session at Lubondai. It had been my purpose to go to them and ask them what the Congolese sentiment was about our reopening the school so I could report it to the assembled brothers and sisters at Mission Meeting. Now I had to go with a different approach. I simply said it seemed evident that the Congolese did not want the school at Lubondai and that I presumed it would not be opened.

This caused quite a flurry in various directions, and the church leaders went to Chief Ntolo to express their profound dismay over what had happened. They frankly told him that if he couldn't do something about the looting, they would propose to the rest of the tribe to look for a new chieftain. The sub-chiefs all came to see us to say how unhappy they were over the situation, and to express their staunch support of the mission presence among the Bakwa Tshipanga. So I wasn't surprised when about midnight they returned, bringing all the stolen articles back. They had apprehended the thieves, two young fellows, who were sent to Dibaya and put in jail.

The chieftainship was actually in a rather precarious position for twenty-four or forty-eight hours. They got out the leopard skin, just about the strongest medicine they could conjure up. Anyone sitting on the skin and questioned will surely die if he lies. Now questionable characters were placed on the skin to express their friendship for the mission, and the assurance that they would do nothing to impair said friendship. It is not a comfortable experience for Christians who look to a wise and powerful God for guidance and protection to find themselves under the safekeeping of a leopard skin, but at times God uses even the wrath of man to praise him, and I must say we were free from further molestation for quite a while!

During these months Charlotte came home from Rift Valley Academy. She got so caught up in all the excitement of reopening

Central School that she decided to stay home and take her senior year at the Lubondai school. We agreed, and when school opened in August she was the lone senior, and perforce president of the student body. When she came home from class feeling elated she enjoyed reminding us that she was at the very top of her class, but when she was down in the dumps she groaned that she was smack dab at the bottom of her class.

School started with thirty-five students who arrived from several different mission groups. It was like old times once more. A dedicated faculty, sent out by our mission board in the U.S., carried on an excellent teaching program, and the kids enjoyed each other with games and contests plus picnics and swimming at the dam for extracurricular activities.

The luggage we brought out with us in February finally arrived in mid-July. Aboard ship with us it took only three weeks from Knoxville, across the Atlantic Ocean to Belgian Congo, but it took five months to traverse the inland journey from Matadi to our home at Lubondai. Better late than never! We were grateful to see the crates and barrels of clothing and other personal articles, but especially the wholesale food order!

In mid-July distressing news came from our family in Knoxville. My Dad, eighty-three years old, was rapidly failing. He had a complete heart block with marked bradycardia and the impaired cerebral circulation was causing mental and behavioral problems which Mother couldn't handle at home alone. It was necessary to put him in a nursing home, and this he couldn't comprehend and he resented the treatment. Everyone was distressed with the situation. Missionary commitment feels the greatest strains when the family at home is in distress and needs a helping hand. A medical professional could make so much difference in caring for a beloved father, easing a dear mother's load. But at the same time there is a tremendous need of so many people who need help. So which way do you turn? What do you do? You look to God and seek His guidance, and you walk with Him in the assurance that He does all things well and that if He upholds you in one direction He is also capable of handling the faraway situation in the other direction.

Two important events occurred in our missionary life in late 1962. One was the arrival of Dr. Paul Hodel and his wife, Barbara, coming to share the medical chores with us at Lubondai. The other was my being a delegate to a Consultation on World Missions, held at Montreat, North Carolina, October 13–19, sponsored by the Presbyterian Church, US.

The Hodels were Mennonites from the Elkhart area of Indiana. Paul came as a conscientious objector to serve out the enlistment time for his draft board. They were young and their first child, Martin, was born during their two-year missionary service. Besides the fine medical contribution made by Paul as a physician and Barbara as a registered nurse, they were both also fine musicians. He played the piano and she the violin, and they helped raise the level of our cultural exposure in central Africa. But more importantly, they were beautiful and dedicated Christians who joined wholeheartedly in proclaiming and interpreting the Good News in Jesus Christ. On their return to the States, Paul qualified as a Board accredited anesthesiologist and they gave many years of undeniable "missionary service" in the coal fields of eastern Kentucky.

CONSULTATION ON WORLD MISSION

The consultation on overseas mission was conducted with some two hundred delegates from around the world. Missionaries and nationals were summoned from each of the church's mission fields plus the added staff personnel from the stateside office, clergy and lay leadership from stateside, correspondents from missionary organizations and churches outside the Presbyterian denomination, and resource consultants in various areas of mission. Our delegation from Africa included four missionaries and five Congolese: Messrs Louis Wanya, Pindi Jean-Baptiste, Pastors Tshisunga Daniel, Isaac Kanyinda, and Boo Pierre representing the Congolese Church, and Charlene Halverstadt, Bill Washburn, Charlie McKee, and myself representing the missionaries.

During my brief two weeks in the United States I was unable to see and visit with my mother as she was with my sister, Barbara, in St. Louis, Missouri. I did, however, visit with my son, Bill, who came over from Davidson to travel with me from Montreat to Knoxville where, most importantly, I visited my Dad in the nursing home. The home was located at Maryville, Tennessee. I had the opportunity to take Dad out for an automobile ride a couple of times. We drove around town and stopped to reminisce at various points of mutual pleasure, recalling precious times we enjoyed as a family. A warm and satisfying visit, it proved to be the last time I saw my father in this life. How blessed I have been by a loving and supportive family of parents and siblings! I often wonder how one can stand up to the burdens of this earthly existence without such undergirding.

After the consultation on my way back to rejoin my family at Lubondai, I stopped off for a day or so in Leopoldville occasioned by a contact I had made with an individual who had a Piper Tripacer plane for sale. My friend and colleague, Garland Goodrum, and I were interested in buying it. The value of the American dollar against the Congolese franc was so favorable at the time that we met the price by each one digging up five hundred dollars! Such a bargain was not to be ignored. The man with the plane was quite a character. He was a

Bill Rule with son Paul, 1965.

German pilot, training Congolese soldiers in the art of flying. I don't remember his name but it doesn't matter since I am sure it was an alias and he was a refugee Nazi. I had his money posted to him to a bank in Switzerland. The deal was quickly completed, and I took off for Lubondai by air. It didn't take me long to realize that my Nazi friend had sold me a plane with a defective compass and a nonfunctioning radio! Fortunately the compass trouble didn't show up on my trip home, but the radio never did work.

There was much excitement on the ground as I buzzed the station. Everybody came out to the airstrip to welcome me as I put down. That Tripacer, designated as 90-CIK, came in very handy for the next several years. I used it often for getting quickly from station to station, and because of its presence we were able to open several rural medical clinics for coverage of areas we could never have reached with expediency by auto.

TRIBAL FIGHTING AGAIN

Once more fighting erupted between the Bena Lulua and the Bakete occasioned by the effort of the central government to divide the Kasai Province and create a new *Unite Kasaienne Province* to separate the smaller tribes from the larger Bena Lulua and Baluba. The result was a sort of gerrymander effort which provided a crescent-shaped area, actually larger and more populous than the other two states. The Baluba had originally hoped to annex this territory. The central government moved to prevent them from doing so. The area included the Bakete of the south, then moved west to include the Basala Mpasu, the Bampende and the Batshioke, reached Tshikapa which was to be the provincial capital, then turned north to include Charlesville, Luebo, Mweka, Port Francqui, and all the Bakuba kingdom which was a more isolated group and more awkward to form into an effective government.

The formation of a new province necessarily caused a flurry of excitement. The Bena Lulua at Lubondai saw great opportunity in the situation to push the Bakete back across the Lulua River and they arose to attack. There was only a thin line of Bakete villages west of the Lulua, but they provided Bakete access to the railroad and the tribal leaders sought to protect those villages at all costs. From a military point of view, with the Lulua River at their backs, they were in a vulnerable position, and so the fighting would flare up from time to time during these uneasy years.

The line of demarcation between the two tribes was only ten miles from Lubondai, and we had numerous points of Christian activity in both groups. It happened that Cam Wallace and I chose a day to make the long auto trip to Tshibuaba at the same time the Bakete and Lulua chose to do some fighting. Tshibuaba was far south in Bakete country. It had been an old tobacco curing and packing post deserted by the Belgians, so the church people took it over and turned it into a Christian center with a regional school. I had organized a medical dispensary with a resident nurse in attendance. The work was growing rapidly and we wanted to go and offer encouragement to the church leaders who were running it. Tshimbalanga Moise had been the fine Bakete pastor at Tshimbulu from where he had narrowly escaped with his life, and now he was heading up the work at Kabuabua with excellence.

Cam and I started out on our trip from Lubondai with high hopes of a good day and a good trip, but before we had covered the thirty miles to the railroad, we ran headlong into a large band of Lulua warriors moving north and torching all the Bakete villages as they went. The Bakete had apparently been warned and had fled. We stopped the car, and were surprised by the cordiality with which they received us. When asked where we were going we deemed it wise to make a clean breast of everything, so we told them we were going south to visit Bakete schools and clinics. I fully expected them to turn us around and send us home, but to my surprise they were completely affable and conducted us through their lines, wishing us well upon our way! This is another example of the impossibility of anticipating Congolese attitude in a particular situation. So we proceeded to Tshibuabua for a couple of days of work and observation, but we returned by another route to avoid the fighting.

Some days later I became concerned about a Bakete woman I had delivered by cesarean section. She was about ready to return to her home village and while there had been no overt threats against her during her hospital stay, I was concerned for her safety plus that of the woman helping her with her newborn child. I decided to take them home in my car. The two women with the baby climbed in the backseat and we took off. Just outside the mission station gate I ran into a number of warriors in the roadway. They all had guns over their shoulders.

Among them we happened upon the Chief's son, Ngandu wa Ntolo, and I stopped to consult with him. I told him where I was going and why, and I asked if the way was clear or whether I would run into any trouble. He assured me that everything was okay and to go ahead, so we proceeded without incident to the first of the Bakete villages. All was calm and peaceful. People were sitting around in their yards, and they greeted us with friendly waving of hands and happy smiles. Observing the relaxed atmosphere, the women begged me to continue the several more miles to their home village which I was glad to do, but as we turned a sharp curve and came upon their village area we were shocked to see every hut down both sides of the road furiously burning. I realized in a moment that the Lulua warriors were at the other end of the village and heading north. I certainly did not want to encounter them so I swung my car around and headed back to the village we had passed to warn them. But as I turned I saw a lone soldier standing directly in the road holding a gun. As I faced him he stepped aside and disappeared in the high grasses. I had to pass by him. I didn't want to gun the engine and roar past, but neither did I want to poke along, so I tried to maintain a sedate pace. However, as I drove by there was a loud report in my ear.

I kept moving, not knowing whether I had been hit and the car damaged or my back seat passengers wounded. They were all three on the floor crying at the top of their voices. The soldier either shot into the air to frighten us or he was a very poor marksman since no damage was done except to our nerves.

We raced back to the first village and advised them that soldiers were on the way and they needed to get out as quickly as possible. I also left my passengers with them, and headed back toward Lubondai. I had gone only a few hundred yards when another band of Lulua warriors stepped out of the tropical grass and stopped me. These were Bakwa Tshipanga moving southward. They were bleary-eyed with the marijuana they had been smoking. I knew many of them by name. I was shocked to see they were right on top of an unsuspecting Bakete village, and that between the two groups, one moving south and the other north, the unsuspecting Bakete were in a perilous pincher movement. This new band demanded to know what I had seen down the road, but I wasn't about to tell them of the advancing group of their tribesmen coming northward to meet them.

"Everything is quiet and peaceful," I lied. "The Bakete are not looking for a fight. For the love of God, turn around and go home!"

They gave me a gruff response and told me to get out of there and go on back to Lubondai—which I did! Possibly my entreaty did carry some weight since they did not fight that day but turned around and went home. Much bitterness and enmity was generated by this sort of sporadic fighting, and a number of participants on both sides were killed.

MR. JOBAERT

One day I flew down to Moma where I met Bill Pruitt and he and I made the ninety mile trip by car through rugged back country to visit Mr. A. J. Jobaert at his hideaway home. Mr. Jobaert was an ancient officer of the Belgian army who had lived in Congo for fifty-three years. He had taken only one short vacation to Europe during that span. It was he, with his Congolese troops, who had campaigned in the cannibal country of the Basala Mpasu to bring them under orderly Belgian rule, accomplished but not without casualties. The Basala Mpasu had a strategy of embedding sharp splinters of wood coated with a paste which contained dried bile of the crocodile. Crocodiles eat carrion and a large percentage of them have tetanus spores in the bile. This is generally known by Africans and the gallbladder of the crocodile is greatly feared as strong medicine. Mr. Jobaert's troops campaigned barefooted, and when he recognized that a number of them died with the typical symptoms of tetanus, he guessed the cause and ordered shoes for them from army supplies. Thus shod they proceeded without further mishap and conquered the Basala converting them, eventually, into an orderly political group.

Jobaert was a great hunter and for many years was the game warden in Kasai Province. Mr. Carroll Stegall became one of his close friends and shared with him the gospel message of salvation. Jobaert was converted and Stegall baptized him. Four years prior to our visit, Jobaert, this old soldier, a bachelor recluse in the hinterland he loved so sincerely, suffered a stroke and was left badly paralyzed except for the movement of his head and one arm. Still, he chose to remain where he lived, with his native helpers, expecting to die in the land which had been his home for so long. A renegade political leader had come by two years earlier and made off with most of his earthly possessions including his car, refrigerator, furniture, cooking utensils, and even his bed! We had packed food and clothing to take to him. That morning we worshipped with him and served communion. Tears of gratitude flowed, and he was surely encouraged in his Christian faith by our visit. He did not live much longer, but passed on to an even fairer land.

MEDICAL NEEDS CONTINUE

It had been our hope and expectation to reopen the *infirmier* school at Lubondai, but it was impossible to find well-qualified students for the advanced courses, so we settled for teaching at a lower level of *Garde Malade* (Caretaker of the Sick). This was more on the level of practical nurses. The class began in December and they received a year's training at Lubondai. The following year it became possible to reopen *infirmier* training and these students were reassigned to Bibanga to complete their courses.

During all these times our clinical work was not restricted and it kept us more than busy. I remember an emaciated patient who was brought in with vomiting and dehydration, all the signs of a gastrointestinal obstruction. He was obviously a poor surgical risk, but his only hope was for us to relieve the obstruction. We rehydrated him with IV fluids but at surgery he proved to have a hopelessly extensive cancer of the stomach.

A gastroenterostomy was performed to bypass the obstruction, but his respiration failed and we had to do his breathing for him. We had none of the complex equipment used today for life support, but with a tube in his throat we kept pumping oxygen into his lungs. His heart action remained slow and steady all afternoon so long as we gave him artificial respiration. Time passed and it became necessary to conserve our precious supply of oxygen, so we breathed directly into the tube to keep him going. Nine hours passed and he still did no breathing without our stimulating him.

It was getting on into the evening as I stood by his bedside contemplating the weaknesses of the flesh. How little I knew and how little I could do, after all, to help him. I addressed the Lord in a sort of offhand way, and said, "Of course, Lord, you are not limited. There isn't anything you can't do." And at that moment the patient took a deep inspiration all on his own. I started, and involuntarily I said, "Was that you or him that did that, Lord?" He breathed again, and from there he went on to establish a regular and relatively normal respiration.

After we had returned the patient to the ward, my head medical helper reminded me of the sermon I had given in church the previous Sunday. I had talked about fire falling from heaven in Elijah's day as a demonstration of God's presence and power, and I had pointed out that the God of the Old Testament is not limited or restricted. He is the same today, and His power is the same. We need the fire from heaven to fall upon us in this day and time also. Ilunga said to me, "Doctor, God was just teaching you your own lesson. Fire fell from heaven this evening!" It is good to know that God's fire is still available and that as we work for Him we shall see it!

Then there was the day our children put on the annual Rule Circus, an occasion Billy initiated back during our Bibanga years. Libby was the technical advisor who explained just how things had been done in the past. Barbara was the tightrope walker and the snake charmer. Johnnie was the strong man, the clown, and also doubled for the howling scowling lion! Unfortunately I missed the circus.

Another gastroenterostomy, this time on a woman with a ruptured gastric ulcer and we had to remove a portion of her stomach.

That year, I performed surgery until 1:00 P.M. the day before Christmas! The schedule included a vaginal hysterectomy and repair of a vesico-vaginal fistula.

And there was the time, early in '63, I was finishing up my morning surgical schedule which included a cesarean section plus a total hysterectomy on a mother stricken with cancer of the cervix, when a man was brought in who had been in a fight with his brother. The brother had chopped his head open resulting in two fractures of the skull, and then he had gone to work on his jaw. The lower jaw was almost completely separated and was hanging to one side. He had also been chopped above and below both knees, opening the joints and severing tendons. Besides there were multiple wounds of the chest, back, and arms. I worked on him for three hours, and really have no idea how many sutures we put in that poor guy. We were giving him blood at the same time and were astonished at how well he got along. I am always amazed at the extremity of insults the human body can sometimes weather. I was reminded of the patient a few years earlier who was gored by an elephant. He was disemboweled and all the ribs on one side were completely torn from the sternum. He also lived and recuperated!

DEATH DOTH STING

My father died on July 5, 1963, and four days later the news reached me in the heart of Africa. It was a special day in my life as I went about my busy occupations and felt a warm and precious communion with my dad which I had not felt before. He never in his whole life traveled for any distance outside of the eastern United States, but he had followed me to Africa many times in his mind's eye. Still, he had never seen or visited or experienced the people, places, and practices which were part of my daily missionary life. He would have loved being a participant, and now the gulf was bridged and I felt his presence in a very special way.

This is the letter I wrote to my mother that same day:

Lubondai, July 9, '63

Dearest Mother,

Your telegram arrived this morning. I was in the operating room and had just finished my big case for the morning. Charlene Halverstadt came over from Luluabourg for a committee meeting and brought the telegram to me. Of course the news did not come as a great surprise or shock as we have realized that Dad was in a rather precarious condition for months now. But it took no less adjustment to realize that one's father to whom one has looked with admiration and confidence for council and aid for more than fifty years, is now no longer an inhabitant of this mortal vale.

I have been extremely busy all day, but Dad's presence has seemed more close and real than it ever has before here in Africa. I realize that he has now bridged the many miles that have separated us; that he has visited us and watched us and enjoyed the experience. I also am comforted by the realization that he is no longer feeble and handicapped. He no longer has a heart block or mental confusion. Even the days that I knew him, at the height of his mental and physical vigor, are not to be compared to his present status, for he has entered into the perfection of the Eternal and I am happy and contented with him.

So this evening it is to you back at home, who have been left behind, that my thoughts turn; and my prayer for you is that a loving Heavenly Father will bless you and fill your loneliness and hurt with all the sweet balm of his presence and his fellowship. I have thought of you and of Gunby, who has had to bear so much of the responsibility and burden of this experience, one in which I should have shared with him. I have thought of Barbara and of the probability that she is still with you and of the peace and strength which I know that her quiet efficient presence lends. I have thought too of young Bill and of the possibility that you called him from camp and that he was there to represent the African family. My love comes with this to you all. How I could wish that the good Lord might have seen fit to let me be with you at this time, but I do not question his ways.

When I got home for lunch I gathered the children at the table and told them the news. I thought that perhaps Johnnie would be the least affected, remembering his Knoxville days with a blurring of memory, but he was the first to burst into tears. Barbara too had to be comforted by her Daddy. Then we had prayers together remembering you all and thanking God for Poppy and for all that he has meant to us, remembering that he is so really a part of each one of us.

I am very grateful to God tonight for the Dad that he gave me. I remember the honesty and the purity of his character. I remember his gentle spirit of love, exhibited in the home, first for you and for each of the children. I remember his unselfishness, and that he was always more willing to give than to receive. He was never grasping or self-assertive in his dealings with men. He truly practiced the Golden Rule. Mostly I am grateful for his Christian faith and that he sought to make the Lord Jesus the center of being for us all. I shall miss his presence when I return home again. But I shall join him again some day in a fairer home, and enjoy him again, forever.

God bless you, my dear, and keep you in the hollow of his hand. I love you too—very, very, very much!

Bill

In October of 1963 we reopened the school for *infirmiers* (inactive for two years) at Lubondai. Ten students were admitted, all of whom had completed three years of secondary school, so it was a well-qualified class. They came to us from various parts of Kasai Province, representing several different tribes. We felt this was a real encouragement. At the time Effie and I were both up to our chins with teaching. The *Menagere* school (home economics) had been dumped in Effie's lap, and she lay awake nights figuring out how she could teach and demonstrate cooking, sewing, and other homemaking skills. My teaching program would have been an impossibility if it had not been for the presence of Dr. Hodel at Lubondai. Paul labored long and hard with an unreasonably heavy hospital load plus a valiant effort to surmount the language barrier. I was freed to do the necessary teaching chores, and his wife, Barbara, also helped us in the operating room and in the pharmacy where she processed and reassembled large quantities of sample drugs we had received from concerned groups in the home church.

This was also the fall that we in Africa heard the news of the assassination of President John Kennedy. We were shocked and grieved, and myriads of our African friends came around to offer their condolences.

Our last Christmas at Lubondai, where we had so many happy previous ones, eventually rolled around. Christmas sort of creeps up on your blind side in the Congo. There is little to engender Christmas sentiment or Christmas cheer until almost too late. No snow, no ice. Not even blustery weather. No downtown decorations. No shops crammed with Christmas merchandise. No Salvation Army Santas on street corners. No Christmas spectaculars on radio and television. No, Christmas all but arrives unannounced and unanticipated as it did that first Christmas long ago. Meanwhile activities on an African mission station maintain a certain

William Rule Jr.

humdrum normalcy until the day finally arrives at which time the momentum suddenly shifts into a higher gear. Native groups come around singing Christmas carols. Children of our family are up at daybreak to see what the contents of dangling stockings might be, and to squeal over inventions that pondering parents have thought up to fill a gap. But all this activity is suspended when it is time for church service because Christmas in Africa brings a warm and worthwhile feeling that it is not so much a holiday as a genuine holy day.

MILESTONE SIX
EXPANDING THE
MEDICAL MINISTRY

"And Jesus went about all the cities and villages, teaching in their synagogues, and preaching the gospel of the kingdom, and healing every sickness and every disease among the people" (Matthew 9:35).

17 MEDICAL MISSIONS MIGHTY THROUGH GOD

For the weapons of our warfare are not carnal, but mighty through God, to the pulling down of strongholds; casting down imaginations, and every high thing that exalts itself against the knowledge of God, and bringing into captivity every thought to the obedience of Christ (2 Corinthians 10:4–5).

One of the most important concepts which must be understood and accepted about mission programs and mission activity is that the perspective is constantly changing. Mission is not a static situation. Policies and methods must repeatedly be examined and updated. The work remains always in a state of flux. It must be versatile and adaptable in order to meet the needs and capture the attention of a changing people.

As a small boy I wanted to be a medical missionary to Africa, and in the providence of God this desire was realized. I never changed. For twenty years I prepared myself for this goal. I concerned myself with all that I could learn about Africa. I read books and talked to and corresponded with missionaries to Africa. But when I finally reached the mission field I was amazed to find that some of my information and ideas were twenty years out of date! I had completely overlooked the factor of cultural change and advancement. I thought I was going to be a pioneer missionary, but I was a generation too late! So don't be static in your concept of missions. The work is not the same now as it was twenty years ago, and it won't be the same twenty years hence. It is not the *gospel* which changes. That is the good news which comes to us from God and it is the same yesterday, today, and forever. But our modes and methods for presenting it must repeatedly change to keep pace with the times.

With the updating there come new needs for new gimmicks, materials, and other accoutrements with which to do the job. How often have I realized there in the heart of Africa that a particular piece of medical apparatus or surgical instrument or recently discovered medication, if available, might be the difference between success and failure— between life and death. I have been tempted to discouragement

189

because some material tool I desperately needed was not available, and on such occasions I learned to turn to a particular verse of promise in the Bible which encouraged and sustained me on many occasions.

> For the weapons of our warfare are not carnal, but mighty through God, to the pulling down of strongholds; casting down imaginations, and every high thing that exalts itself against the knowledge of God, and bringing into captivity every thought to the obedience of Christ (2 Corinthians 10:4–5).

After all, the weapons of our Christian warfare are not carnal, or material. They are not utensils we manipulate with our hands or see with our eyes. They are primarily spiritual in nature, and with them we are mighty through God. If we will permit Him, God can take the things we do or have in our hands to perform with them better than we can imagine.

ILUNGA TSHIKELE

The Medal Chief Tshikele was paramount chief over all of the area near our Lubondai mission station, but he lived near the Catholic mission, Hemptinne. The priests had built him quite a pretentious brick house with a metal roof, and they had acclaimed his village as a uniquely Catholic village. Tshikele never had been a particular friend of the Protestant constituency. He had never allowed any of the Protestant evangelists to locate in his adjacent villages, but when his eldest son Buadi was old enough to go off to school, he chose to attend our school at Lubondai. Several months passed before the Catholics awoke to what had happened, and then they went to Chief Tshikele and expressed their disapproval. The chief sent word to Lubondai for Buadi to come home and attend the Catholic school. The boy dutifully returned.

A year or so later the chief's second son, Ilunga, completed the primary grades taught in the local village, and faced the decision to pursue further education. He too chose to go to Lubondai. He was able to complete his studies and receive his diploma, at which point I took him into the hospital as a student nurse. The Catholics had not realized all this time that the boy had come to us, and again they went to the chieftain about it. Again Tshikele sent word for his son to come home, but Ilunga respectfully replied in the negative. He explained that he was happy with his life at Lubondai, that he had made a public profession of faith and joined the church, and that he was presently engaged in medical training which interested him very much. Of course Tshikele was not happy to be refused by his son, and he publicly expressed his displeasure and anger. So for some time that was how things stood.

Then word came that the old chieftain was not well. He had a lingering illness and seemed to be slowly going downhill. Ilunga was concerned about his father and urged him to come to Lubondai for examination and treatment. In spite of the differences which existed between them, the old chief finally responded to his son's urging and he presented himself for a physical exam. As I went over him I was amazed to find that he was in a far advanced stage of pulmonary tuberculosis. There was very little that could be done for him, as this was before the days of specific antitubercular medications. We put him on a well-rounded, nutritious diet and administered vitamins in large quantities. We built him a small thatch hut just to one side of the hospital to save his having to walk or be carried for his treatments. But there was little improvement of his general condition and after a month or so he chose to return to his village to live out his remaining days.

Finally the message came to Ilunga that his father was dying. Ilunga asked for time off so he could go be with him. Every day we expected to hear of the chief's death, but about a week later I received a note from Ilunga. He reported that his father was very weak and miserable but still alive. "If you could possibly do so," he wrote, "it would please my father and it would please our people for you to come and pay him a visit to see if there is anything else you can do for him." I was not in the habit of making thirty-five-mile house calls, but here was a situation which might be strategic for the work of God's kingdom. I prayed for guidance and the conviction grew that I should go.

In the evening, after completing my day's work, I drove to the village where I found Chief Tshikele on the ground, propped against the side of his house. A large crowd of his village people were standing by, quiet and respectful. He could scarcely speak to me because of the congestion. I listened to his chest; it was the site of massive cavitation. I gave him an injection to ease his constant cough, and I left a potion with Ilunga to administer by mouth. As I worked I talked to him about his soul's salvation, prayed with him, and got up to leave. But as I moved away he held up his hand to stop me and, clearing his throat and with extra effort he spoke to his assembled people.

"I have never been a friend of the church at Lubondai. I have never allowed their evangelists to live and work in our villages. In spite of this the doctor has tried to help me. He has come all the way over here tonight and has given me medicine and prayed with me. Now what I want to say to you, my people, is this: don't refuse the message of the mission. Invite them to come. Listen to what they have to say, for they want to be our friends and help us."

By the following week we had placed evangelists in three or four of Tshikele's villages, and they have worked there among those people from that time to today. But that is not the end of the story. Back at Lubondai I expected to hear of the old chief's demise within a matter of hours, but he didn't die. He improved. In fact he lived for another year. Ilunga came back to work, and a year later, to the very month, his father became desperately ill once again. Ilunga went to be with him, and again he wrote asking me to come, and again I responded. This time the old chief was not in the village, but his retinue had rigged a crude sort of isolation. They led me for a quarter of a mile through the forest to a small hut, where the sick man was huddled beside an evening fire. I examined him again and, if possible, he was in a more critical condition than I had found him a year earlier. Once again I treated him as best I could to make him comfortable, and once again I reminded him of the saving grace of the Lord Jesus, and once again I prayed with him.

It was yet several months before the old chief finally succumbed to the ravages of his pulmonary disease. Ilunga had demonstrated his respect and affection for his father, and he had faithfully attended and ministered to him during his long drawn-out affliction. Chief Tshikele had recognized and appreciated this loyalty, and before his death he named Ilunga to succeed him in the chieftainship of the tribe. As Ilunga prepared to leave us at Lubondai, he attended Sunday worship as was his custom, and during the service he stood to wish his friends farewell and to ask for their prayers. He opened his Bible and read the prayer of young King Solomon, making it his own for the occasion: "O Lord my God, you have made your servant king in place of [Tshikele] David my father, although I am but a little child; I do not know how to go out or come in. And your servant is in the midst of your people whom you have chosen, a great people, that cannot be numbered or counted for multitude. Give your servant, therefore, an understanding mind to govern your people, that I may discern between good and evil; for who is able to govern this your great people?"

It so happened that these events took place in Africa just at the time that President Franklin Roosevelt died and Harry S. Truman was sworn in as the new chief executive in the United States. Mr. Truman quoted the same biblical passage at his inauguration, and one of our missionaries wrote to the president, bringing to his attention that both the president of a mighty nation and the chief of a small African clan were each looking to the same source for the wisdom and strength for their task. Mr. Truman sent a fine leatherbound Bible to Chief Ilunga, and inscribed on the title page: "To Chief Ilunga Andre from Harry S. Truman, President of the United States of America." Truly, the weapons of our warfare are mighty through God—*to the pulling down of strongholds*!

KOKESHA ALBERT

Kokesha Albert had served for years in the *Force Publique*, a combination national guard and standing army of the Belgian Congo. He had lived a rough life. Never married, he had taken his pleasures where he found them, and he had been moved from pillar to post. The time finally came for his retirement from active military service and he was heaped with retirement gifts by the army which included a warm blanket, shoes, raincoat, and other clothing, as well as a cash bonus in hand. He began to wend his way homeward to a village near our Bibanga mission station.

Kokesha's relatives and enlarged family heard he had returned and they descended upon him bringing greetings, and also to each get his or her share of the good things he brought with him. The great problem was that Kokesha had more relatives than he had gifts, and he was quickly divested of all his separation benefits. But still relatives came, arriving late, and they found no gifts for their greetings, and they were incensed! They expressed their anger, saying: "All right, you have not counted our family relationship as anything of value—to be guarded and protected—so we will get even with you. We are going to make medicine against you and it will eat your life away!"

These are devastating words in the Congo culture, and they strike terror to the mind and heart to which they are directed. The angry relatives drove two stout stakes into the front yard of Kokesha's hut and the significance of this act was not lost upon him. He knew this meant that when the stakes decomposed and wasted away, so, too, would he die. Quickly he pulled them up from the ground, wiped them clean and covered them with protective wrapping and kept them in his house where they could be carefully guarded. But, as fate would have it, another crisis beset him. He began having epileptic seizures. Of course he was convinced that these were the result of the curse put on him.

Kokesha came to me at the Bibanga hospital literally frightened to death over what appeared to be happening to him. He brought the stakes to show me and asked in imploring accents if there was anything I could do for him. I tried to level with him. "Kokesha," I said, "I don't know much about the medicine in those stakes nor how much power they might have, but I do know this: no matter how powerful they are, I have something that is stronger and greater. I have the power of the Lord Jesus Christ." And so saying, I told him the story of salvation and concluded by inviting him to come and let me treat him for his seizures. I assured him that if he would be patient and persevere with me, I felt sure I could help him. I put him on daily

medications which we insisted on administering ourselves to be sure
he was getting the correct amounts at the right intervals, and so his
convulsive attacks were brought under control. But since this treatment might take months and perhaps years, Kokesha needed an
occupation with income to provide for himself. I gave him odd jobs
around the hospital and discovered that he was an exceptionally diligent and able worker. His years in the army corps had provided him
with gifts of initiative and forcefulness. He had learned to set himself
to an assigned task until it was completed, and this placed him in a
cadre considerably above the ordinary worker. I found myself leaning
on him, more and more depending on him.

Once Kokesha wanted to take a journey of several days to another
part of the country. He was afraid I would not agree to this since it
would interrupt his treatment, but he wanted to go so much that he
didn't consult me but simply struck out, AWOL. While he was away he
had one of his convulsive seizures, the first in a long time. He came to
me to humbly confess his infraction and the results. He never missed
another medication, and he never had another convulsion.

Kokesha got his life straightened out in many good ways. He made
a profession of faith and joined the church. He found a steady Christian
widow who caught his attention, and we helped him accumulate the
dowry necessary to marry her. They were united in Christian wedlock.
I'm not going to say that Kokesha was the greatest Christian I have ever
known. Like the rest of us, he had his faults and he made his mistakes.
But I will say that he came out of one of the least conducive backgrounds into a full and joyful faith which enriched his life, and I shall
always be grateful for the honor that was mine of interacting with him
as my Christian brother.

In 1954, when our family was instructed by the mission to leave
Bibanga and return to serve at Lubondai. I called Kokesha to say good-
bye and to wish him well. "Oh no!" He said, "I'll go with you." I
explained to him that wasn't a good idea. We would be in an entirely
different part of the country, inhabited by different tribal people. I told
him he ought to stay right there at Bibanga. But this didn't suit Kokesha
at all, and since I wouldn't take him, he and his wife set out for
Lubondai on their own. He established himself there, found a job on
the mission compound, and when we arrived as a family a few weeks
later, Kokesha was a member of the welcoming committee and helped
escort us to our new home! Thus I had several more years of daily
association with this very special friend of mine in the bonds of
Christian fellowship. How true it is that the weapons of our warfare are
mighty through God—*casting down imaginations, and every high thing
that exalts itself against the knowledge of God.*

MUKEBA ANDRE

Pastor Mukeba Andre was our dedicated and godly pastor at Bibanga. I sat under his ministry and was blessed by his Christian leadership for a number of years. His influence was quite profound on many members of the church family in the Bibanga area.

I recall going with him on a weekend of itineration where we arrived in a village on a Saturday afternoon prior to our conducting the Sunday morning service. Mukeba told me he had a Christian friend nearby who ran a village *magasin* or outpost store, and he was sending a man on a bicycle to tell him of the Sunday worship so he could join us. In due time the man on the bike returned with a note from the storekeeper expressing his disappointment that he was not able to attend. With the note he enclosed quite a handsome offering for the collection plate. Mukeba understood that his friend was on the horns of a dilemma: Sunday was a prime day for commercial activity. The friend anticipated too good a financial opportunity to miss by closing his doors to go to church. So Pastor Mukeba put the money back in the envelope and wrote the following note: "God doesn't want your money. God wants YOU." The bike courier delivered the note to the weak church member, and the next morning he was present, sitting on the front row. This little episode shows something of the character of Pastor Mukeba Andre.

But Mukeba developed an illness and he came to the hospital for help. He had become weak and listless with no appetite. He had lost weight and had begun to have all sorts of vague aches and pains. A careful physical examination and a checkup with all the laboratory work at our command revealed nothing. Medications were given to eliminate the possibility of malaria or intestinal parasites as the problem. We gave him special feeding formulas with nutritional value and vitamins in adequate amounts, but he did not improve. Finally I sent him to the doctors over at the Bakwanga diamond mines where they were better equipped with X-ray facilities. They submitted him to another battery of tests but nothing showed up. Then a very strange thing occurred when suddenly Pastor Mukeba broke out with an eruption over his entire body. It was the most acute example of lepromatous leprosy I ever saw during all my years in Africa.

Later I had occasion to pass through Bakwanga where Mukeba was hospitalized, and I went by to see him. He was in excruciating pain. Usually we think of leprosy causing an anaesthesia since nerve fibers are deadened, but before this occurs the fibers may be the seat of inflammation which is extremely painful. I was distressed to see his discomfort and I expressed my sympathy and tried to encourage him, reminding him of the higher power to which we can turn in over-whelming trouble. We prayed together. I bid him farewell and departed, never again to see my friend in this world. But before he died he sent me a letter, thanking me for coming to visit him and telling me how much it had meant to him.

"But the main reason I am writing to you," he said, "is because I am worried about the state of mind I presented to you when you were here the other day. I was in pain and was discouraged, and I'm afraid I gave you the impression that I had doubts about the goodness of God's hand upon me. I don't want you to think that. It's not true at all. I say to you in all sincerity, if it is God's will for me to have leprosy then I know that it is good that I have leprosy!" The weapons of our warfare are mighty through God—*bringing into captivity every thought to the obedience of Christ.*

18 THE TEACHING PRIORITY

And the things that thou hast heard of me among many witnesses, the same commit thou to faithful men, who shall be able to teach others also (2 Timothy 2:2).

As the difficulties of independence passed into history and the United Nations military force moved out of Congo, missionary families returned to again take up the thread of their missionary activities. The leaders of the church sat down to evaluate the situation of the moment and to discuss effective directions for the future. We in the medical field set our vision to the years ahead, looking for answers to some long-range questions. What would we like to see in the advancement of our medical work during the next five years? The next ten? The next twenty-five? Where were we going with the medical program? Where would we like to go? What was the Lord calling us to do?

Surveying the field with its many needs and limitations brought us back again and again to the conclusion that health care and mainte-nance in the Congo would never be adequately met by expatriate missionary effort. The final solution to the problem rested with the people of the land. We could double our medical missionary force, or triple or quadruple it, but we would still be playing around on the fringes of the gigantic need. More and more the conviction came to us that our real priority should be to multiply our roles among the indigenous peoples of the land; to transmit our knowledge, our skills, our zeal, our faith, into the minds and hearts of African students who would eventually mature and transmit in like manner. Of course this predicated a teaching program, and teaching required a school facility, and a school meant concentration of personnel for administration and instruction.

This position met with both approval and opposition. Concentration of medical personnel would mean the withdrawal of professional help in isolated areas. Missionaries were concerned about possible accidents or sick children. The Africans reminded us of their limited means of transportation. The sick had to travel many miles to the nearest hospital. This was the short, immediate view. But we had to recognize the long view—the hope for permanent health care improvement throughout the land. This perforce would mean the formation of a growing cadre of competent professionals to do the teaching job.

There was only one other medical doctor besides myself in the territory of Dibaya, which would be comparable to a county in the United States with perhaps a population of 175,000. One could travel 85 miles to the city of Luluabourg and find three or four more doctors. Then 150 miles to Bakwanga, 200 miles to Tshikapa, and no telling how far south into the Katanga Province to find another doctor. The previous year at Lubondai station we had performed over two hundred major operations, and while this is no large number by U.S. standards, it is quite a load for our staff which must handle everything else including administration and teaching. I was seeing over one hundred patients a week in my prenatal clinic. A day never passed that we did not see patients coming to us from Luluabourg by train, by automobile, by bike, or on foot.

Use of a light plane made it possible to extend our services for hundreds of miles which would have taken us several days in any direction by car. I could attend to the needs at the hospital in the morning, fly fifty miles and visit a rural dispensary during the afternoon, and be back home for supper with my family. Dr. Mark Poole had inaugurated this sort of medical service at Bulape. He had been so successful that others of us were prompted to follow his example. I had earlier established a dispensary at Kasonga across the Lulua River from Lubondai, among the Babindi people, and we had a fine work going there plus an active church. It was impossible to reach them by car without driving all the way to Luluabourg or to Hemptinne to cross the river. We cleared a dirt air strip and I was there in minutes. Another dispensary at Tshibuabua among the Bakete was also a fine work. These two posts were manned entirely by Congolese *infirmiers*. We also served the needs of our two mission stations in the southwest, Kasha and Moma. In all of these places smallpox was still encountered, and our flights were often made to vaccinate thousands of people against a disease which was eventually eliminated all over the world.

URBAN RELOCATION OF THE IMCK

Independence in the Congo did not bring a cessation of tribal conflict. It just temporarily transferred the scene of action from military maneuvers to the field of politics. Most of our Baluba constituency had been eliminated from Lubondai and there was a mounting feeling that they should not be allowed to return as students enrolled in the IMCK.

Late in 1962 when it was generally learned that we would be reopening the school the following year, I was waited upon by a delegation of three church leaders from the local village speaking to me in the name of adjoining villages, the Bakwa Tshipanga. They recounted some of their grievances related to the IMCK. It seemed that only one or two of their number had ever been admitted to the school, and we had flunked them out. So, there were no Bakwa Tshipanga graduates of IMCK—a school which had existed for six or eight years right in their midst! They had come to tell me they wanted the majority of the students in the school to be young people from their clan. They told me they didn't want to be unreasonable about it and we might take in a few from other tribes, but from here on out the majority of graduates of IMCK should be Bakwa Tshipanga.

Our exchange was gentle and without rancor. I pointed out to them that the students were chosen by competitive examinations and, to date, the local boys and girls had not been well enough prepared in their basic studies to successfully compete with students from other areas. I suggested that their concern should be with upgrading their local primary and secondary schools. I gently explained that the means of entry would not be changed, and that we envisioned the school serving the whole nation and we would hopefully receive students from all regions. They did not back away from their position nor I from mine, and we thanked each other and concluded the meeting.

From time to time the mission had discussed the advisability of moving the school from a rural to an urban location. One point in favor was increased accessibility, but perhaps a more important consideration was that over the long haul the school and an adjunctive hospital would come closer to self support in a metropolitan center. Now since the ugly head of tribal coercion had been raised, it seemed to me the die was cast. We must move.

Luluabourg was our obvious destination. The Provincial capital boasted a large modern airport, railroad, and intersecting roads which fanned in all directions. It was a rapidly growing city approaching a population of two hundred thousand. We joined with the Congolese church leaders in seeking facilities which might be converted into a school and eventually accommodate a teaching hospital. We approached the government to see if they would be willing to turn over an old one-story vacant hotel which was located on the main square of town. We had no idea where funds would come from to accomplish such a venture, but at least we were investigating and gathering information. At first our request was favorably received and for a while it looked like they might cede the property to us. We even began to clean up the place and to lay out plans for utilizing the space. But then the government decided to make it the headquarters for their own Board of Education, which function it still serves today.

One of the elders of the church who worked with us on this project most faithfully was Mr. Bitema Jean. I mention his name to give him the full credit he is due since I consider that he, perhaps more than any other member of the church, is responsible for the excellent location of the IMCK today. Bitema was indefatigable in going from government office to government office, sitting patiently for hours while waiting to put in a good word for the placement of IMCK at Luluabourg. He was the one who finally brought word from the governor that they were willing to talk turkey.

Bitema was trained at Mutoto as one of our nursing aides, and from there went to work for Belgian doctors. When independence came in 1960, there were vacant government offices everywhere and no trained personnel to fill them. Grammar school graduates and relative illiterates were thrust into positions of solemn responsibility which they were utterly incapable of filling. This was the number one tragedy of the new Republic of Congo. Bitema was named the director of the city hospital's clinical laboratory and, while he had few skills and little training for the job, he was at least sincere and honest and the lab continued to rock along performing the tests which had long been practiced. As time passed, workers began to arrive with college educations the original job occupants began to find their jobs threatened. Many were dismissed from noteworthy positions with no place to go.

As we sought a location for the school, a series of truly miraculous events occurred which broadened our horizons and brought us exciting new hopes. As I have looked back at that period of time through the years, my heart has continued to stand amazed at the mighty hand of God as He intervened on our behalf. I have known miracles in my life on numerous occasions when God has answered prayer in marvelous ways, but these days were certainly the pinnacle of my personal experience.

The first one occurred in March 1964 when the provincial government at Luluabourg advised us they would be willing to turn over to us an abandoned school at Tshikaji as the site for the IMCK. It was Bitema Jean who came with the news, and on March 27 I journeyed from Lubondai to Luluabourg where Bill Washburn and I, along with several dignitaries of the African church, were invited to dinner with the governor of the province plus some members of his cabinet. They told us that the Tshikaji

An aerial view of Luluabourg, 1952.

campus was rapidly falling into deterioration and destruction from vandalism and looting, and the value and usefulness of the location was threatened. Therefore they offered to give us full title to the property if we would move our school to Luluabourg and there establish the course for *Infirmier Diplome.*

Tshikaji is about eight miles from downtown Luluabourg. The campus was established by the Belgian government for instruction of the sons of village and tribal chieftains. Practically speaking, these boys and young men would advance, by inheritance, into positions of governmental responsibility, so it was logical to train them at an early age. Since they were sons of the African royalty, the school was more imposing than most. It was completed and began its teaching program in the late 1950s, but when independence occurred in 1960, all the teachers in the school left the country. It had not functioned since.

So now what were we to do? The government had called our hand. They had offered us a school site which would obviously require considerable renovation and repair before we could begin a year of teaching, and we had absolutely no funds. Would we simply thank them and turn down their generous offer? How we agonized and prayed over this question!

Then came the second miracle! Out of the blue we received an unexpected message. The First Presbyterian Church in Winston-Salem,

North Carolina, wanted to make us a present of $27,392.00! A completely unrestricted gift. We could use it any way we saw fit. We got down on our knees to thank the Lord for this wonderful blessing; then we rose and went to the governor saying if he meant business so did we. To underline our position we said, "If you give us the property today, we'll go to work on it tomorrow!" The governor was impressed, and the deal was completed.

Now it was time for action if we were going to be able to open a new school year at Tshikaji in October. In late May, Garland Goodrum and I made a trip in the mission plane to Salisbury, Southern Rhodesia, where we indulged in an unrestrained shopping spree for equipment and furnishings for the new school. We bought cots and mattresses, metal lockers, bedside tables for the dorm rooms; twenty desks for each of four classrooms; dining room tables, chairs, dishes and cutlery, and kitchen utensils; a diesel generator for lights; 1,200 panes of glass for windows plus a ton of putty; wood-burning stoves for the central kitchen and each of the faculty residences; metal shelves for the library; and a new pump to hoist water from a stream in the valley to the reservoir tower in the middle of the station to supply our running water. We rented an enclosed freight car, locked our purchases in it, and headed it for Luluabourg. Then we flew home.

However, there was yet a big ugly fly in the ointment. The government had ceded Tshikaji to us but it was occupied by Congolese soldiers and their families. Even the governor was restrained in his dealings with armed soldiers. He could give us the property, but getting the residents relocated was our problem! We too were aware that we must be circumspect and diplomatic as we dealt with the matter.

July rolled around and the class of first year student nurses we had admitted to the reopened IMCK at Lubondai had completed their first year of studies. The time was also at hand for the Rule family to think about their own vacation, and it occurred to me that we might spend it at Tshikaji. This would at least remind the incumbent soldiers that we now considered it our domain and were making plans for early occupation. I hesitantly posed this vacation possibility to my good wife, rather expecting a categorical veto. But I was belittling the stuff she's made of. She recognized the strategy involved and promptly agreed. So we piled the kids who were still at home into a truck and we made for Tshikaji.

The Tshikaji campus comprised an area of approximately twenty hectares, or about fifty acres. Included in this area were eighteen permanent buildings with walls and roofs in good condition, an administration building, a central kitchen and dining hall, two student dormitories, two classroom complexes with six classrooms each, and ten residences for faculty. Most of the doors were gone and all the windows had been knocked out. Much of the plumbing was broken. But we recognized that this was a fabulous gift which had been offered to us outright, and which we could not have duplicated for many hundreds of thousands of dollars.

In July of 1964 when we arrived, the place was in a sad state of repair. The entire campus was grown up head high with tropical grass and through it were only winding trails between the houses. Soldiers and their families were in all the living spaces that were anywhere near respectable. We looked at a residence off to one side which was in a worse state of deterioration than the others because even the Africans had shunned it, and we appropriated it for our two-week "camp out."

The house was in such filthy condition that I hired two or three water carriers from the nearby village, and we scrubbed down the place with abundant soap and water medicated with lysol. Then we set up our cots and mosquito nets, draped the empty window frames, and barricaded the doors for the night. Since there were no kitchen facilities we put our folding table and chairs on the front porch and cooked over an open fire in the front yard.

I set to organizing a work line of laborers, and we began to clear off the landscape, cutting down the high grass and marking off straight pathways plus wider roads to allow access for cars and trucks. This afforded conveniences for the resident soldiers as well, so that they tolerated our presence and activities with a sort of detached amusement.

However, I was considerably disturbed by one of their activities. The Congolese military, moving continually and on short notice, cook their meals over a round-handled iron stove which is about the shape and size of a water bucket. It is called a *babula*. The fire in it is fueled with coal or charcoal which they either buy or prepare themselves. The soldiers here were cutting down all the trees on the compound to make charcoal. The process is to stack wood and cover it loosely with dirt and clay so that, fired from beneath, oxygen is limited and the wood burns incompletely. Thus charcoal is formed. It was apparent to me that all the lovely trees which had been planted by the Belgians would soon be fed into the maws of the multiple *babulas*. It became more urgent to vacate the squatters.

A THIRD MIRACLE

The third miraculous intervention related to the political activities. On June 30, 1964, the United Nations concluded their four years of military occupation in the Congo and withdrew all their troops. This afforded an unhampered arena in which various Congolese groups could vie for power and authority. After his training in terrorist tactics in Communist China, Pierre Mulele had returned to his homeland of the Kwango-Kwilu districts and had organized the bully youth groups called *Jeunesse* whose pillaging and destructive forays had terrorized the countryside. In January they attacked the Baptist Mid-Missions station of Manungu and murdered Irene Ferrel, a single lady missionary. To the northeast, General Nicholas Olenga had organized his Simba army and was rapidly overrunning Stanleyville where many more were soon to die. Seeking to shore up its bulwarks and to present a united front to these rebel campaigns, the central government invited its chief opponent, Moise Tshiombe, of the breakaway Katanga Province, to come to Leopoldville and become prime minister. Tshiombe had accepted. So this was the general political picture at the time our plans to occupy Tshikaji were coming to a head.

The Mulelists were pushing northeastward while the Simbas moved in a southwest direction. If the two could join forces they would effectively cut the Republic of Congo in two. Tshiombe would be separated from his own home territory in the Katanga and the central government would surely fall. The midpoint between these two advances and the destination for unification was Luluabourg. Naturally our attention was divided as we kept one eye on developments at Tshikaji and the other on the ominous national scene.

The Simbas were having more success and moving more rapidly than the Mulelists. They advanced into the Batatele country, the seat of the missionary endeavors of our Methodist brethren, and provoked a general exodus of all the missionaries except for six men at Wembo Nyama whom they held as hostages. When our dear friend Burleigh Law flew in to the station to see if he could help with evacuation, they shot and killed him. From there they advanced on to Lusambo, crossed the Sankuru River, and they moved relentlessly toward Luluabourg. Their radio messages to the white population of the city were reassuring: "Don't run. Everything's going to be all right. We'll be there in a day or two, but we're not going to hurt you." Reassuring? Councils of strategy were held. Rolling stock was checked to be sure it was roadworthy at a moment's notice. And through all of this we proceeded with our plans to occupy Tshikaji and begin a new school year within a month or six weeks!

One reason for the continued military successes of the rebel contingent was the widespread propaganda that the Simbas had an invincible "medicine" which made them immune to enemy bullets. The government troops accepted this wholeheartedly and they were deathly afraid of the rebels. At the first encounter, the government soldiers would turn tail and run. The invaders were now only a day's journey from Luluabourg, and there must be some sort of show of opposition. Local troops were piled into a line of trucks and started forth on the road to Lusambo. Some forty miles after departure, at the village of Mutombo Dibwe where there was a sharp turn in the road, they swung around it and came face to face with a line of vehicles bringing the Simbas to them. They were upon each other before they knew it, and there was no line of retreat as trucks in the rear were bearing down and blocking the way. There was nothing to do but open fire and, wonder of wonders, the government troops began to see rebels falling! Their "medicine" was not working after all, and the state combatants pushed their attack with a shout. The rebels were forced to retreat back across the Sankuru to Lusambo, and even here their supply lines were so long and vulnerable that they began a slow withdrawal toward Stanleyville. Luluabourg and the Kasai country were delivered from invasion. We were free from imminent danger and could continue our efforts to occupy Tshikaji. God had provided us with this third miracle!

A few weeks later the welcome news arrived that Dr. Henry Nelson and his nurse-wife, Katie, were on their way from furlough in the U.S., and would be available to replace us in the hospital work at Lubondai. This meant I was now free to go and settle at Tshikaji and get ready for the October opening of school—*if* I could get the soldiers out!

OCCUPYING TSHIKAJI

I loaded a truck with schoolbooks, didactic material, and school furniture and made my way to Tshikaji. Upon arrival I sent a peremptory message to the sergeant-in-charge advising him that the doctor had come and was ready to take up his abode at Tshikaji. While waiting for his answer, I busied myself with unloading the truck. Shortly a reply came that they were vacating one side of a house for me. Well, at least that was getting a foot in the door, and I quickly moved into the space allocated to me. It was the largest residence on the compound, and originally a dwelling for two families. My quarters, here again, required vigorous scrubbing, and as I mopped I surreptitiously sloshed some of the soapy suds under the door which separated me from the adjoining occupants. My suds were liberally mixed with lysol and the strong odor soon permeated the entire house. Less than an hour later I was informed that the other occupants were leaving and had abandoned the entire place! I have no idea what they thought the "medicine" I was using on them would do, but it worked the trick!

The soldiers were still occupying most of Tshikaji station, and the date to open the school and receive boarding students was drawing nearer and nearer. We went to the colonel who commanded troops at Luluabourg and presented him with our dilemma, but he simply countered that he had no other lodgings wherewith to billet his men. A week went by while we spun our wheels, and then on September 10 the colonel sent word that he had found facilities for relocation but had no rolling stock to transport them. We jumped at the opportunity, telling him we would move the Tshikaji squatters for him!

Garland Goodrum came with a second truck from Luluabourg, and late in the day we began loading soldiers and their families and earthly possessions. It seemed to us that we loaded dozens of huge sacks of charcoal per family on the trucks. It took a long time for the people to pack their belongings and corral scattered children, chickens, and goats, and squeeze as many as possible on a truckload. Night caught us and arrangements proceeded even slower in the dark. Garland and I made our first trip and returned for a second. Then a third was necessary. We worked until well after midnight, completely worn out from helping to hoist heavy loads and then unload at the point of destination. But it wasn't fatigue which gave us the most concern. There was a considerable risk factor involved in transporting armed soldiers. Each had a rifle slung over his shoulder, and in the darkness they could be challenged at any moment by sentries who didn't know whether they were friend or foe. Our route circumvented the Luluabourg airport where there were numerous armed guards, and I must admit my uneasiness as I sat behind the steering wheel and thought about who might pull a trigger first and ask questions afterward! But the good Lord was with us and we made the transfer of personnel without incident.

Day dawned on September 11 and Tshikaji was totally ours! After a whirlwind of preparation incoming classes arrived two weeks later. The instruction of *infirmiers* began at Tshikaji at last!

19 THE TSHIKAJI YEARS

And let us not be weary in well doing: for in due season we shall reap, if we faint not (Galations 6:9).

The year we moved to Tshikaji, 1964, was one of the chaotic, restless years of early Congolese independence. On June 30, the nation's Independence Day, the United Nations formally withdrew all armed troops which for four years had been the glue holding together a frag-mented-prone country. Also on Independence Day the compromise prime minister, Cyrille Adoula, saw the handwriting on the wall and surrendered up his three years of authority, resigning with his cabinet. All of a sudden there was no central government, and this at a time when ominous signals were being sounded from the northeast (Stanleyville) and from the southwest (Kwango-Kwilu). Discontent and rebellion were in the air.

President Kasavubu and his Binza Group of advisors and policy makers were desperately looking for a remedy to the situation and, realizing that they could ill afford a challenge on a third front (revival of threatened Katangan pullout), they were forced to conclude that to keep Moise Tshiombe from capsizing their floundering ship the only logical move was to place him at its helm. Tshiombe became the nation's leader a week after Adoula's resignation. He immediately engaged a unit of mercenary soldiers to move toward Stanleyville in an effort to quell the rising rebellion in that area, but they never quite made it. Congo was destined to an upbeat of war and butchery.

Antoine Gizenga assumed the cloak of the fallen Lumumba and moved to Stanleyville to set up a hostile government, enemy to the one in Leopoldville. He received the blessing of the USSR as well as cold cash, though the Soviets were less capable of supplying his landlocked state with such basically needed materials as rolling stock, guns, ammunition, and all other accoutrements of warfare. This fact determined their ultimate defeat.

Gizenga was the charismatic name in this neo-communistic effort, but he was quickly upstaged by several new figures who pushed their dreams and goals to much more radical conclusions than the more reasonable Gizenga would have envisioned. Christophe Gbenye headed a shadow government of the People's Republic, assuming the title of president. Gaston Soumialot was second in command. He was the military leader of the Simba army which advanced from the south and eventually overran Stanleyville. *Simba* is the Swahili word for "lion" and Soumialot's soldiers always considered themselves to be veritable lions. The Simba army had started out from Albertville (now called Kalemi), on the western border of Lake Tanganyika, and it was here that Jason Sendwe was murdered. Soumialot's fellow traveler was self-styled "General" Olenga, and these three—Gizenga, Soumialot, and Olenga—perpetrated the murders of dozens of Christian missionaries and thousands of defenseless Congolese. Trumped up trials were conducted at Stanleyville with daily executions at the foot of the Lumumba monument in the center of the city. Many Congolese Christians lost their lives for simply standing aloof from the frenzy.

Members of the European population and missionaries on isolated stations were attacked. During the closing weeks of 1964 some thirty Protestant and seventy Catholic missionaries lost their lives in the northeastern sector of Congo. A sixteen-year-old girl came out from England that summer, during her school vacation, to visit with her missionary mother and father. All three were shot and their bodies were thrown into the river. Another mother and father and two small children were massacred in the same manner with only their blood-stained clothing found on the riverbank to confirm the story.

DEDICATION OF THE TSHIKAJI CAMPUS

And so it was during these tragic times that we opened the IMCK school at Tshikaji in late September. We had twenty-six students divided into two classes. We admitted the first girl to attend the training school. Life was rather primitive. We were still in the throes of getting doors onto their hinges, glass into vacant windows, adequate water from the stream in the valley for cooking, cleaning, bathing, and for proper sewage disposal. We had electric lights only at night for two or three hours of

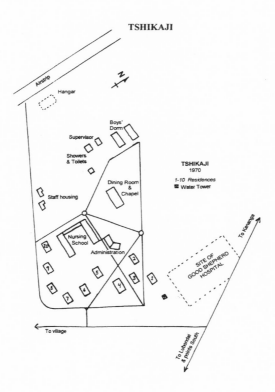

Tshikaji map.

study, but the current had not been run to all the houses. So in the evenings we often found ourselves sitting under the stars whiling away the time in conversation and contemplation. On a clear night it was interesting to watch for satellites making their way across the heavens. Perhaps because we were so close to the equator we could easily recognize spacecraft trajectories appearing overhead, and night after night we counted them—two, three, sometimes four or more in one evening.

With news leaking about the desperate circumstances of foreigners in Stanleyville, there was rumor that Belgian paratroopers would be dropped to secure the airport during evacuation. These troops would be ferried in American Air Force planes. Sure enough, before dawn on the morning of November 24 Effie and I were wakened by the hum of a motor brigade passing overhead. We turned to one another and confirmed, "This is it!" Subsequent news reported that the paratroopers had dropped, but before they could take the city, the retreating Simbas had massacred some forty European prisoners. Among them was Dr. Paul Carlson who had been one of the physicians we recruited for the Operation Doctor effort in 1961. He served with the Swedish Evangelical Church at Karawa, and he was so enamored with the opportunities for Christian service that he and his wife volunteered for full missionary service. During the uprising while he was away from his home base supervising the medical work at an outpost, he was captured and transported to Stanleyville where he was the primary hostage used by the Simbas to try to extract concessions from the United States. He was maltreated, beaten, and finally condemned to die unless the U.S. came to terms with the rebels. When the Belgian troops put down, Carlson managed to escape but was shot in the back and killed.

During these crisis days the IMCK program moved along. The teaching staff busily prepared lessons and organized classes on a definite schedule. Effie had her hands full preparing three meals a day for the two dozen resident students. Others in those opening days were Lucille McElroy, teaching the nursing arts, and Ruth Worth, our laboratory instructor. I taught the medical subjects. Garland Goodrum worked like a Trojan clearing roads and walks, installing doors and windows, providing water, and some limited electricity at night so the students could study.

December 12 was appointed to be the gala celebration day, the dedication ceremony for the school. Printed invitations were extended to many prominent people in the community, a program of celebration was organized, and a large quantity of refreshments was planned to encourage a spirited period of socializing following the ceremony. Many leaders of the church were present. Messages were addressed to the assembled guests by the legal representative of the mission, by the provincial minister of health, and by the governor of the province. The students had organized a choral group which sang with gusto, and we gave thanks to God for His provision and for His protection. The First Presbyterian Church of Winston-Salem, North Carolina, was also represented at the festivities by two physicians from the congregation which had contributed so handsomely to help make this all possible.

ADDITIONAL ACQUISITIONS

The establishment of IMCK at Tshikaji, the increasing importance of Luluabourg (now often called Kananga and soon to be officially designated by this name) as a seat of government and railroad and roadway hub, and the often unpredictable political and tribal relationships in the hinterlands for the next few years brought a considerable urban buildup. Many Belgians, increasingly discouraged by the financial and political difficulties in Congo against which they were continually forced to wrestle, were giving up the struggle. They were selling their properties and businesses to return to their homeland. The *Bonne Auberge* had been one of the more popular inns with an attractive cuisine. Now it was on the market for a song. Even more available if bought with American dollars. So the mission purchased the property, transforming it into useful church offices, accommodations for church-related travelers, and a dining room available to all. The cinema, an adjunct of the original inn, became a meeting hall,

Students at the IMCK, 1965.

and a congregation was organized for Sunday French worship.

A book and stationery shop in the downtown area was also bought and accommodated offices for the church treasurer and the legal representative. It also housed some of the church staff, and served as a storage area for incoming freight and baggage.

The Methodist bishop set up his office in the city and today there are numerous churches making an important Methodist presence in Luluabourg. The Mennonites have made huge advances with printing activities and media distribution. They built a studio for recording music and prepared programs for radio and television. Both Methodists and Mennonites joined us in the teaching program at Tshikaji. Dr. and Mrs. William Hughlett came from the Methodist mission and later Dr. and Mrs. John Zook and nurse Hulda Banmann from the Mennonites. They worked long and hard with the IMCK to help make a quality institution. Mrs. Zook, a highly-trained registered nurse, was director of our IMCK nursing school for a number of years.

During these years the teaching program for *infirmiers* was expanded and the course was lengthened from three years to four. This was considered a culmination of secondary school education as well as vocational nurses' training. At the conclusion, certificates were awarded for both high school and nursing school graduations. This secondary school emphasis also meant that along with our customary teaching of medical subjects and Bible study, there would be other secondary school curriculum. African sociology, physics, chemistry, and history were added as well as both French and English. We had to scramble for added teachers, both missionary and Congolese. I found myself in the unenviable role of teaching algebra, geometry, and biology.

There was another phase of our teaching which presented us with more difficulties. This was the practical application of the nursing program to include hospital participation and bedside nursing care. We had no hospital at Tshikaji nor any hospital facilities anywhere nearby. In order for our students to obtain supervised experience, it was necessary to transport them 100 miles to Lubondai or 150 miles to Bulape where missionary nurses could teach and oversee their clinical work on the spot. This meant that quarterly there was a complete turnover of the student body and classroom schedule for the third and fourth year students. This kept the school in a confusing state and prevented the IMCK program from ever becoming a truly-effective medical teaching unit.

About this time the Congolese government came across with the first significant monetary assistance to the IMCK. The inspector of medical education informed us that the government was allocating a credit of *ten million francs* for any needed materials for the school! This was the equivalent of about twenty-thousand U.S. dollars. Immediately we ordered a lot of badly needed metal furniture for student dormitories, and really comfortable mattresses (for the first time). A school bus was also purchased.

The American ambassador from the capital city paid us a visit and he seemed to be quite impressed. Later he wrote us: "I want to thank you again for taking the time to show me the medical school at Tshikaji. Your work and the work of your colleagues at the school is inspiring. It is a credit to the United States and a lasting service to the Congolese people. You may be sure of my full support and profound admiration for your efforts."

PRESIDENT MOBUTU TAKES OVER

In November of 1965 General Joseph-Désiré Mobutu pulled off a *coup d'etat*, deposing Kasavubu and establishing himself as President of the Republic. The following year, Prime Minister Tshiombe was chased into exile where he mysteriously died while under detention in Algeria. For the next thirty-two years, Mobutu was the undisputed dictator of the country. His tenure saw the nation sink ever deeper into bankruptcy. Support for schools, the health system, and all means of transport dwindled to practically nothing. The nations' currency devalued over and over again, driving the already low standard of living into devastating poverty. Mobutu conducted a studied displacement and regular relocation of public figures to assure that no personality appeared to becloud the complete autonomy of the president. To accomplish this purpose a number were incarcerated, some fled the country, and not a few disappeared without explanation from the face of the earth. However the capital crime of this high-handed tyrant, fashioned from the same political and moral mold of a Shah Mohammad Reza or a Ferdinand Marcos, is that he systematically drew his personal wealth from the potential riches of a developing country, sucking the means of livelihood from an already poverty-stricken people. This conduct has inspired and encouraged a system of corruption in Zaire today that can hardly be equaled anywhere else in the world. Services of any sort must be bought with "money under the table" so to speak. This goes from being waited on in a store to obtaining your already-made plane reservation, boat, or other public conveyance. The attending nurse in the hospital must be bribed to give medicine which the doctor has already ordered on your chart! This is Mobutuism!

Soon after his ascendance to power, Mobutu instituted an Africanization policy for the nation. Name changing was one of its main principles. All names with any suggestion of the old Belgian regime were replaced with African equivalents, reasonably derived from tribal usages which antedated the arrival of any European administration. Leopoldville, the capitol, regained its ancient tribal name of Kinshasa.

Elizabethville became Lubumbashi. Stanleyville became Kisangani. Coquilhatville was changed to Mbandaka. Costermansville became Bukavu and Thysville, Mbanza-Ngungu. Even Luluabourg, named for the nearby river, had to get rid of that offending suffix "burg," and so became Kananga. These are only a few of the larger cities. Renaming also included lakes and rivers.

Mobutu let his tribal prejudices hang out. He was born at Lisala on the northern most arch of the great river in Equatorial Province. Up there the river was not called the Congo, a name it had derived from the Bacongo people near its mouth. It was called the Zaire which was a name David Livingston wrote into some of his early maps. Mobutu not only changed the name of the big river to the Zaire but he renamed the country Zaire, and the same word was adopted for their national unit of currency.

The president changed the popular mode of men's style of dress. No more European-style business suits or coats and ties. Today Zairians effect a tropical jacket, short-sleeved and open at the neck, worn outside of pants with pockets on either side. These jackets are often highly decorated with fancy multicolored stitching around neck and shoulders. Certainly it's a more reasonable garment in a tropical country.

A great flap was occasioned when Mobutu insisted that all Zairians divest themselves of their European or Christian names and replace them with their family and ancestral titles. He led by discarding his names Joseph-Désiré and becoming President Mobutu Sese Seko. This change ran afoul of the Catholic Church's sacraments of Baptism and Confirmation, which are designated and recorded by name and not to be changed. The Catholics publicly criticized such measures and wrote extensively against them in their church communications and, although Mobutu had been reared a Catholic, he was enraged by this turn of events. He immediately suppressed and censored all religious publications which caught us all by surprise.

As time went by and the heat of the disagreement simmered down, restrictions were lifted and the church presses returned to normal function. But most of the president's edicts stood the test of time and were accepted and practiced by populace.

In one matter he did overreach himself. He arbitrarily took over all the mission schools to make them national or public schools. The great bulk of primary and secondary education in the land had been carried on by the Catholic and Protestant churches. The emerging nation was not yet ready to shoulder such responsibility and the schools quickly fell into complete academic and administrative disarray. Before long the government was forced to admit failure and asked the churches to once more take over the education of their people.

THE COMING OF SAMBO

In early October of 1966 I made my regular weekly visit to the rural dispensary of Kasonga to see patients, and also to take supplies to our resident *infirmier*, Kalonga Samuel. There was a crowd of people who had come out to meet me at the airport. I joined Kalonga and on our short walk to the dispensary hut he told me that the night before, October 4, some village people had brought in a woman who had borne her baby in the village. She had a retained placenta and was severely bled out. Kalanga had managed to extract the placenta but had no supportive treatment for his patient, and she had died.

"We have a newborn baby boy here," Kalonga said. "What are we going to do with him?"

The baby had little or no chance of survival in the village. But I had a lot of patients to see and needed to get on with my work, so I dismissed the matter for the moment. I nodded to Kalonga and said, "Let's get started with the patients."

I was fully occupied all afternoon seeing people, and the shadows had begun to lengthen by the time I decided to quit and make my way home so as to avoid flying after dark. I gathered up my medical bag and started for the plane before I remembered the matter of the newborn baby. "Where is that baby?" I asked Kalonga who was at my side.

The *infirmier* pointed to a man silently walking through the crowd holding a small bundle in his arms. I went to the man and threw back the top fold of the scrap of cloth covering a sleeping infant, and once more I was overwhelmed by the innocence of the baby and the help-lessness of the father. It is not uncommon for a newborn child to be buried with a dead mother.

I spoke impulsively to the father. "Do you want me to take the baby and feed him?"

He hesitated only a moment and then extended the bundle to me without a word. I laid the baby on the backseat of the airplane, started the motor, and took off. I began to consider what I had done. Was it a foolish thing? I didn't even know the father's name, or what village he came from. I had no papers to verify the transaction. I could be charged with kidnapping!

The baby's name was Makenga (grief or suffering) Samuel. That immediately translated into Sambo for us. We hadn't had a baby under our roof for ten years! Baby bottles and infant clothes were no problem as they could be found in our White Cross supplies. Milk for formula could be bought in town. We did, however, need to borrow a crib and a baby carriage.

Effie Rule with Sambo.

On my next trip to Kasonga I took along a carefully worded attestation which I had Sambo's father sign in the presence of witnesses. I learned that his name was Mukumbi and that he was from the village of Kabau in the tribal area of the Babindi. I learned further that he and his dead wife, Kandobole, were the parents of thirteen children, only three of whom had survived. One older girl was married and raising her own family. He had another daughter, Tshituke, about twelve or thirteen, and Mukumbi magnanimously informed me he was sending her home with me to be the nurse for her little brother. Now we had two new additions at home. Tshituke was a lovely child to have around. She was quiet and gentle and, at first, awestruck by all the material conveniences of modern living. She had to learn how to use a knife and fork, how to use a flush toilet bathroom, how to make a bed, open and close windows, cook on a wood-burning stove. She found it quite an adventure to simply go about the house and turn on and off the lights, and she enjoyed the unbelievable experience of a hot bath. Tshituke ate our Western food and learned to passably like it, but occasionally she needed to slip away to the village for some *bidia* and *tuishi* (cassava dough and cooked eels).

Unselfishness within the family is an admirable African trait. They teach it to one another and Tshituke taught it to Sambo. I can remember an evening when Sambo was sitting in his high chair and just he and I were at the table. I had given him a cookie and he was thoroughly enjoying it. When I reached over to put my hand on top of his, he interpreted the movement as my wanting part of the cookie, and without a moment's hesitation he took it from his mouth and extended it to me. I couldn't help wondering what one of my kids would have done if I asked for part of their cookie. Probably drawn back with a negative expression implying, "Go get one for yourself." This may be just one of the results (even disadvantages) of affluent living.

We deeply enjoyed those two years with Sambo and Tshituke. But after his mouth was full of teeth and he could handle the ordinary fare fed to him, we decided it was time for him to return to his own village environment. The longer we waited the more difficult it would be for all of us. Tshituke was the perfect bridge to connect the two cultures. She mothered him on their return to the Babindi, and when she married, he went to live with her in her new home.

MEDICAL CONFERENCE WITH DR. NUTE

In that same October (1966) that Sambo came to live with us, a significant event took place in Kinshasa. Some thirty missionary doctors, nurses, and Zairian *infirmiers*, under the auspices of the Congo Protestant Council, met with Dr. William Nute from the World Council of Churches. He came to take a good look at missionary medicine in the Republic of Zaire, and to see if there might be lessons to learn together for the days ahead. The whole question of medical education was examined. Government administrators were also invited to share in the discussion in order to show directions in which the government might be moving. What was going to happen to the *auxilliares* program and to the aides program? While there was the possibility of eventually eliminating these, there was a practical need for them at the present time.

Officers of the Congo Protestant Relief Agency appeared before the group to make their report which was more impressive and reassuring. During the six years of its existence CPRA had provided sixty-seven doctors on short assignment through the Operation Doctor part of its program, and a total of approximately one million tons of medicines and hospital equipment had been supplied to various hospitals and dispensaries.

Leprosy work was discussed, and the latest medication and management of the disease was propounded by experts. Then Dr. Nute addressed the group and reported on his recent tour of inspection, touching mission medical installations throughout the country. He elaborated on the healing ministry of the entire church as presented particularly by the Tubigen Consultation of 1964 and declared that the healing ministry is intimately bound-up with the evangelical ministry. God wants the whole man healthy and complete and perfect.

Further, Dr. Nute emphasized the importance of consultation and cooperation in medical missions. He spoke at length about hospital

The clinic at Konko.

administration and about the importance of hospital statistics. He
touched on accounting, and the vital importance of adequate water
sources. The problem of sanitation came under scrutiny, and he delivered himself at length on the chronic missionary problem of
over-extension. A doctor is under constant pressure to overextend,
often pushed by churchmen or even board members who have little
capacity for judging sound over-all medical policy. He wound up talking
about family planning and about medical teaching. Bill Nute's visit to
Zaire was a most helpful experience for many mission medical
workers, surely adding to the quality of services in Zaire.

During the 60s every effort was made to enlarge the medical presence of IMCK in the Kananga area, and to inaugurate some clinical
services which would effectively serve the people of the community.
Only two miles from Tshikaji, directly on the main road to town, there
was a government dispensary which had been abandoned since independence. It was located in the village of Konko where there were also
offices of the Secteur, analogous to county administration in the United
States. We approached the officers of the Secteur and, at the same time,
the Ministry of Health in Kananga, and offered to take over the dispensary, to equip it, to supply our own medicines, bandages, and other
material. Since it was sitting idle with no immediate prospect of government employment, it was rather reluctantly turned over to us. We
installed our *infirmiers* there on a full-time basis with one of our doctors
in attendance at regular scheduled intervals. A large clientele quickly
developed and crowds of people were treated at Konko for a number of
years. Eventually our outpatient dispensary in the city over-shadowed
this work and demanded all of the professional time and effort which
we could give to it. Konko was relinquished to the government once
more.

The following year after we opened the work at Konko we recognized that we should be working in the city proper where many more

people would have access to our services. We rented a long building on the main avenue leading to the airport, just behind the old Hotel des Aviateurs. It consisted of a series of rooms which could be turned into reception/charts/records, laboratory, bandages and dressings, examination area, pharmacy, injections, cashier, and storage. Four doctors and seven African *infirmiers* served the dispensary in regular shifts, and word quickly spread through the city. Crowds came and we were almost inundated. Within a few months we were treating five hundred people a day, and actually had to limit the number of new cases to thirty per day. With another two hundred being seen each day at Konko we were sometimes handling as many as a thousand patients a day.

About this same time we bought some property just a couple of blocks away. It was first used as a central clinical laboratory but later was turned into a dental clinic. In the backyard was a large, well-built storage building which we equipped with multiple shelves. This became our central storage for medical supplies for, not only our in-town dispensary, but also for the steadily growing number of rural dispensaries appearing in association with our rural churches. People were crying for convenient medical help.

Another area we sought to expand medically was in the large Kananga city hospital. This facility had served the entire city for a number of years and was in much need of repair. The screens had rusted out of all the windows which allowed flies and other insects to invade the wards. There had been no painting or real cleaning for ages. The supply of medications was dangerously low since the staff helped itself to sell them on the black market. Little or no surgery was done because there were no qualified staff surgeons. We at Tshikaji offered our expertise for a limited degree.

Occasionally we brought our own patients in for surgery, but the big problem was their post-op care. Nurses, hired by the government, had precious few medicines or other materials, and what they did have was only available to patients who could tip them. This kind of medical ethics was offensive to us but we had no authority whatsoever over the government-hired nurses. If they ignored our orders, we were powerless to correct the situation. Therefore I came to the hospital with the stipulation that I would bring my own bedside nurse to work with me.

Dr. Hugh Farrior and I were both particularly trained and interested in obstetrics. We worked with them in this specialty. Hugh handled a number of their difficult deliveries and I often conducted their large prenatal clinic. We had excellent assistance from the Catholic nuns who were well-trained and devoted to their work. I was handling the prenatal clinic one day when a patient lay down on the examining table and complained of abdominal pain and extreme weakness. Examination revealed the abdomen full of liquid. Her pulse was fast and thready. She was obviously bleeding abdominally with a probable ruptured ectopic gestation, and she needed surgery immediately. At the time I was the only doctor in the hospital, so it was up to me to operate. We sent word upstairs to prepare the operating room and I informed my clinic patients I had an emergency so they would need to sit and wait a while for their examinations. In surgery I noted that the nuns had started an intravenous drip, but we had no blood for transfusion which we needed badly in this case. It could mean the difference between life and death.

On opening the abdomen a great wave of free blood welled up and I began to suction it out as rapidly as possible to get to the site of the hemorrhage. To my surprise I saw one of the nuns calmly taking the blood from the suction machine receptacle to pour it into the intravenous drip suspended above the patient's head. She was giving the lady a transfusion of her own blood taken from her abdomen and she surely did need that blood! I hurried to locate the ruptured ectopic, remove it, stop the bleeding, and close the abdomen. After surgery I left the patient in the gentle hands of the nuns and returned downstairs to finish the prenatal exams. Our patient survived her emergency operation and was discharged in good condition, thanks to the wisdom and ingenuity of a dedicated Catholic Sister.

EVENTS IN THE FAMILY

In the States, Charlotte's roommate in nursing school was Beth Hutton from Florida. She was a year ahead of Charlotte and was herself an honor member of the Women's Honor Organization. She was the one, in fact, who tapped Charlotte into membership. Among the many subjects to talk about together, they had on occasion discussed life in Africa. Together they wheedled the school and some church folks into helping send Beth out to Tshikaji for the summer to help with the medical work.

We met the plane at Kananga airport on a bright June day, 1967, and a lovely young lady stepped off the plane with a warm smile and an eager attitude. Beth not only brightened our home for three months, but she was a big help with the work. She spent hours in the pharmacy unpacking, repackaging, and labeling drug supplies. She undertook what is always a big job—the classification and storage of White Cross supplies, i.e. all the linens and dry goods used in the school and in dispensary work. Actual hospital experience in the treating and care of patients was in scarce supply since we had no local hospital facilities. Finally an opportunity came to take her to Lubondai for an emergency surgical procedure.

One of my prenatal patients was the wife of a Zairian army major. She was having some troubles in the early months of her pregnancy and after examination I was convinced she was carrying an extrauterine gestation. To protect her life prompt surgical intervention was required, but at the time I had no operative facilities in Kananga. I could take her to Lubondai to the hospital there, but another complicating factor added to the confusion. Recently there had been guerrilla activity and the military was sort of jumpy. They decreed no movement of expatriots out of the urban area. I explained to the major how the land lay and what the emergency meant and he hesitated not at all, assuring me he would get permission for us to make the trip to Lubondai. I insisted that we should go in two cars and he should travel with his retinue in the advance car to clear the way. He agreed and the arrangements were made. Beth and one or two others went with me. En route we got separated and when I drove into Lubondai Station, the major had not yet arrived. The airstrip was covered with empty gasoline drums and I was thankful we had not tried to make the trip by plane. There was also a squad of armed soldiers guarding the field and they promptly surrounded my car, demanding to know who I was and by what authority I was traveling. I tried to explain but only made matters worse. Just as they had decided to line us up and march us off, the major's car arrived and he soon put them straight.

I called the medical boys and set up surgery for the following morning. As I concluded they shook their heads in awe and disbelief as they informed me they had had a woman in difficult labor for the past two days. She had made no progress and before our arrival her relatives had put her on a cart to wheel her to her home village where she would die. "They left here only minutes ago!" the boys exclaimed.

"Well go and bring them back," I urged. "And set up the operating room at once. We'll deliver that baby by cesarean as soon as they are here."

It did not take long to scrub, prepare the patient, and put her on the operating table. The labor had been too long and difficult for the baby, but we saved the mother's life. The following day we operated on the major's wife and eliminated the danger hanging over her. I was especially pleased that Beth finally saw some real Central Africa medical emergencies and was able to help alleviate them. A few weeks later when Effie and I put Beth on the plane to go back to America, I told my wife, "There's the kind of girl I'd like for a daughter-in-law." Though my remark was casual it was prophetic. After graduation Beth and Charlotte roomed together in Atlanta, and soon our son Bill's field work with the Department of Health, Education, and Welfare was moved to Atlanta. He and Beth met and before long they were engaged. They became husband and wife on March 16, 1968. Effie and I gloried in the goodness of the Lord who had permitted us to know and love Beth even before Bill did.

Later that same year we had the joy of another family visit when Libby came out for several weeks. Becky Moorman (my sister Barbara's daughter) accompanied her. Becky was sent by the churches in Missouri Presbytery with the understanding that she would take

Bill and Effie Rule in front of their home in Tshikaji, 1968.

pictures and show slides of the work upon her return.

In November Bill was inducted into the U.S. Army as a medic and six months later was sent to Vietnam where he slogged it out for a year in frontline combat. He did not opt for this since he signed up as a medic, and he requested his draft board to defer him as a conscientious objector. They refused on the basis that he had not originally been so classified. Bill reminded them that a person can honestly change an opinion at any point in time, at which point they told him, "You are not the right denomination to be an objector. Presbyterians don't object." And they pushed him right on to the front.

In December, Charlotte and Dr. Steve White were married. She met Steve at Emory while he was a medical student. When they were wed he was doing a surgical residency at Emory.

On October 15, 1969, a grievous cloud fell across our family circle. Effie's brother, The Reverend Paul E. Crane, and his oldest son, David, were killed in an automobile accident. This was a terrible shock to Effie and she grieved because she was so far from home and unable to help comfort and console her mother and Paul's widow, Dorothy.

The next year Paul Rule arrived in Africa to handle Joe Spooner's industrial and maintenance work during Joe's furlough year, and Charlotte came out with her brand new husband so she could show him from whence her roots had come. This meant that all our children except Bill had recently been with us in Zaire. Charlotte and Steve brought Steve Crane, Effie's nephew, with them. We enjoyed having him with us, and he stayed on for a couple of months to travel home with us. On that return trip we had the pleasure of visiting Rome, Switzerland, Paris, and London.

Perhaps the hardest thing in a missionary's life overseas is the surrender of the children. It is painful to send them back across the seas to a more sophisticated society. Not that one surrenders confidence and assurance in ultimate results. God is too faithful for that. But one recognizes that there will be struggle and often bewilderment. Yes, even discouragement. And one laments that the distances prevent standing shoulder-to-shoulder to offer encouragement and even occasional advice.

THE GOOD SHEPHERD HOSPITAL

As the medical teaching program progressed at Tshikaji and as the student body continued to increase, it became more and more evident that a teaching hospital in conjunction with the school was an absolute imperative if the institution was to ever become the first class facility envisioned. But building a modern hospital from scratch is no simple job, especially in the heart of Africa. Materials are not easy to come by, and it was estimated that six months of accumulation of stocks and supplies, of timbers and tools, of bricks and beams would be necessary before the first ground could even be broken. Then there was the great question of who would do the job. No contractors' signs hang out in Kananga. The skill and know-how combined with the ability to boss a work crew in the Tshiluba language can't be found at just any old corner. The greatest problem was *money*. Where would the funds come from?

Hopes and dreams were immediately directed to the Women of the Church in the homeland. This organization has had a long and illustrious history of annual birthday celebration by generous giving to both home and foreign mission causes. Over a period of fifty years they have given a remarkable total of more than thirteen million dollars. Would they help us build a hospital at Tshikaji?

A trial balloon was floated. We requested consideration of such a project. Our job was to first sell the idea to our own mission board back in the States, and then to the ladies. This was initially a matter of letters and commentaries from the field, circulated to one and all who might have influence in making the decision. The first year we requested consideration we were not chosen and this left us feeling crestfallen and discouraged. But we prayed a lot and kept on writing letters. To our great joy and encouragement our hospital was selected as the major project the following year.

We began to take pictures and to gather testimonials for promotional material back home. Miss Evelyn Green and Miss Janie McGaughey came to Zaire to examine the entire project for adequate presentation. The date for the women's offering was May of 1969, and I was to go to America for April and May to encourage women's groups in churches across the Assembly.

After parking John and Barbara at Central School, Effie and I departed. From New York we proceeded directly to Knoxville, and I began my itineration across the southland. For the next eight weeks I hardly stopped to catch my breath. I visited all fifteen states where there were Southern Presbyterian Church congregations. I was in sixty-eight churches in forty-three towns or cities, and spoke ninety times. We estimated that these talks reached about eight thousand people, mostly women. I did speak to several small groups of doctors and medical people under the auspices of the Medical Benevolence Foundation. As a result almost four hundred thousand dollars was given toward building the hospital in Zaire. This was the second largest donation ever made by the Women of the Church. Of course while in the States we had the added pleasure of visiting with our family members. It was a special time which Effie will always hold dear because it was the last time she saw her brother Paul. He died five months later in the auto accident.

Now we had to secure land on which to build the hospital. A fine level plain lay just north of the school and fronted the main road leading to Kananga. It is a commanding site of fifty acres which looks toward the lights of the city eight miles away. At the time, there were about twenty African families living on the land. We needed to go to the Land Title Office and get representatives to visit them with us. Their property was assessed, and we paid them about one hundred dollars per family to move and relocate. This was necessary before the government would deed the property to us. Next we had to visit the several tribal chieftains who claimed some tribal ownership of the land. To get their signatures each was given a *matabishi*. This is a very important word in the Tshiluba language. It translates into English as a "tip." It is almost impossible to transact business in the Kasai without the *matabishi*. And so we got the property, but it was another six years before the Good Shepherd Hospital was built.

There was one other piece of business to arrange in order to put IMCK and its proposed hospital into full and stable orbit, and that was the procurement of *personnalite civile*. This means incorporation in the eyes of the government. Up to now the IMCK had existed in the bosom of the APCM. But the mission was giving up its incorporation and the IMCK needed legal recognition simply to carry its own bank account. This effort placed us at cross purposes with some of our church leaders. They wanted IMCK to remain under the incorporation of the church so they could handle affairs and call the signals. But such an arrangement would have been disastrous. The financial and administrative responsibilities of a medical training institution is not a money-making proposition, contrary to the thinking of our African brethren. We did not want it to be a millstone around the neck of a young and struggling church. Also, IMCK would undoubtedly be able to get more help from foundations and other secular financing bodies if not directly under the auspices of the church.

In 1968, John Miller and I made repeated trips to Kinshasa taking papers galore in search of *personnalite civile*. We visited the minister of health and the minister of justice and other high ranking officials, and in due time our papers arrived on President Mobutu's desk. We figured the objective was well within our grasp, but it was not until November 30, 1970, that our certificate of incorporation finally came through.

At this juncture of our missionary lives we began to seriously consider what the future might hold for us. We were nearing the thirty-year mark of missionary service, and our question before the Lord was whether He proposed for us to continue in this work or whether He had some new avenues of endeavor He was saving for Effie and me. I had been, for some time, an outspoken advocate that the Board requirements for retirement and full pension benefits needed revising. They were antiquated and unrealistic. At that time the criteria for full pension was forty years of service or seventy years of age. Too often I had seen members of the missionary force having rendered yeoman's service through the years, try to hang on a little longer to get a little more retirement assistance. I felt that it was demeaning for the mission to search for an adequate spot for a missionary who was being replaced, simply to keep him on the field another year or two to afford him a little more security back home. Now here I was reaching the three decade status, so was it time for me to put my feet where my mouth had been?

There were other angles to the question besides the purely physical one. In that day of multiple and rapid changes probably the major requirement of the missionary was the capacity to remain supple and adaptive in making a maximum contribution to the Kingdom. Those of us who had served longer under the old regime and who harbored greater arteriosclerotic deposits might have more difficulty along this line than some of the younger folks. So perhaps we should step aside and let them carry the ball. Or, more realistically, step aside so that the indigenous church could carry the ball.

Finally, there were tuggings from the home direction. My mother was eighty-five years old. She lived alone, drove her own car, and took care of her personal errands and interests. She was doing a good job of it, but it couldn't last forever. She represented a need for us to be at home in the States. Our children were another reason. Two had finished college, two were still in college, and two would soon be ready for college. This was a strain not only on the family equanimity but also on the family pocketbook. There is always a parental yearning to remain in close contact with the children. This was a strategic time to be stateside because of our children.

But more important than all these considerations was the bottom line—what was the leading of our Heavenly Father? This is what had taken us to Africa and only this could lead us home. So we concluded our sixth term of service in Zaire not knowing if we would return.

MILESTONE SEVEN
PICKING UP PERKS

"There is no man that hath left house, or brethren, or sisters, or father, or mother, or wife, or children, or lands, for my sake, and the gospel's, but he shall receive an hundredfold now in this time . . . ; and in the world to come eternal life" (Mark 10:29–30).

20 GOD'S WILD WONDERFUL WORLD

For ye shall go out with joy, and be led forth with peace: the mountains and hills shall break forth before you into singing, and all the trees of the field shall clap their hands (Isaiah 55:12).

Anywhere that one journeys across the face of the earth, the sensitive soul is impressed with the beauty and the magnitude of God's creation. A beloved African friend traveled with me to the Great Smoky Mountains National Park where we drove to the state divide at Newfound Gap to view the repeated ranges of mountain peaks stretched before us on a bright, clear day. He stood and gazed for several minutes without saying a word, then he shook his head in wonder and turned to me with the brief comment, *"Nzambi udi munene!"* (God is great!) Simply to look upon the handiwork of the Almighty bonded his attention to the Creator.

Traveling over the mighty continent of Africa, one can but respond in like manner. Whether it be the power unleashed by a dust storm in the Sahara Desert or the columns of smoke rising from a grass fire on the pampas plains of the Kasai or the brilliant twinkling of the Southern Cross as it shines in the night sky. All of these pictures generate feelings of awe and worship.

Congo forests are beautiful beyond description, but perhaps the geographic feature closest to my own heart are Central Africa's great rivers. How I loved to leave the tug and tension of a demanding medical and missionary program and go absorb the silence and solitude of a peacefully flowing Lubilanji, Mbushimayi, Lulua, or Lubi Rivers. Each of them flowed in its proper sequence toward the mighty Congo, thence through the Crystal Mountains down an unbelievable course of rapids and waterfalls to the Atlantic Ocean.

It is always surprising to find how little visible wildlife there is on the river. The twittering and call of birds can be heard from the forest which blankets both sides of the stream, and occasionally a few monkeys can be seen swinging through the branches. Sometimes a herd of hippos is seen, always bobbing up and down in the water and always moving away as you approach. They present the tops of their heads for a momentary inspection as they blow out a cloud of moisturized air and inhale a new supply before ducking under again. A snake may slither through the water to cross from one side of the river to the other, and a large lizard may drop into the water just ahead from a branch on which he has been sunning himself. That's about all we see. It is always assumed that crocodiles are around, but they are seldom seen. Crocs are wily creatures. They always know where you are, but you seldom know where they are.

The larger animals apparently have had enough brushes with man to teach them to stay out of sight. Antelope are seldom seen unless a determined drive is made to force them out of the forest fringe and high grass. Wild hog, buffalo, leopards—never. I only saw elephants one time in my forty years! They were feeding along the Lulua River.

CAST A HOOK; GET A BITE

The great rivers are teeming with fish. To catch, smoke, and then transport them to sell in the multiple Congo markets provides one of the principal sources of protein-rich food in an otherwise deficient diet. The rivers rise and fall regularly with the rainy and dry seasons, and the fish tend to move up the small but swollen tributaries while the arterial streams are in full flood. During these periods the Congolese fishermen try to block the confluence with sticks and vines and even nets woven from the fibers of certain trees. When the waters recede and the streamlets dwindle to dry-season puddles, the fish return to the rivers. This is when the fishermen wade into the shallows to catch armfuls of fish as they approach the barricades. They pitch the fish onto the bank where others dress them for smoking.

One of the most common small fish is the *tilapia*, and it proves to be good eating. We enjoyed fishing for *tilapia* either from a boat or from the bank of Lake Munkamba. The Tshiluba designation for them is *bikele*. One virtue of this species is that it eats the snails which carry the liver flukes of schistosomiasis, and for this reason, as well as for their culinary qualities, the Belgians stocked small lakes and ponds with them. They also taught the Congolese how to cultivate them in fish reservoirs.

A much more game fish and more thrilling to catch is the *hydrocyon* or tiger fish. It resembles the salmon, but it has a formidable set of sharp teeth and a fiery red tail. It is a carnivore and will strike the line viciously, then fight with fury. It breaks the water, seeking to shake off the hook while in the air. The small tiger might tip the beam from three to five pounds. The larger ones are ten pounds or more. These tigers were fairly common in the rivers. They are also excellent food.

One day Bill Worth and I were fishing on the Lubilanji River, and I caught a fine tiger fish and pulled it in. We got the hook out of its mouth and I held it up while Bill took a picture. It was still morning and we wanted to keep it alive as long as possible toward having it fresh when we got home, so Bill took the fish in his two hands and splashed it through the water a couple of times to force water through its gills. On the second pass the fish wiggled slightly and because the body was slick Bill's grip slid back toward the tail. I saw a sudden look of apprehension as he realized he couldn't let go to get a tighter hold, and we had no gaff or net. By now the fish was getting more oxygen and it wiggled again, and once more Bill's hands slipped. Gradually the fish paddled itself loose and we stood watching as it slowly and drunkenly swam into deeper and deeper water.

"Tell me, Bill," I asked him. "How large do mine have to be before you decide not to throw them back in?"

Big brother to the tiger fish is the goliath. It also has an amazing set of teeth and a red tail, and in size it exceeds the tiger over and over again. Most of the ones we caught were in the forty pound range, but they can go up to twice that size. I came across a book some twenty years ago titled *Game Freshwater Fish of the World*. If my memory is correct, it promoted the goliath as the gamest of all game freshwater fish of the world. It further recounted that the most promising spot in the world to catch this renowned specimen was at the confluence of the Fwa and Lubi Rivers in the Belgian Congo. The hair stood up on the back of my neck! This was the exact location where we had caught them over and over again.

Lake Fwa is one of the most wildly beautiful spots on the face of the earth. It is formed by gigantic underwater springs. The water is crystal clear and myriads of schools of fish can be seen darting in all directions. From its source it winds some three or four miles eastward and empties into the Lubi River which flows north. All along its banks there are virgin forests with giant trees where monkeys and exotic birds may be spotted. The Lubi is a red muddy river where the Fwa feeds into it, and the two sources flow side by side for maybe a hundred to two hundred yards, gradually mixing together.

It is in this area that the goliaths habitually hide out in the muddy water, waiting for unsuspecting smaller fish to drift down with the flow of the Fwa. This is the place where we cast our baited lines from a boat with a silenced outboard motor.

When fishing for goliath, it is imperative to use heavy deep sea quality tackle. My Knoxville sporting shop friends were always amazed

at the size hooks and thirty to fifty pound tackle I asked for to thread my
deep sea reels. This was necessary because the remarkable speed and
strength with which the goliath strike always jars to the bone and feels
like a freight train is on the line. Also, the river is narrow, only some
thirty to fifty yards wide and branches from giant trees are strewn in its
bed. There is little room to play your hooked fish, and multiple opportunities for fouling a line.

One day after I cast my bait and fouled the line, I moved to the bank
on the clear side of the Fwa to unravel it, forgetting to pull in my hook
which was spinning around in eddies on the bottom. Suddenly there was
a mighty tug and my heavy line was snapped as though it was thread. A
goliath made off with bait, hook and line. On another occasion I did the
same thing, but with pole in hand I was trying to untangle knots in the
reel. This time the blow completely snapped my heavy pole in two!

I should explain that the goliath has a very bony mouth, and it is
only by chance that the hook becomes well seated in the flesh. Once in

Bill with a tiger fish.

a while I boated a goliath which when gasping, opened its mouth and the hook fell out on the boat's floor. His greed for the bait kept his mouth closed and got him into trouble! I estimate that for every ten goliath strikes, you only boat one.

John Miller, his son Jim, and I took his boat one day the thirty-five miles from Lake Munkamba to Lake Fwa, put it in the water, and floated down to the Lubi to fish. We had been at it an hour or so with no catch when we began to hear a strange noise. It sounded like a motor, which puzzled us as we were many miles from a road and for somebody else to be on the river would be quite a coincidence. The noise grew louder and louder until suddenly a helicopter flying quite low proceeded down river coming from the south. We immediately recognized that it was a police craft from the diamond mines, and it was doubtless looking for wildcat diamond diggers along the river bank as this was forbidden by law. They hovered above us and we waved to convey, "We're not looking for diamonds, just fish!" They waved in return and proceeded on up the Fwa.

About that time we got a strike and landed a big, beautiful goliath, probably forty pounds. We put it on a steel leader, attached it to the boat, and dumped it back in the water since goliath's die very soon out of water. The helicopter came back down river and as it approached us I reached down, pulled up the big fish, and proudly held it aloft. There, I thought, now you can see for yourselves what we are doing. Our only diamond is this beauty! They stopped the craft dead still right over us, tipped it to one side for a better view. We could see the pleasure and surprise on their faces before they flew off.

Later that day we caught a second fish which was an identical twin. I was working rather carefully to remove the hook from his mouth with a pair of pliers. Bill Worth had his knee torn open by the sharp teeth one time when he landed a goliath, and it took quite a while to heal. My fingers slipped and the pliers slid down into the fish's stomach. It carried that belly full the rest of the day until we returned home that evening and surgically removed the offending tool. When we got it home to the States a year or so later, I turned it over to a taxidermist. My catch became quite a conversation piece except when our grand-children came to visit. Then we had to hide it because they were disturbed by the ferocious face.

Of course the most delectable of all fish is *kapitene*, also called Nile perch. This is the largest of the river fish in Central Africa, running 25 to 50 pounds where we found them, but the record spec-imen caught in Lake Albert weighed 250 pounds. We didn't see them very often as they were rare in our part of the country. I caught only one in all my years of Congo fishing. Belgians call *kapitene* "the king of table fish" and because of their size there is a lot of meat.

It would be improper to cut short our ichthyological index without reference to that common denizen of the deep, the widespread, and bewhiskered catfish. Yes, he lives in Africa too, and grows to a formidable size, sometimes over a hundred pounds. Unlike the tiger or goliath, he does not thrash furiously or break the surface. He just stays down on the bottom and pulls with all his might, and the fisherman must set his feet and apply back and arm muscles to keep from being tugged out of the boat.

One day my son Paul and I were floating downstream fishing on the Lulua River. I hooked a big cat and Paul and I played him for half an hour, passing the rod back and forth to rest from the constant pull. When we finally landed the monster I was actually trembling with exhaustion (mixed with some excitement).

A little further down river we fouled our line under a rock. We motored back upstream, reeling in the played-out line as we drew nearer. Just as we reached the rock and circled to its upper side to disengage the hook there was sudden movement and the line started playing out again, going down river at a rapid rate. It never stopped. Before I could right my rod and reel the entire length of fishing tackle was pulled out, and as it came to the end it snapped like a thread. I was left with rod and reel but with all my fishing line gone in a matter of seconds. Even a goliath can't exert that amount of force. I suspect it was a crocodile under that rock with my bait in its mouth, and it swam off down river and took it all!

THE RIVER HORSE

Today one can live for a lifetime in Central Africa and never see any of the large wild animals associated with Africa. The rhinoceros is an almost hopelessly endangered species, and buffalo, elephants, and lions have also been forced back on a dwindling domain almost to the point of extinction. But the one big animal still easily found is the hippopotamus.

These huge pachyderms usually patrol the riverbanks at night, feeding on tropical herbs and grasses. During the daylight hours they are in the water, bobbing up and down, actually sleeping while they bob. When they come to the surface they exhale a breath of air with such force that it makes a geyser-like spout which can be seen hundreds of yards away, and this is accompanied by a grunt or snort— all of which tells you that you are approaching a herd of hippos long before you can see them. They are not particularly aggressive unless the female is protecting her young, and then you'd better be cautious.

I had my introduction to hippos early on as a young missionary because I lived on the station with Roy Cleveland who was a renowned hunter and an excellent shot. From time to time he went to the river seeking hippo meat to feed the students in our boys and girls homes, or to feed a meeting of the Presbytery, or to feed the mission workmen and their families as well as local village people. Everybody was always hungry for meat, rarely available, and a nearby hippo meant tons of meat!

Once Mr. Cleveland went to the river, found a herd, and shot a large hippo. It sank out of sight and Cleveland patiently waited for it to float to the surface. The hippo stomach is always loaded with silage in the process of decomposition and digestion which forms large quantities of gas. Usually within fifteen minutes to a half hour the buoyant body pops to the surface where it can be tugged to a sand bank and butchered. But time went by and the animal did not appear. The hunter waited until nearly dark before returning home empty-handed. The following day he was busy with other matters and asked me to go find it and bring back the meat.

So after attending to a few urgent hospital matters, I made the twenty-mile trip to the river crossing where I found Cleveland's crew of helpers. They told me in excited rehearsal that the hippo had been found but it had floated a considerable distance down river and we would have to hike out after it. That was some hike—cutting through underbrush and wading streams. There was no hint of a pathway! I lumbered along and as the sun climbed higher, sweat poured from my face and down my neck. I told myself that the fourteen-mile hike of my Boy Scout days couldn't hold a candle to this. Several hours later we reached a clearing at the riverbank where a native canoe was tied up. The Africans of my entourage, now numbering more than a dozen, went into a huddle and came out with the suggestion that I should continue the chase by boat. Of course I asked how far and no one knew. I looked at the setting sun and thought of the long walk back to my car. I chickened out. I arrived home well after dark.

Later I learned that a large band of villagers found the hippo, and they tied long vine ropes to it to take it downstream as fast as they could go to keep it out of the hands of the "white missionaries." One of our men, Matamba, followed them, and they stopped on a sandy island to rest. He had joined them and when he asked them if they didn't think the meat belonged to the mission, he was met with such hostility that he shut up. As he told me later, "Doctor, if I had continued to challenge their possession of all that meat, you might never have seen me again."

Thus the Africans vie for food. It was always sort of a nip and tuck contest between us and the local residents to see who would get the lion's share of a kill. I conceded that the best way to protect my public relations was not to brawl with them, but to give in and let them have the major portion. After all, there were more of them. Usually I took one hind quarter back to the mission station, and that was half a ton right there. Then I took the two tenderloins from each side of the backbone for our several missionary families. Each one was at least five feet long and fed a company of people for a number of days. The rest belonged to the villagers, but they were still greedy as Bill Pruitt and I found out.

One day we killed a hippo and waited for it to surface, but it never did. So we went home. But the following day we were back at the river asking the villagers if they had seen our kill. They said no. We took out our boat and cruised down river, looking among several islands and in all the coves and backwashes to see if the carcass was hung up somewhere, but we found nothing. We returned to where our car was parked. There were a number of men nearby working with their fishing nets and some vine ropes. I noted that two fellows were standing side by side in water up to their hips, and they just stood there, not moving. I knew there were crocodiles in the area and I was concerned for their safety so I urged them to get out. Oh no, they said, they were very comfortable. I mentioned the possibility of crocodiles but they just shrugged without moving an inch. Then I began to smell a rat. There was some good reason they wouldn't move and I wanted to know what it was. I demanded that they come out of the water and reluctantly they left their stand. As they came forward a hippo head floated to the surface. As I had thought, they were standing on it to keep it out of sight! The jig was up and they confessed that they were in the process of butchering our hippo on the facing island, so we crossed and retrieved our rightful share.

Another interesting factor of this kill was that we had unfortunately shot a female. We try to avoid this, presuming the larger and darker-hued animals are males. This time we goofed and we found a hippo fetus. I had never seen one before. It was maybe a foot long and weighed about ten pounds. We took it back to our *infirmier* school where we preserved it in formaldehyde, exhibiting it for the students' elucidation.

When our oldest son, Bill, reached his teenage tribulations, I took him out one day to hunt hippo. Just the two of us were in the boat cruising up river until we came on a herd of big fellows. We tied the boat to an overhanging tree limb, and Bill had a clear view of the bend in the river. I took to the bank and made my way beyond the cavorting animals in order to show myself and invite them to move on down river into Bill's line of fire. This worked out just right, and a few minutes later I heard the gunfire and saw a hippo thrashing in the water and watched it sink. This meant we had achieved our purpose, so we broke out our lunch and waited. Sure enough, about the time we finished, the hippo bobbed to the surface. We got a rope on one foot and hauled it down stream to where a group of Africans were waiting on a wide sandy strand. Before long they had their share and we had ours.

In celebration of Bill's success we had a hippoburger roast at our house and invited all the Central School kids. There was one big platter of hippoburgers and then, in case hippo meat failed to excite some-body's taste buds, we had a platter of beef burgers. I was amused to see that they never stopped to consider which burger they had. For kids a burger is a burger, be it hippo or cow, and is the ultimate in gastro-nomic heaven.

Another time Sid Langrall, Bob Gould, and I went hunting. We got our hippo way up river and had to drag it quite a distance to a rather uninviting sand bank extending far out into the river under two or three feet of water. We had a lot of trouble heaving the heavy hippo body out of the stream and onto the dry bank. We used ropes around the body to roll the big animal, with numbers of Congolese straining at the pull of each rope. Bob Gould and I were in the water, directing the drag for almost an hour, and once again those crocodiles were in the back of my mind because the blood of the hippo would surely attract them. But we managed to get our kill safely onto the bank, and butchered it. The meat was divided among all present and everybody went home happy.

At this point it would seem that I have indicated that our only interest in the hippopotamus was to kill him. However that is not entirely true. The Rule family had a sincere affection and concern for this huge aquatic animal, and the expression of it was centered in an imaginary hippo named *Tubby Nguvu*. In Tshiluba *nguvu* is the word for hippopotamus. When our children were small, Tubby became a friend of ours and often visited with us around the table at meal time. One of the kids would start by saying, "Daddy, tell us a Nguvu story." Then the others would chime in with, "A Nguvu story! A Nguvu story!" So it was up to me to come up with one of Tubby Nguvu's adventures then and there.

Not only have we enjoyed Tubby and his African playground but we have had the pleasure of meeting many of his forest friends. Tubby is a kindhearted hippo, so naturally he has many friends. In our many years in Africa, we met and loved a number of those friends.

SOME OF TUBBY'S FRIENDS

Some of Tubby's best friends were African wild animals that came to live with the Rule family at various and sundry times. Alexander the python graced our backyard at Bibanga for several months. There were often rabbits and monkeys that came for abbreviated or extended visits.

At one juncture we had two monkeys the children insisted on naming Darby Fulton and Jas. A. Jones. I cringed and hoped the two dignitaries of our church never heard about their namesakes.

Of all the small animals we encountered in Africa, the most outgoing and endearing was the mongoose. The mongoose is a ferret-like animal that eats rats and snakes. Its species was immortalized by Rudyard Kipling in a story about Rikki tiki tavi. The mongoose resident of Lubondai Station was W. W. He roamed the pathways between the houses and was known by all. He didn't really belong to the Rule family, but most mornings he came to the hospital to make rounds with me. As I passed down the ward from patient to patient, W. W. scurried along under the beds. He maintained his proper post until examinations were completed, and only left the room when I did.

Of course we took W. W. on our vacations at Lake Munkamba. One bright and shining morning several of us were walking down the path with W. W. frisking along, sometimes ahead and sometimes behind us. As we passed a dense clump of grass and bushes, W. W. made a sudden dive into it and disappeared. We heard the great sound of scuffle and thrashing and we knew a fight was taking place between W. W. and a snake, but our timidity kept us from parting the bushes to watch. We waited for several minutes, listening, and finally W. W. dragged himself out to us. He was obviously in bad shape and walked unsteadily with his head held low to the ground. His body began to swell and eventually he became surprisingly bloated. We knew that his fight had been with a poisonous snake. We feared this was the end of W. W., and we petted him and fed him liquids for several days until the swelling began to recede. He made a complete recovery, but we never knew what kind of snake bit him or whether he killed it.

W. W. was an accepted member of the mission station family for many months until one day he disappeared and was never seen again.

SHIMBI, THE NIGHT PROWLER

Another special wild pet of ours was *Shimbi*. This is the Tshiluba name for a ringtail genet cat which is really more like a weasel than a cat. It has a long slender body and short legs, about a foot and a half in length, and weighs less than five pounds. It is often confused with civet cats, but is about third cousin, in zoological classification, to the already discussed mongoose. It is a nocturnal hunter and feeds on frogs, rats, mice, and insects.

Shimbi was brought to us by one of the Congolese boys when it was a tiny baby genet, and we nursed the little life along with milk from a medicine dropper. The little animal prospered and grew and he was quickly tamed. He loved to climb up on your shoulder to be petted. Soon he learned to come into our bedroom at daybreak and have a rollicking play time with Effie and me while we were in bed. He would bound onto the bed and fly up the curtain at the window in a second. From his lofty perch he would look down at us, then let go and pounce.

Son John had a young pup that followed him everywhere. John corrupted the word "pup" and called his dog "Blup." In the evening it was amusing to watch Shimbi play with Blup. The dog would be dozing beside a footstool and the genet would creep up from behind and nip him on the foot. In an instant the dog would jump up and whirl around to confront his agitator, but Shimbi would have moved more quickly to the opposite side to nip him again in the rear. The poor dog was completely frustrated by the pestering Shimbi and never came out the winner.

One day we noticed that little Shimbi was getting around with difficulty. His fore legs seemed weak and he was pushing along mainly with his hind legs. As we watched for several days, the paralysis increased and affected all his limbs so that he finally couldn't get out of the small box which served for a bed. We had to hand feed Shimbi for a week or two and concluded that this was probably going to be the end of him. But he began to gradually move, and function returned to his limbs as mysteriously as it had disappeared. He made a complete recovery to the delight of the entire household.

Meanwhile we had concluded what caused his disability. As Shimbi grew his hunting instincts grew also, and he would pounce on grasshoppers or beetles or roaches which tend to invade houses in tropical lands. To stem this invasion we used insecticide sprays and powders which contained DDT, and as Shimbi ate the insects he was also imbibing the poison which would have eventually killed him. So we stopped the insecticides, scrubbed all the floors, and cleaned out all the insects we could find, and the genet cat had no further trouble.

Shimbi was with us for more than a year. As he matured his predatory instincts increased and he wanted to go out at night. Whatever was normal shimbi-life was his right and we would not stand in his way. At first we let him out early and he would disappear into the darkness, but he always came back before we went to bed. But the forays became longer and longer, so we went to bed and left the door cracked and in the morning we would find him high on the top shelf of our hall closet which he had appropriated as his own bailiwick. Finally there came the night he did not return. Since he was a night prowler we knew he would not move around by day to return, but would we ever see him again? Then the second night he reappeared, back home again! So it went on for a while. He could be gone for several days and eventually show up. But he was becoming wilder and now would only climb onto Effie's shoulder. Sometimes he looked lean and shaggy as if life were not as easy out in the real world.

Following an unusually long interlude he came dragging one foot behind him one night. He was gaunt and had no animation. He only wanted to eat and sleep. We tried our best to feed him and get him back to normal because in a week we were going away to Lubondai for Mission Meeting and would be gone a number of days. I had rigged a shelf on our front porch which was too high for dogs or goats, and we left snacks on it for Shimbi. He had visited this shelf many times so we put out palm nuts for him. Before we left we fed him a big supper and bid him good-bye. He was beginning to look more like his normal self. He wasn't quite ready to go out and wanted to stick around, but since we were leaving in the morning, it was necessary to make him go into the dark. With a prick of conscience I gently pushed him out the door and closed it. We never saw Shimbi again.

KANKU AND MBUYI

The last fellowship we established with any of Tubby Nguvu's African friends came late in our missionary life. Effie and I were serving our last stint at Bulape and our daughter Barbara was visiting with us during December 1977. One day some Congolese lads came bringing us a couple of puffballs from the forest which turned out to be African Gray Parrot hatchlings. They didn't have one feather between them, but were covered with downy fuzz. It was obvious that they were just fresh out of the egg. They couldn't peck or pick up any food, but just sat with their mouths wide open for a contribution. Believe it or not, we fed those little birds milk for several days, and they began to gain and develop instinctive movements. Bulape was at the northern extremity of our mission area and at the southern edge of the tropical forest primeval. African Grays nest high in the gigantic trees, and to rob a nest is a difficult feat. The African risks life and limb to climb the breathtaking height, and occasionally, if the tree is small, will cut it down. Often this injures the birds. I recall they brought me one with a broken wing, an injured eye, and a crooked beak. We applied splints and doctored the bird and it became an active and normal pet. We frequently saw them flying overhead in coveys, screeching and cawing with all their might. I had constant requests from friends and acquaintances for one or more of these highly prized birds.

African Grays are quite distinguished birds. They are neither as large nor as gaudily colored as the South American cockatoos and macaws, but the gray sheen of their handsome feathers is enhanced with the white around their eyes and bill, plus a brilliant red tail. Their prime accomplishment is that they are the most gifted talkers of all the parrots. They can concentrate on various sounds and in a short time learn to bark like a dog, meow like a cat, and pronounce complete word phrases they hear in the home. Their vocabularies grow to dozens of words, and the most remarkable thing is that they use them in context much of the time.

We named our two new parrots Kanku and Mbuyi. These are Tshiluba names always given to twins. We never knew for sure but we always assumed that Kanku was female and Mbuyi male. Kanku was smaller, and she preened more completely. She was more finicky about what she ate, and she was more reserved and sedate, but also more aggressive in new situations and places. We assigned this quality to the female instinct for safe and adequate nesting. On the other hand, Mbuyi was a more raucous character. He would come at you with his feathers all ruffled like he was going to eat you alive, but at the last minute he would back off to show he was just a big bluff. He was a hearty eater. As they grew they soon picked their own friendship figures. Kanku chose Effie and would have very little to do with me, while it was reversed with Mbuyi. He was mine. (Or I was his.)

We enjoyed watching them play when they were very young. We had two or three small toy cars on wheels which we put on the floor with the parrots, and they quickly learned to push them around. They even fought over a particular car. How we laughed watching them tug in opposite directions, trying to take the car away from one another. Just like two children.

As their pinion (flying) wings began to grow, we cut them on one side to create imbalance, and put the birds out in the front yard trees to soak up the sunshine. During such times we had to watch for hawks that might come to carry one of them off.

Effie and I had to make a six-week visit to the States in September, 1978, and we decided to take the parrots along. We made a small lattice-work box in which to carry them and proceeded to Kinshasa. At the airport they were placed on the plane in an animal compartment for transport to Brussels. There we retrieved the box and had to wait for several hours for a flight to Atlanta. While we waited we took the birds from the box so they could exercise. Many people came and stood watching them. I am sure they brought memories to a few, of earlier days also spent in the Congo.

Sabena Airlines was concerned about entry to America. They produced large books filled with intricate regulations and they poured over them. Time for departure kept getting closer and closer and finally,

Bill with Kanka and Mbuyi, 1978.

as they were making their last call, the attendants threw up their hands and said, "Go ahead with them. If the Captain lets you take them, then you are all aboard!" We ran to board and find our seats. There was barely room enough at my feet to stow the box-cage, and those blessed parrots didn't make a peep during the entire flight across the Atlantic.

In the Atlanta International airport we first had to visit immigration to show our passports and sign in. The line was long, and about this time our birds came to life. Every few minutes there was a resounding "Hello!" issuing from the box. People turned to see who was greeting who, and I kept my eyes on the ceiling and heard nothing. Next was Customs to check our baggage, and when I told the official I had two parrots in the box, he did a violent double-take and exclaimed, "You can't bring those parrots in here!"

I could think of no other rejoinder than, "Well, it looks like I've already done it."

Atlanta had just been declared an international reception terminal and they had no facilities for admitting animals. There was no attending veterinarian. The upshot was that the parrots could not be admitted without authentic veterinary permission. The Sabena officials who had allowed this faux pas were called. They were as polite and reassuring as they could be, and they promised Effie and me that they would take the parrots to their office and protect them until a veterinarian could come the following day to examine them. Effie and I had direct connections to Knoxville where I had an appointment to see a doctor, so we decided that she would stay over to wait for the birds and I would go ahead.

Early the following morning when Effie poked her head in the Sabena office, all she found was a secretary at her typewriter. "Is this where the parrots are?" Effie asked.

The secretary's eyes widened with astonishment. "Is *that* what is in that box?" she exclaimed. "I've heard noises all morning over there and wondered what in the world it was."

The veterinarian finally arrived and said the birds would need to be in isolation for a month, but he allowed Effie to take them on to Knoxville and to keep them isolated. Another official there visited us at the end of the month to determine that they were in good health. All this caution because some South American parrots brought to California carried a gastrointestinal plasmodium which had spread into the poultry industry, causing millions of dollars worth of losses. Now parrots were taboo. We were extremely fortunate since ours got through just before regulations were tightened so that it is still practically impossible to import parrots.

We loved Kanku and Mbuyi. They lived with us longer than any other African animal friends we ever had—almost twelve years. They not only blessed our home but also the homes of our children. They attended family reunions, and bird conversations graced our gatherings. The telephone never rang that a parrot didn't answer, "Hello?" Often they continued with a one-sided recitation. "Hi there! . . . Oh yes . . . Okay." Sometimes one of the birds would start down from its perch on the outside of the cage which sat on an old kitchen table, and on down the table leg. Effie or I would say, "Get back up there!" This became a standard remark between the two of them. If one started down the table leg the other would say, "Get back up there!"

I'll never forget the night I happened to go through the room in a hurry where their cage was located. I was on my way to the car and I called back over my shoulder, "Night night!" as I went out the door. There was a moment of silence, and then the reply, "See you later!"

They not only mimicked the words they heard, but also the inflection and register of the voice. When they called, "Beee-ill!" they sounded like Effie calling me. But when they called, "Eff-eee!" they sounded like me.

We loved Kanku and Mbuyi. They are gone now but they blessed our lives for many years as did others of God's wild wonderful world.

21 CONGO KILLERS

*Offer unto God thanksgiving and pay thy vows unto the most High:
And call upon me in the day of trouble: I will deliver thee, and thou
shalt glorify me (Psalms 50:14–15).*

During my years in Congo/Zaire, I was much interested in studying
snakes and trying to correlate the Congolese identification and
names with the scientific ones. Africans were not particularly
concerned with Latin classes and subclasses, but rather grouped
them by appearance, habitat, and behavior patterns. There was some
overlap here, so they were inclined to align snakes according to the
personal experiences they had with them, which of course varied
with the individual. During the years I was associated with Dr. John
Miller my knowledge of snakes was considerably expanded. He
approached herpetology correctly, as a science. He counted scales
and plates, examined eyes and fangs, and assigned each to its proper
category. John is quite myopic and I can still see him with his glasses
pushed up on his head, squinting at close range to find tiny telltale
signs in the serpentine anatomy. He offered prizes to African boys
who could bring him undamaged snakes, dead or alive, and he
collected them in remarkable numbers. John wrote a monograph
entitled, *A List of Serpents of the Kasai Comprised of 875 Specimens
Collected by J. K. Miller.* Beyond a doubt John knew more about the
snakes of Kasai Province than any other person.

I must admit, our snake collecting exuberance sometimes went
beyond the bounds of propriety. We had a tall, round cardboard barrel
with quite smooth walls in our office at Lubondai, and we dumped
small snakes in it to wait for a leisure moment when we could study
and classify them. It was impossible for the snakes to get out. At least
it was until the afternoon an office attendant stashed a broom in the
barrel, locked up, and left. The next morning when we arrived there
were, of course, no snakes in the barrel. We were sorry to lose our
wiggling collection, but presumed they had escaped to the great
outdoors. At least this was our casual conclusion until Aurie, John's
wife and our lab technician, came to work. She was poking into a
cupboard for some pans or glassware to run an examination. We heard
a startled exclamation which sounded more like a yelp, and the last we
saw of Aurie she was walking resolutely up the path toward her house

where she sent back a curt message that she wasn't coming back to work until we cleared snakes out of the laboratory.

On another occasion John and I were traveling on Air Congo's commercial flight from Luluabourg to Kinshasa, and John had a big batch of newly born pythons he wanted to take to the capital city. We carefully put them in a small cardboard box, sealed it with scotch tape, and punched small holes in it. Then we smuggled them aboard the plane with no one the wiser. Nothing untoward happened on our two hour flight, and we delivered our cargo to its proper destination. I did have some uneasy moments en route as I thought about our twenty-five or thirty baby pythons getting loose and slithering throughout the cabin.

NONVENOMOUS SNAKES

The nonvenomous snakes were the most numerous in John's study. Most common are two small members of the *Colubridae* family, the West African House Snake (Tshiluba name, *Mulualua*) and the Slender Green Snake (Tshiluba name, *Kolombo*). The type he identified more often than any other was the green snake. It is alert and quick-moving, measuring up to six feet. They were most often observed it the palm trees. We approached it with some caution because sometimes it can be confused with the green mamba, a very dangerous snake.

The various members of the *typhlops* family are an interesting group. These are shiny types, perhaps a foot long, which burrow in the ground or in windblown rubbish. They are blind and the head and tail are so similar it is difficult to tell them apart. The Africans call them *Kusuma Kubidi* which means "two mouths," and the Europeans also designate them as the "two headed snakes."

But the truly spectacular snakes of the nonvenomous group are the Pythons (Tshiluba, *Moma*). The African Rock Python was ten to twelve feet long, but might grow up to be fifteen feet or more. They have needlelike teeth and when they bite it's like being stuck with pins—a good deal of bleeding but no lasting lesion. The python does not really crush its victim by fracturing, it simply wraps itself around the chest and squeezes, smothering its prey to death. In this enveloping position it has a lot of muscular power, but not very much when its body is extended. So no matter how large the python, two men have no trouble holding it by its head and tail, stretched out, and it cannot pull itself together from that position.

The python can swallow a goat or small antelope. After the snake swallows such a large mass whole, it must retire for a week or so to digest its meal. During this time it is considerably in danger concerning its own protection. This is when the African catches his python, which gives rise to their proverb, *Kudia kudi kufua*, "To eat is to die."

At Bibanga we had a chicken house with a wire fence around it. One night a python found a small hole in the fence, made its way into the house, and swallowed a good-sized turkey we were saving for Thanksgiving. But then it couldn't get out through the hole, and the following morning we found and captured Mr. Python and put him in a box. Our son Billy, then four, named him Alexander. Billy used to drag Alexander by the neck all over the yard, pulling his length along. Our sentry brought up the rear, of course, to be sure everything was under control.

Some years later when we lived at Lubondai where Dr. Miller and I were organizing and instructing the IMCK, a contingent of messengers came from the village of Beya Nkuna about four miles down the road, to say they had spotted a large python and would show us where it was. Miller was teaching a class, but when I sidled up to the open door and mouthed the word "snake," he turned to the students and with a very straight face dismissed the class and came hurrying out to me asking, "Where is it?"

We got in a truck with our African friends and as we passed Beya Nkuna village they showed us a large ant hill in the middle of a manioc field where, they said, the snake lives in the base of the ant hill. It suns itself beside the mound and if disturbed it retreats down into the ground. We knew we must be as stealthy as possible until we were right on it. We drove the car a little further down the road and got out to begin quietly creeping toward the ant hill. About ten yards away someone yelled, "There it goes!" and sure enough we could see it moving. We made a rush just in time for John and me to catch the tail since most of the snake had disappeared. It had a lot of strength and resistance, but we dug our heels into the soft earth and held on. As we exerted steady traction we noted with interest that the snake was experiencing muscular fatigue. When it let up a little we would pull and gain two or three inches, and this was repeated until after about fifteen minutes we pulled the python out, put it in a sack, and proudly carried it home. It was a twelve-foot specimen.

Pythons are quickly mollified and make gentle pets. But one day I let Alexander out too close to a parked automobile. It made a dive for the machine, disappeared into its under parts, and wrapped itself around the axle of a rear wheel several times. I couldn't budge it and had to jack up the car and take off the wheel in order to recover the python!

VENOMOUS SNAKES

The venomous snakes constituted 28 percent of John Miller's list. First of all are the vipers, characteristically heavy and rather slow moving.

They often have triangular-shaped heads which are distinctly differen-tiated from the rest of the body, and they have unusually long fangs. The venom of vipers is characterized as a hemotoxin which means it poisons the blood. It attacks and causes massive coagulation, blocking the circulatory pathways and depriving the tissues of oxygen, minerals, and other life-sustaining ingredients. The destruction is primarily local but may be so extensive as to cause eventually alarming systemic effects.

The Mole Viper or Burrowing Viper, belonging to the family *Anactaspis*, is a small specimen, usually less than a foot long with black coloring. It has hinged fangs which are extremely long for its small mouth, and by retracting its lower jaw it can expose the fang, usually on one side only. So if this snake is held with fingers just behind the head, the most common way to hold a snake, it can jab your finger without moving its head. I learned this the hard way. When I encoun-tered my first Mole viper, I picked it up with my usual aplomb to look it over and suddenly felt a painful prick in my finger. The end of my finger was swollen considerably. If you have ever hit this portion of your anatomy with a hammer, you know that such swelling can be extremely uncomfortable. There was no systemic effect from this little fellow's poison, but I can tell you I slept very poorly that night.

Another larger viper, which also is not life-threatening but which carries a stronger venom, is the Night Viper (Tshiluba name, *Kadiabiula*). As the name indicates it is a night prowler, and the bare-footed African often steps on this snake in the dark. We missionaries were thoroughly sensitized to the proposition that you don't walk around at night without a flashlight—even wearing shoes! The Tshiluba name means "toad frog eater," and it is an accurate moniker. I was always surprised at how often the ones I caught regurgitated half-digested toads in an effort to escape.

The puff adder has the official name, *Bitis Arietans* (Tshiluba name, *Ditshiula*), and is a much more dangerous character. This is quite a heavy snake with a short tail. The average length is three feet, but they may grow to five feet. They have formidable fangs and the venom is a powerful blood poison. When excited they exhale with an audible hissing sound which gives them their name.

The puff adder is surely a dangerous opponent. The young daughter of one of our evangelists was bitten on the foot by a viper. They lived in a village far from professional help. The evangelist knew to apply a tourni-quet to prevent spread of the venom, but what he didn't know is that you can't leave it tightly applied indefinitely because it also inhibits circulation of the blood. It must be loosened from time to time. When they reached us, three or four days after the accident, the child's entire lower leg was

Bill Worth and a friend.

already in an advanced state of gangrene. Eventually we had to amputate, and while she was growing to adulthood she was fitted with artificial limbs of various sizes and lengths, all of this thanks to Mr. Puff Adder.

The most forbidding snake in appearance is another viper with the title, *Bitis Gabonica* or Gabon viper. This one has a gaudy array of colors and patterns on its head and body, has nasal horns, and can grow to even greater size than the puff adder. The venom is also more active and may contain a mixture of hemotoxin and neurotoxin. These snakes were not as common in our part of the country as the puff adders, but I remember walking along the path one day at Lubondai and coming upon one of these vipers. An African was running toward me and I yelled out the one word, *"Nyoka!"* (Snake!). But when he saw the object of my agitation and warning, he stopped running, turned, and calmly walked back in the other direction.

"Where are you going?" I called.

"I'm going after a stick. That lazy snake will still be there if I don't come back until tomorrow!"

A third *bitis* we encountered is the *Bitis Nasicornis* or Rhinoceros viper. It is quite similar to the above two in size, shape and movement, but its distinctive feature consists of two enormous nasal horns, much more pronounced than those of the Gabon viper. These three constitute the truly dangerous members of the viper family in central Congo.

The more deadly African snakes are those of the *Elapine* family which include the cobras and mambas. These snakes possess a neuro-toxic venom which acts directly on the nervous system. When the bite is an effective one, a sufficient quantity of injected poison affects the respiratory and circulatory systems, eventually arresting the breathing movements and the heartbeats. Africa is the land of the cobra. True, the vaunted King cobra, largest of the venomous snakes, is a denizen of the Orient, particularly India. But there are at least eight full species of African cobras and several subspecies which are classified.

I was out hunting and fishing with my son Bill one day, and we were scouting across an island in the Lulua River when our Congolese guide suddenly held out his arm to stop us. He showed us dead ahead in some bushes an enormous black snake entwined in the branches. It was lying perfectly still, apparently asleep. Bill had his small .410 shotgun over his shoulder, so he unlimbered it and blew the snake in two. It was a fully six-feet-long forest cobra.

At Bibanga I was called one night to Alec and Peggy McCutchen's house where they told me there was a snake in their chicken house. We went out to investigate, and with the aid of a stick and a flashlight we found that there was a fairly large black snake under a low plat-form of reeds and branches. It had already killed two chickens. I dragged the snake out with the stick, pinned down its head, and got it by the neck. Then I took it to my house where I put it in a wooden box with a wire face and left it in the storage room hut out back, plan-ning to make a closer examination by daylight. But during the night an auto arrived from Lake Munkamba calling me out on an emer-gency visit. One of the children of Lachlan and Winnie Vass, our missionary friends, was acutely ill and I stayed with the family for several days until she was out of danger.

On my return to Bibanga I resumed my daily tasks, so it was another day or two before I remembered the snake, waiting now for more than a week. I took the box out in the sunlight and held it up close to my face to get a good look through the wire netting, and it reared its head and neck and spread its hood in typical cobra fashion. I was so surprised I almost dropped the box! I had no idea I had a cobra, and here it was right before my eyes for minute observation. I raised the box again with my face close to the mesh, and as I did so the serpent opened its mouth wide and its head came forward with a swishing sound. I caught it in both eyes from the spitting cobra. I washed out my eyes with water repeatedly and thoroughly, but they still swelled almost shut. For a day or two I discovered how a blind doctor practices medicine.

Later I learned that washing out my eyes with milk would have been more effective. I got a full charge in the face but its only effect was local. There are no symptomatic results from poison spit into the eye. It must penetrate into the tissues with a bite to reach the blood stream. The snake aims this load in expectation that surprise and discomfort will give it a chance to escape when its cornered. It wasn't a pleasant experience, I assure you, and the lesson was not wasted on me. I never gave another cobra such a chance.

Cousins of the cobras, and even more alarming, are the mambas. They are aggressive and move rapidly. The toxicity of their poison tests very high. We encountered two of them in the Kasai, generally spoken of as the green mamba and the black mamba. The green mamba is also identified as Jameson's mamba and the scientific name is *Dendroaspis jamesoni*. The African name in Tshiluba is *Tshianga*. This snake tends to be arboreal in its habits and runs from six to eight feet in length.

Another venomous snake that is not a mamba but closely resembles Jameson's species is the Boomslang (Afrikaans for "tree snake"), and officially listed as *Dispholidus typhus*. The Africans often cannot tell the difference and also call this snake a *Tshianga*. It is also green and also is arboreal. It spreads no hood like a cobra but when aroused it puffs up its throat. Its fangs are located posteriorly in the mouth and for this reason it has difficulty biting quickly and injecting a quantity of venom. Therefore it is not as deadly a snake as the cobras and mambas. If it can get a good chewing bite, it is very dangerous.

I have saved the most perilous of them all until last. This is the black mamba, officially the *Dendroaspis polylepis*. It has color variations and may have a dark-olive shading which appears black. Since it resembles the black cobra, the Africans do not differentiate between them but call all of them by a common name *Nyoka wa ntoka*. The black mamba is terrestrial in its habits, and is the largest of these venomous snakes, sometimes ten or twelve feet. One time an African was walking through the forest toward the Mutoto mission station when without provocation a mamba charged out of the overgrowth on the side of the road and bit him. He never reached Mutoto, but died from the toxic effects there in the path.

Even accidental and trivial injections of the poison can be life-threatening. A mamba was killed in a native village and its head was chopped off. A crowd gathered to watch the death gyrations of the body. A schoolboy ran up to see what they were watching. He accidentally stepped on the severed head and was pricked by the mamba fang. Villagers brought him to the Good Shepherd Hospital in coma and with respiratory activity almost gone. He lived only because professional doctors attended him all night long with artificial respiration and added oxygen supply.

I was traveling alone in my car late one day from Luluabourg to Lubondai, and decided to stop off briefly at Mutoto to see the Vasses. While Lach and I sat in his office talking, several Congolese came running to tell us with great alarm that there was a mamba in one of the married student's houses at the Bible School. Lach had a long pole and some flexible wire filament and we quickly put together a noose. We immediately spotted a large snake up in the rafters at the ridge of the roof. We snagged the snake's head in the wire loop and secured it in a heavy tow sack. I was delighted to have such a fine mamba specimen to take on to Lubondai for a closer examination, but I did not relish taking the sack with me in the car. So, I dumped it under the hood in front of the radiator, behind the front gratings. When I reached home, long after the family was asleep, I simply parked the car in our backyard and went on to bed.

The next day was Sunday. The first thing I did was to look up John Miller and tell him that I had a big black mamba in my car.

He thought for a minute and said, "We'd better transfer it to a cage while everybody is in church. That way we won't run the risk of having a crowd standing round if anything goes awry."

So John and I armed ourselves with stout sticks and opened the hood of the Chevy. To our utter surprise there lay the mamba contentedly coiled around the air filter! It had chewed a big hole in that heavy sack and escaped! I had no idea a snake could do such a thing. When we began to poke at him he glided downward and disappeared in the innards of the motor. A little banging stirred him and suddenly here he came out from under the front fender on my side. He turned in front of the wheel to hide again back in the motor, and as he did I grabbed him by the passing tail. So there I stood with the tail of a mamba in my hands, much more interested in where the head might be. I let go. That was the last we saw of the mamba. We poked and banged and walked all around, but he did not appear again.

Finally we decided we could search for him better if we put the car up on a rack so we could see under it. I drove the Chevy slowly to the garage and John walked along behind to see if the snake dropped out and made off in the grass. It didn't, and we got the car high enough to get under it. John, on his side, poked into all the cracks and crevices on my side while I watched to be sure the snake didn't blindside him from above. Then I did the same thing from my side while John watched. We worked for more than an hour trying to route out that mamba, and finally we gave up the hunt. We drove the car away from the station, well out in the tropical grass where we parked it, presuming that as time went by the mamba would leave its motorized seclusion and seek a fairer place in which to reside. We left the car out there all day Monday. But that's not the end of the story!

Effie had promised to take a group of Central School boys and girls out to a favorite hideaway across the plains which they had christened "Walden." Since the group would more than fill the station wagon, it was necessary to attach the two-wheel trailer for the boys to bump along in. We retrieved the parked car, hooked up the trailer, and off they went in a cloud of dust. The load was heavy, the road was full of soft sand, and the Chevy was laboring and getting hot in the process. Then Effie missed a turn in the high grass and they had to back up. To do this they had to unhitch the trailer. As she slowly backed and turned, her right rear wheel dropped off into an evacuated termite nest, and the Chevy's back axle rested on the ground. Effie gunned the motor but the car didn't move. It did get hotter though. Now the boys cut poles to put under the back end and prize up the disengaged wheel and move the car forward. They heaved with might and mane while Effie reved the accelerator. Chevy shimmied and shook and began to creep forward a bit. As it did so the mamba suddenly dropped down from the under side of the car, almost in the midst of the laboring boys. It was a critical moment, but that snake wasn't for waiting to pay any respects. It had gotten so hot under that car that all it wanted was wide open space, so it hit the ground and took off at top speed into the high tropical grass. Effie and the kids continued their trip. As for me, I learned my lesson well: that God takes care of missionaries—and fools!

CROCODILES CAN BITE TOO

Despite the plethora of venomous snakes in Africa and the hair-raising tales about them, I am convinced that the title of number one animal killer does not belong to the serpent but to the crocodile. Basically the snake is afraid of man and shuns him. The crocodile does not. He looks for man to be his next meal. The Nile crocodile is a wily, patient creature seldom seen, but stalking its prey, sometimes day after day. He will float silently with only his eyes above the surface of the water. Then, at the optimum moment of attack there is a mighty slap of his powerful tail or a sudden snap and tug of the fang-infested jaws, and the victim is pulled under and trapped until drowned. The carcass is cached under submerged logs or brush so the crocodile can return and dine at its leisure.

The Africans become prime targets of this cycle because all of them must perforce go to the water where the crocodile is waiting. Africans go to bathe, to wash their clothes, to collect gourds of water which they carry on their heads to the village, or to simply get a drink. They even go to exercise and play. I have often caught my breath watching African children swimming in the murky waters of a large stream, and have wanted to scream at them to get out and stay away from danger. But they would only be perplexed by my reactions. Their danger is probably analogous to mine when I get in my car and drive the interstate highways of my homeland. People are killed every day on them, but I never give it a thought when I turn on the ignition. It's just an indispensable part of my culture. So are the waterways to the African.

The crocodile is the large and aggressive relative of its more docile cousin, the alligator. The latter's diet is predominantly fish and rarely does it attack man. Anatomically the alligator's snout is more blunt and wide, and its lower jaw or mandible is hinged like yours and mine. The croc's lower jaw is fixed to its spine and body, and it is the upper jaw which is hinged and raises to take a bite. The croc has an interesting attack method when it is trying to pull under a human victim who has hold of a tree or the side of a boat. It furiously gyrates its body, turning over and over while holding onto a leg. On occasion I have repaired the wounds of a Congolese who has been torn and injured by the croc, but saved by helpful friends. Not only must lacerations be closed, but often hips and knees have been torn from their sockets and must be straightened and immobilized for healing.

Crocodiles eat carrion. One night as we were traveling up the Lulua River in a motor boat, we smelled the stench of rotting flesh. It became stronger and stronger until we turned a bend in the stream to come upon the decaying body of a hippopotamus lying in the shallows. A dozen crocodiles were gathered around it, gobbling their fill of the voluminous vile vittles!

A South African fellow who was a professional crocodile hunter visited us at Lubondai. He came in his big truck with a large metal boat loaded on it which he could lower into the water with a hand winch and when through hunting, reload it the same way. He had a team of two or three trained Africans with him who carried all the gear necessary for skinning crocs and treating the hides to preserve them until they were sold. Only the hide of the belly was useful and the soft under-covering of a moderately large croc could bring a hundred dollars. Crocs were considered to be nuisance animals at that time and were not a protected species.

Some of us were curious about the man's hunting methods, so he invited us to come along and observe. He hunted crocs in the dead of night with a powerful spotlight mounted on his forehead. With the light he combed the riverbanks and the surface of the water ahead. He stood in the prow of the boat. One of his assistants handled the outboard motor and tiller while another stood beside him with a long lance-like gig with a coiled rope attached to it and to the side of the boat.

Hunting can only be done when there is no moon. A nearby croc can see the light and hear the motor, but it does not associate this with danger. It is curious and remains stationary staring into the light. The light beam catches the eyes of the prey and they appear as two small cherry red dots close together. So the hunter gives a signal and the man steers directly toward where the beam is zeroed on the water. All aboard are silent so as not to alarm the crocodile. The boat can approach within a few feet of the unsuspecting victim. The hunter raises his rifle and the assistant readies his harpoon. They have worked together for so long that their movements are almost simultaneous. The gun explodes and the harpoon sinks into the leather-covered body. All that is left to do is pull the dead crocodile into the boat. Since we missionaries were not hunting crocs for profit, we modified some of the methods we learned, but by and large they became the basis for many fun nights we spent on the river.

An interesting paradox-of-risk has been that we felt much safer on the rivers at night in proximity of the crocs than in the daylight hours. This is because at night we know where all the crocs are but they don't know where we are. By day this is dangerously reversed.

One time two visiting ministers from the homeland were with us, and Bill Pruitt and I decided to take them crocodile hunting. This was after Congolese independence and expatriots no longer had the freedom to use firearms as they had under the Belgians, so we were carrying no guns. I was the forward observer, Bill was steering, and our two guests were amidships. We were scarcely afloat when we spotted a four-foot crocodile. I gouged it with a pole and it slithered away. Rocky Young, a stout fellow with an athletic history, asked in an accusing voice, "Why didn't you catch it?" His question galled me a bit. What did Rocky Young know about catching crocodiles? But I had to admit to myself that I had never attempted to catch one that large.

We had scarcely gone another two hundred yards when I spotted the second set of cherry red eyes. It was almost the twin of the first, lying in shallow water near the bank. As we neared, I jumped over the side of the boat and onto the back of the croc. I got my hands around its neck and wrestled with it while it spanked me vigorously with its tail. I won the wrestling match and we hauled it into the boat, securing it in a heavy tow sack.

Up river we sighted a third croc and as we approached we found it was a triplet! Rocky was so enamored by my accomplishment that he proposed to catch this one himself, so he followed the script. After much tugging and grunting and shouting and hauling, we had his animal in a second sack.

We sighted no more cherry red dots traveling up stream, but as we returned down river we saw the first croc again. So, we caught that one too, and had three sacks of crocodiles to carry home. These were the largest I had ever captured and I built a brick fence to put them in at Tshikaji, much to the concern of missionary mothers with small children. We had trouble finding food for them since we wouldn't feed them meat which the populace would like to have. Then we happened on the happy solution of toad frogs. Africans not only won't eat them, they won't touch them. They believe that contact with a toad frog reduces human libido. So we gave little African boys large colored magazine pictures for each toad they brought in. They set traps for them and caught them with string lassos. I am sure that our three crocodiles decimated the toad frog population at Tshikaji for several years in the early '70s.

We were living at Lubondai and a group of Central School children and teachers planned a trip to "Virginia Falls." My son Paul and I planned to hunt crocs that night after the school crowd had finished supper and gone, so we took the boat and all the equipment. However, about the time we got there, Paul came down with a rip-roaring malarial fever. He needed to get home. So I turned to my good wife and asked her to pilot the boat. She recoiled.

"But I've never handled a motor boat, and besides it's night! I just can't do it!"

I assured her there was nothing to it, and that I would show her everything. I would navigate it out into the river and bring it back. With tears in her eyes she displayed her devotion and faithfulness to her husband and climbed into the boat.

This time I had a gun. I had managed it in a diplomatic manner. I had an old 12 gauge shotgun I had given to my friend and medical worker, Muwaya Simon, with the understanding that he would "lend" it to me sometimes. I had loaded it with a single slug in case we did encounter a croc.

Our first find was a small one but with Effie's inept control of motor and steering we missed our approach. Our second find was a larger croc and I blasted it before it could get away. We hauled it into the boat. Up river we encountered shallow rapids with many rocks, and Effie was about at her wits end trying to manipulate the craft. Just then I spotted a crocodile lying on a large rock on the other side of the river. The rapids were between us and as I was advising Effie how to set the angle of the idling boat so the current would carry us toward our prey, we felt a big bump. The pin in our propeller was sheared off by one of the rocks, and we bumped helplessly down the river. We were still eighty yards from the croc and that was too far for a 12 gauge slug, but I took a pot shot and saw the animal disappear on the far side of the rock.

Now it was time for Effie and me to change places so I could work at replacing the pin. The boat drifted out of the rapids and into quiet water, then a side current moved us toward the far bank. I saw that we were drifting right to the rock where the croc had been.

"Grab that line in the prow," I told Effie. "Get on that rock and hold us still until I finish this job."

Obediently she did as she was instructed, but as she stepped off onto the rock she screamed. She was standing with one foot on the dead crocodile! My pot shot had blown its brains out. It was a good ten foot model, so we rolled it into the boat too, and I subjected Effie to no further trauma. We went home.

Years earlier I was out at the river fishing all by myself. I had spent the night in my bedroll and expected to do some casting at dawn. A couple of Congolese fellows appeared and as we sat around the evening fire they told me of a large female crocodile that made a nest, deposited her eggs, and slept on it at night to guard it. They said they knew the exact spot and could show me. I knew that meant getting up before daybreak to hike to the place before the sun rose to make it too warm. Crocodiles are cold-blooded and are quite sluggish and slow of movement during the cold hours. I set my portable clock and we took off before five o'clock. We hiked and hiked, crossing small streams and cutting our way through thick underbrush. Questioning an African about distance is always discouraging. They have little use for comparisons. It's sort of like in East Tennessee—everything is just over the next mountain!

Eventually we came to a clearing by the Mulafidi River. The boys signaled silence, and one of them crept forward to peek over a narrow sand dune. He came hurrying back to say she was on her nest, directly in front of us. Now it was my turn. I went slowly and quietly and was rewarded with the sight of a very large crocodile lying side view before me. I took aim and shot her in the shoulder. She raised her head, opened her mouth wide, but never moved from the nest. We found fifty eggs in her nest. We cut off the crocodile head and buried it in the ground. Weeks later, when insects had eaten all the flesh, someone brought the skull to me at Lubondai. I still have that crocodile skull.

Bill Rule enjoyed many outings on the rivers of Congo.

22 AROUND THE WORLD IN MANY WAYS

The Lord is my rock, and my fortress, and my deliverer; my God, my strength, in whom I will trust; my buckler, and the horn of my salvation, and my high tower (Psalms 18:2).

The missionary's opportunity to travel often leads through foreign lands and distant places. Sabena Airlines was particularly gracious in allowing stopovers at landing points for any reasonable length of time and picking up a subsequent flight at no extra cost.

Because it was such a remarkable experience I have already written at some length of our first journey back to the United States during World War II, and of our return the following year after hostilities had ceased. We came home with one baby boy and for Effie and me to meet our respective in-laws. We returned to Africa with two children, Billy and Charlotte. During the next four years while at Bibanga, Libby and Paul were added to our entourage, and when we started home again in the summer of 1950 we cut quite a figure—like a drake and his spouse with four small ducklings. Two had never set foot on the pathways of twentieth-century urbanity, and the other two had no recollection of having done so. We really were bringing four small heathen into a completely new culture.

We left Leopoldville late in the afternoon and stopped in the middle of the night at Kano in Nigeria to refuel. I got off the plane to stretch my legs while the rest of the family slept. It was a moonless night, dark as pitch, and I had to feel my way along, step by step, but even so was shortly outside the confines of the tiny airport. Suddenly I heard a snort and felt a jerky movement directly in front of me. I halted just in time to avoid running over a camel resting on the ground. Its keeper, with hand on bridle, was also dozing. I've had bumping accidents with automobiles and streetcars, and with chickens, goats, pigs, and sheep. Once I hit a hyena in the night and another time an antelope. But this was my first camel!

Early in the morning we stopped again to take on fuel at Tunis, and then proceeded to cross the beautiful blue Mediterranean. It was a clear day and we had excellent visibility of the islands of Sardinia and Corsica, plus a breathtaking flight over the snow-covered Alps with the massif of Mount Blanc squarely in the center of the picture. We landed in Brussels during the early part of the day and since our plane for New

York didn't leave until evening, Sabena put us up at an elegant downtown hotel. The "little heathen" Rule children began to examine their surroundings.

First they found double beds with innerspring mattresses, and when their bouncing activities were curtailed by parental mandate, they went outside to the staircase. In Africa they had seen two or three steps at a time, but never two or three stories or more! Up and down they went as fast as they could manage until the squeals of delight began to reverberate through the hallways and it was time to put a stop to that activity.

I began to figure they needed to get out of the building and walk off some of that vim and vigor. So I took them over just across the public highway to a botanical garden, and we traversed its paths with several round trip excursions. On our return to the hotel I noticed that the noonday traffic had picked up considerably. The children were running on ahead of me and I became concerned.

"Stop at the corner!" I called.

But to my consternation I saw them bolt out into the street without hesitation. Fortunately there was a lull in the flow of traffic and they made it across without mishap, but when I caught up I scolded them with vigor.

"I told you to stop at the corner!" I growled.

Billy's seven-year-old eyes opened wide and he looked at me with a puzzled expression as he asked, "Daddy, what's a corner?"

I hadn't stopped to think. Of course he didn't know what a corner was. We didn't have corners at Bibanga.

Two-year-old Paul had not gone with us. His mother decided to give him a bath and when she put him in the shiny slick porcelain tub he began to slide around. He couldn't keep his footing or his balance and he began to cry. The room was closed with tile walls which magnified sounds, and the reverberating noise frightened the little fellow even more. He had quite a fit about being bathed in that deluxe bathtub, and it amused us to think that he preferred his rough old cement tub at Bibanga.

Downstairs in the handsome lobby with five-year-old Charlotte, a lady came sweeping by us graced with fine furs over her shoulders and flowing out behind her. Charlotte asked the lady why she was wearing animals around her neck. As I made a dive to cut off further embarrassing questions, I failed to hear the lady's reply, but Charlotte's rejoinder was, "Well, who killed them?" I heard the answer in perfect English mixed with a slight accent, "Little girl, I don't know who killed them but you can be sure *I* didn't!"

Since we had to leave for the airport before dinner, the hotel served us a special meal. Just the Rule family. We will never forget that meal.

It was very special. All that was brought to us was two giant dishes. One was filled with various fresh fruits: apples, peaches, strawberries, grapes, mangos. The other was piled high with ice cream and ices of many flavors: vanilla, chocolate, mocha, neapolitan. All you could eat, in any combination you wanted. We all made pigs of ourselves since we had a lot of catching up to do on eating ice cream.

We left Brussels and stopped at Manchester, England, before continuing to Shannon, Ireland, for the last refueling before the hop across the Atlantic to New York. It was late when we reached Shannon and the kids were sound asleep. An obliging hostess urged Effie and me to deplane and get sandwiches and coffee. She assured us she would not leave the cabin and would keep close watch on the kids, so we went to the waiting area and our wait lengthened from thirty minutes to an hour, and then to two and longer. Some mechanical problem with the plane was the delay. The crew kept coming back to the passengers and apologizing. I thought of that long flight ahead, over the north Atlantic, and of the precious cargo of mine they were carrying, and each time they came I urged, "Don't apologize. Just take all the time necessary. We sure don't want to leave here until everything is in perfect order."

Finally we were ready, and we flew to New York without further mishap. Our Rule family holed up at the Prince George Hotel, awaiting railroad reservations to Charleston, West Virginia. In the morning Mrs. Julia Lake Kellersberger came to our rescue and took us to her New York apartment for a fine breakfast. But jet lag was catching up with the kids, and it was hard for them to sit at the table and keep their eyes open. Later in a Pullman car they were out like a light until waking the next day in Charleston where they were hugged and kissed by Grandmama and Granddaddy Crane who drove them home for a year of Stateside visitation and schooling.

BRITAIN AND BELGIUM

After a year of furlough we were again on our way to Africa, but not directly. The Belgian government had allowed me to proceed to medical service in the Congo ten years earlier without the prescribed orientation courses given in Belgium. Now I was to make up that lost instruction, and we would be in Brussels for several months before returning to Bibanga.

Our itinerary called for us to make the trip to Europe by boat and we had the great fortune to book passage on the most magnificent passenger ship afloat, the *Queen Elizabeth*. It sailed from New York to Southampton, and then we traveled by train to London where we lodged for a week at the South Kensington Hotel in Queen's Gate Terrace. This gave us and the children easy access to Hyde Park where we admired the statue of Peter Pan and watched young sailors maneuver their toy ships on the round pond. We also had time to visit the zoo, Westminster Abbey, and the gigantic and amazing Museum of Natural History. One day I slipped away and went over to St. Paul's Cathedral to hear General Ike Eisenhower who was speaking. I had glimpses of the Queen Mother and the two young Princesses, and after the ceremonies I toured the cathedral which still suffered extensive areas of damage from World War II. Large stones torn from the building were still lying in the courtyard, and as I came up Ludgate Hill toward the church I had observed whole blocks of ruins. For two blocks behind the cathedral one could see only gutted buildings and rubble in every direction.

These were the days of a World's Fair in London, so naturally we attended. There were great crowds and large areas to cover, and the inevitable happened. Our family was separated. I had baby Paul on my shoulders and Effie was with the other three children. For some time we searched for each other, but had no success. Paul and I eventually caught a taxi back to the hotel, and Effie and her seventeen-year-old cousin, Lisa Steiner, pooled their assets for taxi fare.

One other London experience I record with some hesitation and embarrassment. We chanced upon an attractive little restaurant not far from our hotel. It provided a quiet and sedate atmosphere, an excellent cuisine, and reasonable prices, so we dined there one evening. We were so pleased with the place that we returned the next evening for supper. When we went for a third time, the meticulously groomed ladies who ran the place approached us with some unease. They told us they had a number of elderly boarders who had been with them some years and who highly prized their decorum and tranquility while dining, and would we please not bring the children there any more. We withdrew, of course, taking our injured dignity with us. It was the first eating joint I had ever been kicked out of.

On July 5 we caught a train at Victoria Station for the two-hour trip to Dover where we boarded a Belgian ferry for Ostend, enjoying the lovely sight of Dover's famous white cliffs receding as we crossed the English Channel. The train to Brussels arrived about 10:30 P.M. and we went to a hotel before finding the next day a "pension" where we could room and board during our stay in the city. This was Pension Ten Bosch at Place Albert Leemans in the community of Ixelles, and we thoroughly enjoyed our stay there. The proprietors were a jovial Flemish couple, and she served us several Belgian dishes we liked and learned to anticipate. One was artichoke leaves, pulled from the main cluster and scraped between the teeth to remove the succulent coating. Another was small bites of cheese and bread crumbs fried in deep fat. I don't know what they are called in Flemish, but we nicknamed them

Bill and Effie with Billy, Charlotte, Libby, and Paul.

"cheese-its." *Frits* are the Belgian version of French fries, and we could always buy a folded paper of them from street vendors, as well as delicious cherries and giant strawberries.

Effie and I engaged tutors and settled in for diligent and daily study of the French language. I had picked up a smattering in the Congo, but Effie was even behind me. I also attended colonial courses conducted by the government for Congo-bound missionaries, and because of my ten years of medical work already performed, they sort of went easy on me. I was not required to take examinations but only monitor the courses, and at the conclusion was awarded a certificate of full recognition by the Belgian authorities.

The studies over, Alec McCutchen and Ted Stixrud and I set out on a bicycle tour of western Belgium. Our first day's stop, southward, was Mons, a quaint little town built on a hill which saw heavy fighting in both world wars, and which exhibited an interesting war museum. We swung westward and spent the second night at Tournai, an important provincial capital in the days of Charlemagne. Tournai was severely bombed by the Germans in 1940 because of troop concentrations there. Over 1,500 buildings were destroyed, and even ten years later there was still more damage than any other place we saw in Belgium. The cathedral was still being restored, and was the largest and most impressive that we saw. The third night we spent in Courdrai, and here again the vestiges of bombings were more than apparent. This time they were of allied origin.

The following day we moved to Ypres which brought us into the heart of Flanders. Ypres is a town which has become a special shrine for the British. The Ypres salient was held throughout the 1914–1918 war by the British against repeated German assaults. Over 160,000 British soldiers were killed in this vicinity, and the tremendous victory arch raised at Ypres is inscribed with the names of 58,000 men who lie in unknown graves! Well-kept British cemeteries dot the countryside and Ypres has profited over the intervening years by annual pilgrimages of Englishmen. English is spoken almost as commonly as French, and poppies still grow in profusion. The city was leveled to the ground in the early war and the cathedral was rebuilt only to be gutted again in the more recent war.

From Ypres we biked on to Dixmuid which was on the same line in World War I, but was held by the Belgian army. It was even more completely destroyed than Ypres, and for months the Belgians and Germans lay in trenches across a small river from each other, practically a stone's throw. The Belgian trenches were still in a fine state of preservation and very interesting to explore. So atrocious was the stand at that point they were still referred to as the "Trenches of the Dead." We cycled on to the coast and turned north to Ostende where I was initiated into the delicacy of *moules* (mussels). We visited the docks but did not stay overnight. We moved on to Bruges.

Bruges is perhaps the most picturesque city in Belgium. A mighty seaport in the Middle Ages, its approaches from the ocean silted up and left it a quaint relic of an ancient era. One feels the enchantment walking its streets. The city is filled with canals which are made lovely by artificial lights at night. The clock tower is very impressive, and the Basilica of the Sacred Blood is visited by large crowds because of its most holy relic. Supposedly an ancient knight brought back from the crusades actual drops of Jesus' blood. They are displayed on special occasions, and tradition has it that for many years they liquefied each Friday. Of course they don't do it any more! Bruges is now a highly-commercialized town and, next to Brussels, probably the most popular tourist spot in Belgium.

From Bruges we proceeded eastward to Gant. This too was a powerful Middle Ages city. Its main attraction was the castle of the Counts of Flanders which had been carefully restored. It took the better part of a day to see. The halls, parapets, towers, kitchens, stables, dungeons, torture chambers, and instruments of torment all contributed to recalling a vivid picture of life in another day. From Gant we returned to Brussels, some seven nights and eight days on the road! It was strenuous, sometimes even harrowing, but I recommend it as a most delightful way to see a strange country and to truly see what it is like.

Now it was Effie's turn, and she and Lisa had a week in Switzerland while I kept the kids. Belgium is such a fascinating small country that one can spend weeks, even months, sight-seeing. We, of course, visited Waterloo and examined the terrain of Napoleon's downfall. The children grew tired and restless so we returned to the city, but I could have stayed on for a week soaking up the historical glamour. The trip to Tervueren was a must and although we had ten years' experience in Congo under our belts, we were amazed at the multitude of artifacts and historical relics on display at the Colonial Museum. The grotto at Han-Rochefort was most beautiful and impressive, rivaling our own highly commercialized caves of Virginia and Kentucky.

During our last days in Belgium I made another cycling foray to the east rather than the west, with my friend Eric Bolton. Eric and I traveled in higher style and rented motor bikes. From Brussels to Namur where we visited the imposing Citadel with its rows of ancient cannon guarding the river below, and then we followed the flow of the Meuse northward. The small village of Huy was a complete surprise and perhaps the most picturesque spot I visited in Belgium. I was enthralled by its quaint beauty, its profound atmosphere of peace and quiet, and the gentle *milieu* it extended. I think I could go live in Huy indefinitely.

Liege was, of course, a much larger, cosmopolitan, and busy city. We enjoyed visiting the great university there, and I was particularly interested in the medical school. From Liege we turned westward again toward Louvain, close to Brussels. Here was another great university, particularly well-known in the Congo because it extended its services by founding a medical school at Leopoldville called Luvanium until after independence. But we didn't make the short run back to Brussels. Instead we turned north once more and visited Malines. The massive cathedral tower in this town bears silent contemplation of the herculean effort required to construct it. Its world-famous carillon bell tower is soothing and refreshing. Just across the street I passed a small shop with black and white caricature sketches of a couple of musicians in the window—a violinist and a conductor. I went in, asked the price, and bought them after which I concluded from the proprietor's manner that he had others. I asked him about another one and he demurred. I pressed him and finally he came forth with a third one. I bought it and asked about a fourth. This was a great game which took about forty-five minutes, but I finally bought six interesting drawings and eventually gave them to my music-critic brother, Gunby, and he finally gave them to the then-conductor of the Knoxville Symphony Orchestra, Mr. Van Vactor. Sometimes I wonder what became of them and I still relish the effort I made to wheedle them out of that merchant in Malines. From Malines, Eric and I returned to our families in Brussels.

Time had run out and we packed, ready to head for the dark continent. We took the train to Antwerp, our point of embarkation, but we had a side trip in a rental car north into Holland for the day. We saw the sights in Amsterdam, the capital, and we purchased the inevitable four pairs of wooden clogs before we returned to Belgian soil and boarded the S.S. *Leopoldville* for our trip to Matadi. This was one of Belgium's luxury liners and again we luxuriated with its many handsome trappings. A fabulous play area was provided for the children so we had no problem keeping them occupied every day of the trip. It was on this voyage that I not only learned to eat *bifsteck americain* but actually relished it. I am sure this expression of American beef steak must come from down Argentina way, but since it carries the geographic nomenclature *americain*, we North Americans are also associated with it.

The dish consists of rich and finely ground raw beef crowned with a raw egg. It is liberally garnished with pepper and various sauces, spices and seasonings. I enjoyed it.

The Bay of Biscay seas were a bit choppy and a stomach here and there felt rather queasy, but nobody missed a meal. On the way southward we stopped off at Teneriffe in the Canary Islands and there was time to make a two-hour auto trip up the mountain of volcanic origin. The view from its summit was magnificent and made the narrow breathtaking roads more than worthwhile.

Our car was waiting for us on the dock at Matadi. Lisa and I bundled Effie and the children off to the railroad station so they could begin their long, hot ride to Leopoldville. Then we hurried to get our baggage through customs and proceeded to the capital by road. Helen

Norwood, a new Presbyterian missionary, was also with us. She had spent the better part of a year in Belgium. In Leo we put Effie and the youngsters on a plane for Luluabourg before the two young women and I started the drive through the country to Bibanga. It was a difficult and interminable journey. The roads were quagmires and it took hours to cross the rivers. More than once we got stuck and had to unload all the baggage to get the car through. Finally at midnight we reached Kikwit, knocked on the doors of a friendly mission, and exhausted, fell into bed without even stopping to bathe! Early in the morning we were off again and reached Tshikapa by evening. The following day we arrived at Bibanga where we found Effie and the kids already ensconced and keeping house. My speedometer read 1,600 miles!

ROME VIA CAIRO

Five years later we took our next trip back to the States for another furlough with an added family member, baby Barbara, nearly two years old. On the first segment of our journey we flew from Luluabourg eastward to Usumburu, the capital of Rwanda-Urundi. We were really aiming for Stanleyville from whence we would fly with Sabena up the east African airways to Egypt, but there were no flights from Luluabourg to Stanleyville, so we had to detour. We enjoyed the day in a tiny country which we had never visited, and were much impressed with the long views of mighty Lake Tanganyika. In fact we made a special trip to the water's edge where we removed our shoes and socks to wade and splash.

From Usumburu we flew to Stanleyville where we were amazed at the prodigious force of the cataracts and falls in the Congo River just above the city. The Africans build flimsy systems of scaffolding with poles and vines just above these turbulent waters and nimbly traverse the area carrying large woven baskets of fish—and they catch some whoppers.

The trip from Stanleyville to Cairo was a night flight with stopover at Khartoum. The kids were all asleep but I had to deplane and implant my feet on the soil of Sudan, another new country for me. In Cairo we had no trouble getting to our prearranged hotel where we were greeted by our guide who was to show us the city for the next four days. He was the most amiable guide we ever had. He guided us into all the displays of the unbelievable Egyptian antiquities, including King Tut and his golden coffin and the inscrutable mysteries of the pyramids and the Sphinx. He also wisely advised which artifacts and traditional semiprecious stones and jewels were worth the price and which were rip-offs. He crowned his service above and beyond the call of duty when he took us out one evening to an elegant Egyptian multi-course dinner! I wish I could remember his name. I'd preserve it for posterity. He deserves it!

Our next stop was Athens, and this ancient city was somewhat disappointing since it was sandwiched between Cairo and Rome, such fabulous places. In Athens we visited several points that were less than exciting, but we did of course ascend the Acropolis and walk through the Parthenon and other temple relics. We stood on Mars Hill and reread Paul's great manifesto. We took note of the various military and festival costumes we saw on the streets. The food was nothing to brag about, and we began to set our sites toward Rome.

THE ETERNAL CITY

For all its eccentricities Rome is the number one truly great city of the European mainland. Paris has its artistic heirlooms, but Rome is the historic hub of ancient, medieval, and modern exploration. I could spend a year in Rome and never see the same things twice. The Vatican Museum alone would take a month. It can only be favorably compared with the Museum of Natural History in London.

One of the genuine serendipities of this trip, along with our Egyptian guide, was the housing arrangements in Rome. Our reservations were not in a hotel but with an Italian family which rented short-term tourist accommodations in their modest home which was called Villa Eva. They spoke English which quickly bridged the gap between them and our children, and they took them into their arms and hearts. With enthusiasm they assured Effie and me that we could go anywhere we wanted in the evening and stay as long as we liked. They would baby-sit the whole crowd! But that wasn't the only perk we received from them. Apparently they were resistance activists during the war ten years earlier, or at least they claimed to be, and when we came home from an evening out to find the kids all tucked away and sleeping, we would visit over a glass of wine and they regaled us for hours on end with their hair-raising war stories. If only I had had a tape recorder. I could sell those stories for a pretty penny!

We saw all the correct panoramas and places in Rome—the Coliseum, the Forum, the various fountains, Bernini and Trevi and Esedra, the Altar of the Fatherland, the Pantheon, the Holy Stairs, the Catacombs, Trinita of the Mount with its Spanish steps, and numerous parks and cathedrals. We had our night at the opera, and we traveled the Appian Way.

One day as we piled into a bus for the day's excursion, I motioned for Charlotte, sitting opposite me, to come sit on my lap so someone could have her seat since it was very crowded. She came and was replaced by a gentleman who began to look at me with a quizzical eye. As he did, I felt some suggestion of recognition myself, and finally he leaned toward me.

"Aren't you Bill Rule?"

"Charlie Peckinpaugh!" I exclaimed. Such amazement to run into an old friend and classmate of junior high days (and we probably had not seen each other since) on a bus in Rome, Italy, instead of on a street in Knoxville, Tennessee!

While we were in Rome we learned that the Pope was going to make one of his rare public appearances, and we were at St. Peter's Square in full force and on time. Sure enough, the Pope appeared on the balcony of his papal chambers to bless the cheering crowd of some ten thousand voices. We were able to duck into the Basilica where standing room only was a gross understatement. The feeling of excitement can hardly be described when shortly the Pope appeared enthroned and carried on the shoulders of his throne-bearers. Wonder of wonders, he came directly toward the Rule family! Paul was in front and could have easily touched the august prelate as he passed by. We were much taken by the show and were jabbering excitedly when suddenly I realized that Paul was nowhere to be seen. Ten thousand people and a seven-year-old was lost in their midst! I stationed Effie and the other four kids by an easy-to-identify statue and took off to look for my son. Where to look? Follow the Pope's entourage, of course. So I did, and sure enough, there was Paul walking along aside him, completely mesmerized by the unique experience.

Of course we visited the Sistine Chapel and were captivated by the beauty and magnitude of Michelangelo's paintings. He was truly the artist of the ages. But it is interesting that he considered himself primarily a sculptor, and here I cast my vote. For me, the greatest and the most awe-inspiring creation of his fabulous career is not his David nor his Pieta, but his majestic Moses in St. Peter's in Vincoli.

One more thing to say about Rome before we leave. It is my observation that the most skillful motorists are those who maneuver the congested city streets of that metropolis. In Brussels they are the worst. In Rome, the best. The traffic down Rome's arterial avenues is fast and furious, but let a momentary obstruction appear, even a minor one, and the whole flow of traffic for two or three blocks back, gracefully swerves to adjust to the situation, causing no confusion and no loss of speed. Another amazing accomplishment is the bus driver who carefully takes his vehicle through the terribly narrow streets where cars are parked or waiting at all angles, and he makes it without bumps or bashes or even a scratch. You would have said it was an impossibility!

Rome is truly the Eternal City, or as Henry Wadsworth Longfellow so aptly put it:

>   . . . There may be other cities
>   That please us for a while, but Rome alone
>   Completely satisfies. . . .

The final segments of this memorable trip to America were without incident. We flew from Rome to Brussels and after several hours there, on to New York. We spent the year in Knoxville in a house next door to my parents.

FISHING IN LAKE KARIBA

In 1965 our son Bill graduated from Davidson College. My own school year at Tshikaji was not finished in time for me to make it to the ceremonies, but that did not deter his mother. She bundled her two youngest on a plane and arrived in good time to stand proudly with her cap-and-gowned firstborn.

This left me in Africa with Libby and Paul, with time to leisurely plan a furlough trip to the States. Paul and I had heard of the fabulous tiger fishing in Lake Kariba on the Zambezi River, formed by the great hydro-electric dam there, between Zambia (old Northern Rhodesia) and Zimbabwe (Southern Rhodesia). We decided to travel south in order to reach home in the northern hemisphere! A classmate of Libby's, Sarah Gay Stockwell, also on her way to the States, went with us, making us a party of four.

The first leg of our trip was the train ride to Elizabethville where we stopped overnight to tell the Congo good-bye, continuing by train to Victoria Falls. Once again there was for me that awe-inspiring experience of watching the mighty plunge of waters create "the smoke that thunders." Every angle is a new wonder to stop the breath in your throat. This was my second visit to Victoria Falls, but the first for the children and they were duly impressed. We took a boat trip up the river and watched monkeys in the trees and hippos and crocodiles in the water. Guarding our dearth of funds, we had rented a tent-like pavilion to save on the hotel tax, and we bought food at the store and stashed it away before we left to scout around. But we forgot to close the gate, and we hadn't walked a dozen steps when we heard a commotion behind us and turned to see a big ape making off with our loaf of bread!

Again we traveled south by train and visited the Wankie Game Preserve where we were bused through open country to see lions and elephants and other African wild life. We had to stop and wait for the lions and then the elephants to clear the path. We took a small plane from Wankie to Lake Kariba where we camped and fished for several days. For a reasonable price we engaged a boat and fishing gear and a guide. We did catch some tiger fish which the hotel prepared and

Libby and Sarah Stockwell, posing with David Livingston at Victoria Falls, 1965.

served to us. One catch was particularly amusing. The tiger was hooked, not in the mouth but in the tail! Apparently it jumped from the water to shake loose the hook in its mouth and the flying hook was firmly imbedded as it flapped its tail. It could swim directly away from the pull of the reel which made it a particularly strong catch.

From Lake Kariba we flew to Salisbury, the capital, and from there we flew Air France to Paris where we spent a day or two and took in some of the sights. We viewed the city from the top of the Eiffel Tower, we visited Notre Dame Cathedral, and saw Napoleon's tomb at the Hotel des Invalides. We rode the metro and made the trip to Versailles where we did the palace and gardens. Then it was time to catch the plane for New York where we all holed up in one room at the Prince George Hotel.

But we couldn't give up and go to bed quite yet. Why? Because the World's Fair was in progress and this was our one chance to see it. Nothing would do but that we catch the train for Flushing Meadow and see the sights. As we entered the fair grounds area I saw a bandstand with seats for an audience, and who should be playing on that band-stand but Guy Lombardo and his Royal Canadians! Imagine the amazement and thrill which coursed through my auricles and ventricles! Guy Lombardo was the class dance band of my college days. I knew the run downs on all his musicians, and I knew most of the hit tunes he played, and now here he was playing them again right before my eyes and ears! I told the kids I was stopping right there and that they could go ahead and see all the displays they wanted. When they were finished they were to come back to me at that spot. I'd still be there. So they returned at closing time and we took the train back to town.

But what we had forgotten was that jet lag was working on us. Back in Paris where we had started, it was well into the next day, and we had been up and going a full twenty-four hours. In our hotel room we tumbled into bed and were out like the lights.

I was the first awake, about noon. I raised my head, squinting, and looked around. Something was strange. Things weren't like I remembered them when we went to bed. Then I saw the door standing slightly ajar, and I began to realize that we had been visited, indeed, probably robbed! That turned out to be the case. We didn't really have much for a thief to take. Whoever it was had only wanted cash, and most of our things were intact. Looking out in the hall, we saw all of the contents of Libby's handbag strewn along as the intruder had walked away. It was necessary for me to explain this to the hotel management and then call my dad for money to get us home. This accomplished, we became a completed family once more, ready to start a furlough year with Effie's parents in Athens, Georgia.

INCLUDING THE SWISS ALPS

Our travel adventures will conclude with this account of a final tourist trip which was part of our return to the homeland after completing thirty years of missionary life, in the year 1970. You will recall that Charlotte and her husband, Steve White, came out to visit us, and they brought along Effie's teenage nephew, Stephen Crane. When the time came to bid good-bye to Tshikaji and to each other, Steve and Charlotte went their separate way, and Stephen Crane joined forces with our group, which included Barbara and John, making our party a quintet. We headed first for Rome. The kids were all eyes and questions, and nearly walked the legs off Effie who is not a great walker under any circumstances. Probably our greatest triumph during that Roman visit was the discovery of a popular plebeian cafe-teria where we could get a lot of food at a moderate price, and we gorged ourselves on huge slabs of watermelon!

After Rome we traveled to Geneva, Switzerland. This was my first visit to that heavenly little country—heavenly from the point-of-view of both its beauty and its location. Perhaps it is closer to God than most other places! We marveled at the memorial statue to the Reformation, and blessed the heroic spirit of the Calvins and Knoxes and others who paid the price of assuring us our rich Protestant heritage. We found a delightful little restaurant where we introduced the children to the delicacy of cheese fondue. We rode a bus around the lake, viewing the ancient castles and visiting Lausanne.

Our chief destination was Interlaken with the primary goal Jungfrau mountain. Merely looking from the street or through a window up at that mighty snow-covered peak gave one goosebumps. Of course we took the narrow gauge railroad, and that was a never-to-be-forgotten trip through a tunnel in the mountain which is an engineering wonder in itself. At the top we unloaded in a well-heated building with a restaurant and shops as well as rest and viewing accommodations for the scores of tourists. To step through a door onto an open balcony ushers one onto the very brow of the Jungfrau. You are suddenly on the summit of its glacier and experience subzero temperature and an icy blast of wind. Down below you can see groups of mountain climbers roped together, toiling upward to conquer the famous peak.

The building is not actually at the very summit. The mountain's altitude is 13,600 feet, and you can still see several hundred feet of rugged crags above your head, covered with snow and ice, but believe me, you are high enough and cold enough and close enough to the real thing standing on that balcony to make you feel like you have ascended like those you can see below! This was our highest moment, both figuratively and literally.

From Interlaken we took the train to Zurich and caught a plane to London where we spent several days visiting the capital of our English-speaking kinsmen. We visited Westminster Abbey and the antithesis, Madame Tussaud's famous waxen figures. We visited a large ornate church on Sunday evening and were amazed at only the handful of a dozen or so worshippers.

In London, we came to a shop sign that caught our attention. It read: *Tennessee Pancake House*. Obviously it was expedient that we go in and case the joint. At a table we opened the bill of fare and read with amusement the special pancakes: a Memphis Special, Chattanooga Choo-Choo Conglomeration, and other specialties named for Nashville and Knoxville.

Once more it was time to head for home. We knew the Boeing 747 Jumbo Jets had recently come into service and our two boy-passengers, Stephen and John, were determined that we fly on this huge new model. So we changed reservations and finally flew to Dulles Airport in

Washington and from there to Atlanta where Effie's parents and Stephen's mother were to meet us. After hours of delay at Dulles they finally told us the flight had been cancelled and they were ferrying us to National where we would need to catch another flight. At National airport time went by again but we finally boarded a slow plane that touched down at every small air strip in North and South Carolina before we reached Georgia in the wee small hours of the morning. They had waited most of the night and we were so sleepy from jet lag we hardly made good sense, but we had a joyous reunion and revived for a happy ride to Athens, Georgia.

MILESTONE EIGHT
REACHING FOR
THE SUMMIT

"I delight to do thy will, O my God: yea
thy law *is* within my heart" (Psalms 40:8).

23 THE INTERIM PERIOD

I can of mine own self do nothing: as I hear, I judge: and my judgement is just; because I seek not mine own will, but the will of the Father which hath sent me (John 5:30).

On arrival back in the United States in 1970 we were fortunate to have a home arranged for us at Mission Haven, a complex of apartments for furloughing missionaries, adjoining Columbia Theological Seminary in Decatur, Georgia, and financed and controlled by a number of dedicated women of the church. Our two youngest children were with us; Barbara a junior in the local high school and John in junior high. The other children were scattered. Bill was just back from one year as a medic in the army in Vietnam to resume his work with the Department of Health and Human Services in Washington, D.C. Charlotte's doctor husband, Steve, would soon be on his way for a similar military service hitch. Libby was winding up her studies at the University of Georgia with a fine arts degree. And Paul was way out in Congo putting a roof on the Bonne Auberge at Luluabourg plus other industrial and maintenance work for the mission.

But our well-accommodated family in Decatur didn't last very long. My old colleague in the Congo, Henry Nelson, was now engaged in the new specialty of emergency medicine in Knoxville, and his group was seeking to expand. He called on me to come on home and join the effort. Effie and I had been thinking and praying about what we should do at this juncture. Should we separate ourselves from missionary work and seek to erase some of our piled-up indebtedness? This seemed to be an option which we took as a clear leading from the Lord, so I accepted. Effie had to remain in Decatur to mother the two kids now busily occupied in school, while I moved to Knoxville, roomed at my own mother's house, and became a member of the Knoxville Emergency Physician's Group where I divided my working hours between two hospitals: St. Mary's Catholic and Fort Saunders Presbyterian.

Once more we were a divided family, but my colleagues were most considerate giving me the opportunity to double up work hours during the week so I could have the long weekend for life with my family in Decatur. I kept that road between Knoxville and Decatur hot for almost a year!

It was a pleasure to work in the KEPG with the fellows who became my partners. Some of them I had known for a long time. Nelson had been my colleague for twenty years in Congo. Aster Jenkins and I were in the high school band together for three years. He was a class behind me and became the band captain the year after I graduated. He and his wife, Betty, continue to be friends of ours. Fred Carr is a fraternity brother. He attended the University of Tennessee where he was on the swimming team with my brother Gunby. A gun collector, he took a fancy to my African rifle. I figured I'd do no big game hunting in the U.S. so I swapped it to him for a 20 gauge pump gun. There were others who joined our group later and with whom I had special and previous affiliations. David Dorr had been a missionary in Yemen and Gaza, and Merrill Moore was also a missionary in the Gaza strip. Harry Ogden and I are members of the same church and have served as elders on the session. His mother was a Lapsley, niece of our Congo pioneer missionary, Samuel Lapsley.

In early 1971 we began to look for a permanent residence in Knoxville. Mother was eighty-five, still living alone, and driving her own car, but those days were bound to come to an end and I wanted to include her in our plans. We found a place in a charming neighborhood. The house had roomy first-floor accommodations with a downstairs apartment which suited Mother. So we bought the place.

Effie and I were amused to think, here we are a thirty-year married couple with six kids proceeding like newlyweds with our first home. We had never owned property nor furnished a house, and now we were starting from scratch. We had to buy a refrigerator, dishwasher, washer and dryer, and a television! We had to acquire furniture we had never before possessed—our queen-size bed, a built-in bookcase to accommodate our stereo. This was only a start. Two automobiles were in the offing. How do real newlywed young people accomplish all this? After the school year in Georgia my family finally joined me in our new home, and once more we became a more stable and normal family.

The decade of the '70s saw profound changes in our intimate family which should certainly be recorded. There were marriages and births and deaths considerably altering our corporate character. Paul came home from Africa to enroll in the area technical training school in Atlanta to study aviation mechanics. He had made the decision to throw his inborn talents and his concentrated efforts toward aviation, and he did a good job of it as he graduated at the head of his class. But he made another even more important decision. He fell in love and decided to marry his childhood sweetheart whose parents were also Congo missionaries. Paul and Roxie Stixrud had grown up on the mission field together. She was now also living in Atlanta and working in a local bank.

Of course we knew her mother and father, Beng and Shirley Stixrud, and so arrangements were made to tie the knot at Lookout Mountain Presbyterian Church in Chattanooga, Tennessee, where Roxie had attended during her school years. Chattanooga is only a hundred miles from Knoxville, so the scattered family gathered at the homestead to make the trek southwestward for the ceremony.

Three years later our Libby married Jim Woodruff. Jim's family was prominent in the community of Columbus, Georgia, where his father was a successful businessman. The two lovers each attended the University of Georgia but did not meet there. Both were drawn from city life and the Establishment to homesteading in the mountains of western North Carolina. An art major, Libby was intent on developing mountain crafts with the women of the hills. Jim believed in self-sufficiency and organic farming. They met where they were working in a small mountain community not far from Asheville, North Carolina.

Libby chose to be married in the beautiful garden of her Crane grandparents' wooded residence in Athens, Georgia. Her grandfather, Dr. William Crane, was the officiating minister. The reception, with small tables and chairs scattered on the patio, was a lovely party in the flowering bower behind the Crane house. At the reception there was quite a family gathering including Rowlands, Rules, and Woodruffs.

WEDDINGS MEAN GRANDCHILDREN

As some wiseacre once remarked, "If I had known that grand-children were going to be so much fun I would have had them first!"

Four of our six children were now married and it was inevitable that grandchildren would begin to appear. The decade of the 70s was a great time for us in this respect. We greeted seven during the seventies.

The first grandchild to bless our advancing years was Anne Rule, daughter of Bill and Beth. She was an April baby in 1971 and she lost little time in coming to see her grandmamma and her grandpappa. We took her up to Gatlinburg to see the mountains where it was rather cool at that altitude. Her granddaddy had to hug her close and cuddle her to keep her warm!

Five days after Anne put in her appearance, Seth White, son of Charlotte and Steve, joined her to pursue their lifelong search for true meaning in this wobbly old world. Seth was born in Atlanta, Georgia, where his mother was temporarily living with her mother, Effie, because Steve was with the armed forces in Vietnam. Under such circumstances Grandmother Effie had the rapturous responsibility of helping to care for newborn Seth, a job she still remembers with a great deal of pleasure.

Karen, Anne's baby sister, was almost a 1973 Christmas gift, only four days too late. Thus endeth the reproductive renditions of our two eldest.

Our next grandchild followed in the footsteps of most of the Rule children. He was born in the Republic of Zaire where Paul and Roxie were missionaries for the Presbyterian Church. Paul was a pilot based in Kananga (formerly Luluabourg). Kevin, their firstborn, was delivered at the Good Shepherd Hospital at Tshikaji on March 1, 1975. They were far from family but had many friends in the missionary and African community.

The banner year of 1977 brought us two new grandkids within a month. Jennifer Woodruff was born in January at a hospital in Fletcher, North Carolina. That was not far from Knoxville so Grandmamma Effie made a beeline there and participated in all the formalities of bringing up a brand new baby in the way it should be. One month later Timothy, Kevin's little brother, arrived. He was born in Atlanta, Georgia, because his parents were back in the United States.

The final grandchild addition during the decade of the '70s was Logan Woodruff. He brought the total number to an imposing seven. His mom followed her mom's example for a home delivery and all went well. But by the time baby Logan was a couple of weeks old it was obvious something was wrong. He was having trouble breathing and had to be rushed to the emergency room in Asheville where his problem was diagnosed as coarctation of the aorta. They flew him to the Duke Hospital in Durham, North Carolina, and wonder of wonders, they operated on this tiny baby, removed the narrowed portion of the aorta, reattached this vital artery to the heart, and a week later discharged him from the hospital!

A TIME TO BE BORN, AND A TIME TO DIE

This same decade saw several vacancies appear in our family circle bringing the inevitable grief of separation, but at the same time giving cause to praise God for the assurances of Christian victory. In 1972 my sister Barbara's husband, Bill Moorman, collapsed and died suddenly on his way home from work, riding in a car with a fellow worker. The man tried desperately to get him to the nearest hospital emergency room, but he was pronounced DOA (dead on arrival). Bill had been diagnosed some twenty years earlier with an aortic coarctation, the same circulatory anomaly baby Logan had been born with. Strange that two people within one family but with no blood relationship, should have been born with this same rather rare condition. Bill's was surgically repaired, but he had developed other heart problems and was under the care of a heart specialist. When he died he was only weeks away from a routine check-up with his doctor. Eighteen days later my brother, Gunby, also died suddenly of a heart attack.

Charlotte Gunby Rule.

The third departure from our midst was that of my mother, Charlotte Gunby Rule. This was the year of her ninetieth birthday. She died on a Sunday morning in June of 1976.

These breaks in the family circle served to convince Effie and me even more completely that we had been providentially led to return home and reestablish our roots when we did. One of the tremendous experiences of the abundant life in Christ is to watch the unfolding of the pathway, in the providence of God, and to realize once again that all things truly do work together for good for those who love the Lord. The words "lucky" or "unlucky" should not even be part of the Christian vocabulary!

What more shall I tell of family affairs? There were some graduations in the '70s to be mentioned. Barbara was graduated from high school in 1972 and then she enjoyed two years at Emory Junior College in Oxford, Georgia. She was active in campus activities, performed special work on their annual publication, and was included in a national compilation of outstanding junior college students. We were delighted for her to have this experience since her high school education had been so interrupted and moved around that she had never felt the fulfilling flow of things. Following junior college she transferred to Knoxville and the University of Tennessee where she graduated in 1976. John, following his sister by three years, played on the varsity football team at Bearden High School in '74 and graduated in the spring of '75. Elizabeth had received her Bachelor of Fine Arts degree in 1972. Thus the '70s also encompassed several Rule graduation events.

EMERGENCY MEDICINE

Our arrival to take up residence in the United States coincided with the emergence of a newly recognized specialty in medical practice, emergency medicine. In its early days, the practice of emergency medicine in the various hospital emergency rooms meant that staff doctors, saddled with emergency service on a rotation basis, could now turn them over to emergency teams employed to man the emergency demands around the clock. Doctors for these specialized teams were applying themselves with a vigorous program of continuing medical education. At first the emphasis was not as uniquely on true emergencies as it is today.

Typically, patients arrived with the whole gamut of physical complaints. They soon recognized the advantage of waiting until after work or household duties to come to the hospital in the late afternoon or early evening and thus avoid loss of prime time sitting and waiting a turn in a doctor's office. The hospital waiting room began to fill up regularly and examinations often ran late into the night before the grumbling crowd was treated and dispersed. Walk-in clinics have relieved this glut of hospital patients, but at that time the emergency room was itself a veritable walk-in clinic.

This does not mean that we did not get our share of crises and trauma victims. There were always the numerous lacerations from knife fights after payday to be sewn up. Automobile accidents took their toll with everything from cuts, bumps, and contusions, to fractures, concussions, and injured organs of chest and abdomen. Motorcycle accidents appeared on the register with alarming regularity, which always meant massive abrasions.

Acute asthmatic distress always came to us in the middle of the night. It seemed possible to tough it out during the day, but in the darkness of the night with insomnia complicating the picture, courage ebbed and aid was sought.

Overdoses appeared every day or so. Sometimes they represented serious efforts to shuffle off this mortal coil of tears and depression, but much more often they were cries of confusion and an appeal for recognition and compassion and help.

Medical practice is like most other activities of life with its ups and its downs—its good days and its bad ones. One of my good days was when they brought in a little old lady complaining of mild chest pain. She was alert and rather joking about her own symptoms while the nurses began to undress her and prepare her for examination. A thermometer was stuck in her mouth, and then it happened in a flash. She bit the glass tube to pieces as she went into cardiac arrest. We had to fish the glass out of her mouth while performing CPR, in order to insert an endotracheal tube. Our cardiograph, near at hand, showed that she was fibrillating and we shocked her with the electric paddles which converted her back to normal rhythm. She was transferred to the cardiac care unit and eventually made a good recovery. The good feeling comes in realizing that she suffered her myocardial infarction right there in our emergency department with all the life-saving equipment right at hand. If it had happened at home she probably never would have arrived at the hospital alive.

Bad days often come with the inebriated patients. Alcohol plays such a major role in the emergency situations. Certainly a high incidence of automobile and highway accidents are alcohol related. I remember a great big hulk of a fellow who came in one night after a fight. He had been carved up in extensive fashion with a lot of blood loss, and it took me an hour or more and hundreds of stitches to get all the gaping lesions properly closed. As I finished he got up off the table and growled through his clenched teeth that he was now going out to find the guy and give him back some of what he had received.

I remonstrated, telling him, "You are in no condition to protect yourself, much less to inflict damage on your adversary. What you need to do is go home and sleep it off. Tomorrow you can start all over again." But he paid me no mind and later, in the wee small hours of the morning, they brought him back in. This time he had been finished off. I only needed to pronounce him dead.

Working with the police was also an interesting experience. Since they were each different they obviously had different outlooks and insights about the affairs of victims they dealt with. Some were hard and cold and punitive. Others were more considerate, even indulgent. I never will forget what one detective said to me one night. It has come to my mind over and over and seems the epitome of contrast between the mind of the world and the mind of God. He had brought in some casualties of an automobile accident and no one was significantly injured. Only bumps and bruises which would ache for a few days. "Why don't you just forget this whole thing?" I asked him. "Nobody's really hurt and there's no legal action that needs to be taken." But he was unwilling to just let things go.

"Can't you give me some kind of a diagnosis that we can make some noise about?" I told him I couldn't, and asked why he was pushing me. What difference did it make? It was his reply that I have remembered, not only my lesson for that day but for many days since. He smiled faintly and said, "Do unto others, before they do unto you." And there you have it in a nutshell. God's way—to do *for* others; man's way—to do *against* others. No wonder the Lord said, "My thoughts are not your thoughts, neither are your ways my ways. For as the heavens are higher than the earth, so are my ways higher than your ways and my thoughts than your thoughts" (Isa. 55:8).

During the seven years that I practiced emergency medicine in Knoxville I had occasion to serve as president of the Knoxville

Emergency Physicians Group. I was also chairman of the Medicine & Religion Committee of the Knoxville Academy of Medicine; had membership on the Medical Care Evaluation Committee, the Emergency Advisory Committee, the Infection Control Committee, and the Executive Committee at St. Mary's Hospital; and finally was named president of the Tennessee chapter of the American College of Emergency Physicians. Like I said, I sort of got in on the ground floor!

EXTRACURRICULAR EXCURSIONS

During this period of time I did the most traveling in the United States I had ever done. There were frequent seminars on emergency medicine to update practitioners in relatively new duties. I attended meetings in Richmond, Philadelphia, Atlanta, Miami, and Scottsdale, Arizona, to mention a few. But there were four special trips we took as a family or fractions thereof which I must share. Two of them were in 1972: first to Explo '72, conducted by Campus Crusade for Christ in Dallas, Texas, and the second, to the International Congress of Christian Physicians in Toronto, Canada.

We traveled to Canada by car, taking both our still-at-home children, Barbara and John. We had an interesting stopover in Detroit where we visited the huge museum of automobiles, ancient and modern. At London, Ontario, we made a side trip to a game preserve with all sorts of wild animals. It was a novel experience to ride in a protected bus through prides of lions, herds of antelope and buffalo, and other varieties of creatures far up in the northern climes of Canada!

The series of medical-religious meetings in Toronto were most stimulating. Program leaders included Dr. Paul Brand, missionary doctor from India who is a pioneer in the development of surgical reconstruction of the hand among his leprosy patients. Brand co-authored two remarkable bestsellers: *In His Image* and *Fearfully And Wonderfully Made*. He was finally engaged as Chief of Rehabilitation at the U.S. Public Health Service Hospital in Carville, Louisiana.

Another outstanding speaker, widely known in the medical world, was Dr. Dennis Burkitt who was a missionary doctor in Uganda and who first described Burkitt's lymphoma. In more recent years he has been the prime exponent of a fiber-rich diet as prophylaxis against G-I carcinoma.

We were in Toronto during their great World's Fair, so of course we took that in and visited many wondrous displays and amusements. Calling their fair Expo '72, they continue to use the moniker "Expo" for their professional baseball team.

This was our first family visit to Canada and we decided to make the most of it, so instead of heading homeward when the congress concluded, we nudged our way north toward the great Canadian expanses. John and I wanted to wet a hook and try our hand at fishing, so we spent a couple of days at Huntsville, Ontario, a region with a confluence of several lovely lakes. We rented a boat and fishing gear and between the four of us we caught enough fish to enjoy a special meal at the accommodating hotel where we were staying. From Huntsville we drove deep into the Algonquin National Park, marveling once again at the wonders of Almighty God's artistic handiwork.

From there we headed south and homeward, but of course we had to stop off at mighty Niagara Falls. What an awesome display of nature it presents! We viewed the falls from both Canada and from the U.S., from upstream and down, even from the bowels of the earth where we watched it thunder down over our heads. Finally, when we were completely surfeited with views from every angle, we turned our faces toward Knoxville, Tennessee.

The last trip to record was the longest and in many ways the most exciting. Effie and I traveled back to Zaire to participate in the dedication of the just-completed Good Shepherd Hospital. Since we had shared in dreaming the original dream and in raising funds for the original construction, some dear Christian friends made the trip possible for us.

We left Knoxville on January 2, 1975, traveling from Atlanta to Brussels and on to Kinshasa. At Kananga we stayed with our own kids; Paul, the mission pilot, and Roxie. We were there with them just a month before their son Kevin was born.

At the Good Shepherd Hospital I had the opportunity to meet with groups of doctors and nurses and present some illustrated lectures on cardio-pulmonary resuscitation, and also on the reading of electro-cardiograms. On January 20 we attended a grand outdoor celebration at the main entrance of the new hospital. Speeches were made by the Governor of the State, leaders of the hospital staff, and dignitaries of the church. It was an inspiring event for those of us who had put so much blood, sweat, and tears into the planning and construction of the building. We were grateful to God who, in his good providence, made it all happen. Five days later we were back in Knoxville to resume our normal life.

One more important factor touched our lives during this first seven years out of overseas missionary service. Membership and participation in the home church was a blessing. For the first time in our adult lives both Effie and I were active members of the sending church, not the receiving church. Yes, we had often been in the home church during our furlough years, but we were visitors. We had been in the role of guests who were outside looking in. Now we were an integral part of the congregation which meant among other things, revising our concepts to some extent. We truly had to undergo a period of orientation and adaption.

Where would we fit into the picture as members of a home church? What were our gifts? How could we contribute? Where should we serve?

We prayed and sought the Lord's leading and we believe he instructed us and showed us the way. We grew in our Christian experience, receiving new blessing in our walk of faith. Both Effie and I served at one time or another on the church Session, the church governing body. In our particular church Effie was the first woman elder elected to serve, paving the way for numbers of others in the years since. Most of all we were blessed by the fellowship and loving interaction with many other believers in the congregation. We felt the warmth and the moving of the Holy Spirit in our midst, and we now realize that we have enjoyed a fuller, richer Christian experience by being members of the home church than if we had always remained as missionaries in Zaire. God blesses his children in many many ways, in whichever direction they turn!

24 BULAPE AND THE BAKUBA

Jesus saith unto them, My meat is to do the will of him that sent me, and to finish his work (John 4:34).

In 1977 word came to us through the Presbyterian Board of Missions that the church in Zaire was anxiously looking for a doctor to take over the management of Bulape hospital. The Board was wondering if I might be available. Of course Effie and I were interested. We talked about it and prayed, and as we surveyed our options we realized there was a real freedom for us to go. Mother was gone. The children were now adults, most of them in their own homes. John was the last one at home and studying architecture at the University of Tennessee. My emergency work was a job I had walked into without undue preparation, and I could leave it just as conveniently. So we accepted the appointment and returned to Zaire for what we assumed at the time was a one-year stint. It stretched into three years.

Our arrival at Bulape was hardly a first time. We had visited the station on numerous occasions. But it was the first time we unloaded our baggage there and began to put down roots. Bulape was to be our home and the headquarters of our medical and missionary work. Effie and I were both excited since this was an entirely new sort of adventure for us, and we sought to adapt as we went along. Even leaving home had been a new experience. We leased the upper floor of our house and left John in Mother's downstairs apartment to keep an eye on things and to collect the rent. Effie and I departed with only the suitcases and bags we could carry between us. A far cry from all the other departures when we trooped onto boats or planes with a passel of kids and trunks, boxes, and drums of extensive baggage. This time we determined to live off the land and also to live closer to the people. We looked forward to our new venture with keen anticipation.

Bulape is the northernmost station of our inland Presbyterian group. It lies just on the southern edge of the great tropical rain forest less than five degrees below the equator. This is the heart of the Bakuba country or, the Bakuba Kingdom. The Bakuba people are an extremely interesting tribal group. In an intriguing story about them in his book, *The Leopard Hunts Alone*, Conway T. Wharton borrows a scriptural phrase to describe them as "A people tall and smooth." He quotes a Mr. Hilton-Simpson, an English traveler and author who says, "The Bushongo [Bakuba] are a most interesting people . . . quite one of the most interesting tribes of Central Africa." Certainly they are the peerless artisans of all Africans we encountered and today our home is proudly decorated with their angular designs on palm-fiber weavings and tapestries, wooden cups, and ivory ornaments.

The Bakuba are governed, not simply by a paramount chieftain as are other tribes, but by a veritable king. Outsiders call him by a Tshiluba appellation, "Lukengu," but the Bakuba themselves employ the Bushonge title, "Nyimi." His word is law. He functions under the principle of divine right of kings. He maintains and supports a harem of some three hundred wives, and his capital village is Mushenge, only thirty-five kilometers north of Bulape. The current Nyimi was better educated as a school boy than his predecessors, and when the new government was formed after independence the African officials reasoned, "Since he is the hereditary ruler of the region why not make him the administrative officer as well?" So now he wears two hats (or crowns). He is King of the Bakuba and also the Administrator of the Zairian Territory of Mweka. This is the Nyimi who was our neighbor and with whom I formed a friendship while I was at Bulape.

Another interesting fact about Lukengu is that he is never succeeded by his own son. The government recognizes matriarchal succession and the next king will be a son of one of Nyimi's sisters. At the time we were at Bulape, the queen mother, an extremely important and venerated person in the hierarchy, was a Christian and an elder in the church at Mushenge.

LAPSLEY MEMORIAL HOSPITAL

The hospital at Bulape was similar to those I had directed at Lubondai and Bibanga. Lapsley Memorial consisted of a group of rectan-

Bakuba warrior.

gular one-story brick buildings with metal roofs and cement floors. Uncovered, paved walk-ways connected the group. The two largest buildings were Administration which comprised doctors offices and an examining room, X-ray, surgery suite, storeroom for supplies, and area for White Cross (linens) storage in the attic; and the Outpatient Dispensary to accommodate the large ill but ambulatory crowds. At the dispensary, the *Infirmier Diplome* saw many patients and assigned some to a smaller peripheral room for medicines, others to a room for external treatments and bandaging, and still others to the area for injections. One large portion of the dispensary housed files of medical and business records with an office where patients paid their bills. The clinical laboratory was also located in the dispensary.

The next largest building was Maternity comprising labor and delivery rooms plus a large room for postpartum patients. The Pharmacy was also appended to the maternity building. Three buildings with rows of beds for hospitalized patients were the Men's Ward, Women's Ward, and Pediatrics. A seventh building contained a classroom for medical lectures, and several small private and semiprivate accommodations for the few who could pay the extra tariff.

Finally, there was a row of four or five small one-room structures to meet the urgent isolation needs, plus a hospital chapel with a full-time chaplain where regular worship services were held for ambulatory and outpatients and their family members. Professions of faith were often made in this chapel.

We reported our hospital as an institution of approximately 120 beds. An exact count was impossible since we almost always were full with an overflow of patients on improvised floor mats.

A description of Lapsley Memorial Hospital is not complete without mention of the outpatient camp adjacent to the complex which we called the *lazaret*. This was a group of twenty or more mud and stick huts with thatch roofs for patients and their families if detained at the hospital over a period of days or weeks. Keep in mind that many patients came to us from long distances and often on foot. Because we had no hospital kitchen, family members had to feed their sick. So the entire family came bringing their manioc flour and chickens and they "camped out" in a hut. We of the Christian mission were able to introduce the gospel of Jesus Christ to these large contingencies of visiting families. Obviously this outlay was no mean contribution to the physical and spiritual health of the local and not-so-local people. Hospital statistics for 1977 disclose that 6,640 individuals were treated during that calendar year.

I was both frustrated and often amused as I studied this annual report and tried to compile the various pathological conditions which had been encountered. A correct list of diagnoses was thwarted at every turn by the inadequate notations affixed to the charts. Often I had no inkling whatever about illness and treatment. I first encountered the concept that a

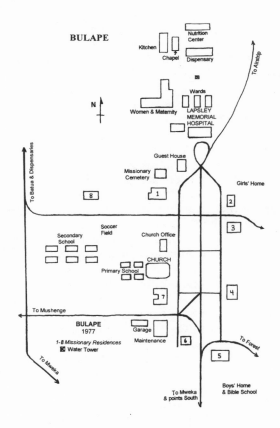

Bulape map.

surgical procedure might constitute an adequate diagnosis. But "hysterectomy" or "D&C" or "cesarean section" doesn't tell me what was wrong with the patient. Even worse was the entry "laparotomy," which simply says, "We looked into the abdomen." Even more inadequate than using operations to record diagnosis is using symptoms the same way. "Convulsions" gives me a very poor lead for naming the disease. The unadorned word "fever" was occasionally listed, also "icterus" and "dyspnea." Three times I came across the entry "edema of the feet." Expressions like "pain in the eye" or in the abdomen or the thorax, or "generalized weakness" served as erudite diagnostic conclusions. Perhaps the most amusing in this category was the offering "fluctuation!"

Also medical procedures and treatments sometimes served to name pathological conditions. "Cystoscopy" or "biopsy" were enlightening entries along this line. Once I got the prize comment, "catheterization." Several times the diagnostic conclusion was simply "amenorrhea," though for the life of me I couldn't figure out why this would have required hospitalization. And finally there was the classic, "six months pregnant!"

We were greeted at Bulape by Dr. Stuart Anderson, a young Scottish physician, who was working at the hospital. Stuart was quite a personable and friendly fellow. He had offered for service shortly out of medical school as a Volunteer In Mission, giving two years of enthusiastic and dedicated work. We enjoyed the last seven months with Stuart before he hung up his stethoscope and returned to England to continue his medical practice.

One of the most important members of the Bulape medical team was beloved Mukulu Mikobi Jacques. Mikobi was a layman and one of the finest Christians I have ever known. We became fast friends. The term "Mukulu" is a title word indicating an elder in the church. For fifteen years Mukulu was treasurer of the Presbyterian Church in Kasai. I never heard a word of doubt or accusation concerning his integrity or honesty during our time there. This was a tribute only he alone could claim. He was kind and considerate, sensitive to the feelings of others, and humble and patient. And he was the administrator of my hospital! I had never enjoyed a hospital administrator before. It was a beautiful experience.

"Kampanda failed to come to work today? Well, tell Mukulu."

"Not enough water to sterilize the linens for surgery? Ask Mukulu to get us some."

"You think someone is stealing sheets off the beds? Report it to the administrator, Mukulu."

"Not paid your full salary this month? Take your complaint to Mukulu Mikobi. That's his department."

I shall always thank God for those three years I had with Mukulu in the medical work at Bulape.

Ngongo Elias was our *Infirmier Diplome* at the hospital. He was a graduate of IMCK and the first product of the school at Tshikaji with whom I had the pleasure of working. I had supervised the hospital duties of students and stagaires, but here was a graduate with several years of experience behind him and it was a genuine pleasure to observe his superior take-hold ability, and his general medical knowledge was a level above African nurses I had worked with in the past. He could conduct an outpatient clinic or visit distant dispensaries with the good judgment to know what he could take care of himself and what he should refer to me for consultation. I had the advantage of his assistance for nearly a year before it began to become apparent that he was loosening his ties and going to leave. I was distressed and looked for a reason for this departure. Obviously he could find other jobs where he would make more money, but was that the only reason? Didn't he feel a Christian calling of witness to bind him to the mission program? Gradually the real reason began to filter through. It was the old entanglement of polygamy. He already had his recognized wife by Christian marriage, but he also had a couple of unpublicized ones on the side.

Polygamy is a strong way of life in black Africa, and always difficult for the Christian community to deal with. The basic status symbol of chieftains and other important village leaders is plural marriages. Clans and families demand this sign of excellence from any outstanding relative. Ngongo finally came to me. He told me he knew he had done wrong and he was sorry about it. He confessed his Christian faith and explained that one reason he was leaving was because he realized that his marital status compromised his Christian leadership, bringing shame to the Church of Christ. He cited family pressures but he didn't rectify his position, and he left us. I reminded him that family ties are important but that there is another tie with Almighty God through the Lord Jesus which is more important. Before he took his leave we had a departing prayer together.

We lost Ngongo and his teaching capacities just as we were preparing to start a new school for *infirmieres auxillaires* (nurse assistants) at Bulape. The African church had asked us to undertake this new work in light of the fact that IMCK at Tshikaji was graduating such a small number of students annually who were so easily able to find better paying outside work with government and commercial companies who were gobbling them up. It left very few to fill vacancies in the church's medical program. We needed workers, a cut below the *Infirmier Diplome* level who wouldn't be drawn away and who, incidentally, wouldn't demand as high a salary. So entrance examinations were prepared and given across the church area, and an inaugural class of ten boys and ten girls was selected.

Now I must need scurry around and find an *Infirmier Diplome* to replace Ngongo and help me with the teaching. Burdened with my clinical load, it was too much for one person to handle that and the teaching as well. The Lord blessed us and we found two aides instead of one! Probably Birch Rambo and Ralph Shannon at Tshikaji were having compassion on us and prodding some help in our direction. At any rate, two promising young *infirmiers* came from IMCK to live and work with us. Lumboko Meshongo and Tshibangu Mvita were nice fellows, and they were not only medically well-trained but they were musically gifted. They had enjoyed choral singing and continued with us when we were able to obtain a guitar for each of them for accompaniment.

Shambe N'shake was our charge nurse in the operating room. He kept things reasonably clean and in order with sterile supplies ready for emergency surgery. He was my skillful assistant at the operating table. Years of assisting with the same operation over and over had made him qualified to handle many procedures himself. Many minor surgeries were left entirely up to him. When I suffered arthritis with acute pain in wrists and hands late in 1978, I was forced to call on Shambe for a few major interventions, and while I stood by to give advice or even step in if necessary, he performed several inguinal herniorrhaphies where further temporizing might have meant rupture of the bowel. I even tapped him one day to do a cesarean section. Mother and baby got along fine!

MEDICAL TREATMENT

The pathological conditions encountered in central Africa are basically the same as those we see in the homeland. It is not that they are alien orders of change, but they are often more exaggerated and thus more spectacular. Sure, there are the tropical vectors of disease like the tsetse fly and the falciparum mosquito, but more often it is ignorance and poverty and neglect which change the character and appearance of illness.

A case in point is a patient who came to me the day I arrived at Bulape. A tumor growing in his throat was making an obstruction so that he could breathe only by consciously exerting all his muscles of forced respiration. If he stopped making the effort he stopped breathing. This had been going on for days, gradually becoming more difficult. He had had no sleep nor rest and was beside himself with total exhaustion and overwhelming fear. Obviously the only means of relief was a tracheostomy to introduce a metal tube into his airway below the obstruction. This we did and he took a long smooth breath of air, relaxed, fell asleep, and stopped breathing! His sleep debt was so great and his muscles so weary that when the cessation of the blockage was eased the entire breathing process decided to take a vacation! We had to go to work to breathe for him, and an air bag was employed for an hour or two until he had a little rest and was able to resume breathing on his own.

The following day a patient with a bleeding placenta previa came in and I did my first cesarean section in ten years! Two days later I reviewed over three hundred cases of tuberculosis, a disease almost eliminated in the United States. Many of these cases were glandular and bone infections. We saw a lot of Pott's disease. And all of this with hardly any X-ray assistance. Film and reagents were hard to come by.

A month later a woman arrived at 4:00 P.M. who had been in labor since morning. She had undergone a C-section with her three previous pregnancies, and lost two of those babies. She had never been to our hospital and I had never laid eyes on her. She had sought no prenatal care. So we sectioned her through a mass of adhesions, the omentum adherent all over the anterior uterine surface. We got a premature baby weighing 1.83 kilograms, and with our primitive facilities this meant only a 50–50 chance of survival. You can be sure that this time I asked permission to tie her tubes!

In December of 1977, a man was brought in with lower right quadrant pain and exquisite tenderness. His temperature was 104 degrees. He was vomiting and there were only occasional bowel sounds. We opened him up and found free pus in the abdomen. There was an appendiceal abscess with so much necrosis of the cecum that it was necessary to remove it and do an anastomosis. Fifteen minutes after the surgery was completed he had a voluminous liquid bowel movement while still on the operating table—a beautiful sight!

A woman came in who had experienced no period for seventeen months. Early on she had felt the movements of pregnancy but for four months she had felt none. Surgery revealed a moderately macerated fetus, 45 centimeters in length, lying free in the abdomen. It had ruptured through the fundus of the uterus and the uterine tear had then healed itself with closure around the umbilical cord. The placenta had remained implanted within the uterine cavity. The mother had experienced no other symptoms except her amenorrhea and the cessation of movement.

Another time, a Zairian lady arrived with a tense and uncomfortable mass in her lower abdomen extending up above the umbilicus, and a history of only one week's duration. We had operated her five months earlier for a ruptured ectopic pregnancy, and had evacuated huge blood clots. The rapid growth of this tumor created suspicion that this might again be blood, but her hematocrit was thirty-five which was fairly respectable by Bantu standards. Her WBC was sixteen thousand and she had no fever. An I.V. drip was started and I told the nurses to insert a urinary catheter and take her to surgery. But before operating I was anxious to know more about what I was dealing with, and so I introduced an exploratory needle into the swelling and I got back urine! When I asked what was the matter with the catheter the reply was, "Oh, we haven't put it in yet." So I handled the matter personally and got back a quart of urine!

This of course reduced the size of the mass but there was still a lower abdominal and pelvic tumor with a distended and fluctuating cul-de-sac. This I incised and fastened in a rubber drain, and we got almost as much fluid from this incision as we did from the catheter. We removed a large cystic tumor at a later date, but for the time being all was going well. That morning she had thought she was dying, and I was not so sure but maybe she was right. But that afternoon she was sitting up in bed eating bidia!

I operated on a woman with a fibroid uterus, intending to do a hysterectomy. As I opened the peritoneum I inadvertently nicked a loop of small intestine and a large ascaris poked its head out, or maybe it was its tail. I fished it and four others from that tiny opening, sewed it up, and closed the abdomen to do the hysterectomy another day.

The first operative case one morning was thought to be a prostatic hypertrophy. It turned out to be a calcium encrusted wad of gauze in the bladder! The patient had been operated at Mweka three years earlier for an inguinal hernia. Obviously they had gotten into the bladder, stuffed in a sponge, and forgot to take it out.

A fellow was brought in who had been shot a couple of weeks earlier with an ancient muzzle loading gun sported by so many Congolese hunters. Black gun powder is tamped down the barrel and several metal slugs are added which may be nails or screws or small bits of copper beaten into small balls. A flintlock spark sets off the whole load. He took five of these slugs, two in the back, two in his seat, and one which penetrated his left flank and lodged in the groin or femoral area. This last one was causing him pain which radiated down into his foot. X-ray showed it well down near the femur but the point of entry was not marked and I had little indication of relative direction or position. Under spinal anaesthesia a probe was introduced along the pathway of the ball, but no foreign body was felt. The tract was enlarged and I tried to feel it with my finger, but no success. I continued the probing for almost an hour, but by this time considerable hemorrhage had been started and any visibility was zero. I was thoroughly discouraged and ready to quit but I breathed a short prayer, "Lord, I have no idea where to search and am ready to give up, but I'm going to try one more time. If you want me to get this thing out it's entirely up to you. But please, let's get on with it!" Again I felt. This time just a bit higher, and under the tip of my finger something firm moved! Within thirty seconds I had the rough little piece of metal plus the most immediate answer to prayer I ever experienced. It's so good to have the Lord on your side!

MEDICAL OUTREACH

Not all of Bulape's medical service took place within the walls of Lapsley Memorial Hospital. Bibola Ngoma, whom I taught at IMCK, was the nurse who headed up the Public Health program so ably organized by Dr. Richard Brown, my predecessor at Bulape. Bibola traveled regularly by motor bike to distant villages to conduct "under-five" clinics to administer polio and whooping cough shots to the little fellows. He also did surveys for tuberculosis and leprosy for early detection and treatment. Shamba Bidiaka was mentioned in the introduction. He was our faithful and dedicated keeper of the pharmacy. Mingashanga Tula was the nurse who surprised and delighted us at Christmastime when he brought one of the classic Bakuba woven mats with the words spelled out in English, MERRY CHRISTMAS! We still get it out for display at every birthday of our Lord.

Health services reached well out into the hinterland of Mweka Territory and beyond. This first became a reality when Dr. Mark Poole had the vision of bringing to central Africa a means of local transport by plane. Dr. Poole was the doctor at Bulape for a twenty-year span, from 1942 to 1962, and he saw the possibilities of clearing air strips on Congo's vast plains to extend his medical and surgical reach to villages fifty miles and more from Bulape. He flew the first light single motor plane in that part of the world and established dispensaries at Batue, Mbelu, and Shongamba—three different directions from Bulape. A nurse was stationed at each dispensary for daily treatments, and a doctor made flying weekly visits to replenish medicines and supplies, and to see difficult and serious cases. People swarmed to these dispensaries in ever-increasing

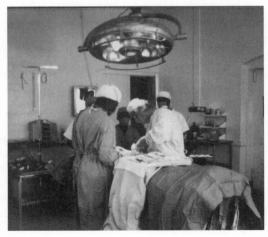

Bill in the operating room at Bulape.

numbers, becoming a part of Bulape's ballooning medical statistics. A plane also afforded the life-saving ministry of flying seriously ill or emergency patients to the hospital for help they never would have received back in the village.

A decade after Dr. Poole's service, another form of outreach was organized by Dr. Richard Brown when he set up public health surveys in numerous outpost villages. These activities were composed of two separate and distinct efforts. One was a systematic survey looking specifically for open cases of tuberculosis and leprosy. Drugs are available today to treat these two similar infections rendering them nontransmissable, thus protecting the general public from a spread of the diseases. This treatment can be done under supervision in the village without disrupting home life by a long visit to the hospital. The other effort was toward protecting small children against contagious diseases. Children no longer getting their mother's milk are almost always hypoproteinemic—prime targets for whooping cough, chicken pox, and pneumonia. The numbers who succumb are appalling. Vaccinations to protect them are given and weight gain or loss is recorded to judge the presence and extent of malnutrition. Because of the age group involved we refer to these as "under-five" clinics. Both of these Public Health services, as well as the outpost dispensaries, expand the effective work of the hospital into many villages within a fifty-mile radius of Bulape.

SCHOOL FOR AUXILIARY NURSES

Six months after our arrival at Bulape the church approached us with the request that we start a school for *infirmiers auxillaires*. This was an entirely new thought which would shift our medical service into a distinctly higher gear. Effie and I had anticipated a year in Zaire when we left Knoxville. This would doubtless be a two-year course and would presume our presence to see it through and, hopefully, to put it on a permanent and continuing basis. We were rather aghast.

The church was not without reason with the request. The IMCK had filled the need for training nurses at a higher professional level, but its output of graduates continued to be only a trickle, and, as I have said, many of these better-trained individuals were wooed away to higher paying jobs. The needs of the church hospitals and dispensaries were not being met, and church leaders realized that a flow of workers trained at a somewhat lower level, would fill the gaps. In years past we had called the lower level graduates "nurses' aides." The government chose to designate them as "auxiliary nurses."

So the church asked us to inaugurate a new school to meet our own needs, but they offered us no funds with which to do the job! We had no didactic materials, no facilities to house students, no money to hire a cook or buy food to feed them. The familiar and oft repeated activity of scrounging around for help went into full force. Eventually we wheedled some relief from the church, the government, and augmented with unsolicited gifts from folks in the home church. The Bible School for training village evangelists opened its dormitory doors to include our male students and we turned over a residence on the station to the girls, and also used the kitchen and dining area for all the students. I have written of the two fine *infirmiers Diplomes* who came to help with the teaching load. Instruction for the ten boys and ten girls was begun in such subjects as anatomy, pathology, bacteriology, general nursing care, and the much needed but little comprehended medical mathematics. I also taught a required class of Bible study.

One of our urgent needs was for more skilled instruction in bedside nursing care, so we asked Lucille McElroy in North Carolina to come back and help us. Lucille had first taught hospital nursing care at Lubondai, then at Bulape, and finally at Tshikaji at IMCK. She had been back in the States in North Carolina for seven years, but when we called her she bent an ear to the voice of the Lord and concluded that he was really doing the calling, so she returned to Africa. She reached Bulape in February 1979 and we were already well into that first year of instruction. But she pitched in with a will, doubled her class load, and adequately completed the prescribed work in June.

We got through the year in relatively good shape. A few floundered and were dismissed. A few became discouraged and dropped out. But the larger body of the class survived and prepared for the second year of instruction and for regular contribution in the hospital. At the end of the first year the church sent further instructions which we had anticipated but dreaded. They wanted us to take in another first-year class! This would mean doubling the student body, doubling the teaching load, and doubtless doubling costs. So we gave another entrance exam and chose another class while desperately looking around for more help. We had a new doctor working with us at Bulape, Dr. Tshiswaka Kayembe. He would share with the teaching load and this, more than anything else, made it possible to begin with another class. They arrived in September 1979. Nine girls and fourteen boys. And now it was my turn to double up on my instruction and finish my courses the first half of the school year because I was going home! This was more than adequate motivation, and I completed the job!

THE COMING OF TSHISWAKA

One of the fondest dreams a missionary doctor can have is to see the day when African physicians join him and move in to take over the leadership in medical ministry. Dr. Tshiswaka Kayembe was from the Katanga region of Zaire, now called Shaba, where his father was an employee of the government-controlled copper mines. He was of the Baluba tribe, but had spent his boyhood in the cosmopolitan environs of Elizabethville (Lubumbashi). He spoke Kiswahili and impeccable French, but did not know his own tribal language of Tshiluba. He had done well in secondary school and was accepted into the medical school in Kinshasa where he made a new friend, Tshibangu Mangala, also a first year student from the Shaba area. Tshiswaka's family had Catholic connections but his own relationship to the Catholic Church was at best casual. On the other hand, Tshibangu was a devout Protestant Christian, and he shared his personal beliefs with Tshiswaka. He urged him to attend church services and invited him to youth meetings. Tshiswaka was impressed with the earnestness and sincerity of his friend concerning spiritual matters. He realized that it was a strength he did not possess, and finally he was moved to make a new commitment to Jesus Christ as Lord and Saviour. Such is the beautiful story of two medical students in central Africa, and how one brought the other into a saving Christian faith.

As a result of his newfound Christian commitment, Tshiswaka decided he would not seek a lucrative medical practice in the huge capital city of Kinshasa, a location to which most graduating young doctors aspired. He would look for some place where the need was great and where he could best serve a host of needy people. With this goal in mind he appeared at Kananga to ask questions and gather information from the Christian leaders, and they directed his attention toward Bulape, telling him, "Bulape is an important and far-reaching medical complex. It is being directed by Dr. Rule who came out on an interim contract and only a holding basis. In nine months he will be leaving to return to the United States. If you go there it will give you time to work with him and learn policies, procedures, and practices. Then you can take over and run the hospital." This appealed to Tshiswaka, and so he came and established himself at Bulape.

Tshiswaka stepped into the medical chores with enthusiasm. He took his share of making rounds, promptly began to pick up surgical procedures, conducted outpatient clinics, taught two or three courses to the nursing students, and made many of the flying visits to outpost dispensaries. It was a blessing to have him around!

Then a sudden and disturbing interruption broke into the program. Tshiswaka came to tell me he must make a trip back to Kinshasa because he had some personal business that needed attention. He said he might be gone several weeks. The question immediately ran through my mind, Is this the end of a sweet honeymoon? Is he leaving for good? But there was nothing I could do about it. He was his own boss. So we wished him Godspeed and sadly watched him go.

Days lengthened into weeks and we heard nothing from our doctor. We tightened our belts and carried on the best we could until one day we were incredulously delighted when he appeared again with his friend in tow. He introduced us to Dr. Tshibangu Mangala whom, he said, had come to help us with the medical work! The story goes that when Tshiswaka reached Kinshasa he looked up his good friend and announced, "Tshibangu, I've come to get you and take you back to the Kasai where you are going to help me run a hospital!" Now my cup was truly running over. I had *two* African doctors as colleagues, and I had never expected to have even one.

Drs. Tshiswaka and Tshibangu were the first two Zairian physicians with whom I had the delightful experience of working, but let me hasten to add that they were not the first African doctors to serve in our medical mission complex. Dr. Katambue Nkonu, a graduate of the government medical school in Kinshasa, returned to the church of his childhood where he volunteered for missionary service. He was assigned to Bibanga hospital where there was no longer an expatriate physician in residence, and at this writing he has been the faithful and effective medical and administrative head of that institution for twenty-five years.

Benoit Nzengu was one of the most outstanding graduates of the IMCK nursing school. He was recognized as a candidate of M.D. caliber and was sent to the United States for a year of high school to perfect his mastery of the English language. As the first black student at Davidson College he was a star soccer player. He studied medicine in Belgium, took residency in Alberta, Canada, and returned to Zaire as a member of the staff at Good Shepherd Hospital and a faculty member of IMCK. Dr. Ngoi Kadima, another graduate of the Zairian government medical school, served at Good Shepherd Hospital. He took postgraduate surgical training in the United States and returned to become chief-of-staff at the hospital.

These are the outstanding Christian physicians of Zaire that I knew during my closing years in that land, and with whom I worked in a professional partnership. It is with deep gratitude to God that we have watched them take over a vital aspect of the Christian witness among their people.

OTHER AREAS OF MINISTRY

The American Peace Corps was another group with which we had pleasant and fulfilling interaction while at Bulape. Of the young ladies and men there were always three or four teaching in our local schools. Outlets for extracurricular activities were limited. No theater. No television. And almost no caucasian friendships outside their small, close-knit group. Transportation was almost nonexistent, and food selectivity boiled down to the same old thing day after day.

If things got bad they turned to Effie, and she responded to them in her understanding and untiring manner. She became the sounding board for their problems and complaints. She was their counselor and offered sage and balanced advice. She became their arbitrator in matters of contention and compromise. But most important of all, she became their hostess and offered home-cooked meals and special surprise goodies. Thanksgiving and Christmas and Fourth of July became special efforts to fill a painful void and soon the word got around. Peace Corps kids came from miles away, turning either their shoe leather or bike tires toward Bulape, and on many of these occasions we had rousing "family times" together.

Another area of ministry in which Effie rendered dedicated and effective service was in the feeding of many malnourished people. Most folks in our affluent western culture have no concept of what it would be like to have starving victims come to their back door. Effie had them all the time. Most of these pitiful specimens were small children, but there were also many adults. We had a nutrition center at the hospital where meals were prepared for malnourished kiddies. Their mothers came with them and learned how to take the foodstuffs, available from the local gardens or marketplace, and prepare nourishing meals. But there were always children who had been deprived of food so long, weeks and months, that their digestive processes had simply ceased to function. I would send these over to the house to Effie and she would try to coax teaspoonfuls of milk or soup down them without their regurgitating. These children were not hungry. They were not snatching at any morsel and bolting it down. In fact they were sort of disgusted by the thought of food, and they were starving to death.

The stunted state of some of these chronically deprived children was almost beyond comprehension. I recall two five-month old babies. One weighed 8 1/4 pounds, not much above birth rate. The other weighed 11 pounds. But there were worse cases. One two year old weighed only 10 pounds! Mikobi was a one year old who weighed 9 3/4 pounds. Tshisubu was 14, hopelessly physically and mentally deformed. He weighed 37 pounds.

It was for cases such as these that Effie was called upon to provide. She responded with such loving and tender care that the number seeking aid steadily grew, and when we had been at Bulape only a year she was feeding twenty-five hungry people a day. Rice was ladled out, some times with a suggestion of gravy on it. Hot tea was fortified with sugar and milk. Some had hot grits. This wasn't much but it served to ease aching stomachs and in some cases afforded the few extra calories necessary to keep body and soul together. On one occasion a year later I counted seventy participants by actual count!

Little Bawoto was a special child that Effie worked with assiduously over a period of months. She was slowly weaned back from the very sill of death's doorway. She began to digest her food and put a little flesh on her ribs and limbs. We thought she was over the hump and sent her home with her mother and grandmother, giving them explicit instructions about continued feeding. But it didn't work out. They either forgot or never grasped the importance of what they had been told. And worse, they were negligent about bringing the child back for Effie's care. When they finally came, Bawoto was in an even more appalling state than the first time, and in spite of all efforts to coax food down her for nutrition, her progress was steadily downhill. There had already been so much cellular and functional degeneration that it became an irreversible process. There was probably liver damage beyond saving. Little Bawoto slipped away in Effie's arms while Effie whispered to her that Jesus loved her.

The major groups of patients in our pediatric ward were the malarias, pneumonias, diarrheas, and the malnutritions. Every Zairian baby lives so close to the line nutritionally it cannot afford to contend with any of the other circulating illnesses without slipping down into the malnourished class. The chronicity of this condition is appalling. One prime little member of our collection was a pitiful three year old who had suffered the limit of nutritional restriction with its stunting effect on brain and brawn. He could not stand nor sit nor speak, but lay only in a fetal position. His sole activity was the movement of his eyes which regarded one and all out of a stolid and expressionless face. His weight, 11 pounds. His hematocrit was 20.

MORE INTRODUCTIONS

The patriarch of our church family was the aged but alert Pastor Mishenge, along with his equally aged wife, Baba Kama. They had presided over the congregation at Bulape for many many years. Pastor Mishenge personified faithfulness to the Lord encountered from the early days of the gospel message in central Africa across four or five generations of Christian believers. Well into his eighties, he was still there, and he was still faithful.

Baba Kama was a cheerful neighbor and a gracious hostess when it came to offering us the finger lickin' good items of an African cuisine. Medically she was a particular concern of mine because she possessed the most stubborn and resistant hypertension I ever encountered. Her diastolic pressure was invariably well above a hundred and I never once clocked her systolic pressure below two hundred. We tried her on all the antihypertensive medicines in our possession, pushing them to their limits of tolerance, but I never had the slightest intimation that her BP was affected. I carried the anxiety from day to day that she would fall victim to either stroke or heart failure or perhaps urinary shut-down or some other crippling or concluding accident. But day by day we encountered her broad smile and when we departed from Africa she was still going strong.

Mulami Mabudi was our sentry. The title *Mulami* means caretaker and is the word used for deacons in the church. Mabudi was not only our caretaker, but he was also a faithful deacon. As sentry he was charged with protecting the place against intruders, cutting and gathering wood for the kitchen stove, clearing and tending our garden, pumping water from the cistern to overhead barrels in the attic for gravitational flow into the house, and for taking care of odd jobs as they appeared. He was our "telephone." If there was a message to be sent to the hospital or elsewhere on the station, his legs carried the written communication.

Mabudi and his family lived in a sun-dried brick house in our backyard. He and his wife had six children who all became part of our household, and who participated in the small jobs according to their age and size, profiting from handouts of food, clothing, and toys as they came to Effie. A special time that we enjoyed with the Mabudi family was an evening celebration on Christmas Eve. It was an annual tradition with us to invite the Mabudis for this party. They washed and dressed up and trooped into the house to sit on chairs or the floor as space presented itself. Mabinshi was the teenage daughter who married and had a baby while we were there. Mayu and Davidi and Nambudi Muana and little Bionyi were all attractive children and we thoroughly enjoyed them. Five-year-old Woto wasn't at a very appealing stage as he whined and cried too much. He still had some growing up to do.

Effie prepared various sorts of goodies including cookies, fudge, bananas, and other fruits, Kool-aid for the kids and special hot tea for the adults. We always had rubber balloons to blow up, bat around, and eventually burst. These were a special delight for the children since they only played with them once a year. There were other surprises and squeals of appreciation as Effie collected and produced them for this special event. We always read the Christmas story together from the Tshiluba Bible, and while Effie played the piano we sang Christmas carols. All of this eventually put the smaller ones to sleep and they had to be collected from wherever they were draped over furniture, along with their new acquisitions, and carried out of the house before electric lights were cut off at 10:00 P.M. It was a special time with Mabudi and his family.

My list of African introductions could be much longer but I will conclude the roll of honor with the name of a most unique and engaging villager, Mbaya Tshiala Benyi. Mbaya he is called and the appropriated *Tshiala Benyi* might roughly translate as "Guest House" or "Host of Guests." Mbaya was a middle-aged man, rather small and spare, with a touch of gray hair. He wore the traditional Bakuba dress which consisted of a full, gathered skirt woven from palm tree fibers, with a woven four-cornered skull cap or *lutshieta*. His feet and torso were bare. This man was wholly dedicated to what he considered to be his Christian vocation—providing for strangers and travelers. Daily he housed and fed numbers of them. At church on Sunday he looked for strangers he could take home to dinner. He cleared and planted large fields simply to produce sufficient food for this ministry. And it was no afterthought. It was his full-time job and he applied himself tirelessly. This was the basic (and very real) practical expression of his faith.

VISITS FROM THE FAMILY

We were delighted to have our own Barbara with us for a few weeks during this final term of missionary service. In Kananga when we first arrived we heard that a number of the Peace Corps volunteers were at Lake Munkamba where they were studying the Tshiluba language under the skillful guidance of Virginia Pruitt. Barbara was gung ho for joining them. First, to brush up on her neglected Tshiluba. Second, to meet and make new friends. And third, to again embrace the beauties of our beloved Lake Munkamba, site of so many childhood happinesses. So we parted company with Barbara as she headed for Munkamba.

It was another month before she joined us again in our new home at Bulape and we began to prepare for the first African Christmas in eight years. We enjoyed evenings of relaxation and fellowship while we sat around the table yakking and playing such games as yahtzee, hearts, sequence, or even put together a jigsaw puzzle or two.

But time passed all too quickly and Barbara left us in January to fly back for an eight-month sojourn in Kinshasa, the nation's capital, where she was engaged in a disciplined Christian witness in an effort to draw African believers, old and new, into a cohesive church group. In order to pay her own way during this period, she took a secretarial job at TASOK which was the American high school she had attended her first two years. This work provided her with room and board. She thoughtfully kept her eyes open for tasty edibles and incidentals she could pass along inland to her mamma and daddy, and we were often surprised by various delightful goodies. In August she packed her bags to return to life in the United States.

But when Barbara departed Bulape we were not long devoid of family, for within two weeks the Woodruff family arrived to spend a month. Elizabeth had prevailed upon husband Jim to venture into central Africa to get a glimpse of the land of her childhood, and they brought along their year-old baby, Jennifer. Libby helped her mother with the sewing classes Effie conducted for Congolese women. Jim, an outdoors man, enjoyed jaunts to the forest with our house sentry who went to cut and haul fuel for our wood-burning stove and outside-bath water heater. Jennifer happily concentrated on the effort to step on the baby parrots which needed some protection from her little bare feet.

Finally it was time to start the trip back to the States, and herewith another example of the essence of airline incompetence. The Woodruff tickets had been carefully verified and their reservations were to leave Kananga on February 27 on a 5:30 P.M. flight, but at 11:00 that morning we learned that the schedule had been changed, without notice to anyone, and the plane had already gone! Don't think for a moment that means it wasn't fully charged. There are always many waiting, without reservations, and a plane can be filled at a moment's notice. There was nothing to be done but to make new reservations for a flight two days later.

These were some of our experiences included in the medical work at Bulape. We will always be so deeply grateful to our Heavenly Father for giving us the high privilege of laboring in that field, and we continue to pray that He will take that effort and use it in the building of His kingdom.

25 THERE ARE MANY ADVERSARIES

Trust in the Lord with all thine heart; and lean not unto thine own understanding. In all thy ways acknowledge him, and he shall direct thy paths (Psalms 3:5–9).

Being a foreign missionary is not always the glamorous undertaking it is cracked up to be. As in most other occupations repetitive activities can veil the true significance of underlying dreams and goals, and bring into center focus only the drudgery of daily duties. Besides, there are a myriad of divergences which distract attention and draw our energies and concerns into secondary, even trivial channels. I recall a day of this kind at Bulape which will always remain a lesson in my memory.

I was awakened about 2:30 A.M. by a whole herd of cows outside my window. I jumped out of bed, grabbed a stick, and chased them all the way across the compound in my bare feet. Back home, I washed my feet and went back to bed. A few minutes later I heard a cow in the garden, and again I rose and went forth in the bright moonlight to do battle with the beast. She just sidled quietly into the bushes and disappeared. I stood very still and hoped she would come forth close enough for me to lay a mighty blow across her back, or whatever portion of her anatomy she might present. As I stood waiting I became conscious of the insects. Tiny biting gnats swarmed all over me. The discomfort increased and I yielded the field to my tough-skinned antagonist. Again I washed my feet and crawled into bed.

But by now I was so mad I couldn't sleep. Those Presbyterian cows, predestined to be the destruction of Effie's garden, had become an acute pain in the neck. Already they had trampled down our fence and devoured our corn. Now I kept casting about in my mind for just how I might murder a cow. It would have been a most satisfying accomplishment. But I couldn't come up with any dignified means. All I did was lie there for a couple of hours thinking critical and uncomplimentary thoughts . . . like:

Reasons Why a Refined and Self-Respecting
Doctor Would be Unwilling to Associate Himself
With the Work at Bulape Hospital.

1. Because it is extremely dirty.
2. Because there is habitually a lack of water on hand.
3. Because patients are seldom given a bath.
4. Because there is no adequate program to combat lice and bedbugs.
5. Because hospital linens are changed only when thoroughly soiled.
6. Because dressings saturated with blood or drainage are shamefully neglected.
7. Because no hospital windows or woodwork are ever cleaned.
8. Because there is no metal polish and fixtures are always dull and rusty.
9. Because all cupboards, closets, and drawers serve primarily for the collection of trash and cockroaches.
10. Because the hospital plumbing is continually out of order.
11. Because children (and probably adults) defecate in the grass.
12. Because goats, dogs, and chickens have free run of the compound and corridors.

I could go on . . .

Finally, that morning I got up with a headache from lack of sleep and proceeded to the hospital to perform the three major operations scheduled for the day. My distractions of lesser matters left me somewhat impaired for the priority performances of the day.

Speaking of the cattle problem leads me to comment on a subject I dealt with earlier, which is the capacity of a young church in a developing country to handle its own business and keep its household in order. I am speaking of improvidence—the inability to look ahead and plan for the future. The attitude of affluence is entirely different from that of poverty. The haves are occupied with keeping what they have, or watching it grow. They look to the future and preserve what they have.

On the other hand the have-nots take little thought of the future. Their crisis and concern is right now: today's bread and today's shelter. Their constant living on the edge inclines them to use today whatever comes to hand, and they are alarmingly improvident about tomorrow.

This attitude spills over into hospital administration, chiefly concerning medicines and supplies. My attitude was to husband them with all my might. But let it be known that a new shipment of drugs had arrived and my African cohorts wanted to give them in generous dosage to every patient who darkened the door! The same went with linen and dry goods supplies. Their reasoning was new sheets for all the beds and several new baby blankets to go home with each newborn. I contended that we must take inventory and calculate how long our supplies would last. They thought that was a lot of foolishness.

Looking at the situation at Bulape and contemplating on the long range goals and hopes of the church, I considered there were four signals in the wind which read that the road to ordered management and success was still a long and rocky one. These signals were the unattended cows, the Presbytery's relatively new but unusable Land Rover, the ever-present problem of water, and the sad and dilapidated condition of Bulape's church building. Taking them in order, I shall elaborate.

The cows belonged to the Presbytery. They made up a herd of about fifteen head, and were doubtless envisioned by the divines as a money-making enterprise for the Lord's work. After all, look at all the lush grass on the compound to serve as inexhaustible fodder for a growing group of cattle. There was no herdsman and the cows had never enjoyed the snug confines of a corral at night, in spite of the fact that buying barbed wire and selecting a circular group of trees to wrap it around was all it would take. No one even took them to the streams in the valley for water, and they suffered with thirst, particularly in the dry season. They marauded gardens and trampled fences, but any correction of the situation would be embarrassing since they belonged to the church. So much for a poorly conceived and totally unattended cattle project.

Another deficient property of the Presbytery was a Land Rover, the British equivalent of an American four wheel drive Jeep. It was a vehicle which had seen limited use and was in good mechanical condition, but during the three years we were at Bulape it sat either in front of the pastor's house or in the garage in my backyard, and never ran so much as one kilometer. The reason? A mileage charge had never been made for its use and so a maintenance fund was never accumulated to keep it running. Those responsible for the vehicle felt a reticence to charge for its use. That would seem grasping and un-Christian. It apparently never occurred to them that there are other costs of motorized transportation besides gas and oil. If tires wore out or the battery gave up the ghost, casualties often occurring on the unimproved roads and in a tropical climate, there were no funds for replacement. So the Land Rover just sat and collected rust and was still parked by the side of the road when we left Zaire.

The hospital water supply was another problem. We had a couple of large cisterns set in the ground which collected rainwater off roofs of surrounding hospital buildings. Enough could be accumulated during the raining season to see us comfortably through the dry season. Also there was a fine water tank which stood twenty feet above the ground with both an electric and hand pump to lift water from the cistern to overhead reservoir where gravitational flow supplied the various needs of a busy hospital service. I had envisioned that fine water tank being full of water at all times, ready to meet any and all medical needs at a moment's notice. Daily pumping should replenish the fraction used and top it off full once again.

But alas, my idealism along such lines was completely thwarted. In my household, water is an essential item. The African family is no exception. They need it for cooking, drinking, bathing, washing, and they must travel to the water and haul it on their heads to the village. So when they saw all that water accumulated in the tower, their universal reaction was "It must immediately come down from there and be put to good use." And instead of daily replenishing a full tank, we only pumped up a pittance to wet the bottom before it was all drained off again. But the situation was worse than that. Dozens of village people came daily to the hand pump and our dry season reserve was compromised so that we had to pay out hundreds of zaires to either pump water from the valley with a diesel motor or pay water carriers to haul it to the hospital.

This same mentality of community rights and community ownership is common in various other situations. We had a lovely orange tree in our front yard at Bulape and each year it was loaded with oranges. Village children began to pluck them as soon as they first appeared. Still too green to eat, the picker would take one bite, pucker up lips, and throw it down. We tried to refrain from fussing or pointing out that they were taking our oranges. We even went easy on reminding them that the fruit should be left on the tree until it was ripe. We simply hoped that in due time there would be some good oranges. But when the fruit matured the crowds increased and I had to send forth a picker to gather our share.

This is part of the culture in which we lived. It's like the water problem. Water is for everybody. Who is to say that the cistern is to hoard only for the hospital, or only for any few? That is not *ethical.* And the orange or papaya or mango tree is in the same category. No one needs to ask if he or she can have some. Everyone can take some. It's their right.

Now let me say a word about the church building. It was constructed in the 1920s by Mr. Lawrence DeLand and has been an imposing and attractive edifice through the years. Its high, steep roof was originally covered with grass, but because grass roofs need constant repair a metal one was later laid over the thatch. Inside, large woven mats with Bakuba designs and figures decorated the wall behind the pulpit. The effect was most impressive, but time and termites took their toll. Supporting timbers had become weakened and bowed. Storms had blown off some of the sheets of roofing which left holes for rain to pour in. At one time an initial sum was collected for repairs, but some lean and hungry deacon ate it. And so the structure stood neglected and little used when we left Bulape.

Sad to report, this is the story of many buildings on the former mission-controlled stations. After the Presbyterian Church U.S. turned over to the Zairian Presbyterian Church some two hundred buildings in the 1960s, there has been little or no maintenance or renovation and only a small amount of new construction. All buildings are gradually running down, wearing out, and will eventually be written off. Lost. Gone. The church will be back to its grassroots in more than one way, but hopefully its members will have a greater spiritual vision and a deeper love and loyalty to the Lord Jesus Christ.

ARTHRITIS, TENDONITIS, AND MEDICAL FURLOUGH

One day in September 1978 while I was operating I began to feel some discomfort in my right knee. I thought it was the awkward angle at which I was standing. Probably the table hadn't been pumped up high enough. It was an old-fashioned table with a hand pump which couldn't be manipulated without disarranging all the sterile drapes, so I fussed at the nurses and requested a stool to sit on to finish my surgery.

By that evening I had a fever, judged it was malaria and took my camoquin. But the following day I was still febrile with some chills, and was having pain in a finger that gradually began to swell and throb so that I had to immobilize it with a splint. The painful joints began to multiply. My wrists were especially painful and I bound them both with ace bandages to limit mobility.

I was hampered with these ailments for a week, and then one morning I woke with the inability to extend my left thumb. It just lay there in the palm of my hand. I could extend it with the other hand but on release it flopped back in my palm. This really shook me. I went to the hospital, found my white blood cell count elevated, and took a big shot of bicillin in my hip. Then I went to the short-wave radio transmitter to look for medical help. I caught pilot Jim Branch and Dr. Henry Nelson just getting into the plane at Bibanga, and they came straight to Bulape. I was so grateful to Henry for taking over for me while plans were initiated to get Effie and myself on our way to the States as soon as possible.

As soon as I arrived in Knoxville my dedicated Christian physician, Dr. Glen Kennedy, put me in the hospital where they aspirated my knee and took 10 or 20 cc of a thick bloody fluid that was put through all the tests. Nothing was cultivated from it and to this day nobody knows just what it was. Examination of my hand convinced the doctors that I had suffered a rupture of the extensor tendon of the thumb, weakened by extension of the arthritic inflammation. A month following our arrival an orthopedic surgeon, John Bell, who was another fine Christian friend of mine, operated on my hand and did a tendon transplant giving me a replacement muscle for extending the thumb. Six weeks after our sudden departure from Africa we were on our way back, my hand in a light splint to protect it for a few more weeks of healing.

ENCOUNTERING THE GRIM REAPER

Benjamin Franklin observed " . . . in this world nothing is certain but death and taxes." He was a wise man to list death first. Death is still the last enemy to be conquered and until that day our tears and sorrow and loneliness and grief are its counterparts.

In Africa death seemed to be so much with us. I remember an experience involving one of the Zairian soccer players. He was on the nation's team which would compete in the Olympics. Since the country was relatively bankrupt, the members of the team were called on to raise some of their travel expenses to Moscow, and this fellow had the idea of going into the forest to buy captured Gray African Parrots which he would sell for hundreds of dollars profit. At Mweka he explained his mission to the authorities and requested some means of transportation. They obliged him with a truck and chauffeur, and he headed for our part of the country. He reached Patambamba, nine kilometers from Bulape, about noon. He stopped and bought a meal of bidia from one of the village women, then proceeded to Banzebwe, the village just adjacent to Bulape compound.

When the chauffeur stopped the truck, he noted that his passenger was asleep on the seat beside him. He decided not to disturb him, and got out to greet and chat with the village people. An hour or so later they went back to the truck to waken the soccer player, but he was in a deep coma. So they brought him to me at the hospital where we judged he had been poisoned by something he ate or that had been somehow introduced into his body.

We washed out his stomach, started an I.V. drip, and tried to stimulate diuresis. He lived for nearly twenty-four hours without regaining consciousness. We sent his body back to Mweka. The affair raised quite a ruckus in the capital city. What really happened? Was he the victim of drug overdose that he himself took? Or was he poisoned by someone seeking to rob him? He must have had a significant amount of cash on him with which to buy birds, but we found none when he reached the hospital. Was the chauffeur involved? It would certainly appear so. The poor woman who fed him was severely chastised but I think unjustly so. As far as I know this mystery never was solved, nor any reasonable explanation for the sequence of events ever offered.

Lucille McElroy was the daughter of missionary parents, and had grown up as a "mish kid" in the Congo. After training, she returned as a missionary nurse and spent twenty-seven years in that calling, much of it teaching at the IMCK. Back in the States and after seven years of nursing in North Carolina, she was returning to help with the classes for auxiliary nurses. In spite of the fact that she arrived late in the school year, she doubled her class time and caught up her class work to finish in June.

On the morning of June 29 she came to the hospital in a disturbing condition. Her left leg was markedly swollen and cyanotic, and she had a lot of pain. She had obviously suffered a thrombophlebitis of the femoral vein and was in serious condition. We bundled her into the car, took her home, and put her to bed where she was treated for her discomfort with the limb elevated. Intravenous heparin was begun. But in spite of treatment she went into profound shock and never recovered, dying during the night.

The Christian community had responded, this time for one whose natural family was far away in the States, but whose missionary family and African family were near at hand, expressing their love and grief in many ways. Her body was conducted to the church by all her boy and girl students serving as pallbearers, and a Christian memorial service was held after which the earthly remains were laid to rest in the small Bulape cemetery for missionary families.

Only God, in His goodness and grace, knows the answers to perplexing questions raised by our poor minds at such times as these.

Lucille McElroy's funeral service at Bulape.

We can only put our trust in Him and remember that death for the Christian, even though fraught with grief and loneliness, is not a time of defeat but one of great and joyous victory in the Lord Jesus Christ.

ABUSE OF CRIPPLED AND DISABLED CHILDREN

Effie's jobs were so demanding, physically and emotionally, that I sometimes was concerned about her good health and humor. Often she looked tired and haggard and found it difficult to sleep. All of her feeding programs, plus sewing classes, plus care of White Cross supplies, plus giving out linens at the hospital, plus visiting patients on the wards, plus a constant stream of visitors at the house, plus constant care of me were enough to get anybody down. So besides all that, she took on another job—mothering and caring for a little crippled girl named Mayinda.

Mayinda was about nine or ten years old with partial paralysis of one arm and leg. She walked with a limp and was hampered in properly grooming herself or performing various activities since one arm and hand didn't function properly. Possibly she had polio before we knew her, or she may have suffered a birth injury. Her mother had died and her father remarried, but the stepmother wouldn't allow the child to live in their house, so she slept in her grandparents' hut. She was filthy, dressed in rags, and malnourished since she truly got only the cast-off crumbs. Such great need attracted Effie's interest as she talked with the child at our back door when she came for a hand-out.

She had been taught to steal and lie and had developed the mentality that those are the tools one uses to get along in the world. She had never gone to school. She had never known love or friendship from anybody. Other children teased her and picked on her. Adults ignored her. This was Mayinda's miserable lot in life.

Under Effie's care she began to respond physically with improved nutrition. Her bones became padded with new overlying tissue and her skin and hair began to show the glossy blackness of Central African good health. But she needed more than food. She needed training to adapt to the culture from which she had been excluded. She needed to know and believe principles of goodness and righteousness. She needed to develop some self-dignity and worth, and a desire to do well. She needed to hear the gospel.

So I took her to church. She sat by me because otherwise she probably would have been excluded. Her seat by me was her ticket of admission. But she smelled bad, and so the next week we gave her a bucket of warm water and a square of soap and asked her to wash thoroughly before the service. Effie also supplied her with panties and a simple cotton dress, but when she went home her stepmother took the clothes to give to some "more respectable" child. Mayinda came back in her dirty, evil-smelling rags. So it was necessary to change the routine. When she arrived each Sunday morning, she not only bathed herself but washed her rags and hung them up to dry. She dressed for church in clothes supplied by Effie. After worship she changed back to her clean rags, then washed her dress for Effie to keep for her. This was her Sunday routine when she went with us to church. I would give her a coin during the service so she could go forward and drop it in the collection plate. Her look of contentment and appreciation because she was being accepted as a legitimate member of the congregation paid for the weekly coin donation a thousand times over! And it was glorious to anticipate her ultimate acceptance of the One who loves her more than anyone else, and whose outstretched arms welcome her into His family of love—forever!

Yes, there are many adversaries along the pathway of proclaiming the Good News to a stumbling and stricken world. The adversaries of ignorance, of poverty, of greed, of falsehood, of thievery, of illness, and even death. But the door is open! No one can close it because Jesus says that He *is* the door. Through Him the sheep are gathered into the shelter of the fold, and through Him they venture forth to find the pasture of daily involvement with Christian experience.

26 THE HARVEST FIELD LIES WAITING

Then saith he unto his disciples, The harvest truly is plenteous but the labourers are few; pray ye therefore the Lord of the harvest, that he will send forth labourers into his harvest (Matthew 9:37–38).

The ministry of witnessing to the glorious message of salvation in Jesus Christ is more easily performed on the overseas mission field than in the homeland. It quickly becomes a natural and spontaneous approach. It is expected of you. It's why you are there and seldom brings forth a negative or offended response. Within this less sophisticated society the existence and transcending importance of a Creator God is almost universally accepted and information or ideas concerning Him are worth listening to.

As Effie and I stepped back into missionary life at Bulape after a seven year layoff, we were delighted at the avenues of witness which opened to us. The immediate opportunity which came to me was during the early morning meeting of the hospital staff when we heard the night report of those going off duty, and also made any particular work assignments for the day. The meeting also included a time of brief worship together with a short spiritual message or Bible study and a period of prayer.

As soon as I arrived on the scene and greeted my fellow workers, I was asked to give the spiritual commentary at these meetings, so throughout most of the next three years I led the group in various Bible studies and discussions. They were most receptive and seemed to count this time together as instructive in their Christian concepts. Several of them commented about their new insights into Scripture gained from these few minutes of Bible study in the morning.

Teaching the word of God is like a stone thrown into a pond. There is an ever-extending circle of wavelets reaching out toward the shoreline. God's word can be counted on to operate in the same manner.

Some of the hospital nurses were impressed by our morning meditations and they talked to friends in the village about them. They were concerned that we were such a limited group and that the time was short, and they came to ask if I would be willing to give a Bible study in the village for a volunteer group. Their leader was Kongo Iodi and, with his wife, Mbulu Mantshiumba, they had gathered fifteen or twenty people who were interested. Effie and I were delighted to meet with them a couple of afternoons a week. I started out emphasizing the importance of the Bible and impressed upon them how our understanding of the word of God comes to us from instruction of the Holy Spirit. Their attention was quickened by mention of the Spirit. Many Africans look for a mystic and emotional experience in their Christian walk. Well, it's there, in spite of the fact that we Anglo-Saxon Presbyterians tend to gloss it over and cover up our Teutonic embarrassment. So I welcomed the opportunity to give a Bible-centered presentation of the Holy Spirit including His indwelling presence and His filling dynamic.

The rippling circle continued to widen. Kongo Iodi came to say that our Bible classes should be extended out into other villages. His home village was Patambamba, only five miles from Bulape. He asked if I would be willing to go there once a week if he would make the arrangements and gather the people. I agreed and we began a series of Bible studies at Patambamba. We never drew a very large crowd of worshippers, but the faithful few who attended seemed to get a spiritual blessing from the time we spent together.

But five miles is not enough for a spiritual ripple, and two of the graduate nurses came to suggest a series of evangelistic services at Christmastime. Lumboko and Tshibangu were both gifted with musical talent, both playing the guitar and singing. They organized a group they called the Chorale Evangelique and proposed that we go to outlying villages every Sunday for a month before Christmas. They provided the musical adoration in abundance and I brought a message attuned to the Advent of the Lord Jesus. We drew some large and enthusiastic crowds, up to four or five hundred at one stop, where a number of people came forward to make a profession of faith or to renew their dedication to the Lord. These trips took us out forty to sixty kilometers from Bulape. The rains were upon us and the roads were horrible so that fifty kilometers meant two hours of hard driving. However I was surrounded by good hands and strong backs to dig us out of the mud, and we accomplished our missions with pleasure and satisfaction.

The waves continued to spread. We were invited to make a Sunday visit to Mushenge to hold our service in the king's compound. This meant a visit within the walled-off area which housed his huge harem of wives. Such is the new day and the new opportunity in Bakubaland. In the early days of this twentieth century if a missionary had set foot within this enclosure he probably would have been decapitated for his presumption.

Now we found a church shed located in the center of the compound and it was obvious that some of Lukengu's wives were professing Christians. They were waiting for us with Bibles and song books in hand. We had a hearty song and worship service and I noted that a number of the women had their offering envelopes which they put in the collection plate. I brought the message "Unto us a child is born; unto us a Son is given," and there was reverent attention throughout the service.

From there we went outside and held a second service in the regular village chapel, and at 1:30 in the afternoon we were still worshipping! When the service concluded they showed their appreciation for our efforts by feeding us bidia and chicken. The Chorale Evangelique had come with me to add the prayer and praise portion of the service, and late in the afternoon we all returned to Bulape with an inner glow from feeling it was a job well done for the Lord!

But opportunities down the road were not the only ones for passing along the word. There were opportunities at home as well. Every Saturday evening we had a worship service in our home, conducted in English and attended by all who, with some command of the English language, wanted to attend. We were gratified by how regularly the Peace Corps people worshipped with us. Some of them were Jewish and were responsive in sharing Jewish attitudes and interpretations of Scripture passages plus descriptions of Jewish rituals. Some of our African friends with enough command of English to follow along, also joined our company. In all of this we reveled in the fact that the fields are white unto the harvest and God had granted us the glad privilege of laboring in such fields.

SHARING THE GOSPEL, ONE ON ONE

A poor old fellow came into the clinic one afternoon with his whole upper abdomen filled with a hard immobile tumor which was obviously malignant and obviously way beyond any possibility of correction. I began to talk with him. I asked him if he was a Christian. He didn't know what I was talking about. I asked him if he knew who Jesus Christ was. He was apologetic.

"I may have known at one time," he said, "but I am an old man and have forgotten."

I asked him if he knew his wife's name. Oh yes, he knew that. I asked if he knew his tribal chieftain's name. He knew that too.

"Well," I continued, "I was asking you if you knew about someone who is closer to you than your wife and who loves you more dearly. He is also the strongest of all chieftains. So your greatest interest is to know His name and to know Him." Then I explained the way of salvation and prayed with him that the Spirit of God might deal with him and instruct him and bring him into the family of the redeemed. I fully believe that the Lord heard and answered my prayer.

One day as I walked past the pediatric ward I heard through the window the clear treble voice of a small child singing. The tune was surprisingly true and the words, "Allelujah! Allelujah! Allelujah!" floated into my soul. If a sick child in a hospital ward can sing a message of praise then we can rest assured that the Good News does sometimes fall on fallow ground and bring forth fruit, even a hundred-fold!

One Sunday morning Effie and I walked the mile from our house through Banzebue village to worship at Luebo Church. The service started at 10:00 A.M. and concluded at 12:15 P.M., and it was an impressive sight. Before a full house, forty boys and girls joined the church. Half of them were also baptized. These young people had studied and recited the catechism, and had made their profession of faith. It is interesting to speculate and ask how this instruction plus dozens of gospel songs learned without song books plus the Bible reading and study they had done, would move in ordering and governing their lives in the years which lay ahead. As the Holy Spirit performs an effective work of saving grace in their hearts it is our fond expectation that many of their lives will be vitally touched and they will never be the same again. Thus the gospel of Jesus Christ moves out into the people of the world.

MOTIVATION FOR MISSION—THE BOTTOM LINE

Wilbur Hawkins was an exuberant and dedicated dentist from Dallas, Texas. He and his wife, Frances, gave a month of their time in Zaire to ease the burden of overworked Dr. Kabamba at Kananga. We were blessed by their visit to Bulape and their help with dental needs among the local people. One evening after supper Wilbur and I were stretching our legs in the moonlight, enjoying the glow of an almost full lunar profusion. We talked together of the missionary enterprise in Zaire and of the medical and dental contribution in particular. Abruptly Wilbur turned and shot me a question which had been brewing for some time. "Bill, why are you out here in Africa?"

This brought me up rather short with no ready response. It was apropos of nothing in our conversation. Nor was I sure that I had ever addressed myself to such a question or formulated an answer. So I pondered the matter. Wilbur finally broke the silence with an explanation for his query. "I just wondered. You had a fine education at one of the outstanding medical schools in the United States, and you could have engaged in a highly successful practice and enjoyed the good life of affluence and social position. Instead, you came out here to live in the lap of squalor and poverty. Sure, to help people who really need you but who can offer little or nothing in pay." He shook his head and once more asked, "Why?"

With a little time I had been sifting the sands and had come up with the answer. "Wilbur," I said, "there is only one reason why I am here. It alone gives me complete contentment and peace of mind on the matter. I am here because God called me to this work. I am sure that I am where He wants me to be—and for that reason I wouldn't be anywhere else." This is the bottom line, and it makes all the difference in the world between effective and ineffective missionary ministry. Commitment.

Jesus taught us the ultimate lesson on commitment. One day He was on a journey from Judea to Galilee accompanied by His disciples. They trudged the hot, dusty road all morning and arrived at Sychar in Samaria hungry and thirsty. His disciples went into town to look for food, while Jesus rested by a well. A woman came to draw water and during their conversation Jesus revealed to her that He was the long-awaited Messiah. Her true hope of eternal life.

When his disciples returned with food, he told them, "I have meat to eat that you know not of . . . My meat is to do the will of him who sent me, and to finish his work" (John 4:32, 34).

He repeated this motive for mission over and over again. It was the cornerstone of His human life and behavior.

This is the breathtaking goal toward which we, His followers, stumble and strive. This is our ultimate milestone. I contemplate on my own ministry in Zaire over a span of forty years, and the true motive which took me there. Yes, I wanted to follow in the steps of my beloved Saviour, and to preach the gospel of the kingdom, teach in the schools and churches, heal the sicknesses and diseases among the people—as He did. He gave me magnificent opportunities along all these lines. I had the high honor of proclaiming the Good News in villages, in hospital wards, in the home church, and in one-on-one situations. I saw people make a profession of faith in Christ and watched while their lives were turned around in the receiving of His fullness. But this is not the result that gives me most satisfaction and it is not the deepest reason I went to Zaire.

I had many opportunities to teach and to expound to those hungry for knowledge which had eluded them. I taught school. I taught the Bible. I even taught a few to read and write. I was one of the primary founders of a school for paramedical workers which is highly regarded in Zaire today. But teaching did not bring me my greatest satisfaction, and it is not the motive for my going to Africa.

In the providence of God I studied medicine and was equipped with the skills to meet a myriad of physical needs which would never have been met if I had not been on the scene. There were newborns who lived to adulthood, cripples who walked into a better life, and dying patients who received the needed medicines or surgical interventions to cure their illnesses and send them home well once more. Thank you, Lord, for this dimension of my services! But again, this was not my primary fulfillment, and it is not the reason I went to the mission field.

My reply to Wilbur Hawkins is still valid and true. The reason I was out there was because God had called me. It was His will for my life, and it was the motive which moved me to missionary service. The deepest satisfaction I have today is that I perceived the command and I obeyed it.

The greatest joy which could come to me from recounting my own experiences would be the possibility of some young doctor or nurse or technician or worker with different skills to be moved by perusal of these pages to give his or her life to carry the gospel of Jesus Christ out across cultural and linguistic barriers to other people who have never heard. There are still many out there. God willing, that young person just might be one of my own children or grandchildren whom I might only contact in this earthly life through these written pages.

AU REVOIR

In the early days of 1980 Effie and I began to set our house in order and to prepare for that final trip back to the United States and home again. These were bittersweet moments. We were departing from what had become a treasured home which God had given to us for our life's work. It was here in Africa we met one another, fell in love, and wed. It was here in Africa we reared our family. It was here in Africa we made many beloved friends, black and white. It was hard to turn our backs on such a land woven into our lives. One cannot give thirty-seven years of service in a particular place and walk away without leaving something of one's self behind.

But on the other side of the ocean we had children and grand-children, family and friends, church home, and longtime brothers and sisters in the faith. The anticipation of such reunions was exciting and joyful, as it had always been with previous homecomings.

First we must dispose of accumulated household goods and impedi-ments which we had collected across the years. This brought on a rush one might compare with California's in '49. The Africans, deprived of even the ordinary niceties, were ever on the lookout for unexpected favors. We were asked for everything, including the kitchen sink. I didn't want to seem apathetic, so I jotted down their requests. But how to fill such a plethora of need? Or how meet one and leave ten others disconsolate? I counted some 130 requested items which included 96 blankets, 205 sheets, 22 pillows, and 20 mattresses.

They asked for more than a hundred table settings, including dishes, cups and knives, forks and spoons. Add to that 80 towels, 56 kitchen pots and pans, 35 suitcases, and 43 pairs of shoes. I could go on enumerating, but you can see why we had some sentiment about slipping away unob-served and without farewells.

Fortunately this did not occur. I was invited to speak at a meeting of Lutshuadi Presbytery to bid the brethren good-bye. There was warm comraderie between us, and I realized I will not see some of them again until we sit down together at the marriage feast of the Lamb.

One week later we were in Kananga, completing the first lap of our homeward journey. I was asked to give a sort of "farewell address" to the missionary community at their Sunday evening gathering. Effie and I held the longest tenure of missionary service and were probably looked on as father and mother figures by some of the younger personnel. I used the text from 2 Corinthians 4:18, "We look not at the things which are seen, but at the things that are not seen: for the things that are seen are temporal, but the things that are not seen are eternal."

I was also invited to speak to assembled leaders of the church at Tshibashi Presbytery which was in session. I had another heart-warming time with them, reminiscing on my days in Zaire and bidding them adieu. Dr. Wakuteka asked me to come out to the Bible School at Ndesha where I spoke to the students on three different occasions about personal witnessing for Christ. We went out to Tshikaji, of course, and there was a chapel service where good things were said about Effie and myself regarding our part in founding the IMCK schools. All of these opportunities of final sharing with others came to us unexpectedly, and I was humbly grateful to God for the way the Spirit moved through our testimony in those concluding days.

On March 17, 1980, we were up at 4:30 A.M. and off to the airport in time to observe a last beautiful Zairian sunrise.

The Titan airplane of MAF arrived and took aboard three missionary doctors, three Zairian doctors, as well as Effie and myself. We were on our way to a Continuing Medical Education seminar in Kenya. The Christian Medical Society in the United States had been extremely helpful in arranging this seminar to help missionary and local Christian physicians keep abreast of the rapidly evolving innovations of modern medicine.

Drs. Hull, Rambo, Shannon, Katambue, Ngoi, and Tshiswaka were aboard. They would return to the Kasai. But Effie and I would continue from Kenya to Europe and then on to the United States. Enroute to Kenya we stopped to refuel at Goma, the breathtaking beautiful lake and volcanic region of Rwanda, crossing majestic Lake Victoria to arrive in Nairobi, the capital, about 2:30 P.M. From there we were transported by bus the twenty-five kilometers to Brackenhurst, a Baptist conference center which would provide housing and board for the seminar.

For a week we were exposed to a rather stringent schedule of medical lectures which were interspersed with some lighter social occasions and worship sessions. It was a well-prepared and well-presented program. Outstanding Christian specialists in various fields

Bill and Effie, 1990.

of medicine had given of their time and, at their own expense, had come to Africa to share new developments in our profession. Nearly a hundred participants came from all over Africa with a few from the Near East to profit from these presentations. Not least among the advantages of the occasion was making acquaintance and sealing friendships with many godly people who blessed our lives. Some of these we have kept in contact with during the succeeding years.

Although Effie had visited Kenya once, this was my first encounter, and we didn't want to miss the opportunity of seeing some of its fabled natural and animal life, so we said farewells to our Zairian companions and purchased a travel package from Menno, the Mennonite travel agency, for a couple of touring days. We boarded their Volkswagen bus and descended the amazing geographical escarpment into Great Rift Valley. Traveling with us were Dr. Walter and Charlene Moore, missionaries in Nigeria and Ghana. They had also attended the seminar. Driving along we immediately began to see many antelope and giraffe. We traveled southward one hundred kilometers on paved road, and then another one hundred kilometers on dirt road, arriving at Kikorok Lodge in the Masai Mara Game Reserve. This was a delightful experience—delicious food as we watched baboons romp across the lawn, and saw one lone elephant plus many antelope grazing on the next hill. That afternoon we traveled over hill and dale for three hours, not sticking to any roads. We drove right into the middle of a herd of buffalo which must have numbered three hundred. Giraffe, wart hogs, zebra, hyena, elephant, and one cheetah were encountered.

The following morning we began again at 6 A.M. Yesterday's animals were out again in full force. We added jackals to the list and a river full of hippos, but we missed the big cats and the rare rhinoceros. We returned to the lodge for a late breakfast and then set out for Nairobi.

From Nairobi Effie and I flew by KLM to Amsterdam where we spent a couple of days visiting the art museum, touring the city, watching them cut and polish diamonds, and enjoying Dutch food.

Then on to London and, of course, to the British Museum of Natural History—the most awe-inspiring one in the world. I am sure I could profitably spend a year in that institution and see only a small part of it. We also took in the planetarium and Madame Tussaud's, and of course the zoo. All of these we had visited in times past but would not want to pass up yet again. We did the British Museum and St. Paul's Cathedral. Then Westminster Abbey. I went immediately to what, to me, is the most hallowed spot in that plethora of hallowed spots—the grave of David Livingston.

> Open the Abbey doors and bare him in
> To sleep with king and statesman, chief and sage,
> The missionary, born of weaver kin,
> But great by work that brooks no lower wage.
>
> He needs no epitaph to guard a name
> That men will prize while worthy work is known.
> He lived and died for good, be that his fame;
> Let marble crumble, this is living stone!
> —Unknown

From London we traveled by rail to Edinburgh, stopping off overnight at York to meet Stuart Anderson who drove 150 miles from Wales to meet us. With him was his fiancee, Elizabeth Searls, and we were delighted to meet such an attractive young lady. We lunched together and then visited the imposing York Minster Cathedral. This huge structure was 250 years in the building, and was completed 18 years before Columbus discovered America. Its stained glass windows are the finest in Britain. The cathedral was in a bad state of repair with renovations in progress so that we could not tour the entire edifice. However, we were able to visit its underground excavations. The church was built on the ruins of an old Roman fortification, and the ancient foundations plus many uncovered artifacts were most interesting.

Stuart and Elizabeth put us on the train for Edinburgh where we visited the Palace of Holyroodhouse. The richness of its draperies, paintings, and furniture was rather staggering. This is the official residence of Queen Elizabeth in Scotland. At the other end of the Royal Mile we climbed the ascent to the Citadel which overlooks the city. A small, shiny cannon was fired every day at exactly 1:00 P.M. Some lady asked the guide why one o'clock had been chosen rather than noon, and his reply was one of the best "last words" I had heard in a long time as he drew himself up and with deliberate dignity said, "Madame, you must remember that we are Scotchmen and it is less expensive to fire the gun one time rather than twelve."

We were in Edinburgh on Easter Sunday, an eminent opportunity to worship in the cradle of Presbyterianism, so Effie and I conducted

The Rule family.

ourselves to St. Giles Cathedral. This beautiful church is the site of John Knox's ministry where he held forth through tumultuous years of Scottish change, both political and religious.

As we were seated we observed that it would be an Easter Communion celebration. This was a very moving experience for me. The Elders marched with pomp and dignity down the center aisle, at least half of them ladies in flowing shiny black gowns, and many of the men wore their Scottish kilts to display their family tartans. They carried the heavy silver pitchers and trays containing the loaves and the rich red wine, and as I participated, my mind harked back to the small tin cups and the watery fruit juice with which we had only recently celebrated the same sacrament with our black brethren in Africa. Once again I realized that God has beloved children everywhere in all the lands of this old sin-sick world, and Jesus holds out His arms of welcome to all. I walked away from St. Giles with a smile. Participating in communion on Easter Sunday at the mother church of John Knox I felt that my Presbyterianism had come full flower!

BIBLIOGRAPHY

Anderson, Vernon A. *Still Led in Triumph*, Board of World Mission, PCUSA.

Bakole wa Ilunga, Mgr. *Chemins De Liberation*, Edicitons de L'Archdiocese, Kananga, 1978.

Baldwin, Monica. *I Leap Over the Wall.*

Bryant, John. *Health & the Developing World*, Cornell U. Press, Ithica, 1969.

Calder, Ritchie. *Agony of the Congo*, Victor Gollance Ltd, London, 1961.

Carpenter, George W. *Highways for God In Congo*, LECO Press, Leopoldville, 1952.

Carter, S. & Mrs. R. N. William, editors. *Four Presbyterian Pioneers in Congo*, Private Printing, Selma, Ala., 1965.

Chesterman, C. C. *In the Service of Suffering*, 1912.

Cowan, L. Gray. *The Dilemmas of African Independence*, Walker & Co., N.Y., 1964.

Crabb, John H. *The Legal System of Congo-Kinshasa*, The Michie Co., Charlottesville, Va., 1970.

Crawford, Dan. *Thinking Black*, Morgan & Scott, Ltd., London, 1912.

Crawford, John R. *Protestant Missions in Congo*, 1878–1969, Private Printing.

Ditmars, Raymond L. *Snakes of the World*, The McMillan Co., N.Y., 1942.

Dowdy, Homer E. *Out of the Jaws of the Lion*, Harper & Row, 1965.

Gerard-Libois, Jules. *Katanga Secession*, Univ. of Wis. Press, 1966.

Hege, Ruth. *We Two Alone*, Thomas Nelson & Sons, 1965.

Hennessy, Maurice N. *The Congo, A Brief History and Appraisal*, Frederick A. Praeger, publisher, N.Y.

Hunter, Frye & Swartzwelder. *A Manual of Tropical Medicine*, W. B. Saunders Co., 1966.

Isemonger, R.M. *Snakes of Africa*, Thomas Nelson & Sons, 1962.

Italiaander, Rolf. *The New Leaders of Africa*, Prentice-Hall, Englewood Cliffs, N.J., 1961.

Kabeya, Samuel. *Muoyo ne Lufu Bia Muambi Daniel Moody Tshisungu*, LECO Press, Kinshasa, 1970.

King, Maurice. *Medical Care in Developing Countries*, Oxford Univ. Press, London/Nairobi, 1966.

Law, Virginia. *As Far as I Can Step*, Word Books, 1970.

Legum, Colin. *Congo Disaster*, Penguin Books, Baltimore, 1961.

Lingle, Walter L. *Memories of Davidson College*, John Knox Press, 1947.

McLean,David A. *The Sons of Muntu*, Thesis, Univ. of Witwatersrand, So. Afr.

Merriam, Alan P. *Congo, Background of Conflict*, Northwestern Univ. Press, 1961.

Pruitt, Virginia G. *New Nation, New Church*, Private Printing.

Shaloff, Stanley. *Reform in Leopold's Congo*, John Knox Press, 1970.

Vass, Winifred K. *Doctor Not Afraid*, Nortex Press, 1986.

Washburn, Hezekiah, *A Knight in the Congo*, Bassett Printing Co., Bassett, Va., 1972.

Weiss, Herbert. *Political Protest in the Congo*, Princeton Univ. Press, 1967.

Weissman, Stephen R. *American Foreign Policy in the Congo 1960-64*, Cornell Univ. Press, 1974.

Wharton, Conway T. *The Leopard Hunts Alone*.

Wharton, Ethel Taylor. *Led in Triumph*, John Knox Press, 1952.

Willoughby, W. C. *The Soul of the Bantu*, Negro University Press, Westport, Conn., 1970.

Wood, Michael. *Different Drums*, Clarkson N. Potter, Inc. N.Y., 1987.

Yancy, Phillip. *Where Is God When It Hurts?* Zondervan, Grand Rapids, 1977.

Young, Crawford. *Politics in the Congo*, Princeton Univ. Press, 1965.

Cowan, L. Gray. *The Dilemmas of African Independence*, Walker & Co., N.Y., 1964.

ARTICLES AND RECORDS

American Presbyterian Congo Mission. Minutes of Annual Meetings, 1941–1964.

Executive Committee of Foreign Mission. Presbyterian Church US, Annual Reports.

Department of the Navy. "Poisonous Snakes of the World," U.S. Govt. Printing Office, 1962.

Grolier Incorporated. *The New Book Of Knowledge*, 1980.

Miller, J. K. *Une Liste des Serpents du Kasai Comprennant, 875 Especes Collectonnes.*

Rule, William. "A Medal And A Miracle," *So. Pres. Journal,* Oct. 15, 1945, Vol. IV, No. 8.

Rule, William. "Able To Save To The Uttermost," *Presbyterian Survey,* June 1949, Vol. 39, No. 6.

Rule, William. "The 'Raison d'Etre' of Medical Missions," *Congo Mission News,* Oct. 1955, No. 172.

Rule, William. "Report From The Congo," *Presbyterian Survey,* Feb. 1961, Vol. 51, No. 2.

Tourist Bureau for the Belgian Congo and Ruanda-Urundi. "Traveler's Guide to the Belgian Congo and Ruanda-Urundi," Brussels 1951.

INDEX

326

Bontrager, Robert, 137–39, 147, 150
Borsinger, Mr., 141, 149
Bowers, Lee, 62
Boyd Junior High School, 8
Branch, Jim, 305
Brand, Paul, 120, 280
Brantley, Maurice, 41
Brooklyn Bridge, 66
Brown, Richard, 291–92
Brussels Palais de Justice, 173
Bryn Mawr Hospital, 26–27
Bukasa, Samuel, 165
Bulape station, 103, 130–31, 210, 238, 282–83, 286–88, 291, 291, 292–95, 297, 299–306, 309
Bunche, Ralph, 135
Burkitt, Dennis, 280
Burns, Brantley, 94

C
Calder, Duncan, 22, 26
Camp Sequoyah, 23, 173
Carlson, Paul, 208
Carper, Day, 44, 150
Carr, Fred, 274
Carson, Katharine, 18
Catholic Archbishop Bakole, 99
Central School, 46, 48, 52, 53, 133, 173, 175–76, 221, 233, 235, 250, 253
Chapman, Dave, 8
Christian Association, 23
Christian Medical Society, 21, 162, 315
Church World Service (CWS), 144
Churchill, Winston, 63
Cleveland, Roy, 233

Cocheran, Robert, 121–22
Columbia Theological Seminary (Decatur, Ga.), 273
Congo Christian medical relief program, 137
Congo Evangelistic Mission, 158
Congo Protestant Council, 118, 130, 164, 213, 215
Congo Protestant Relief Agency (CPRA), 138–39, 142, 147, 149–50, 157, 162, 165, 215
Corbitt, Duvon, 144
Cousar, Dr., 59, 77
Craig, Allen, 45
Crane, Bill, 50, 66, 93, 133, 257
Crane, David, 220
Crane, Dorothy, 220
Crane, Hank, 143
Crane, Katharine, 50, 66, 93, 220, 257
Crane, William, 275
Crane, Paul E., 220, 222
Crane, Stephen, 220, 268–70
Crouch, Will, 8, 9
Crystal Mountains, 44, 227
Currie, Colonel, 62–63

D
Dambreville, Dr., 148
Daniel, Tshisunga, 169, 177
Davidson College, 13–14, 19, 22, 115, 163, 173, 177, 266, 295
Davis, Bill, 144
Davis, John, 144
Dayal, Rajeshwar, 135
Deaf and Dumb School of Knoxville, 8
DeLand, Lawrence, 304